THE OXFORD BOOK OF

LONDON

THE OXFORD BOOK OF
LONDON

Edited by

PAUL BAILEY

Oxford   New York

OXFORD UNIVERSITY PRESS

1995

Oxford University Press, Walton Street, Oxford OX2 6DP

Oxford New York
Athens Auckland Bangkok Bombay
Calcutta Cape Town Dar es Salaam Delhi
Florence Hong Kong Istanbul Karachi
Kuala Lumpur Madras Madrid Melbourne
Mexico City Nairobi Paris Singapore
Taipei Tokyo Toronto
and associated companies in
Berlin Ibadan

Oxford is a trade mark of Oxford University Press

Published in the United States by
Oxford University Press Inc., New York

Introduction, editorial material, and selection © Paul Bailey 1995

British Library Cataloguing in Publication Data
Data available

Library of Congress Cataloging in Publication Data
The Oxford book of London / edited by Paul Bailey.
p.   cm.
Includes index.
1. London (England)—Literary collections.
2. London (England)—Social life and customs.
3. London (England)—Description and travel.
4. English Literature—England—London.
I. Bailey, Paul, 1937–   .
PR1111.L6094   1995   820.8'032421—dc20   95–4310
ISBN 0–19–214192–9

10 9 8 7 6 5 4 3 2 1

Typeset by Graphicraft Typesetters Ltd
Printed in Great Britain
on acid-free paper by
The Bath Press
Bath, Avon

For Joan Bailey and Pat Keen

FOREWORD

The Oxford Book of London begins in 1180 or thereabouts, with a monk named William Fitzstephen enumerating the delights of the capital, and ends in the present day. This anthology has been designed more or less chronologically, with the intention of giving the reader some sense of the ways in which the city has developed and expanded over eight centuries. It is possible to read it from cover to cover, but it is also—in common with other anthologies—a book to dip into. There is much here that is familiar—Spenser's 'Prothalamion'; John Evelyn's unrivalled description of the Great Fire; Wordsworth awestruck upon Westminster Bridge; the sonorous opening of *Bleak House*; Eliza Doolittle's first encounter with Professor Henry Higgins—but there are, I hope, surprises too. Among these are passages from Yevgeny Zamyatin's surrealist novella *The Fisher of Men*; the opening scene of Ben Jonson's rarely performed satire *The Devil is an Ass*; a letter, written in English, the Italian businessman Ettore Schmitz—who as Italo Svevo is the author of *Confessions of Zeno*—sent to his wife in Trieste; poems by Isabella Whitney and Charles Morris, and Mark Twain's comments on Family Hotels: 'They are a London specialty. God has not permitted them to exist elsewhere.'

Certain famous events have been included, but my main concern has been with quotidian history, memorably recorded. I chose Froissart's account of the Peasants' Revolt and the death of Wat Tyler because it is a vivid piece of writing, and Charles Dickens's fictional recreation of the Gordon Riots, in *Barnaby Rudge*, for the same reason. Since the Plague and the Fire inspired Defoe, Pepys, and Evelyn to incomparable prose, it would have been foolish to exclude them. A. C. Benson's sketch of Edward VII's coronation was chosen for its attention to telling detail and its gossip, and Jack the Ripper is present because the sobriquet he gave himself in an advance communication to the news agencies concerning his next murder has guaranteed him a curious immortality. Otherwise, it is everyday high life and low life I have sought to capture in this selection from a wealth, a huge mass, of material.

The book comes in three parts: the first encompasses the period between the twelfth and eighteenth centuries; the second is devoted to the nineteenth century, when London grew larger and yet larger; and the third starts in 1900 and comes to a halt in the 1990s, with the city still in a state of flux. The London of Part I is a relatively confined place; in Part II it is the hub of the British Empire, on which the sun will never set, with a prosperous middle class asserting itself and demanding accommodation in what were to become the suburbs, and in Part III the sun—against every prediction and expectation—has gone down, has finally disappeared, but London remains.

I have attempted to make *The Oxford Book of London* a flowing narrative, for all that its content is diverse, peculiar, idiosyncratic. The great poets and novelists chose themselves: Blake, Spenser, Wordsworth, Clare (Epping Forest was near enough to London, and greatly loved by venturesome Londoners), Dunbar, Chidiock Tichborne (a solitary masterpiece can afford a poet greatness), Defoe and Dickens and Thackeray. The opinions of distinguished foreign visitors—by turns enchanted or exasperated—have been respected: those of Leopold Mozart, Chateaubriand, Haydn, Dostoevsky, and Alexander Herzen, among others. Of the marvellous painters who detected beauty in London, I have selected passages from the letters and recollections of Van Gogh, Monet, Derain, and Pissarro. And I feel no need to apologize for the inclusion of jottings by the likes of 'Bon Viveur' and Barbara Cartland, who both reflect the chauffeur-driven spirit of the times they are recounting.

I have limited explanation and explication to the minimum, only providing information and footnotes when necessary. Perhaps I should explain, however, why I have given London's poor such prominence. The Cockneys described by Henry Mayhew, Arthur Morrison, V. S. Pritchett, and Jack London are not lovable, forelock-touching stereotypes, but real people with scissor-sharp voices. They constitute a particular aspect of London's durability. The art that gave them succour from the 1850s to the 1950s was that of the music-hall, and I have acknowledged it, briefly. Defoe—a writer who thrived on financial embarrassment—and Dickens honoured them, as did Jonson and a host of lesser talents. Peter Reading in the poem I have taken from *Perduta Gente* honours them, too, to the accompaniment of the last five notes of Sibelius's Fifth Symphony, with five terror-inducing words.

Some anthologies are composed of tantalizing titbits, and this one offers several, in the form of diary entries and stray paragraphs of exceptional brilliance. Every so often, though, I have elected to quote at length, because the quality of the prose or poetry, and the sheer interest of the subject-matter, commands that I do so. That is why the entire first act of *Pygmalion* and a whole chapter of *Vanity Fair*, for instance, appear unscathed.

I have learnt much in the course of editing this book. I have become acquainted with authors—Dorothy George, especially—hitherto unheard of, and the acquaintance has proved both profitable and pleasurable. I am conscious of serious omissions, as a serious anthologist ought to be.

ACKNOWLEDGEMENTS

My thanks are due, first, to Judith Luna of Oxford University Press for inviting me to edit this book, and for exhibiting immeasurable patience during the years it took me to put it together. I am also indebted to the staff of the London Library, to Deborah Rogers, to David Miller, and to Oliver Reynolds. To Jeremy Trevathan I owe immense gratitude.

CONTENTS

I suggested a doubt, that if I were to reside in London, the exquisite zest with which I relished it in occasional visits might go off, and I might grow tired of it. JOHNSON. 'Why, Sir, you find no man, at all intellectual, who is willing to leave London. No, Sir, when a man is tired of London, he is tired of life; for there is in London all that life can afford.'

JAMES BOSWELL, *The Life of Samuel Johnson*

Make me feel the wild pulsation that I felt before the strife,
When I heard my days before me, and the tumult of my life;
Yearning for the large excitement that the coming years would
    yield,
Eager-hearted as a boy when first he leaves his father's field,
And at night along the dusky highway near and nearer drawn,
Sees in heaven the light of London flaring like a dreary dawn . . .

ALFRED TENNYSON, 'Locksley Hall'

INTRODUCTION

ON a Saturday evening, in the autumn of 1947, I was taken by my parents to the Grand Theatre at Clapham Junction to see one of their favourite stars of the music hall, Kate Carney. Although she was already in her seventies, she seemed possessed of a defiant vitality as she sang the songs she had made famous fifty years earlier. Hers was the genuine voice of the London poor, and the largely working-class audience recognized and loved its familiar, rasping sound. It did not strike any of her ageing admirers as odd that this old woman should still be singing of her young husband's unfaithfulness with 'another', because for them she had become something of an institution. Indeed, all the singers and comics who appeared on the bill that night looked like survivors from London's past, and I was vaguely aware, at the age of 10, that I was watching them just before they vanished for ever.

At that time, London was a city scarred by war. There were gaps in the streets where houses, shops, and public buildings had once stood. My friends and I played on the nearest of those many bomb sites, defying parental warnings of unexploded bombs. In the spring, the common flowers of London sprouted up out of the rubble: the ubiquitous dandelion; the rarer rose-bay willow-herb, with its deep pink spikes; the pinkish-white London pride. We could almost pretend we were back in the countryside in which we had lived in comparative safety for most of our short lives.

It was not until I was in my second decade that I began to understand and appreciate the huge diversity of the city of my birth. I had visited the Tower, of course, and been to the Zoo, and joined the crowd in front of Buckingham Palace, but mine was otherwise a confined London. But when I was 12, I began to walk beyond the confines of Battersea. For months on end, if the weather was favourable, I explored the dark, silent streets behind St Paul's Cathedral, so noisy with the din of money-making during the week, or the narrow alleyways that led off Aldgate and Whitechapel Road. I strolled down Park Lane, looking up at the hotels where only the fabulously rich—film stars, King Farouk, the Aga Khan—could afford to stay. I went to the museums in Kensington, and to the National Gallery, and developed a lifelong habit of going into the lesser-known churches (every city boasts them) that are seldom mentioned in popular guidebooks. I discovered the smaller Wren masterpieces for myself, and the great extravagance of Nicholas Hawksmoor's Christ Church in Spitalfields (which was boarded up for twenty years), and the modest seamen's church of St Mary's in Rotherhithe, which has carvings by Grinling Gibbons.

Even in the early 1950s, vestiges of a former way of London life were to be detected, especially in the poorer areas. Brewers' drays delivered beer to the pubs, and the milkman's cart was drawn by a horse. The horse trough—a solid stone construction filled with water—was a regular fixture throughout the capital, and it was a delight of childhood to watch the horses taking their hard-earned refreshment at one of them. Tramps used the troughs to perform their ablutions in, free of charge. And I remember two characters who might have been described by Henry Mayhew—a cat's meat salesman, who sold offal from door to door, and a knife-grinder, who kept everybody's carving knives in a permanent state of sharpness.

Our terraced house—which we shared with another family, who occupied the ground floor—was lit by gas, and had no running hot water. The communal lavatory was in the back garden, or yard, where it was not possible to grow many plants thanks to the presence of a concrete shelter that had been hastily built in 1940. From the front room, we could look out at the black chimneys of the gasworks, towering above the roofs and constantly belching smoke, and the rear bedroom window offered a view of the railway line. All the mothers in the street did their families' laundry at a nearby wash-house, the soapy smell of which was at its most pungent on Mondays, when the noise of dozens of mangles being turned rose to a deafening pitch. My mother's face was always beetroot red on a Monday, after hours spent at the tubs, with the steam rising around her.

'Londoners have no neighbours,' M. V. Hughes observes in *A London Child of the 1870s*. She expatiates: 'During our fifteen years in the one house we never had the slightest acquaintance with our "semi-detached", nor with the people round, although we knew several by sight and gave them nicknames.' Molly Hughes's father was not rich, but he was not poor by the standards of his day, either. He had money enough to keep his family in Canonbury, and to employ servants at a very minimum wage. Mr Vivian, his wife, sons, and daughter were consequently a 'cut above' people such as my parents, who were Londoners with lots and lots of neighbours. In Gwynne Road, where only warehouses stand today, everyone knew each other's business—to a certain extent, anyhow. There were waspish neighbours, as the law of averages suggests, but there were also good Samaritans, who tended the sick and the elderly because it was the natural, and decent, thing to do. The word 'community' has been mis-used to the point of meaninglessness recently, but ours was a genuine, close-knit community. That I felt suffocated by it, and was happy when I left it behind me, is no criticism. In west London, where I now live, I greet some of my neighbours, and stop to chat with them. In the south London of my childhood and youth, the neighbours were in and out of our kitchen, and my mother and sister stopped for a quick, or not so quick, cup of tea to return the compliment in the kitchens of Mrs Watts and Mrs Minter. Talking in the street was not a sign of being neigh-bourly—that was mere politeness. True neighbours sat in your chairs, and shared their joys and sorrows.

That community was soon to vanish, along with the horse-drawn carts and the notorious fog that descended on the city each November. The 'pea-souper', as it was called, was feared by sufferers from asthma and bronchitis, and by anyone of a nervous disposition. November was the perfect month for thieves and pickpockets, who were the sole Londoners to mourn the fog's departure with the arrival of the Clean Air Act. London is still, romantically, associated with fogginess: there is a firm in America that manufactures raincoats and overcoats with the label 'Lon-don Fog'; there is the George and Ira Gershwin classic 'A Foggy Day in London Town', which has been recorded by innumerable singers; and films set in London, and made in Hollywood, often have at least one fog-bound scene to satisfy the demands of nostalgia and cliché. To experience a serious fog these days, like the pea-soupers I choked in and crept in as a boy, you have to go to Milan in winter. No matter: London remains the legendary home of the fog, despite its thirty-year absence.

In the 1960s—when London replaced Paris as the centre of fashion—the houses in Gwynne Road were demolished and their tenants dis-persed. My mother's neighbours found themselves in the sky, living in moderate-sized flats on the umpteenth floor of a newly built tower block. The architects and town planners who decided that the relatively poor were better accommodated in close proximity to the heavens demonstrated no indication of moving skywards too. They were content to remain in Hampstead, or Highgate, or Richmond, in their high-ceilinged, spacious houses, in districts where the idea of a quasi-skyscraper would never be countenanced. The beauty of the tower block, the argument went, was that it could contain in a single space more human beings than an entire street of three-storey houses. Now, in the 1990s, that argument no longer seems beautiful or indeed logical. London at present possesses the kind of slums the Danish architect Steen Eiler Rasmussen warned us against erecting in 1937, when he praised the capital for being unique among Europe's major cities. (His warning can be found on p. 322.) A few of the tower blocks have already been razed, and many more are unoccupied. And the terraced houses of south and north London, originally constructed for railway workers, builders, and artisans, have proved that they were built to last, now that their moneyed owners have had them restored to suit their tastes.

London is a city that thrives on change, and I care to think it is thriving today, despite the obvious fact that it has lost much of its power and prestige. It is not all of a marvellous piece—like Venice, or Florence, or Prague. It is varied and various, and that variety has come with expansion and the more imaginative type of development. Londoners have not been protective of their more eccentric and idiosyncratic buildings, as Hermione Hobhouse's saddening collection of photographs, *Lost London*, shows: the destruction of the interior of Soane's Bank of England constituting a particularly philistine act of vandalism. London's music-halls need not have disappeared when the art that kept them in business died with its great practitioners, for the Metropolitan in Edgware Road was an exquisite theatre, with the largest, most capacious bar imaginable, since it was designed for seasoned drinkers. What the Great Fire and the German bombers did not destroy was left to bureaucrats to dispose of, from century to century. Their work was not always misguided, if only because it acknowledged the possibility of future glories, and the fact that art, of necessity, has to reflect some quality or qualities of the age in which it is created. And London, with all its abominations to the discerning eye, is not a museum piece, a dead city that is only alive to tourists. You have to seek out its curious treasures—an East End synagogue; a grand house by the Thames at Chiswick; an eighteenth-century passageway in Soho; a folly resembling Wemmick's castle in

Great Expectations, though without the drawbridge, in Bath Road—in the midst of much else that is dull or nondescript.

London is frequently depicted in fiction as a place of decay, or as a setting for Gothic horrors. Both depictions diminish it, pay no proper imaginative attention to the variety I have referred to. Since Britain gave up, released, or abandoned its colonies, its cities have become far more cosmopolitan than ever could have been envisaged even fifty years ago, and London is at the very heart of that cosmopolitanism. London's great days of power may be past, but then Rome's great days are the subject of ancient history—that is what happens to cities that were once the hub of the universe. The London I see around me is radically different from the city I was raised in, and the main difference has to do with its citizens, who are no longer easily identifiable as Cockneys, or City gents with bowler hats and rolled umbrellas, or any of the other types that constitute London folklore—no, this city that has been opening its gates to the world's dispossessed (the Huguenots; the Jews from Russia, Armenia, Latvia; the Poles, and—for reasons that are not entirely honourable—the Irish) for nearly two hundred years is now a city in the process of drawing its cultural strength from the people who have come to inhabit it from the Empire of which it was for so long the centre. The process is in its infancy, but I am optimistic enough to believe that it will burgeon beyond the millennium.

The one spectacle in London that truly distresses me is of the hosts of tourists, young and old, gathered outside Madame Tussaud's every day of the week, every week of the year. These unfortunates have been assured that the place is a London landmark, where they can thrill to the Chamber of Horrors. What do they see inside but a collection of wax models of infamous murderers and politicians (the two occasionally combined in the same person) and actors and currently fashionable celebrities? London is not in there, I want to shout at them. Ignore it. Tell your tour guides to cease being lazy and show you the real city. And even as I send them my silent message or imprecation, I know that the real London demands time and patience of its visitors as well as its inhabitants.

London is a troubled city, but living cities are usually troubled; it is a city of dreadful night, but so is Paris and so is Chicago; yet it is also a city, as I hope this anthology testifies, of surprise, excitement, enchantment. The city *per se* is among man's grandest inventions, and the grandeur of London is unique, incontestable. I am disposed towards that grandeur, having been born and raised in its midst, and I would like this book to introduce those who are not or never could be Londoners to the complexities of which that grandeur is composed.

P.B.

London
1994

PART I

THE TWELFTH CENTURY TO
THE EIGHTEENTH CENTURY

A MONK'S VIEW OF LONDON

Amid the noble cities of the world, the City of London, throne of the English kingdom, is one which has spread its fame far and wide, its wealth and merchandise to great distances, raised its head on high. It is blessed by a wholesome climate, blessed too in Christ's religion, in the strength of its fortifications, in the nature of its site, the repute of its citizens, the honour of its matrons; happy in its sports, prolific in noble men.

On the east lies the royal citadel, of very notable size and strength; its court and wall rise from very deep foundations, where mortar mingles with animal's blood. On the west are two keeps strongly fortified. The whole way round the north of the city the wall, tall and wide, strengthened with turrets at intervals, links the seven gates of the city, each double-faced. Once London was walled and towered on the south side too; but that great river, the Thames, well-stocked with fish, with tidal flow and ebb, has lapped against the walls over the years and undermined and destroyed them.

Everywhere outside their houses are the citizens' gardens, side by side yet spacious and splendid, and set about with trees. There are also in the northern suburbs of London splendid wells and springs with sweet, healing, clear water. Holywell, Clerkenwell and St Clement's Well are especially famous and often visited; and crowds of schoolboys and students and young men of the City take the air on summer evenings.

The citizens of London are universally held up for admiration and renown for the elegance of their manners and dress, and the delights of their tables. London like Rome is divided into wards; has sheriffs annually appointed for consuls; has a senatorial order, and lesser magistracies; sewers and acqueducts in its streets; deliberative, demonstrative, judicial cases have their individual courts; London has its assemblies on fixed days. I can think of no other city with customs more admirable, in the visiting of churches, ordaining of festivals to God's honour and their due celebration, in almsgiving, in receiving guests, in concluding betrothals, contracting marriages, celebrating weddings, laying on ornate feasts and joyful occasions, and also in caring for the dead and burying them. The only plagues of London are the immoderate drinking of fools and the frequency of fires.

WILLIAM FITZSTEPHEN, Preface to the *Life* of Thomas à Becket, *c.*1180

ANOTHER MONK'S VIEW

I do not at all like that city. All sorts of men crowd together there from every country under the heavens. Each race brings its own vices and its own customs to the city. No one lives in it without falling into some sort of crimes. Every quarter of it abounds in great obscenities . . . Whatever evil or malicious thing that can be found in any part of the world, you will find in that one city. Do not associate with the crowds of pimps; do not mingle with the throngs in the eating-houses; avoid the dice and gambling, the theatre and the tavern. You will meet with more brag-garts there than in all France; the number of parasites is infinite. . . . jesters, smooth-skinned lads, Moors, flatterers, pretty boys, effeminates, pederasts, singing and dancing girls, quacks, belly-dancers, sorceresses, extortion-ers, night-wanderers, magicians, mimes, beggars, buffoons: all this tribe fill all the houses. Therefore, if you do not want to dwell with evil-doers, do not live in London.

RICHARD OF DEVIZES, *Chronicle*, *c.*1180–90

This anonymous poem, sometimes attributed to John Lydgate, dates from the fifteenth century. It was re-transcribed between 1600 and 1625.

LONDON LICKPENNY

To London once my steps I bent,
    Where truth in no wise should be faint;
To Westminster-ward I forthwith went
    To a man of law to make complaint.
    I said: 'For Mary's love, that holy saint,

Pity the poor that would proceed!'
But for lack of money I could not speed.

And as I thrust the press among,
 By froward chance my hood was gone;   *evil*
Yet for all that I stayed not long
 Till at the King's Bench I was come.
Before the judge I kneeled anon
  And prayed him for God's sake to take heed;
  But for lack of money I might not speed. . . .

Unto the Common Place I yode tho   *went then*
 Where sat one with a silken hood;
I did him reverence—for I ought to do so—
 And told my case as well as I could,
 How my goods were defrauded me by falsehood.
  I gat not a mum of his mouth for my meed, *word*
  And for lack of money I might not speed. . . .

In Westminster Hall I found out one
 Which went in a long gown of ray;
I crouched and kneeled before him anon,
 For Mary's love of help I him pray.
 'I wot not what thou meanst', gan he say;
  To get me thence he did me beed: *bid*
  For lack of money I could not speed.

Within this hall neither rich nor yet poor
 Would do for me aught, although I should die;
Which seeing, I gat me out of the door,
 Where Flemings began on me for to cry:
 'Master, what will you copen or buy?   *purchase*
  Fine felt hats, or spectacles to read?
  Lay down your silver, and here you may speed.' . . .

Then unto London I did me hie—
 Of all the land it beareth the prise!
'Hot peascods!' one began to cry,
 'Strawberry ripe!' and 'cherries in the rise!' *on the branch*
  One bad me come near and buy some spice;

Pepper and saffron they gan me beede;   *proffer*
But for lack of money I might not speed.

Then to the Cheap I gan me drawn,
  Where much people I saw for to stand:
One offered me velvet, silk, and lawn;
  Another he taketh me by the hand,
   'Here is Paris thread, the finest in the land'.
   I never was used to such things in deed,
   And, wanting money, I might not speed.

Then went I forth by London Stone,
  Throughout all Canwike Street: *Cannon Street*
Drapers much cloth me offered anon;
  Then comes me one, cried 'Hot sheep's feet!'
  One cried 'Mackerel!'; 'Rishes green!' another   *rushes*
    gan greet.
   One bad me buy a hood to cover my head;
   But for want of money I might not speed.

Then I hied me into East Cheap.
  One cries 'Ribs of beef and many a pie!'
Pewter pots they clattered on a heap;
  There was harp, pipe, and minstrelsie.
  'Yea, by cock!' 'Nay, by cock!' some began cry.
   Some sung of Jenken and Julian for their meed.
   But for lack of money I might not speed.

Then into Cornhill anon I yode,
  Where was much stolen gear among;
I saw where hong mine own hode
  That I had lost among the throng.
  To buy my own hood I thought it wrong—
   I knew it well as I did my Creed:
   But for lack of money I could not speed.

The taverner took me by the sleeve:
  'Sir', saith he, 'will you our wine assay?'
I answered: 'That can not much me grieve;
  A penny can do no more than it may.'
  I drank a pint and for it did pay;

Yet sore a-hungered from thence I yede,
And, wanting money, I could not speed.

Then hied I me to Billingsgate,
  And one cried: 'Hoo! go we hence!'
I prayed a barge-man for God's sake
  That he would spare me my expense.
'Thou 'scapst not here', quod he, 'under two pence;
  I list not yet bestow my alms-deed.'
Thus, lacking money, I could not speed.

Then I conveyed me into Kent,
  For of the law would I meddle no more;
Because no man to me took entent
  I dight me to do as I did before.   *prepared*
Now Jesus that in Bethlem was bore,
  Save London, and send true lawyers their meed!
For whoso wants money with them shall not speed.

ANON.

The following extracts from Jean Froissart's Chronicles, *which were translated by Lord Berners in the 1520s, give a dramatic—though not necessarily accurate—account of the Peasants' Revolt in 1381.*

'A REVEL! A REVEL!'

On 12 June in this same year the peasants of Essex and Kent gathered together in very large numbers. Growing ever denser, they went rampaging far and wide, declaring that Master Simon Sudbury, at that time archbishop and also chancellor of England, was a traitor and that he richly deserved to die. Swooping upon his manor at Lambeth they set fire to most of its abandoned contents, including books, clothes and linen; stove in wine-barrels and drained them, pouring what wine was left on the floor; banged together and smashed all the kitchenware; and all the while accompanied this behaviour as if in self-congratulation on some praiseworthy feat, with shouts of 'A revel! A revel!'

About four in the afternoon on the following day the peasantry, wrought up to a state of sheer frenzy, attacked the Duke's palace of the Savoy, where they burst through every barrier and spared no article of value from destruction either by burning or by being flung out to sink in the Thames . . . As the evening twilight drew on, they made their way to the priory of St John at Clerkenwell and killing everybody who offered any opposition burned down the entire structure.

In view of their aggressive temper and their gross effrontery, the King fell in with their request and went to the place known as Mile End, where the assembled throng of rustics insistently demanded of him that they should be given every kind of liberty and an amnesty for all offences committed up to that time, whether in connection with the insurrection or not. Fearing that if he did not give in to these demands mischief would follow from his refusal, the King bowed to the importunity of the raging mob.

While these events were going forward, a sinister section of the horde of serfs moved on to the Tower of London, from which they dragged out the archbishop, the treasurer and a friar minor who was surgeon to the Duke of Lancaster, brought them to Tower Hill and there beheaded them together with a royal sergeant at arms named John Legg and another victim.

These executions took place on 14 June at eleven o'clock. The heads of the archbishop and the rest were stuck on poles and carried through the city streets before being set up on London Bridge. The hallowed head of the archbishop they set in the middle and higher than the others and to make it especially recognisable among them they nailed on it a scarlet cap.

THE DEATH OF WAT TYLER

The same proper morning Wat Tyler, Jack Straw and John Ball had assembled their company to commune together in a place called Smithfield, where as every Friday there is a market of horses. And therewith the King came the same way unwary of them, for he had thought to have passed that way without London, and with him 40 horses; and when he came before the abbey of St Bartholomew and beheld all these people, then the King rested and said he would go no farther till he knew what these people ailed.

When Wat Tyler saw the King tarry, he said to his people, 'Sirs, yonder is the King, I will go and speak with him.' And therewith he spurred his horse and departed from his company and came to the King, so near him that his horse' head touched the crop of the King's horse . . . Wat Tyler cast his eyes on a squire that was there with the King, bearing the King's sword; and Wat Tyler hated greatly the same squire, for the same squire had greatly displeased him before for words between them. 'What,' said Tyler, 'art thou there? Give me thy dagger.' The King beheld the squire and said, 'Give it him, let him have it.' And when this Wat Tyler had it he began to play therewith and turned it in his hand, and said to the squire, 'Give me also that sword.' 'Nay,' said the squire, 'it is the King's sword; thou art not worthy to have it, for thou art but a knave; and if there were more here but thou and I, thou durst not speak those words, for as much gold in quantity as all yonder abbey.' 'By my faith,' said Wat Tyler, 'I shall never eat meat till I have thy head.' And with those words the Lord Mayor of London came to the King with twelve horses, well armed under their coats, and so broke the press and saw and heard how Wat Tyler demeaned himself, and said to him, 'Ha, thou knave, how art thou so hardy in the King's presence to speak such words? It is too much for thee so to do.' Then the King began to chafe, and said to the mayor, 'Set hands on him.' And while the King said so, Tyler said to the Mayor, 'In God's name, what have I said to displease thee?' 'Yes, truly,' quoth the Mayor, 'thou false stinking knave, shalt thou speak thus in the presence of the King my natural lord? I commit thee never to live without thou shalt dearly abye it.' And with those words the Mayor drew out his sword and struck Wat Tyler so great a stroke on his head that he fell down at the feet of his horse; and as soon as he was fallen, they environed him all about, whereby he was not seen of his company. Then a squire of the King's alighted, called John Standish, and he drew out his sword and put it into Wat Tyler's belly, and so he died.

Then the ungracious people there assembled, perceiving their captain slain, began to murmur among themselves and said, 'Ah, our captain is slain; let us go and slay them all.' And therewith they arranged themselves on the place in the manner of battle and their bows before them. Thus the King began a great outrage; howbeit, all turned to the best, for as soon as Tyler was on the earth, the King departed from all his company and all alone he rode to these people, and said to his own men, 'Sirs, none of you follow me, let me alone.' And so when he came before these ungracious people, who put themselves in ordinance to revenge their

captain, then the King said unto them, 'Sirs, what aileth you, ye shall
have no captain but me; I am your King, be all in rest and peace.' And
so the most part of the people that heard the King speak and saw him
among them were shamefaced, and began to wax peaceable and to depart.

JEAN FROISSART, *Chronicles*, trans. John Bourchier (Lord Berners), 1523–5

THE PILGRIMS GATHER AT THE TABARD

It happened at this season, that one day
In Southwark at the Tabard where I stayed
Ready to set out on my pilgrimage
To Canterbury, and pay devout homage,
There came at nightfall to the hostelry
Some nine-and-twenty in a company,
Folk of all kinds, met in accidental
Companionship, for they were pilgrims all;
It was to Canterbury that they rode.
The bedrooms and the stables were good-sized,
The comforts offered us were of the best.
And by the time the sun had gone to rest
I'd talked with everyone, and soon became
One of their company, and promised them
To rise at dawn next day to take the road
For the journey I am telling you about.

*

Our host gave each and all a warm welcome,
And set us down to supper there and then.
The eatables he served were of the best;
Strong was the wine; we matched it with our thirst.
A handsome man our host, handsome indeed,
And a fit master of ceremonies.
He was a big man with protruding eyes
—You'll find no better burgess in Cheapside—
Racy in talk, well-schooled and shrewd was he;
Also a proper man in every way.
And moreover he was a right good sort,
And after supper he began to joke,

And, when we had all paid our reckonings,
He spoke of pleasure, among other things:
'Truly,' said he, 'ladies and gentlemen,
Here you are all most heartily welcome.
Upon my word—I'm telling you no lie—
All year I've seen no jollier company
At one time in this inn, than I have now.

> GEOFFREY CHAUCER, *The Canterbury Tales*, Prologue, *c*.1387, trans.
> David Wright, 1985

*The following descriptions of London and the Lord Mayor's banquet were written
by Andrea Trevisan, a Venetian diplomat, who visited London in 1498.*

SILVER VESSELS IN THE STRAND

All the beauty of this island is confined to London; which, although sixty
miles distant to the sea, possesses all the advantages to be desired in a
maritime town; being situated on the river Thames, which is very much
affected by the tide, for many miles (I do not know the exact number)
above it: and London is so much benefited by this ebb and flow of the
river, that vessels of 100 tons burden can come up to the city, and ships
of any size to within five miles of it; yet the water in this river is fresh
for twenty miles below London.

Although this city has no buildings in the Italian style, but of timber
or brick like the French, the Londoners live comfortably, and, it appears
to me, there are not fewer inhabitants than at Florence or Rome. It
abounds with every article of luxury, as well as with the necessaries of
life: but the most remarkable thing in London, is the wonderful quantity
of wrought silver. I do not allude to that in private houses, though the
landlord of the house in which the Milanese ambassador lived, had plate
to the amount of 100 crowns, but to the shops of London. In one single
street, named the Strand, leading to St Paul's, there are fifty-two goldsmith's shops, so rich and full of silver vessels, great and small, that in
all the shops in Milan, Rome, Venice, and Florence put together, I do
not think there would be found so many of the magnificence that are to
be seen in London.

A SUMPTUOUS ENTERTAINMENT

The city is divided into several wards, each of which has six officers; but
superior to these, are twenty-four gentlemen who they call aldermen,
which in their language signifies old or experienced men; and, of these
aldermen, one is elected every year by themselves, to be a magistrate
named the mayor, who is in no less estimation with the Londoners, than
the person of our most serene lord (the Doge) is with us, or than the
Gonfaloniero at Florence; and the day on which he enters upon his office,
he is obliged to give a sumptuous entertainment to all the principal
people in London, as well as to foreigners of distinction; and I, being one
of the guests, together with your Magnificence, carefully observed every
room and hall, and the court, where the company were all seated, and
was of opinion that there must have been 1000 or more persons at table.
This dinner lasted four hours or more; but it is true that the dishes were
not served with that assiduity and frequency that is the custom with us
in Italy; there being long pauses between each course, the company
conversing the while.

Andrea Trevisan, repr. in Relation or rather a True Account of the Island
of England, ed. C. A. Sneyd, 1847

TO THE CITY OF LONDON

London, thou art of townes A *per se*.   *the best*
  Soveraign of cities, semeliest in sight,
Of high renoun, riches, and royaltie;
  Of lordis, barons, and many goodly knyght;
  Of most delectable lusty ladies bright;
Of famous prelatis in habitis clericall;
  Of merchauntis full of substaunce and myght:
London, thou art the flour of Cities all.

Gladdith anon, thou lusty Troy Novaunt,
  Citie that some tyme cleped was New Troy,
In all the erth, imperiall as thou stant,
  Pryncesse of townes, of pleasure, and of joy,
  A richer restith under no Christen roy;   *king*

For manly power, with craftis naturall,
    Fourmeth none fairer sith the flode of Noy: *flood of Noah*
London, thou art the flour of Cities all.

Gemme of all joy, jasper of jocunditie,
    Most myghty carbuncle of vertue and valour;
Strong Troy in vigour and in strenuytie;   *strength*
    Of royall cities rose and geraflour;   *gillyflower*
    Empresse of townes, exalt in honour;
In beawtie beryng the crone imperiall;   *crown*
    Swete paradise precelling in pleasure;
London, thow art the floure of Cities all.

Above all ryvers thy Ryver hath renowne,
    Whose beryall stremys, pleasaunt and preclare,   *beryl; clear*
Under thy lusty wallys renneth down,
    Where many a swanne doth swymme with wyngis fare;
    Where many a barge doth saile, and row with are,   *oar*
Where many a ship doth rest with toppe-royall.
    O! towne of townes, patrone and not-compare:
London, thou art the floure of Cities all.

Upon thy lusty Brigge of pylers white
    Been merchauntis full royall to behold;
Upon thy stretis goth many a semely knyght
    In velvet gownes and cheynes of fyne gold.
    By Julyus Cesar thy Tour founded of old
May be the hous of Mars victoryall,
    Whos artillary with tonge may not be told;
London, thou art the flour of Cities all.

Strong be thy wallis that about the standis;
    Wise be the people that within the dwellis;
Fresh is thy ryver with his lusty strandis;
    Blith be thy chirches, wele sownyng be thy bellis;
    Riche be thy merchauntis in substaunce that excellis;
Fair be thy wives, right lovesom, white and small;
    Clere be thy virgyns, lusty under kellis: *coifs*
London, thow art the flour of Cities all.

Thy famous Maire, by pryncely governaunce,
  With swerd of justice the rulith prudently.
No Lord of Parys, Venyce, or Floraunce
  In dignytie or honoure goeth to hym nye.
He is exampler, loode-ster, and guye;   *lode star; guide*
Principall patrone and roose orygynalle,   *rose*
  Above all Maires as maister moost worthy:
London, thou art the flour of Cities all.

WILLIAM DUNBAR (?1456–?1513)

FALSTAFF AND JUSTICE SHALLOW REMINISCE

Fal. Come, I will go drink with you, but I cannot tarry dinner. I am glad to see you, by my troth, Master Shallow.

Shal. O, Sir John, do you remember since we lay all night in the Windmill in Saint George's Field?

Fal. No more of that, good Master Shallow, no more of that.

Shal. Ha, 'twas a merry night! And is Jane Nightwork alive?

Fal. She lives, Master Shallow.

Shal. She never could away with me.

Fal. Never, never; she would always say she could not abide Master Shallow.

Shal. By the mass, I could anger her to th'heart. She was then a bona-roba. Doth she hold her own well?

Fal. Old, old, Master Shallow.

Shal. Nay, she must be old, she cannot choose but be old, certain she's old, and had Robin Nightwork by old Nightwork before I came to Clement's Inn.

Sil. That's fifty-five year ago.

Shal. Ha, cousin Silence, that thou hadst seen that that this knight and I have seen! Ha, Sir John, said I well?

Fal. We have heard the chimes at midnight, Master Shallow.

Shal. That we have, that we have, that we have; in faith, Sir John, we have; our watchword was 'Hem, boys!'—Come, let's to dinner; come, let's to dinner. Jesus, the days that we have seen! Come, come.

FALSTAFF CORRECTS SHALLOW'S LIES

Lord, how subject we old men are to this vice of lying! This same starved justice hath done nothing but prate to me of the wildness of his youth, and the feats he hath done about Turnbull Street, and every third word a lie, duer paid to the hearer than the Turk's tribute. I do remember him at Clement's Inn, like a man made after supper of a cheese-paring. When a was naked, he was for all the world like a forked radish, with a head fantastically carved upon it with a knife. A was so forlorn, that his dimensions to any thick sight were invisible; a was the very genius of famine, yet lecherous as a monkey, and the whores called him mandrake. A came ever in the rearward of the fashion, and sung those tunes to the over-scutched housewives that he heard the carmen whistle, and sware they were his fancies or his good-nights. And now is this Vice's dagger become a squire, and talks as familiarly of John a Gaunt as if he had been sworn brother to him, and I'll be sworn a ne'er saw him but once in the tiltyard, and then he burst his head for crowding among the marshal's men. I saw it and told John a Gaunt he beat his own name, for you might have thrust him and all his apparel into an eel-skin—the case of a treble hautboy was a mansion for him, a court; and now has he land and beefs. Well, I'll be acquainted with him if I return, and't shall go hard but I'll make him a philosopher's two stones to me. If the young dace be a bait for the old pike, I see no reason in the law of nature but I may snap at him: let time shape, and there an end.

WILLIAM SHAKESPEARE, *2 Henry IV*, III. ii, 1600

This striking poem is extracted from the 'Wyll and Testament' of Isabella Whitney. Certain terms need glossing. 'And Pauls unto the head' means 'St Paul's Cathedral to its top'; Canwick Street, also known as Candlewick Street (latterly Cannon Street), was noted for its sellers of woollen cloth; Cheap is obviously Cheapside; 'bongraces' were shades worn on the front of women's bonnets; 'pawn' was the upper gallery of the Royal Exchange; 'Cornwall' was the ground in Vintry Ward; 'Bow', the church of St Mary Bow; 'dags' were heavy pistols; and 'Steel-yard' was the place of business of Hanseatic merchants, who specialized in Rhenish wines.

A BEQUEST

I whole in body and in mind,
　　But very weak in purse,
Do make and write my testament
　　For fear it will be worse.
And first I wholly do commend
　　My soul and body eke
To God the Father and the Son,
　　So long as I can speak.
And after speech, my soul to Him
　　And body to the grave,
Till time that all shall rise again
　　Their Judgment for to have.
And then I hope they both shall meet
　　To dwell for aye in joy,
Whereas I trust to see my friends
　　Released from all annoy.
Thus have you heard touching my soul
　　And body what I mean;
I trust you all will witness bear
　　I have a steadfast brain.
And now let me dispose such things
　　As I shall leave behind,
That those which shall receive the same
　　May know my willing mind.
I first of all to London leave,
　　Because I there was bred,
Brave buildings rare, of churches store,
　　And Pauls unto the head.
Between the same, fair streets there be
　　And people goodly store;
Because their keeping craveth cost
　　I yet will leave them more.
First for their food, I butchers leave,
　　That every day shall kill;
By Thames you shall have brewers store
　　And bakers at your will.

And such as others do observe
  And eat fish thrice a week,
I leave two streets full fraught therewith—
  They need not far to seek.
Watling Street and Canwick Street
  I full of woollen leave,
And linen store in Friday Street,
  If they me not deceive.
And those which are of calling such
  That costlier they require,
I mercers leave, with silk so rich
  As any would desire.
In Cheap, of them they store shall find,
  And likewise in that street
I goldsmiths leave with jewels such
  As are for ladies meet.
And plate to furnish cupboards with
  Full brave there shall you find,
With purl of silver and of gold
  To satisfy your mind;
With hoods, bongraces, hats or caps
  Such store are in that street
As if on tone side you should miss
  The tother serves you feat.
For nets of every kind of sort
  I leave within the pawn,
French ruffs, high purls, gorgets and sleeves
  Of any kind of lawn.
For purse or knives, for combs or glass,
  Or any needful knack,
I by the stocks have left a boy
  Will ask you what you lack.
I hose do leave in Birchin Lane
  Of any kind of size,
For women stitched, for men both trunks
  And those of Gascoyns' guise.
Boots, shoes, or pantables good store   *slippers or overshoes*
  St Martin's hath for you;

In Cornwall, there I leave you beds
    And all that longs thereto.
For women shall you tailors have,
    By Bow the chiefest dwell:
In every lane you some shall find
    Can do indifferent well.
And for the men few streets or lanes
    But body-makers be,
And such as make the sweeping cloaks
    With guards beneath the knee.
Artillery at Temple Bar
    And dags at Tower Hill;
Swords and bucklers of the best
    Are aye the Fleet until.
Now when thy folk are fed and clad
    With such as I have named,
For dainty mouths and stomachs weak
    Some junkets must be framed.
Wherefore I potecaries leave,
    With banquets in their shop;
Physicians also for the sick,
    Diseases for to stop.
Some roisters still must bide in thee
    And such as cut it out,
That with the guiltless quarrel will
    To let their blood about.
For them I cunning surgeons leave,
    Some plasters to apply,
That ruffians may not still be hanged
    Nor quiet persons die.
For salt, oatmeal, candles, soap,
    Or what you else do want,
In many places shops are full—
    I left you nothing scant.
If they that keep what I you leave
    Ask money when they sell it,
At Mint there is such store it is
    Unpossible to tell it.

At Steelyard, store of wines there be
  Your dulled minds to glad,
And handsome men that must not wed
  Except they leave their trade.
They oft shall seek for proper girls
  And some perhaps shall find
That need compels or lucre lures
  To satisfy their mind.
And near the same I houses leave
  For people to repair
To bathe themselves, so to prevent
  Infection of the air.
On Saturdays I wish that those
  Which all the week do drug
Shall thither trudge to trim them up
  On Sundays to look smug.
If any other thing be lacked
  In thee, I wish them look;
For there it is: I little brought
  But nothing from thee took.

ISABELLA WHITNEY, from *The Manner of her Will and What she left to London and to All Those in it, at her Departing*, 1573

AUTUMN

Autumn hath all the summer's fruitful treasure;
Gone is our sport, fled is poor Croydon's pleasure.
Short days, sharp days, long nights come on apace,
Ah, who shall hide us from the winter's face?
Cold doth increase, the sickness will not cease,
And here we lie, God knows, with little ease.
  From winter, plague, and pestilence, good Lord, deliver us!

London doth mourn, Lambeth is quite forlorn;
Trades cry, woe worth that ever they were born.
The want of term is town and city's harm;
Close chambers we do want, to keep us warm.
Long banished must we live from our friends;

This low-built house will bring us to our ends.
From winter, plague, and pestilence, good Lord, deliver us!

THOMAS NASHE (1567–1601)

STEWS AND STRUMPETS

London, what are thy suburbs but licensed stews? Can it be so many
brothel-houses of salary sensuality and six-penny whoredom (the next door
to the magistrates) should be set up and maintained, if bribes did not
bestir them? I accuse none, but certainly justice somewhere is corrupted.
Whole hospitals of ten-times-a-day dishonested strumpets have we clois-
tered together. Night and day the entrance unto them is as free as to a
tavern. Not one of them but hath a hundred retainers. Prentices and poor
servants they encourage to rob their masters. Gentlemen's purses and
pockets they will dive into and pick, even whiles they are dallying with
them.

No Smithfield ruffianly swashbuckler will come off with such harsh
hell-raking oaths as they. Every one of them is a gentlewoman, and either
the wife of two husbands, or a bed-wedded bride before she was ten years
old. The speech-shunning sores and sight-irking botches of their unsatiate
intemperance they will unblushingly lay forth and jestingly brag of,
wherever they haunt. To church they never repair. Not in all their whole
life would they hear of GOD, if it were not for their huge swearing and
foreswearing by Him.

Great cunning do they ascribe to their art, as the discerning, by the
very countenance, a man that hath crowns in his purse; the fine closing
in with the next Justice, or Alderman's deputy of the ward; the winning
love of neighbours round about to repel violence if haply their houses
should be environed, or any in them prove unruly, being pilled and
pould [skinned and shaven] too unconscionably. They forecast for
backdoors, to come in and out by, undiscovered. Sliding windows also
and trapdoors in floors to hide whores behind and under, with false
counterfeit panes in walls, to be opened and shut like a wicket. Some one
gentleman generally acquainted they give his admission unto sans fee,
and free privilege thenceforward in their nunnery to procure them fre-
quentence. Awake your wits, grave authorized law-distributors, and show
yourselves as insinuative-subtle in smoking this city-sodoming trade out

of his starting-holes as the professors of it are in underpropping it. Either you do not or will not descend into their deep-juggling legerdemain. Any excuse or unlikely pretext goes for payment. Set up a shop of incontinency whoso will, let him have but one letter of an honest name to grace it. In such a place dwells a wise woman that tells fortunes, and she, under that shadow, hath her house never empty of forlorn unfortunate dames, married to old husbands.

PRAYER FOR LONDON

Comfort us, Lord; we mourn, our bread is mingled with ashes and our drink with tears. With so many funerals are we oppressed that we have no leisure to weep for our sins, for howling for our sons and daughters. Oh, hear the voice of our howling, withdraw Thy hand from us, and we will draw near unto Thee.

Come, Lord Jesu, come, for as thou art Jesus, thou art pitiful. Challenge some part of our sin-procured scourge to thy cross. Let it not be said that thou but half-satisfiedst for sin. We believe thee to be an absolute satisfier for sin. As we believe, so for thy merit's sake we beseech thee let it happen unto us.

Thus ought every Christian in London, from the highest to the lowest, to pray. From God's justice we must appeal to His mercy. As the French King, Francis the First, a woman kneeling to him for justice, said unto her: 'Stand up, woman, for justice I owe thee; if thou begst anything, beg for mercy.' So if we beg of God for anything, let us beg for mercy, for justice He owes us. Mercy, mercy, Oh grant us, heavenly Father, for Thy mercy.

THOMAS NASHE, The Unfortunate Traveller, 1594

Nothing of much good took place in the Tower of London, except for the writing of this solitary masterpiece.

TICHBORNE'S ELEGY
Written with his own hand in the Tower before his execution

My prime of youth is but a frost of cares,
  My feast of joy is but a dish of pain,

My crop of corn is but a field of tares,
    And all my good is but vain hope of gain.
        The day is past, and yet I saw no sun,
        And now I live, and now my life is done.

My tale was heard and yet it was not told,
    My fruit is fallen and yet my leaves are green;
My youth is spent and yet I am not old,
    I saw the world and yet I was not seen.
        My thread is cut and yet it is not spun,
        And now I live, and now my life is done.

I sought my death and found it in my womb,
    I looked for life and saw it was a shade;
I trod the earth and knew it was my tomb,
    And now I die, and now I was but made.
        My glass is full, and now my glass is run,
        And now I live, and now my life is done.

                                CHIDIOCK TICHBORNE, 1586

Almost 400 years after Tichborne's execution, the architectural historian Ian Nairn described the Tower of London as it appeared to him in the mid-1960s.

THE TOWER

The Tower is London's one big hostage to the unreality of organized sight-seeing. It is lucky not to have more; but the Abbey and St Paul's are too big to be swamped and Buckingham Palace is too much used. All the Tower's history is past, and the chance of a memorable place to look at was lost with the preposterous mock-medieval outer walls of the 1840s, probably by Salvin, every bit as silly as Windsor and far less fun: all subsequent repairs have accentuated the stage-set or comic-opera character. Now, by comparison, the bascules of Tower Bridge feel straightforward. The White Tower itself, heartlessly made over with yellow instead of white stone, has not a fraction of the force of its ruined brother at Rochester.

    Still, if it is a joke, it is at least full-blown farce, and enough historical events have happened to make invention unnecessary. The trouble is that the atmosphere makes even the real events seem phoney: people actually went to their death through that pasteboard Traitors' Gate? Nonsense!

On a stricter level there are two things really worth seeing. One is in the Tudor chapel of St Peter ad Vincula: the wonderfully crisp canopy, of what looks like hard chalk, to the tomb of John Holland (d. 1447) and his wives. Crisp because untouched, not retouched, and every little face and curl of foliage has an angular grace that is one of the most English of English virtues. The effigies themselves are the usual puddingy shop-work.

Nice, but perhaps not enough of a draw to justify the endless croco-diles of tourists and all that armour. But the other thing should be seen by any London visitor. The Chapel of St John is on the first floor of the White Tower, which was built before 1100. Perhaps no other building in the whole of England conveys such an overwhelming effect of early Norman steamrollering mass, the force that produced Domesday Book and fixed the shires. It seems as if it were all hollowed out of one solid block, and had always been in the block waiting to be hollowed, from the heavy plain capitals to the tunnel vault.

IAN NAIRN, *Nairn's London*, 1966

TWICKNAM GARDEN

Blasted with sighs, and surrounded with tears,
    Hither I come to seek the spring,
    And at mine eyes, and at mine ears,
Receive such balms, as else cure everything;
    But O, self traitor, I do bring
The spider love, which transubstantiates all,
    And can convert manna to gall,
And that this place may thoroughly be thought
    True paradise, I have the serpent brought.

'Twere wholesomer for me, that winter did
    Benight the glory of this place,
    And that a grave frost did forbid
These trees to laugh, and mock me to my face;
    But that I may not this disgrace

Endure, nor yet leave loving, Love, let me
    Some senseless piece of this place be;
Make me a mandrake, so I may groan here,
    Or a stone fountain weeping out my year.

Hither with crystal vials, lovers come,
    And take my tears, which are love's wine,
And try your mistress' tears at home,
For all are false, that taste not just like mine;
    Alas, hearts do not in eyes shine,
Nor can you more judge woman's thoughts by tears,
    Than by her shadow, what she wears.
O perverse sex, where none is true but she,
    Who's therefore true, because her truth kills me.

JOHN DONNE (1572–1631)

PROTHALAMION

Calm was the day, and through the trembling air
Sweet breathing Zephyrus did softly play,
A gentle spirit, that lightly did delay
Hot Titan's beams, which then did glister fair;
When I whose sullen care,
Through discontent of my long fruitless stay
In prince's court, and expectation vain
Of idle hopes, which still do fly away
Like empty shadows, did afflict my brain,
Walked forth to ease my pain
Along the shore of silver streaming Thames,
Whose rutty bank, the which his river hems,
Was painted all with variable flowers,
And all the meads adorned with dainty gems,
Fit to deck maidens' bowers,
And crown their paramours,
Against the bridal day, which is not long:
    Sweet Thames, run softly, till I end my song.

There, in a meadow, by the river's side,
A flock of nymphs I chanced to espy,

All lovely daughters of the flood thereby,
With goodly greenish locks all loose untied,
As each had been a bride;
And each one had a little wicker basket,
Made of fine twigs entrailed curiously,
In which they gathered flowers to fill their flasket,
And with fine fingers cropped full featously
The tender stalks on high.
Of every sort, which in that meadow grew,
They gathered some; the violet pallid blue,
The little daisy, that at evening closes,
The virgin lily, and the primrose true,
With store of vermeil roses,
To deck their bridegrooms' posies,
Against the bridal day, which was not long:
   Sweet Thames, run softly, till I end my song.

With that, I saw two swans of goodly hue
Come softly swimming down along the Lee;
Two fairer birds I yet did never see.
The snow, which doth the top of Pindus strew,
Did never whiter shew,
Nor Jove himself, when he a swan would be
For love of Leda, whiter did appear:
Yet Leda was they say as white as he,
Yet not so white as these, nor nothing near.
So purely white they were,
That even the gentle stream, the which them bare,
Seemed foul to them, and bade his billows spare
To wet their silken feathers, lest they might
Soil their fair plumes with water not so fair,
And mar their beauties bright,
That shone as heaven's light,
Against their bridal day, which was not long:
   Sweet Thames, run softly, till I end my song.

Eftsoons the nymphs, which now had flowers their fill,
Ran all in haste, to see that silver brood,
As they came floating on the crystal flood.

Whom when they saw, they stood amazed still,
Their wondering eyes to fill.
Them seemed they never saw a sight so fair,
Of fowls so lovely, that they sure did deem
Them heavenly born, or to be that same pair
Which through the sky draw Venus' silver team;
For sure they did not seem
To be begot of any earthly seed,
But rather angels or of angels' breed:
Yet were they bred of Somers-heat they say,   *summer's heat/Somerset*
In sweetest season, when each flower and weed
The earth did fresh array,
So fresh they seemed as day,
Even as their bridal day, which was not long:
   Sweet Thames, run softly, till I end my song.

Then forth they all out of their baskets drew
Great store of flowers, the honour of the field,
That to the sense did fragrant odours yield,
All which upon those goodly birds they threw,
And all the waves did strew,
That like old Peneus' waters they did seem,
When down along by pleasant Tempe's shore,
Scattered with flowers, through Thessaly they stream,
That they appear through lilies' plenteous store,
Like a bride's chamber floor.
Two of those nymphs, meanwhile, two garlands bound,
Of freshest flowers which in that mead they found,
The which presenting all in trim array,
Their snowy foreheads therewithal they crowned,
Whilst one did sing this lay,
Prepared against that day,
Against their bridal day, which was not long:
   Sweet Thames, run softly, till I end my song.

'Ye gentle birds, the world's fair ornament,
And heaven's glory, whom this happy hour
Doth lead unto your lovers' blissful bower,
Joy may you have and gentle heart's content

Of your love's couplement:
And let fair Venus, that is queen of love,
With her heart-quelling son upon you smile,
Whose smile, they say, hath virtue to remove
All love's dislike, and friendship's faulty guile
For ever to assoil.
Let endless peace your steadfast hearts accord,
And blessed plenty wait upon your board,
And let your bed with pleasures chaste abound,
That fruitful issue may to you afford,
Which may your foes confound,
And make your joys redound,
Upon your bridal day, which is not long:
  Sweet Thames, run softly, till I end my song.'

So ended she; and all the rest around
To her redoubled that her undersong,
Which said, their bridal day should not be long.
And gentle echo from the neighbour ground
Their accents did resound.
So forth those joyous birds did pass along,
Adown the Lee, that to them murmured low,
As he would speak, but that he lacked a tongue,
Yet did by signs his glad affection show,
Making his stream run slow.
And all the fowl which in his flood did dwell
'Gan flock about these twain, that did excel
The rest so far as Cynthia doth shend
The lesser stars. So they, enraged well,
Did on those two attend,
And their best service lend,
Against their wedding day, which was not long:
  Sweet Thames, run softly, till I end my song.

At length they all to merry London came,
To merry London, my most kindly nurse,
That to me gave this life's first native source;
Though from another place I take my name,
An house of ancient fame.

There when they came, whereas those bricky towers,
The which on Thames' broad aged back do ride,
Where now the studious lawyers have their bowers
There whilom wont the Templar Knights to bide,
Till they decayed through pride:
Next whereunto there stands a stately place,
Where oft I gained gifts and goodly grace
Of that great lord, which therein wont to dwell,   *the Earl of Leicester*
Whose want too well now feels my friendless case.
But ah! here fits not well
Old woes but joys to tell
Against the bridal day, which is not long:
    Sweet Thames, run softly, till I end my song.

Yet therein now doth lodge a noble peer,
Great England's glory and the world's wide wonder,
Whose dreadful name late through all Spain did thunder,
And Hercules' two pillars standing near
Did make to quake and fear.
Fair branch of honour, flower of chivalry,
That fillest England with thy triumph's fame,
Joy have thou of thy noble victory,
And endless happiness of thine own name
That promiseth the same:
That through thy prowess and victorious arms,
Thy country may be freed from foreign harms;
And great Elisa's glorious name may ring
Through all the world, filled with thy wide alarms,
Which some brave Muse may sing
To ages following,
Upon the bridal day, which is not long:
    Sweet Thames, run softly, till I end my song.

From those high towers this noble lord issuing,
Like radiant Hesper when his golden hair
In th' Ocean billows he hath bathed fair,
Descended to the river's open viewing,
With a great train ensuing.
Above the rest were goodly to be seen

Two gentle knights of lovely face and feature
Beseeming well the bower of any queen,
With gifts of wit and ornaments of nature,
Fit for so goodly stature;
That like the twins of Jove they seemed in sight,
Which deck the baldric of the heavens bright.
They two forth pacing to the river's side,
Received those two fair birds, their love's delight,
Which at th'appointed tide
Each one did make his bride,
Against their bridal day, which is not long:
   Sweet Thames, run softly, till I end my song.

EDMUND SPENSER (c.1552–99)

In the fourth act of Beaumont and Fletcher's The Knight of the Burning
Pestle, *a servant dresses up as the Maylord and addresses the assembled company.*

THE 'MAYLORD' SPEAKS

London, to thee I do present the merry month of May;
Let each true subject be content to hear me what I say:
With gilded staff and crossed scarf, the Maylord here I stand.
Rejoice, O English hearts, rejoice! rejoice, O lovers dear!
Rejoice, O City, town and country! rejoice, eke every shire!
For now the fragrant flowers do spring and sprout in seemly sort;
The little birds do sit and sing, the lambs do make fine sport;
And now the birchen-tree doth bud, that makes the schoolboys cry;
The morris rings, while hobby-horse doth foot it feateously;
The lords and ladies now abroad, for their disport and play,
Do kiss sometimes upon the grass, and sometimes in the hay;
Now butter with a leaf of sage is good to purge the blood;
Fly Venus and phlebotomy, for they are neither good;
Now little fish on tender stone begin to cast their bellies,
And sluggish snails, that erst were mewed, do creep out of their
   shellies;
The rumbling rivers now do warm, for little boys to paddle;
The sturdy steed now goes to grass, and up they hang his saddle;

The heavy hart, the bellowing buck, the rascal, and the pricket,
Are now among the yeoman's peas, and leave the fearful thicket;
And be like them, O you, I say, of this same noble town,
And lift aloft your velvet heads, and slipping off your gown,
With bells on legs, with napkins clean unto your shoulders tied,
With scarfs and garters as you please, and 'Hey for our town!' cried,
March out, and show your willing minds, by twenty and by twenty,
To Hodgson or to Newington, where ale and cakes are plenty;
And let it ne'er be said for shame, that we the youths of London
Lay thrumming of our caps at home, and left our custom undone.
Up, then I say, both young and old, both man and maid a-maying,
With drums, and guns that bounce aloud, and merry tabor playing!
Which to prolong, God save our King, and send his country peace,
And root out treason from the land! and so, my friends, I cease.

FRANCIS BEAUMONT and JOHN FLETCHER, *The Knight of the Burning Pestle*, IV. v, ?1607

Ben Jonson's play The Devil Is an Ass *was written and performed in 1616. It opens with the Devil making his expected entrance: 'Ho, ho, ho . . .' he booms, before addressing Pug (or Puck), the sprite who must justify to his Master his spritely presence in London.*

SATAN, PUG, AND INIQUITY: A CONVERSATION
Enter Satan, Pug

Sat. To earth? And, why to earth, thou foolish spirit?
    What wouldst thou do on earth?
Pug.   For that, great chief!
    As time shall work. I do but ask my month,
    Which every petty puisne devil has;   *junior*
    Within that term, the Court of Hell will hear
    Something may gain a longer grant, perhaps.
Sat. For what? The laming a poor cow or two?
    Entering a sow, to make her cast her farrow?
    Or crossing of a market-woman's mare,
    'Twixt this, and Tottenham? These were wont to be
    Your main achievements, Pug. You have some plot, now,
    Upon a tunning of ale, to stale the yeast,   *putting (ale) into a tun*

Or keep the churn so that the butter come not;
Spite o' the housewife's cord, or her hot spit?
Or some good ribibe, about Kentish Town,   *old woman*
Or Hoxton, you would hang now, for a witch,
Because she will not let you play round Robin:
And you'll go sour the citizens' cream 'gainst Sunday?
That she may be accused for't, and condemned,
By a Middlesex jury, to the satisfaction
Of their offended friends, the Londoners' wives,
Whose teeth were set on edge with it? Foolish fiend,
Stay i' your place, know your own strengths, and put not
Beyond the sphere of your activity.
You are too dull a devil to be trusted
Forth in those parts, Pug, upon any affair
That may concern our name, on earth. It is not
Everyone's work. The state of Hell must care
Whom it employs, in point of reputation,
Here about London. You would make, I think,
An agent to be sent, for Lancashire
Proper enough; or some parts of Northumberland,
So you had good instructions, Pug.
Pug.   Oh chief!
You do not know, dear chief, what there is in me.
Prove me but for a fortnight, for a week,
And lend me but a Vice, to carry with me,
To practise there, with any playfellow,
And, you will see, there will come more upon't,
Than you'll imagine, precious chief.
Sat.   What Vice?
What kind wouldst thou have it of?
Pug.   Why, any, Fraud;
Or Covetousness; or Lady Vanity;
Or old Iniquity: I'll call him hither.

Enter Iniquity

Ini. What is he calls upon me, and would seem to lack a Vice?
Ere his words be half spoken, I am with him in a trice;
Here, there, and everywhere, as the cat is with the mice:
True *vetus Iniquitas.* Lack'st thou cards, friend, or dice?

I will teach thee to cheat, child, to cog, lie, and   *cheat at dice*
   swagger,
And ever and anon, to be drawing forth thy dagger:
To swear by Gog's nouns, like a Lusty Juventus,
In a cloak to thy heel, and a hat like a penthouse,
Thy breeches of three fingers, and thy doublet all belly,
With a wench that shall feed thee, with cock-stones   *cockle shells*
   and jelly.
Pug. Is it not excellent, chief? How nimble he is!
Ini. Child of hell, this is nothing! I will fetch thee a leap
   From the top of Paul's steeple, to the Standard in Cheap:
   And lead thee a dance, through the streets without fail,
   Like a needle of Spain, with a thread at my tail.
   We will survey the suburbs, and make forth our sallies,
   Down Petticoat Lane, and up the Smock Alleys,
   To Shoreditch, Whitechapel, and so to Saint Katharine's,
   To drink with the Dutch there, and take forth their patterns:
   From thence, we will put in at Custom House Quay there,
   And see, how the factors, and prentices play there
   False with their masters; and geld many a full pack,
   To spend it in pies, at the Dagger, and the Woolsack.
Pug. Brave, brave, Iniquity! Will not this do, chief?
Ini. Nay, boy, I will bring thee to the bawds, and the roisters,
   At Billingsgate, feasting with claret wine, and oysters,
   From thence shoot the bridge, child, to the Cranes i' the Vintry,
   And see there the gimlets, how they make their entry!
   Or, if thou hadst rather, to the Strand down to fall,
   'Gainst the lawyers come dabbled from Westminster Hall,
   And mark how they cling, with their clients together,
   Like ivy to oak; so velvet to leather:
   Ha, boy, I would show thee.

BEN JONSON, *The Devil Is an Ass*, I. i, 1616

This poem was written to mark Robert Herrick's return to London from Devon-
shire, after his ejection from the parish of Dean Bourne on the coming of the
Commonwealth.

HIS RETURN TO LONDON

From the dull confines of the drooping West,
To see the day spring from the pregnant East,
Ravished in spirit, I come, nay more, I fly
To thee, blest place of my nativity!
Thus, thus with hallowed foot I touch the ground,
With thousand blessings by thy fortune crowned.
O fruitful Genius! that bestowest here
An everlasting plenty, year by year.
O Place! O People! Manners! framed to please
All nations, customs, kindreds, languages!
I am a freeborn Roman; suffer then
That I amongst you live a citizen.
London my home is: though by hard fame sent
Into a long and irksome banishment;
Yet since called back; henceforward let me be,
O native country, repossessed by thee!
For rather than I'll to the West return
I'll beg of thee first here to have mine urn.
Weak I am grown, and must in short time fall;
Give thou my sacred relics burial.

HIS TEARS TO THAMASIS

I send, I send here my supremest kiss
To thee, my silver-footed Thamasis.
No more shall I reiterate thy Strand,
Whereon so many stately structures stand;
Nor in the summer's sweeter evenings go
To bathe in thee (as thousand others do).
No more shall I along thy crystal glide,
In barge (with boughs and rushes beautified)
With soft-smooth virgins (for our chaste disport)
To Richmond, Kingston, and to Hampton Court.

Never again shall I with finny oar
Put from, or draw unto thy faithful shore;
And landing here, or safely landing there,
Make way to my beloved Westminster;
Or to the golden Cheapside, where the earth
Of Julia Herrick gave to me my birth.
May all clean nymphs and curious water dames,
With swanlike state, float up and down thy streams,
No drought upon thy wanton waters fall
To make them lean, and languishing at all.
No ruffling winds come hither to disease
Thy pure, and silver-wristed Naiades.
Keep up your state, ye streams; and as ye spring,
Never make sick your banks by surfeiting.
Grow young with tides, and though I see ye never,
Receive this vow, *So fare ye well for ever.*

ROBERT HERRICK, from *Hesperides*, 1648

SOLITUDE AND REASON, IN THE VILLAGE

Thou the faint beams of reason's scattered light,
  Dost like a burning-glass unite,
  Dost multiply the feeble heat,
And fortify the strength, till thou dost bright
  And noble fires beget.

Whilst this hard truth I teach, methinks I see
  This monster, London, laugh at me,
  I should at thee too, foolish City,
If it were fit to laugh at misery,
  But thy estate I pity.

Let but thy wicked men from out thee go,
  And all the fools that crowd thee so,
  Even thou who dost thy millions boast,
A village less than Islington will grow,
  A solitude almost.

ABRAHAM COWLEY (1618–67)

THOMAS HOBBES IN LONDON

Anno 1650 or 1651, he returned into England, and lived most part in Fetter-lane, where he writ, or finished, his book *de Corpore*, in Latin and then in English.

He was much in London till the restoration of his Majesty, having here convenience not only of books, but of learned conversation. I have heard him say, that at his Lord's house in the country there was a good library, and books enough for him, and that his Lordship stored the library with what books he thought fit to be bought; but he said, the want of learned conversation was a very great inconvenience, and that though he conceived he could order his thinking as well perhaps as another man, yet he found a great defect. Methinks in the country, for want of good conversation, one's wit grows mouldy.

JOHN AUBREY, *Brief Lives*, c.1693

MOLL FLANDERS BECOMES A LONDON THIEF

We lived in an uninterrupted course of ease and content for five years, when a sudden blow from an almost invisible hand blasted all my happiness, and turned me out into the world in a condition the reverse of all that had been before it.

My husband having trusted one of his fellow-clerks with a sum of money, too much for our fortunes to bear the loss of, the clerk failed, and the loss fell very heavy on my husband; yet it was not so great but that, if he had had courage to have looked his misfortunes in the face, his credit was so good that, as I told him, he would easily recover it; for to sink under trouble is to double the weight, and he that will die in it, shall die in it.

It was in vain to speak comfortably to him; the wound had sunk too deep; it was a stab that touched the vitals; he grew melancholy and disconsolate, and from thence lethargic, and died. I foresaw the blow, and was extremely oppressed in my mind, for I saw evidently that if he died I was undone.

I had had two children by him, and no more, for it began to be time for me to leave bearing children, for I was now eight-and-forty, and I suppose if he had lived I should have had no more.

I was now left in a dismal and disconsolate case indeed, and in several things worse than ever. First, it was past the flourishing time with me, when I might expect to be courted for a mistress; that agreeable part had declined some time, and the ruins only appeared of what had been; and that which was worse than all was this, that I was the most dejected, disconsolate creature alive. I that had encouraged my husband, and endeavoured to support his spirits under his trouble, could not support my own; I wanted that spirit in trouble which I told him was so necessary for bearing the burthen.

But my case was indeed deplorable, for I was left perfectly friendless and helpless, and the loss my husband had sustained had reduced his circumstances so low, that though indeed I was not in debt, yet I could easily foresee that what was left would not support me long; that it wasted daily for subsistence, so that it would be soon all spent, and then I saw nothing before me but the utmost distress; and this represented itself so lively to my thoughts, that it seemed as if it was come, before it was really very near; also my very apprehensions doubled the misery, for I fancied every sixpence that I paid for a loaf of bread was the last I had in the world, and that to-morrow I was to fast, and be starved to death.

In this distress I had no assistant, no friend to comfort or advise me; I sat and cried and tormented myself night and day, wringing my hands, and sometimes raving like a distracted woman; and indeed I have often wondered it had not affected my reason, for I had the vapours to such a degree, that my understanding was sometimes quite lost in fancies and imaginations.

I lived two years in this dismal condition, wasting that little I had, weeping continually over my dismal circumstances, and, as it were, only bleeding to death, without the least hope or prospect of help; and now I had cried so long, and so often, that tears were exhausted, and I began to be desperate, for I grew poor apace.

For a little relief, I had put off my house and took lodgings; and as I was reducing my living, so I sold off most of my goods, which put a little money in my pocket, and I lived near a year upon that, spending very sparingly, and eking things out to the utmost; but still when I looked before me, my heart would sink within me at the inevitable approach of misery and want. O let none read this part without seriously reflecting on the circumstances of a desolate state, and how they would grapple with want of friends and want of bread; it will certainly make them think not of sparing what they have only, but of looking up to heaven for support, and of the wise man's prayer, 'Give me not poverty, lest I steal.'

Let them remember that a time of distress is a time of dreadful temptation, and all the strength to resist is taken away; poverty presses, the soul is made desperate by distress, and what can be done? It was one evening, when being brought, as I may say, to the last gasp, I think I may truly say I was distracted and raving, when prompted by I know not what spirit, and, as it were, doing I did not know what, or why, I dressed me (for I had still pretty good clothes), and went out. I am very sure I had no manner of design in my head when I went out; I neither knew or considered where to go, or on what business; but as the devil carried me out, and laid his bait for me, so he brought me, to be sure, to the place, for I knew not whither I was going, or what I did.

Wandering thus about, I knew not whither, I passed by an apothecary's shop in Leadenhall Street, where I saw lie on a stool just before the counter a little bundle wrapped in a white cloth; beyond it stood a maid-servant with her back to it, looking up towards the top of the shop, where the apothecary's apprentice, as I suppose, was standing upon the counter, with his back also to the door, and a candle in his hand, looking and reaching up to the upper shelf, for something he wanted, so that both were engaged, and nobody else in the shop.

This was the bait; and the devil who laid the snare prompted me, as if he had spoke, for I remember, and shall never forget it, 'twas like a voice spoken over my shoulder, 'Take the bundle; be quick; do it this moment.' It was no sooner said but I stepped into the shop, and with my back to the wench, as if I had stood up for a cart that was going by, I put my hand behind me and took the bundle, and went off with it, the maid or fellow not perceiving me, or any one else.

It is impossible to express the horror of my soul all the while I did it. When I went away I had no heart to run, or scarce to mend my pace. I crossed the street indeed, and went down the first turning I came to, and I think it was a street that went through into Fenchurch Street; from thence I crossed and turned through so many ways and turnings, that I could never tell which way it was, nor where I went; I felt not the ground I stepped on, and the farther I was out of danger, the faster I went, till, tired and out of breath, I was forced to sit down on a little bench at a door, and then found I was got into Thames Street, near Billingsgate. I rested me a little and went on; my blood was all in a fire; my heart beat as if I was in a sudden fright. In short, I was under such a surprise that I knew not whither I was agoing, or what to do.

After I had tired myself thus with walking a long way about, and so eagerly, I began to consider, and make home to my lodging, where I came about nine o'clock at night.

What the bundle was made up for, or on what occasion laid where I found it, I knew not, but when I came to open it, I found there was a suit of childbed-linen in it, very good, and almost new, the lace very fine; there was a silver porringer of a pint, a small silver mug, and six spoons, with some other linen, a good smock, and three silk handkerchiefs, and in the mug a paper, 18s. 6d. in money.

All the while I was opening these things I was under such dreadful impressions of fear, and in such terror of mind, though I was perfectly safe, that I cannot express the manner of it. I sat me down, and cried most vehemently. 'Lord,' said I, 'what am I now? a thief! Why, I shall be taken next time, and be carried to Newgate, and be tried for my life!' And with that I cried again a long time, and I am sure, as poor as I was, if I had durst for fear, I would certainly have carried the things back again; but that went off after a while. Well, I went to bed for that night, but slept little; the horror of the fact was upon my mind, and I knew not what I said or did all night, and all the next day. Then I was impatient to hear some news of the loss; and would fain know how it was, whether they were a poor body's goods, or a rich. 'Perhaps,' said I, 'it may be some poor widow like me, that had packed up these goods to go and sell them for a little bread for herself and a poor child, and are now starving and breaking their hearts for want of that little they would have fetched.' And this thought tormented me worse than all the rest, for three or four days.

But my own distresses silenced all these reflections, and the prospect of my own starving, which grew every day more frightful to me, hardened my heart by degrees. It was then particularly heavy upon my mind, that I had been reformed, and had, as I hoped, repented of all my past wickedness; that I had lived a sober, grave, retired life for several years, but now I should be driven by the dreadful necessity of my circumstances to the gates of destruction, soul and body; and two or three times I fell upon my knees, praying to God, as well as I could, for deliverance; but

I cannot but say, my prayers had no hope in them. I knew not what to do; it was all fear without, and dark within; and I reflected on my past life as not repented of, that Heaven was now beginning to punish me, and would make me as miserable as I had been wicked.

Had I gone on here I had perhaps been a true penitent; but I had an evil counsellor within, and he was continually prompting me to relieve myself by the worst means; so one evening he tempted me again by the same wicked impulse that had said, 'Take that bundle,' to go out again and seek for what might happen.

I went out now by daylight, and wandered about I knew not whither, and in search of I knew not what, when the devil put a snare in my way of a dreadful nature indeed, and such a one as I have never had before or since. Going through Aldersgate Street, there was a pretty little child had been at a dancing-school, and was agoing home all alone; and my prompter, like a true devil, set me upon this innocent creature. I talked to it, and it prattled to me again, and I took it by the hand and led it along till I came to a paved alley that goes into Bartholomew Close, and I led it in there. The child sāid, that was not its way home. I said, 'Yes, my dear, it is; I'll show you the way home.' The child had a little necklace on of gold beads, and I had my eye upon that, and in the dark of the alley I stooped, pretending to mend the child's clog that was loose, and took off her necklace, and the child never felt it, and so led the child on again. Here, I say, the devil put me upon killing the child in the dark alley, that it might not cry, but the very thought frighted me so that I was ready to drop down; but I turned the child about and bade it go back again, for that was not its way home; the child said, so she would; and I went through into Bartholomew Close, and then turned round to an-other passage that goes into Long Lane, so away into Charterhouse Yard, and out into St John's Street; then crossing into Smithfield, went down Chick Lane, and into Field Lane, to Holborn Bridge, when, mixing with the crowd of people usually passing there, it was not possible to have been found out; and thus I made my second sally into the world.

DANIEL DEFOE, *Moll Flanders*, 1722

Cymbeline and Lud were two of the statues of England's mythical kings which stood on the Ludgate.

'LUSTS OF ALL SORTS'

Should we go now a-wand'ring, we should meet
With catchpoles, whores, and carts in ev'ry street:
Now when each narrow lane, each nook and cave,
Signposts, and shop doors, pimp for ev'ry knave,
When riotous sinful plush, and tell-tale spurs
Walk Fleet Street, and the Strand, when the soft stirs
Of bawdy, ruffled silks turn night to day;
And the loud whip, and coach scolds all the way;
When lusts of all sorts, and each itchy blood
From the Tower Wharf to Cymbeline, and Lud,
Hunts for a mate, and the tired footman reels
'Twixt chairmen, torches, and the hackney wheels.

> HENRY VAUGHAN (1622–95), from 'A Rhapsody, written upon a meeting with some friends at the Globe'

A WHALE IN LONDON, 3 JUNE 1658

A large whale was taken betwixt my land butting on the Thames and Greenwich, which drew an infinite concourse to see it, by water, horse, coach, and on foot, from London and all parts. It appeared first below Greenwich at low water, for at high water it would have destroyed all the boats, but lying now in shallow water incompassed with boats, after a long conflict it was killed with a harping iron struck in the head, out of which spouted blood and water by two tunnels, and after an horrid groan it ran quite on shore and died. Its length was 58 foot, height 16; black skinned like coach leather, very small eyes, great tail, only 2 small fins, a picked snout, and a mouth so wide that divers men might have stood upright in it; no teeth, but sucked the slime only as through a grate of that bone which we call whale-bone; the throat yet so narrow as would not have admitted the least of fishes. The extremes of the cetaceous bones hang downwards from the upper jaw, and was hairy towards the ends and bottom within side: all of it prodigious, but in nothing more wonderful than that an animal of so great a bulk should be nourished only by slime through those grates.

CROMWELL'S FUNERAL, 22 NOVEMBER 1658

Saw the superb funeral of the Protector. He was carried from Somerset House in a velvet bed of state drawn by six horses, housed with the same; the pall held by his new Lords; Oliver lying in effigy in royal robes, and crowned with a crown, sceptre, and globe, like a king. The pendants and guidons were carried by the officers of the army; the Imperial banners, achievements, &c. by the heralds in their coats; a rich caparisoned horse, embroidered all over with gold; a knight of honour armed cap-a-pie, and after all, his guards, soldiers, and innumerable mourners. In this equipage they proceeded to Westminster: but it was the joyfullest funeral I ever saw, for there were none that cried but dogs, which the soldiers hooted away with a barbarous noise, drinking and taking tobacco in the streets as they went.

KING CHARLES II RETURNS TO LONDON, 8 MAY–4 JUNE 1660

8th. This day was his Majesty proclaimed in London, &c.

9th. I was desired, and designed to accompany my Lord Berkeley with the public Address of the Parliament, General, &c. to the King, and invite him to come over and assume his Kingly Government, he being now at Breda; but I was yet so weak I could not make that journey by sea, which was not a little to my detriment, so I went to London to excuse myself, returning the 10th, having yet received a gracious message from his Majesty by Major Scot and Col. Tuke.

24th. Came to me Col. Morley, about procuring his pardon, now too late, seeing his error and neglect of the counsel I gave him, by which if he had taken it he had certainly done the great work with the same ease that Monk did it, who was then in Scotland and Morley in a post to have done what he pleased, but his jealousy and fear kept him from that blessing and honour. I addressed him to Lord Mordaunt, then in great favour, for his pardon, which he obtained at the cost of £1000, as I heard. O the sottish omission of this gentleman! what did I not undergo of danger in this negotiation to have brought him over to his Majesty's interest, when it was entirely in his hands!

29th. This day his Majesty Charles the Second came to London after a sad and long exile and calamitous suffering both of the King and Church, being 17 years. This was also his birth-day, and with a triumph of above 20,000 horse and foot, brandishing their swords and shouting with inexpressible joy; the ways strewed with flowers, the bells ringing, the streets hung with tapissry, fountains running with wine; the Mayor, Aldermen, and all the Companies in their liveries, chains of gold, and banners; Lords and Nobles clad in cloth of silver, gold, and velvet; the windows and balconies all set with ladies; trumpets, music, and myriads of people flocking, even so far as from Rochester, so as they were seven hours in passing the city, even from 2 in the afternoon till 9 at night.

I stood in the Strand and beheld it, and blessed God. And all this was done without one drop of blood shed, and by that very army which rebelled against him; but it was the Lord's doing, for such a restoration was never mentioned in any history ancient or modern, since the return of the Jews from the Babylonish captivity; nor so joyful a day and so bright ever seen in this nation, this happening when to expect or effect it was past all human policy.

June 4th. I received letters of Sir Richard Browne's landing at Dover, and also letters from the Queen which I was to deliver at Whitehall, not as yet presenting myself to his Majesty by reason of the infinite concourse of people. The eagerness of men, women, and children, to see his Majesty and kiss his hands was so great, that he had scarce leisure to eat for some days, coming as they did from all parts of the nation; and the King being as willing to give them that satisfaction, would have none kept out, but gave free access to all sorts of people.

Addressing myself to the Duke, I was carried to his Majesty when very few noblemen were with him, and kissed his hands, being very graciously received. I then returned home to meet Sir Richard Browne, who came not till the 8th, after nineteen years exile, during all which time he kept up in his chapel the liturgy and offices of the Church of England, to his no small honour, and in a time when it was so low, and as many thought utterly lost, that in various controversies both with Papists and Sectaries, our divines used to argue for the visibility of the Church, from his chapel and congregation.

OUT OF THE ABBEY AND INTO A PIT, 30 JANUARY 1661

This day (O the stupendous and inscrutable judgments of God!) were the carcasses of those arch rebels Cromwell, Bradshaw the Judge who condemned his Majesty, and Ireton son-in-law to the Usurper, dragged out

of their superb tombs in Westminster among the Kings, to Tyburn, and
hanged on the gallows there from 9 in the morning till 6 at night, and
then buried under that fatal and ignominious monument in a deep pit;
thousands of people who had seen them in all their pride being spectators. Look back at Nov. 22, 1658, [Oliver's funeral] and be astonished!
and fear God and honour the King; but meddle not with them who are
given to change!

JOHN EVELYN (1620–1706), Diary, first pub. 1818

ON ST JAMES'S PARK,
AS LATELY IMPROVED BY HIS MAJESTY

Of the first paradise there's nothing found;
Plants set by heaven are vanished, and the ground;
Yet the description lasts: who knows the fate
Of lines that shall this paradise relate?
   Instead of rivers rolling by the side
Of Eden's garden, here flows in the tide;
The sea, which always served his empire, now
Pays tribute to our prince's pleasure too.
Of famous cities we the founders know;
But rivers, old as seas to which they go,
Are nature's bounty; 'tis of more renown
To make a river than to build a town.
   For future shade, young trees upon the banks
Of the new stream appear in even ranks;
The voice of Orpheus, or Amphion's hand,
In better order could not make them stand;
May they increase as fast, and spread their boughs,
As the high fame of their great owner grows!
May he live long enough to see them all
Dark shadows cast, and as his palace tall!
Methinks I see the love that shall be made,
The lovers walking in that amorous shade;
The gallants dancing by the river's side;
They bathe in summer, and in winter slide.
Methinks I hear the music in the boats,

And the loud echo which returns the notes;
While overhead a flock of new-sprung fowl
Hangs in the air, and does the sun control,
Darkening the sky; they hover o'er, and shroud
The wanton sailors with a feathered cloud.
Beneath, a shoal of silver fishes glides,
And plays about the gilded barges' sides;
The ladies, angling in the crystal lake,
Feast on the waters with the prey they take:
At once victorious with their lines, and eyes,
They make the fishes, and the men, their prize.
A thousand Cupids on the billows ride,
And sea-nymphs enter with the swelling tide,
From Thetis sent as spies, to make report,   *a sea-goddess*
And tell the wonders of her sovereign's court.
All that can, living, feed the greedy eye,
Or dead, the palate, here you may descry:
The choicest things that furnished Noah's ark,
Or Peter's sheet, inhabiting this park;
All with a border of rich fruit-trees crowned,
Whose loaded branches hide the lofty mound.
Such various ways the spacious alleys lead,
My doubtful Muse knows not what path to tread.
Yonder, the harvest of cold months laid up
Gives a fresh coolness to the royal cup;
There ice, like crystal firm, and never lost,
Tempers hot July with December's frost;
Winter's dark prison, whence he cannot fly,
Though the warm spring, his enemy, draws nigh.
Strange, that extremes should thus preserve the snow,
High on the Alps, or in deep caves below.
    Here, a well-polished Mall gives us the joy
To see our prince his matchless force employ:
His manly posture and his graceful mien,
Vigour and youth in all his motions seen;
His shape so lovely and his limbs so strong
Confirm our hopes we shall obey him long.
No sooner has he touched the flying ball

But 'tis already more than half the Mall;
And such a fury from his arm has got,
As from a smoking culverin 'twere shot.
  Near this my Muse, what most delights her, sees
A living gallery of agèd trees:
Bold sons of Earth, that thrust their arms so high,
As if once more they would invade the sky.
In such green palaces the first kings reigned,
Slept in their shades, and angels entertained;
With such old counsellors they did advise,
And, by frequenting sacred groves, grew wise.
Free from the impediments of light and noise,
Man, thus retired, his nobler thoughts employs.
Here Charles contrives the ordering of his states,
Here he resolves his neighbouring princes' fates:
What nation shall have peace, where war be made,
Determined is in this oraculous shade;
The world, from India to the frozen north,
Concerned in what this solitude brings forth.
His fancy, objects from his view receives;
The prospect, thought and contemplation gives.
That seat of empire here salutes his eye,
To which three kingdoms do themselves apply;
The structure by a prelate raised, Whitehall,
Built with the fortune of Rome's capitol;
Both, disproportioned to the present state
Of their proud founders, were approved by fate.
From hence he does that antique pile behold, *Westminster Abbey*
Where royal heads receive the sacred gold:
It gives them crowns, and does their ashes keep;
There made like gods, like mortals there they sleep;
Making the circle of their reign complete,
Those suns of empire, where they rise, they set.
When others fell, this, standing, did presage
The crown should triumph over popular rage:
Hard by that house, where all our ills were shaped,
The auspicious temple stood, and yet escaped.
So snow on Ætna does unmelted lie,

Whence rolling flames and scattered cinders fly;
The distant country in the ruin shares;
What falls from heaven the burning mountain spares.
Next, that capacious hall he sees, the room   *Westminster Hall*
Where the whole nation does for justice come;
Under whose large roof flourishes the gown,
And judges grave, on high tribunals, frown.
Here, like the people's pastor he does go,
His flock subjected to his view below;
On which reflecting in his mighty mind,
No private passion does indulgence find;
The pleasures of his youth suspended are,
And made a sacrifice to public care.
Here, free from court compliances, he walks,
And with himself, his best adviser, talks:
How peaceful olive may his temples shade,
For mending laws, and for restoring trade;
Or, how his brows may be with laurel charged,
For nations conquered, and our bounds enlarged.
Of ancient prudence here he ruminates,
Of rising kingdoms and of falling states;
What ruling arts gave great Augustus fame,
And how Alcides purchased such a name.   *Hercules*
His eyes, upon his native palace bent,
Close by, suggest a greater argument.
His thoughts rise higher when he does reflect
On what the world may from that star expect
Which at his birth appeared, to let us see
Day, for his sake, could with the night agree;
A prince, on whom such different lights did smile,
Born the divided world to reconcile!
Whatever heaven, or high extracted blood
Could promise, or foretell, he will make good;
Reform these nations, and improve them more
Than this fair park, from what it was before.

EDMUND WALLER, 1661; Amphion's music could move stone; for
Peter's sheet see Acts 11: 5.

THE BEGINNING OF THE PLAGUE

22 August 1665

Up; and after much pleasant talk, and being importuned by my wife and her two maids (which are both good wenches) for me to buy a necklace of pearl for her, and I promising to give her one of 60*l* in two year at furthest, and in less if she pleases me in her painting, I went away and walked to Greenwich, in my way seeing a coffin with a dead body therein, dead of the plague, lying in an open close belonging to Coome farm, which was carried out last night and the parish hath not appointed anybody to bury it—but only set a watch there day and night, that nobody should go thither or come thence, which is a most cruel thing— this disease making us more cruel to one another then we are to dogs.

SAMUEL PEPYS (1633–1703), *Diary*, ed. R. Latham and W. Matthews, 1970–83

'SPARE US, GOOD LORD'

One of the worst days we had in the whole time, as I thought, was in the beginning of September [1665], when, indeed, good people began to think that God was resolved to make a full end of the people in this miserable city. This was at that time when the plague was fully come into the eastern parishes. The parish of Aldgate, if I may give my opinion, buried above a thousand a week for two weeks, though the bills did not say so many;—but it surrounded me at so dismal a rate that there was not a house in twenty uninfected in the Minories, in Houndsditch, and in those parts of Aldgate parish about the Butcher Row and the alleys over against me. I say, in those places death reigned in every corner. Whitechapel parish was in the same condition, and though much less than the parish I lived in, yet buried near 600 a week by the bills, and in my opinion near twice as many. Whole families, and indeed whole streets of families, were swept away together; insomuch that it was frequent for neighbours to call to the bellman to go to such-and-such houses and fetch out the people, for that they were all dead.

And, indeed, the work of removing the dead bodies by carts was now grown so very odious and dangerous that it was complained of that the bearers did not take care to clear such houses where all the inhabitants were dead, but that sometimes the bodies lay several days unburied, till the neighbouring families were offended with the stench, and consequently infected; and this neglect of the officers was such that the churchwardens and constables were summoned to look after it, and even the justices of the Hamlets were obliged to venture their lives among them to quicken and encourage them, for innumerable of the bearers died of the distemper, infected by the bodies they were obliged to come so near. And had it not been that the number of poor people who wanted employment and wanted bread (as I have said before) was so great that necessity drove them to undertake anything and venture anything, they would never have found people to be employed. And then the bodies of the dead would have lain above ground, and have perished and rotted in a dreadful manner.

But the magistrates cannot be enough commended in this, that they kept such good order for the burying of the dead, that as fast as any of those they employed to carry off and bury the dead fell sick or died, as was many times the case, they immediately supplied the places with others, which, by reason of the great number of poor that was left out of business, as above, was not hard to do. This occasioned, that notwithstanding the infinite number of people which died and were sick, almost all together, yet they were always cleared away and carried off every night, so that it was never to be said of London that the living were not able to bury the dead.

As the desolation was greater during those terrible times, so the amazement of the people increased, and a thousand unaccountable things they would do in the violence of their fright, as others did the same in the agonies of their distemper, and this part was very affecting. Some went roaring and crying and wringing their hands along the street; some would go praying and lifting up their hands to heaven, calling upon God for mercy. I cannot say, indeed, whether this was not in their distraction, but, be it so, it was still an indication of a more serious mind, when they had the use of their senses, and was much better, even as it was, than the frightful yellings and cryings that every day, and especially in the evenings, were heard in some streets. I suppose the world has heard of the famous Solomon Eagle, an enthusiast. He, though not infected at all but in his head, went about denouncing of judgment upon the city in a frightful manner, sometimes quite naked, and with a pan of burning charcoal on his head. What he said, or pretended, indeed I could not learn.

I will not say whether that clergyman was distracted or not, or whether he did it in pure zeal for the poor people, who went every evening through the streets of Whitechapel, and, with his hands lifted up, repeated that part of the Liturgy of the Church continually, 'Spare us, good Lord; spare Thy people, whom Thou hast redeemed with Thy most precious blood.' I say, I cannot speak positively of these things, because these were only the dismal objects which represented themselves to me as I looked through my chamber windows (for I seldom opened the casements), while I confined myself within doors during that most violent raging of the pestilence; when, indeed, as I have said, many began to think, and even to say, that there would none escape; and indeed I began to think so too, and therefore kept within doors for about a fortnight, and never stirred out. But I could not hold it. Besides, there were some people who, notwithstanding the danger, did not omit publicly to attend the worship of God, even in the most dangerous times; and though it is true that a great many clergymen did shut up their churches, and fled, as other people did, for the safety of their lives, yet all did not do so. Some ventured to officiate and to keep up the assemblies of the people by constant prayers, and sometimes sermons or brief exhortations to repentance and reformation, and this as long as any would come to hear them. And Dissenters did the like also, and even in the very churches where the parish ministers were either dead or fled; nor was there any room for making difference at such a time as this was.

It was indeed a lamentable thing to hear the miserable lamentations of poor dying creatures calling out for ministers to comfort them and pray with them, to counsel them and to direct them, calling out to God for pardon and mercy, and confessing aloud their past sins. It would make the stoutest heart bleed to hear how many warnings were then given by dying penitents to others not to put off and delay their repentance to the day of distress; that such a time of calamity as this was no time for repentance, was no time to call upon God. I wish I could repeat the very sound of those groans and of those exclamations that I heard from some poor dying creatures when in the height of their agonies and distress, and that I could make him that reads this hear, as I imagine I now hear them, for the sound seems still to ring in my ears.

*

Those who remember the city of London before the fire must remember that there was then no such place as that we now call Newgate Market, but that in the middle of the street which is now called Blowbladder Street, and which had its name from the butchers, who used to kill and dress their sheep there (and who, it seems, had a custom to blow up their meat with pipes to make it look thicker and fatter than it was, and were punished there for it by the Lord Mayor); I say, from the end of the street towards Newgate there stood two long rows of shambles for the selling meat.

It was in those shambles that two persons falling down dead, as they were buying meat, gave rise to a rumour that the meat was all infected, which, though it might affright the people, and spoiled the market for two or three days, yet it appeared plainly afterwards that there was nothing of truth in the suggestion. But nobody can account for the possession of fear when it takes hold of the mind.

However, it pleased God, by the continuing of the winter weather, so to restore the health of the city that by February following we reckoned the distemper quite ceased, and then we were not so easily frighted again.

There was still a question among the learned, and at first perplexed the people a little, and that was in what manner to purge the house and goods where the plague had been, and how to render them habitable again, which had been left empty during the time of the plague. Abundance of perfumes and preparations were prescribed by physicians, some of one kind and some of another, in which the people who listened to them put themselves to a great, and indeed, in my opinion, to an unnecessary expense; and the poorer people, who only set open their windows night and day, burned brimstone, pitch, and gunpowder, and such things in their rooms, did as well as the best; nay, the eager people, who, as I said above, came home in haste and at all hazards, found little or no inconvenience in their houses, nor in the goods, and did little or nothing to them.

However, in general, prudent, cautious people did enter into some measures for airing and sweetening their houses, and burned perfumes, incense, benjamin, rosin, and sulphur, in their rooms close shut up, and then let the air carry it all out with a blast of gunpowder; others caused large fires to be made all day and all night for several days and nights; by the same token that two or three were pleased to set their houses on fire, and so effectually sweetened them by burning them down to the ground; as particularly one at Ratcliff, one in Holborn, and one at

Westminster; besides two or three that were set on fire, but the fire was happily got out again before it went far enough to burn down the houses; and one citizen's servant, I think it was in Thames Street, carried so much gunpowder into his master's house, for clearing it of the infection, and managed it so foolishly, that he blew up part of the roof of the house. But the time was not fully come that the city was to be purged by fire, nor was it far off; for within nine months more I saw it all lying in ashes; when, as some of our quacking philosophers pretend, the seeds of the plague were entirely destroyed, and not before; a notion too ridiculous to speak of here, since, had the seeds of the plague remained in the houses, not to be destroyed but by fire, how has it been that they have not since broken out, seeing all those buildings in the suburbs and liberties, all in the great parishes of Stepney, Whitechapel, Aldgate, Bishopsgate, Shoreditch, Cripplegate, and St Giles, where the fire never came, and where the plague raged with the greatest violence, remain still in the same condition they were in before?

But to leave these things just as I found them, it was certain that those people who were more than ordinarily cautious of their health, did take particular directions for what they called seasoning of their houses, and abundance of costly things were consumed on that account, which I cannot but say not only seasoned those houses, as they desired, but filled the air with very grateful and wholesome smells, which others had the share of the benefit of as well as those who were at the expenses of them.

And yet after all, though the poor came to town very precipitantly, as I have said, yet I must say the rich made no such haste. The men of business, indeed, came up, but many of them did not bring their families to town till the spring came on, and that they saw reason to depend upon it that the plague would not return.

The Court, indeed, came up soon after Christmas, but the nobility and gentry, except such as depended upon and had employment under the administration, did not come so soon.

I should have taken notice here, that notwithstanding the violence of the plague in London and in other places, yet it was very observable that it was never on board the fleet, and yet for some time there was a strange press in the river, and even in the streets, for seamen to man the fleet. But it was in the beginning of the year, when the plague was scarce begun, and not at all come down to that part of the city where they usually press for seamen; and though a war with the Dutch was not at all grateful to the people at that time, and the seamen went with a kind of reluctancy into the service, and many complained of being dragged into it by force, yet it proved in the event a happy violence to several of them, who had probably perished in the general calamity, and who, after the summer service was over, though they had cause to lament the desolation of their families, who—when they came back, were many of them in their graves—yet they had room to be thankful that they were carried out of the reach of it, though so much against their wills. We indeed had a hot war with the Dutch that year, and one very great engagement at sea, in which the Dutch were worsted, but we lost a great many men and some ships. But, as I observed, the plague was not in the fleet, and when they came to lay up the ships in the river the violent part of it began to abate.

I would be glad if I could close the account of this melancholy year with some particular examples historically; I mean of the thankfulness to God, our preserver, for our being delivered from this dreadful calamity. Certainly the circumstance of the deliverance, as well as the terrible enemy we were delivered from, called upon the whole nation for it. The circumstances of the deliverance were indeed very remarkable, as I have in part mentioned already, and particularly the dreadful condition which we were all in, when we were, to the surprise of the whole town, made joyful with the hope of a stop of the infection.

Nothing but the immediate finger of God, nothing but omnipotent power, could have done it. The contagion despised all medicine; death raged in every corner; and had it gone on as it did then, a few weeks more would have cleared the town of all, and everything that had a soul. Men everywhere began to despair; every heart failed them for fear; people were made desperate through the anguish of their souls, and the terrors of death sat in the very faces and countenances of the people.

In that very moment, when we might very well say, 'Vain was the help of man,'—I say, in that very moment it pleased God, with a most agreeable surprise, to cause the fury of it to abate, even of itself; and the malignity declining, as I have said, though infinite numbers were sick, yet fewer died, and the very first week's bill decreased 1843; a vast number indeed!

It is impossible to express the change that appeared in the very countenances of the people that Thursday morning when the weekly bill came out. It might have been perceived in their countenances that a secret surprise and smile of joy sat on everybody's face. They shook one another by the hands in the streets, who would hardly go on the same side of the way with one another before. Where the streets were not too broad, they would open their windows and call from one house to another, and ask how they did, and if they had heard the good news that the plague was abated. Some would return, when they said good news, and ask, 'What good news?' and when they answered that the plague was abated and the bills decreased almost 2000, they would cry out, 'God be praised,' and would weep aloud for joy, telling them they had heard nothing of it; and such was the joy of the people that it was, as it were, life to them from the grave. I could almost set down as many extravagant things done in the excess of their joy as of their grief; but that would be to lessen the value of it.

DANIEL DEFOE, *A Journal of the Plague Year*, 1722

'NO LONGER A CITY': 25 AUGUST–7 SEPTEMBER 1666

In the afternoon visited the Savoy Hospital; where I stayed to see the miserably dismembered and wounded men dressed, and gave some necessary orders. Then to my Lord Chancellor, who had, with the Bishop of London and others in the Commission, chosen me one of the three surveyors of the repairs of Paul's, and to consider of a model for the new building, or, if it might be, repairing of the steeple, which was most decayed.

26th. The contagion still continuing, we had the church service at home.

27th. I went to St Paul's church, where with Dr Wren, Mr Prat, Mr May, Mr Thomas Chichley, Mr Slingsby, the Bishop of London, the Dean of St Paul's, and several expert workmen, we went about to survey the general decays of that ancient and venerable church, and to set down in writing the particulars of what was fit to be done, with the charge thereof, giving our opinion from article to article. Finding the main building to recede outwards, it was the opinion of Chichley and Mr Prat that it had been so built *ab origine* for an effect in perspective, in regard of the height; but I was, with Dr Wren, quite of another judgment, and so we entered it; we plumbed the uprights in several places. When we came to the steeple, it was deliberated whether it were not well enough to repair it only on its old foundation, with reservation to the four pillars; this Mr Chichley and Mr Prat were also for, but we totally rejected it, and persisted that it required a new foundation, not only in regard of the necessity, but for that the shape of what stood was very mean, and we had a mind to build it with a noble cupola, a form of church-building not as yet known in England, but of wonderful grace: for this purpose we offered to bring in a plan and estimate, which, after much contest, was at last assented to, and that we should nominate a committee of able workmen to examine the present foundation. This concluded, we drew all up in writing, and so went with my Lord Bishop to the Dean's.

28th. Sat at the Star Chamber. Next day to the Royal Society, where one Mercator, an excellent mathematician, produced his rare clock and new motion to perform the equations, and Mr Rooke his new pendulum.

Sept. 2nd. This fatal night about ten, began the deplorable fire near Fish street in London.

3rd. I had public prayers at home. The fire continuing, after dinner I took coach with my wife and son and went to the Bank side in Southwark, where we beheld that dismal spectacle, the whole city in dreadful flames near the water side; all the houses from the Bridge, all Thames street, and upwards towards Cheapside, down to the Three Cranes, were now consumed: and so returned exceeding astonished what would become of the rest.

The fire having continued all this night (if I may call that night which was light as day for 10 miles round about, after a dreadful manner) when conspiring with a fierce eastern wind in a very dry season; I went on foot to the same place, and saw the whole south part of the city burning from Cheapside to the Thames, and all along Cornhill (for it likewise kindled back against the wind as well as forward), Tower street, Fen-church street, Gracious street, and so along to Bainard's Castle, and was now taking hold of St Paul's church, to which the scaffolds contributed exceedingly, the conflagration was so universal, and the people so astonished, that from the beginning, I know not by what despondency or fate, they hardly stirred to quench it, so that there was nothing heard or seen but crying out and lamentation, running about like distracted creatures without at all attempting to save even their goods; such a strange consternation there was upon them, so as it burned both in breadth and length, the churchs, public halls, Exchange, hospitals, monuments, and ornaments, leaping after a prodigious manner, from house to house and street to street, at great distances one from the other; for the heat with a long set of fair and warm weather had even ignited the air and prepared the materials to conceive the fire, which devoured after an incredible manner houses, furniture, and everything. Here we saw the Thames covered with goods floating, all the barges and boats laden with what some had time and courage to save, as, on the other, the carts, &c. carrying out to the fields, which for many miles were strewed with moveables of all sorts, and tents erecting to shelter both people and what goods they could get away. Oh the miserable and calamitous spectacle! such as haply the world had not seen since the foundation of it, nor be outdone till the universal conflagration thereof. All the sky was of a fiery aspect, like the top of a burning oven, and the light seen above 40 miles round about for many nights. God grant mine eyes may never behold the like, who now saw above 10,000 houses all in one flame; the noise and cracking and thunder of the impetuous flames, the shrieking of women and children, the hurry of people, the fall of towers, houses, and churches, was like an hideous storm, and the air all about so hot and inflamed that at the last one was not able to approach it, so that they were forced to stand still and let the flames burn on, which they did for near two miles in length and one in breadth. The clouds also of smoke were dismal and reached upon computation near 50 miles in length. Thus I left it this afternoon burning, a resemblance of Sodom, or the last day. It forcibly called to my mind that passage—*non enim hic habemus stabilem civitatem:* the ruins resembling the picture of Troy. London was, but is no more! Thus I returned.

Sept. 4th. The burning still rages, and it was now gotten as far as the Inner Temple; all Fleet street, the Old Bailey, Ludgate hill, Warwick lane, Newgate, Paul's chain, Watling street, now flaming, and most of it reduced to ashes; the stones of Paul's flew like granados [grenades], the melting lead running down the streets in a stream, and the very pavements glowing with fiery redness, so as no horse nor man was able to tread on them, and the demolition had stopped all the passages, so that no help could be applied. The eastern wind still more impetuously driving the flames forward. Nothing but the Almighty power of God was able to stop them, for vain was the help of man.

5th. It crossed towards White-hall; but oh, the confusion there was then at that Court! It pleased his Majesty to command me among the rest to look after the quenching of Fetter lane end, to preserve if possible that part of Holborn, whilst the rest of the gentlemen took their several posts, some at one part, some at another (for now they began to bestir themselves, and not till now, who hitherto had stood as men intoxicated, with their hands across) and began to consider that nothing was likely to put a stop but the blowing up of so many houses as might make a wider gap than any had yet been made by the ordinary method of pulling them down with engines; this some stout seamen proposed early enough to have saved near the whole city, but this some tenacious and avaricious men, aldermen, &c. would not permit, because their houses must have been of the first. It was therefore now commanded to be practised, and my concern being particularly for the Hospital of St Bartholomew near Smithfield, where I had many wounded and sick men, made me the more diligent to promote it; nor was my care for the Savoy less. It now pleased God by abating the wind, and by the industry of the people, when almost all was lost, infusing a new spirit into them, that the fury of it began sensibly to abate about noon, so as it came no farther than the Temple westward, nor than the entrance of Smithfield north: but continued all this day and night so impetuous toward Cripplegate and the Tower as made us all despair; it also broke out again in the Temple, but the courage of the multitude persisting, and many houses being blown up, such gaps and desolations were soon made, as with the former three days consumption, the back fire did not so vehemently urge upon the rest as formerly. There was yet no standing near the burning and glowing ruins by near a furlong's space.

The coal and wood wharfs and magazines of oil, rosin, &c. did infinite mischief, so as the invective which a little before I had dedicated to his Majesty and published, giving warning what might probably be the issue of suffering those shops to be in the City, was looked on as a prophecy.

The poor inhabitants were dispersed about St George's Fields, and Moorfields, as far as Highgate, and several miles in circle, some under tents, some under miserable huts and hovels, many without a rag or any necessary utensils, bed or board, who from delicateness, riches, and easy accommodations in stately and well furnished houses, were now reduced to extremest misery and poverty.

In this calamitous condition I returned with a sad heart to my house, blessing and adoring the distinguishing mercy of God to me and mine, who in the midst of all this ruin was like Lot, in my little Zoar, safe and sound.

Sept. 6th. Thursday. I represented to his Majesty the case of the French prisoners at war in my custody, and besought him that there might be still the same care of watching at all places contiguous to unseized houses. It is not indeed imaginable how extraordinary the vigilance and activity of the King and the Duke was, even labouring in person, and being present to command, order, reward, or encourage workmen, by which he shewed his affection to his people and gained theirs. Having then disposed of some under cure at the Savoy, I returned to White-hall, where I dined at Mr Offley's, the groom porter, who was my relation.

7th. I went this morning on foot from White-hall as far as London Bridge, through the late Fleet-street, Ludgate hill, by St Paul's, Cheapside, Exchange, Bishopsgate, Aldersgate, and out to Moorfields, thence through Cornhill, &c. with extraordinary difficulty, clambering over heaps of yet smoking rubbish, and frequently mistaking where I was. The ground under my feet so hot, that it even burnt the soles of my shoes. In the meantime his Majesty got to the Tower by water, to demolish the houses about the graff [trench], which being built entirely about it, had they taken fire and attacked the White Tower where the magazine of powder lay, would undoubtedly not only have beaten down and destroyed all the bridge, but sunk and torn the vessels in the river, and rendered the demolition beyond all expression for several miles about the country.

At my return I was infinitely concerned to find that goodly church St Paul's now a sad ruin, and that beautiful portico (for structure comparable to any in Europe, as not long before repaired by the late King) now rent in pieces, flakes of vast stone split asunder, and nothing remaining entire but the inscription in the architrave, shewing by whom it was built, which had not one letter of it defaced. It was astonishing to see what immense stones the heat had in a manner calcined, so that all the ornaments, columns, freizes, capitals, and projectures of massy Portland stone flew off, even to the very roof, where a sheet of lead covering a great space (no less than six acres by measure) was totally melted; the ruins of the vaulted roof falling broke into St Faith's, which being filled with the magazines of books belonging to the Stationers, and carried thither for safety, they were all consumed, burning for a week following. It is also observable that the lead over the altar at the east end was untouched, and among the divers monuments, the body of one Bishop remained entire. Thus lay in ashes that most venerable church, one of the most ancient pieces of early piety in the Christian world, besides near 100 more. The lead, iron work, bells, plate, &c. melted; the exquisitely wrought Mercers Chapel, the sumptuous Exchange, the august fabric of Christ Church, all the rest of the Companies' Halls, splendid buildings, arches, entries, all in dust; the fountains dried up and ruined, whilst the very waters remained boiling; the voragos [chasms] of subterranean cellars, wells, and dungeons, formerly warehouses, still burning in stench and dark clouds of smoke, so that in five or six miles traversing about, I did not see one load of timber unconsumed, nor many stones but what were calcined white as snow. The people who now walked about the ruins appeared like men in some dismal desert, or rather in some great city laid waste by a cruel enemy; to which was added the stench that came from some poor creatures' bodies, beds, and other combustible goods. Sir Thomas Gresham's statue, though fallen from its niche in the Royal Exchange, remained entire, when all those of the Kings since the Conquest were broken to pieces; also the standard in Cornhill and Queen Elizabeth's effigies, with some arms on Ludgate, continued with but little detriment, whilst the vast iron chains of the city streets, hinges, bars and gates of prisons were many of them melted and reduced to cinders by the vehement heat. Nor was I yet able to pass through any of the narrower streets, but kept the widest; the ground and air, smoke and fiery vapour, continued so intense that my hair was almost singed, and my feet unsufferably surbated [sore]. The by lanes and narrower streets were quite filled up with rubbish, nor could one have possibly known where he was, but by the ruins of some Church or Hall, that had some remarkable tower or pinnacle remaining. I then went toward Islington and Highgate, where one might have seen 200,000 people of all ranks and degrees dispersed and lying along by their heaps of what they could save from the fire, deploring their loss, and though ready to perish for hunger and destitution, yet not asking one penny for relief, which to me appeared a stranger sight than any I had yet beheld. His Majesty and Council indeed took all imaginable care for their relief by proclamation for the country to come in and refresh them with provisions. In the midst of all this calamity and confusion, there was, I know not how, an alarm begun that the French and Dutch, with whom we were now in hostility, were not only landed, but even entering the City. There was in truth some days before great suspicion of those two nations joining; and now, that they had been the occasion of firing the town. This report did so terrify, that on a sudden there was such an uproar and tumult that they ran from their goods, and taking what weapons they could come at, they could not be stopped from falling on some of those nations whom they casually met, without sense or reason. The clamour and peril grew so excessive that it made the whole Court amazed, and they did with infinite pains and great difficulty reduce and appease the people, sending troops of soldiers and guards to cause them to retire into the fields again, where they were watched all this night. I left them pretty quiet, and came home sufficiently weary and broken. Their spirits thus a little calmed, and the affright abated, they now began to repair into the suburbs about the City, where such as had friends or opportunity got shelter for the present, to which his Majesty's proclamation also invited them.

Still the plague continuing in our parish, I could not without danger adventure to our church.

10th. I went again to the ruins, for it was now no longer a City.

JOHN EVELYN (1620–1706), Diary, first pub. 1818

AFTER THE FIRE

5 September 1666

Thence homeward, having passed through Cheapside and Newgate-market, all burned—and seen Anthony Joyce's house in fire. And took up (which I keep by me) a piece of glass of Mercer's chapel in the street, where much more was, so melted and buckled with the heat of the fire, like parchment. I also did see a poor cat taken out of a hole in the chimney joining to the wall of the Exchange, with the hair all burned off the body and yet alive. So home at night, and find there good hopes of saving our office—but great endeavours of watching all night and having men ready; and so we lodged them in the office, and had drink and bread and cheese for them. And I lay down and slept a good night about midnight—though when I rose, I hear that there had been a great alarm of French and Dutch being risen—which proved nothing. But it is a strange thing to see how long this time did look since Sunday, having been alway full of variety of actions, and little sleep, that it looked like a week or more. And I had forgot almost the day of the week.

*

14 December 1666

Up, and very well again of my pain in my back, it having been nothing
but cold. By coach to White-hall, seeing many smokes of the Fire by the
way yet. And took up into the coach with me a country gentleman, who
asked me room to go with me, it being dirty—one come out of the
North to see his son after the burning his house—a merchant. Here
endeavoured to wait on the Duke of York, but he would not stay from
the Parliament. So I to Westminster-hall—and there met my good friend
Mr Eveling and walked with him a good while—lamenting our condition, for want of good counsel and the King's minding of his business
and servants. I out to the Bell Tavern, and thither comes Doll to me and
yo did tocar la cosa of her as I pleased; and after an hour's stay away, and
stayed in Westminster-hall till the rising of the House, having told Mr
Eveling, and he several others, of my Gazette which I had about me, that
mentioned in April last a plot for which several were condemned of
treason at the Old Bailey for many things.

*

31 December 1666

Rising this day with a full design to mind nothing else but to make up
my accounts for the year past, I did take money and walk forth to several
places in the town, as far as the New Exchange, to pay all my debts, it
being still a very great frost and good walking. I stayed at the Fleece
tavern in Covent-garden, while my boy Tom went to W. Joyces to pay
what I owed for candles there. Thence to the New Exchange to clear my
wife's score; and so going back again, I met Doll Lane (Mrs Martin's
sister) with another young woman of the Hall, one Scott, and took them
to the Half-Moon tavern and there drank some burned wine with them,
without more pleasure; and so away home by coach, and there to dinner
and then to my accounts, wherein at last I find them clear and right; but
to my great discontent, do find that my gettings this year have been 573*l*
less then my last—it being this year in all, but 2986*l*; whereas the last
I got 3560*l*. And then again, my spendings this year have exceeded my
spendings the last, by 644—my whole spendings last year being but
509*l*; whereas this year it appears I have spent 1154*l*—which is a sum
not fit to be said that ever I should spend in one year, before I am master
of a better estate then I am. Yet, blessed be God, and I pray God make
me thankful for it, I do find myself worth in money, all good, above

6200*l*; which is above 1800*l* more then I was the last year. This, I trust in God, will make me thankful for what I have, and careful to make up by care next year what by my negligence and prodigality I have lost and spent this year.

The doing of this and entering it fair, with the sorting of all my expenses to see how and in what points I have exceeded, did make it late work, till my eyes became very sore and ill; and then did give over, and supper and to bed.

Thus ends this year of public wonder and mischief to this nation—and therefore generally wished by all people to have an end. Myself and family well, having four maids and one clerk, Tom, in my house; and my brother now with me, to spend time in order to his preferment. Our healths all well; only, my eyes, with overworking them, are sore as soon as candle-light comes to them, and not else. Public matters in a most sad condition. Seamen discouraged for want of pay, and are become not to be governed. Nor, as matters are now, can any fleet go out next year. Our enemies, French and Dutch, great, and grow more, by our poverty. The Parliament backward in raising, because jealous of the spending of the money. The City less and less likely to be built again, everybody settling elsewhere, and nobody encouraged to trade. A sad, vicious, negligent Court, and all sober men there fearful of the ruin of the whole Kingdom this next year—from which, good God deliver us. One thing I reckon remarkable in my own condition is that I am come to abound in good plate, so as at all entertainments to be served wholly with silver plates, having two dozen and a half.

> Samuel Pepys (1633–1703), *Diary*, ed. R. Latham and W. Matthews, 1970–83; 'tocar la cosa' in Pepys's code, meaning literally 'touch the thing'.

TWO GOOD THINGS

During Charles II's reign the Great Plague happened in London. This was caused by some rats which had left a sinking ship on its way from China, and was very fortunate for the Londoners, since there were too many people in London at the time, so that they were always in bad health.

In the following year, therefore, London was set on fire in case anyone should have been left over from the Plague, and St Paul's Cathedral was built instead. This was also a Good Thing and was the cause of Sir Christopher Wren, the memorable architect.

PEPYS

Among the famous characters of the period were Samuel Pepys, who is memorable for keeping a Dairy and going to bed a great deal, and his wife Evelyn, who kept another memorable Dairy, but did not go to bed in it.

W. C. SELLAR and R. J. YEATMAN, 1066 and All That, 1930

In the second act of Vanbrugh's The Relapse, *Sir Novelty Fashion, who has been newly created Lord Foppington, is being teased by Amanda, the wife of Loveless, on whose virtue he has designs, and her cousin Berinthia, a young widow. Loveless, too, is privileged to hear how the vain fop and lecher occupies his time in London.*

LORD FOPPINGTON'S LONDON ROUTINE

Lord Fop. Naw I think a man of quality and breeding may be much diverted with the natural sprauts of his own. But to say the truth, madam, let a man love reading never so well, when once he comes to know this tawn, he finds so many better ways of passing away the four-and-twenty hours, that 'twere ten thousand pities he shou'd consume his time in that. Far example, madam, my life; my life, madam, is a perpetual stream of pleasure, that glides thro' such a variety of entertainments, I believe the wisest of our ancestors never had the least conception of any of 'em. I rise, madam, about ten o'clock. I don't rise sooner, because 'tis the worst thing in the world for the complection; nat that I pretend to be a beau; but a man must endeavour to look wholesome, lest he makes so nauseous a figure in the side-bax, the ladies shou'd be compell'd to turn their eyes upon the play. So at ten o'clock, I say, I rise. Naw, if I find it a good day, I resalve to take a turn in the park, and see the fine women; so huddle on my clothes, and get dress'd by one. If it be nasty weather, I take a turn in the chocolate-house; where, as you walk, madam, you have the prettiest prospect in the world; you have looking-glasses all round you—But I'm afraid I tire the company.

Ber. Not at all. Pray go on.

Lord Fop. Why then, ladies, from thence I go to dinner at Lacket's, and there you are so nicely and delicately serv'd, that, stap my vitals, they can compose you a dish, no bigger than a saucer, shall come to fifty shillings; between eating my dinner, and washing my mouth, ladies, I spend my time, till I go to the play; where, till nine o'clock, I entertain myself with looking upon the company; and usually dispose of one hour more in leading them aut. So there's twelve of the four-and-twenty pretty well over. The other twelve, madam, are disposed of in two articles: In the first four I toast myself drunk, and in t'other eight I sleep myself sober again. Thus, ladies, you see my life is an eternal raund O of delights.

Lov. 'Tis a heavenly one, indeed.

Aman. But, my lord, you beaux spend a great deal of your time in intrigues: You have given us no account of them yet.

Lord Fop. [*aside*]. Soh, she wou'd enquire into my amours—That's jealousy—She begins to be in love with me. [*To Aman.*] Why, madam—as to time for my intrigues, I usually make detachments of it from my other pleasures, according to the exigency. Far your ladyship may please to take notice, that those who intrigue with women of quality, have rarely occasion for above half an hour at a time: People of that rank being under those decorums, they can seldom give you a larger view, than will justly serve to shoot 'em flying. So that the course of my other pleasures is not very much interrupted by my amours.

Lov. But your lordship now is become a pillar of the State; you must attend the weighty affairs of the nation.

Lord Fop. Sir—as to weighty affairs—I leave them to weighty heads. I never intend mine shall be a burden to my body.

Lov. O, but you'll find the house will expect your attendance.

Lord Fop. Sir, you'll find the House will compound for my appearance.

Lov. But your friends will take it ill if you don't attend their particular causes.

Lord Fop. Not, sir, if I come time enough to give 'em my particular vote.

Ber. But pray, my lord, how do you dispose of yourself on Sundays? for that, methinks, shou'd hang wretchedly on your hands.

Lord Fop. Why, faith, madam—Sunday—is a vile day, I must confess; I intend to move for leave to bring in a Bill, that players may work upon it, as well as the hackney coaches. Tho' this I must say for the Government, it leaves us the churches to entertain us—But then again, they begin so abominable early, a man must rise by candle-light to get dress'd by the psalm.

Ber. Pray which church does your lordship most oblige with your presence?

Lord Fop. Oh, St James's, madam—There's much the best company.

Aman. Is there good preaching too?

Lord Fop. Why, faith, madam—I can't tell. A man must have very little to do there, that can give an account of the sermon.

Ber. You can give us an account of the ladies, at least.

Lord Fop. Or I deserve to be excommunicated. There is my Lady Tattle, my Lady Prate, my Lady Titter, my Lady Leer, my Lady Giggle, and my Lady Grin. These sit in the front of the boxes, and all church-time are the prettiest company in the world, stap my vitals.

Sir John Vanbrugh, The Relapse, or Virtue in Danger, 1696

THE BLACK BIRDS OF ST GILES

In 1690 Katherine Auker, a black, petitioned to be discharged from her master as he was in Barbados. She said that she had been brought to England about six years before by Robert Rich, a planter from Barbados. She was baptized at St Katherine's by the Tower and after that her master and mistress 'tortured her and turned her out; her said master refusing to give her a discharge, she could not be entertained in service elsewhere'. Her master had caused her to be arrested and imprisoned in the Poultry Compter. The Court ordered that she should be free to serve anyone till her master returned.

More fundamental issues were raised by the case of John Caesar, whose wife petitioned the Sessions in 1717. Her husband, she said, had served Benjamin and John Wood, who were printers and embossers in Whitechapel, as a slave without wages for fourteen years. They had very much abused the said John with very hard usage and for the greatest part of the time had imprisoned him in their dwelling-house. Seven years ago he had been baptized, nevertheless he was still detained as a slave, though, 'as the petitioner is advised, slavery is inconsistent with the laws of this realm'. She herself was very poor and destitute and likely to become chargeable to the parish unless her husband was released from his slavery and confinement and so enabled to provide for himself and the petitioner. The Court recommended the master to come to some reasonable agreement with regard to wages, and as the recommendation was not acted upon, in the next Sessions certain justices were ordered to consider what wages ought to be allowed to Caesar.

Difficulties of this kind seem sometimes to have induced the owners of slaves to enter into indentures with them and so secure a property in their labour by a contract recognized in English courts and not open to doubtful constructions. This at all events seems to be the explanation of certain advertisements for runaway negroes, one of which may be quoted:

Run away on Wednesday, the 28th ult., and stole money and goods from his master, John Lamb, Esq., an indentured black servant man about twenty-four years of age named William, of a brown or tawney complexion; had on when he went off, a parson's grey coat, blue breeches, white Bath flannel waistcoat, yellow gilt shoe buckles, and a beaver hat with a white lining.

Whoever apprehends him and brings him to his master at the Rookery House in Lewisham, Kent, shall have ten guineas reward and ten more on conviction in court of any persons harbouring or concealing him either on board ship or on shore.

N.B. He is also the property of his master, and has a burnt mark L.E., on one of his shoulders (1770).

On the other hand we hear of 'a black' as an apprentice boy and apparently as free as other apprentices which is perhaps not saying much. Anthony Emmannuell had been bound in 1723 to one Samuel Johnson, with the consent of his then mistress. Two years later his master petitioned for his discharge as notwithstanding his kindness the apprentice ran away, embezzled money and remained incorrigible in spite of having been put in the House of Correction. There were doubtless many Negroes who were either legally or virtually free, and lived uneventfully as domestic servants; there is the famous case of Dr Johnson's faithful Francis Barber. There seems to have been little prejudice against them on account of their race and colour. There was Ignatius Sancho, born on a slave ship, the butler of the Duke of Montague, afterwards a grocer, who was a well-known London character, his portrait painted by Gainsborough and engraved by Bartolozzi, whose letters (in rather painful imitation of the manner of Sterne) were published after his death. In the earlier part of the century little black boys as pages or playthings were favourite appendages of fashionable ladies or ladies of easy virtue.

Nevertheless there were many derelict unfortunate Negroes in London, and their number was increased by the peace of 1783 when the Negroes who had served with the British forces in America were sent, some to Nova Scotia, some to the Bahamas, some to London, where they quickly fell into distress. Negroes became conspicuous among London beggars and were known as St Giles black birds. Granville Sharp, to whose efforts the Somersett trial was due, was regarded by them as their protector, and he found himself with some 400 black pensioners. The urgency of removing them from London became apparent and a Committee for Relieving the Black Poor was formed with Jonas Hanway as its chairman. A scheme was formed in 1786 for establishing a colony of free Africans and other settlers on the west coast of Africa, and the Government undertook to pay up to £14 a head for their transportation. Applications were invited from those who were 'desirous of profiting by this opportunity of settling in one of the most fertile and pleasant countries in the known world'. Some 700 blacks offered themselves (of whom 441 embarked) and about sixty whites, chiefly London prostitutes, were sent with them, removal to the colonies being a favourite project of the age for reforming and providing for these poor women. This first settlement (1787) at Sierra Leone was an ill-fated one, the climate was not all that had been supposed, and the emigrants were not of the stuff to make successful pioneers.

M. Dorothy George, *London Life in the Eighteenth Century*, 2nd edn., 1966

A DESCRIPTION OF A CITY SHOWER

Careful observers may foretell the hour
(By sure prognostics) when to dread a shower.
While rain depends, the pensive cat gives o'er
Her frolics, and pursues her tail no more.
Returning home at night you find the sink
Strike your offended sense with double stink.
If you be wise, then go not far to dine,

You spend in coach-hire more than save in wine.
A coming shower your shooting corns presage,
Old aches throb, your hollow tooth will rage.
Sauntering in coffee-house is Dulman seen;
He damns the climate, and complains of spleen.

Meanwhile the South, rising with dabbled wings,
A sable cloud athwart the welkin flings,
That swilled more liquor than it could contain,
And like a drunkard gives it up again.
Brisk Susan whips her linen from the rope,
While the first drizzling shower is born aslope:
Such is that sprinkling which some careless quean
Flirts on you from her mop, but not so clean:
You fly, invoke the gods; then turning, stop
To rail; she singing, still whirls on her mop.
Nor yet the dust had shunned the unequal strife,
But, aided by the wind, fought still for life;
And wafted with its foe by violent gust,
'Twas doubtful which was rain, and which was dust.
Ah! where must needy poet seek for aid,
When dust and rain at once his coat invade?
Sole coat, where dust cemented by the rain
Erects the nap, and leaves a cloudy stain.

Now in contiguous drops the flood comes down,
Threatening with deluge this devoted town.
To shops in crowds the daggled females fly,
Pretend to cheapen goods; but nothing buy.
The Templar spruce, while every spout's abroach,
Stays till 'tis fair, yet seems to call a coach.
The tucked-up seamstress walks with hasty strides,
While streams run down her oiled umbrella's sides.
Here various kinds, by various fortunes led,
Commence acquaintance underneath a shed.
Triumphant Tories, and desponding Whigs,
Forget their feuds, and join to save their wigs.
Boxed in a chair the beau impatient sits,
While spouts run clattering o'er the roof by fits:

And ever and anon with frightful din
The leather sounds; he trembles from within.
So when Troy chair-men bore the wooden steed,
Pregnant with Greeks, impatient to be freed;
(Those bully Greeks, who, as the moderns do,
Instead of paying chair-men, run them through)
Laocoon struck the outside with his spear,
And each imprisoned hero quaked for fear.

Now from all parts the swelling kennels flow,
And bear their trophies with them as they go:
Filths of all hues and odours, seem to tell
What streets they sailed from, by the sight and smell.
They, as each torrent drives with rapid force
From Smithfield, or St Pulchre's shape their course;
And in huge confluent join at Snow Hill ridge,
Fall from the conduit prone to Holborn Bridge.
Sweepings from butchers' stalls, dung, guts, and blood,
Drowned puppies, stinking sprats, all drenched in mud,
Dead cats, and turnip-tops come tumbling down the flood.

                              JONATHAN SWIFT, 1710

ADDISON IN THE ABBEY

When I am in a serious humour, I very often walk by myself in West-minster-abbey: where the gloominess of the place, and the use to which it is applied, with the solemnity of the building, and the condition of the people who lie in it, are apt to fill the mind with a kind of melancholy or rather thoughtfulness that is not disagreeable. I yesterday passed a whole afternoon in the church-yard, the cloisters, and the church, amusing myself with the tombstones and inscriptions that I met with in those several regions of the dead. Most of them recorded nothing else of the buried person, but that he was born upon one day, and died upon another; the whole history of his life being comprehended in those two circumstances that are common to all mankind. I could not but look upon these registers of existence, whether of brass or marble, as a kind of satire upon the departed persons; who had left no other memorial of them, but that they were born, and that they died. They put me in mind of several persons mentioned in the battles of heroic poems, who have sounding names given them, for no other reason but that they may be killed, and are celebrated for nothing but being knocked on the head.

> Glaucumque, Medontaque, Thersilochumque.—VIRGIL
> Glaucus, and Melon, and Thersilochus.

The life of these men is finely described in holy writ by 'the path of an arrow', which is immediately closed up and lost.

Upon my going into the church, I entertained myself with the digging of a grave; and saw in every shovel-full of it that was thrown up, the fragment of a bone or skull intermixed with a kind of fresh mouldering earth that some time or other had a place in the composition of a human body. Upon this I began to consider with myself what innumerable multitudes of people lay confused together under the pavement of that ancient cathedral; how men and women, friends and enemies, priests and soldiers, monks and prebendaries, were crumbled amongst one another, and blended together in the same common mass; how beauty, strength, and youth, with old age, weakness, and deformity, lay undistinguished in the same promiscuous heap of matter.

After having thus surveyed the great magazine of mortality, as it were, in the lump, I examined it more particularly by the accounts which I found on several of the monuments which are raised in every quarter of that ancient fabric. Some of them were covered with such extravagant epitaphs, that if it were possible for the dead person to be acquainted with them, he would blush at the praises which his friends have bestowed upon him. There are others so excessively modest, that they deliver the character of the person departed in Greek or Hebrew, and by that means are not understood once in a twelve-month. In the poetical quarter, I found there were poets who had no monuments, and monuments which had no poets. I observed, indeed, that the present war has filled the church with many of these uninhabited monuments, which had been erected to the memory of persons whose bodies were perhaps buried in the plains of Blenheim, or in the bosom of the ocean.

I could not but be very much delighted with several modern epitaphs, which are written with great elegance of expression and justness of thought, and therefore do honour to the living as well as the dead. As a foreigner is very apt to conceive an idea of the ignorance or politeness of a nation from the turn of their public monuments and inscriptions, they should be submitted to the perusal of men of learning and genius before they are put in execution. Sir Cloudesly Shovel's monument has very often given me great offence. Instead of the brave rough English admiral, which was the distinguishing character of that plain gallant man, he is represented on his tomb by the figure of a beau, dressed in a long peri-wig, and reposing himself upon velvet cushions, under a canopy of state. The inscription is answerable to the monument; for instead of celebrating the many remarkable actions he had performed in the service of his country, it acquaints us only with the manner of his death, in which it was impossible for him to reap any honour. The Dutch, whom we are apt to despise for want of genius, show an infinitely greater taste of antiquity and politeness in their buildings and works of this nature than what we meet with in those of our own country. The monuments of their admirals, which have been erected at the public expense, represent them like themselves, and are adorned with rostral crowns and naval ornaments, with beautiful festoons of sea-weed, shells, and coral.

But to return to our subject. I have left the repository of our English kings for the contemplation of another day, when I shall find my mind disposed for so serious an amusement. I know that entertainments of this nature are apt to raise dark and dismal thoughts in timorous minds and gloomy imaginations; but for my own part, though I am always serious, I do not know what it is to be melancholy; and can therefore take a view of nature in her deep and solemn scenes with the same pleasure as in her most gay and delightful ones. By this means I can improve myself with those objects which others consider with terror. When I look upon the tombs of the great, every motion of envy dies in me; when I read the epitaphs of the beautiful, every inordinate desire goes out; when I meet with the grief of parents upon a tombstone, my heart melts with compassion; when I see the tomb of the parents themselves, I consider the vanity of grieving for those whom we must quickly follow. When I see kings lying by those who deposed them, when I consider rival wits placed side by side, or the holy men that divided the world with their contests and disputes, I reflect with sorrow and astonishment on the little competitions, factions, and debates of mankind. When I read the several dates of the tombs, of some that died yesterday, and some six hundred years ago, I consider that great day when we shall all of us be contemporaries, and make our appearance together.

JOSEPH ADDISON, essay in the *Spectator*, 30 March 1711

This description of Hampton Court comes from The Rape of the Lock *(1712).*

Close by those meads for ever crowned with flow'rs,
Where Thames with pride surveys his rising tow'rs,
There stands a structure of majestic frame,
Which from the neighb'ring Hampton takes its name.
Here Britain's statesmen oft the fall foredoom
Of foreign tyrants, and of nymphs at home;
Here thou, great Anna! whom three realms obey,
Dost sometimes counsel take—and sometimes Tea.
　　Hither the heroes and the nymphs resort,
To taste awhile the pleasures of a Court;
In various talk th'instructive hours they passed,
Who gave the ball, or paid the visit last:
One speaks the glory of the British Queen,
And one describes a charming Indian screen;
A third interprets motions, looks, and eyes;
At ev'ry word a reputation dies.
Snuff, or the fan, supply each pause of chat,
With singing, laughing, ogling, and all that.
　　Meanwhile declining from the noon of day,
The sun obliquely shoots his burning ray;
The hungry Judges soon the sentence sign,
And wretches hang that jurymen may dine;
The merchant from th'Exchange returns in peace,
And the long labours of the Toilet cease.

ALEXANDER POPE (1688–1744)

LONDON'S VOICE

'Tis the first Virtue, Vices to abhor;
And the first Wisdom, to be Fool no more.

But to the world no bugbear is so great,
As want of figure, and a small Estate.
To either India see the Merchant fly,
Scar'd at the spectre of pale Poverty!
See him, with pains of body, pangs of soul,
Burn through the Tropic, freeze beneath the Pole!
Wilt thou do nothing for a nobler end,
Nothing, to make Philosophy thy friend?
To stop thy foolish views, thy long desires,
And ease thy heart of all that it admires?
   Here, Wisdom calls: 'Seek Virtue first, be bold!
As Gold to Silver, Virtue is to Gold.'
There, London's voice: 'Get Money, Money still!
And then let Virtue follow, if she will.'
This, this the saving doctrine, preach'd to all,
From low St James's up to high St Paul;
From him whose quills stand quiver'd at his ear,
To him who notches sticks at Westminster.

ALEXANDER POPE, 'Imitations of Horace', Book I, Epistle I, 1738

TRIVIA, OR WALKING THE STREETS OF LONDON

I

The seasons operate on ev'ry breast;
'Tis hence that fawns are brisk, and ladies dressed.
When on his box the nodding coachman snores,
And dreams of fancied fares; when tavern doors
The chairmen idly crowd; then ne'er refuse
To trust thy busy steps in thinner shoes.

   But when the swinging signs your ears offend
With creaky noise, then rainy floods impend;
Soon shall the kennels swell with rapid streams;
And rush in muddy torrents to the Thames.
The bookseller, whose shop's an open square,

Foresees the tempest, and with early care
Of learning strips the rails; the rowing crew
To tempt a fare, clothe all their tilts in blue:
On hosiers' poles depending stockings tied
Flag with the slackened gale from side to side;
Church monuments foretell the changing air;
Then Niobe dissolves into a tear,
And sweats with secret grief: you'll hear the sounds
Of whistling winds, ere kennels break their bounds;
Ungrateful odours common shores diffuse,
And dropping vaults distil unwholesome dews
Before tiles rattle with the smoking show'r,
And spouts on heedless men their torrents pour.

II

When night first bids the twinkling stars appear,
Or with her cloudy veil enwraps the air,
Then swarms the busy street; with caution tread
Where the shop-windows falling threat thy head;
Now lab'rers home return, and join their strength
To bear the tott'ring plank, or ladder's length;
Still fix thy eyes intent upon the throng,
And as the passes open, wind along.

Where the fair columns of St Clement stand,
Whose straitened bounds encroach upon the Strand;
Where the low penthouse bows the walker's head,
And the rough pavement wounds the yielding tread;
Where not a post protects the narrow space,
And strung in twines, combs dangle in thy face;
Summon at once thy courage, rouse thy care,
Stand firm, look back, be resolute, beware.
Forth issuing from steep lanes, the collier's steeds
Drag the black load; another cart succeeds,
Team follows team, crowds heaped on crowds appear,
And wait impatient till the road grow clear.
Now all the pavement sounds with trampling feet,

And the mixed hurry barricades the street.
Entangled here, the waggon's lengthened team
Cracks the tough harness; here a pond'rous beam
Lies overturned athwart; for slaughter fed
Here lowing bullocks raise their horned head.
Now oaths grow loud, with coaches coaches jar,
And the smart blow provokes the sturdy war;
From the high box they whirl the thong around,
And with the twining lash their shins resound:
Their rage ferments, more dangerous wounds they try,
And the blood gushes down their painful eye,
And now on foot the frowning warriors light,
And with their pond'rous fists renew the fight;
Blow answers blow, their cheeks are smeared with blood,
Till down they fall, and grappling roll in mud.
So when two boars, in wild Ytene bred,
Or on Westphalia's fatt'ning chestnuts fed,
Gnash their sharp tusks, and roused with equal fire,
Dispute the reign of some luxurious mire;
In the black flood they wallow o'er and o'er,
Till their armed jaws distil with foam and gore.

Where the mob gathers, swiftly shoot along,
Nor idly mingle with the noisy throng.
Lured by the silver hilt, amid the swarm,
The subtil artist will thy side disarm.
Nor is thy flaxen wig with safety worn;
High on the shoulder in a basket born
Lurks the fly boy; whose hand to rapine bred,
Plucks off the curling honours of thy head.

JOHN GAY (1685–1732); 'Ytene' is the ancient name for the New
Forest in Hampshire.

CLEVER TOM CLINCH GOING TO BE HANGED

As clever *Tom Clinch*, while the Rabble was bawling,
Rode stately through *Holbourn*, to die in his Calling;
He stopt at the *George* for a Bottle of Sack,

And promis'd to pay for it when he'd come back.
His Waistcoat and Stockings, and Breeches were white,
His Cap had a new Cherry Ribbon to ty't.
The Maids to the Doors and the Balconies ran,
And said, lack-a-day! he's a proper young Man.
But, as from the Windows the Ladies he spy'd,
Like a Beau in the Box, he bow'd low on each Side;
And when his last Speech the loud Hawkers did cry,
He swore from his Cart, it was all a damn'd Lye.
The Hangman for Pardon fell down on his Knee;
Tom gave him a Kick in the Guts for his Fee.
Then said, I must speak to the People a little,
But I'll see you all damn'd before I will *whittle*.
My honest Friend *Wild*, may he long hold his Place,
He lengthen'd my Life with a whole Year of Grace.
Take Courage, dear Comrades, and be not afraid,
Nor slip this Occasion to follow your Trade.
My Conscience is clear, and my Spirits are calm,
And thus I go off without Pray'r-Book or Psalm.
Then follow the Patience of clever *Tom Clinch*,
Who hung like a Hero, and never would flinch.

JONATHAN SWIFT, 1726

LORDS OF THE STREET AND A MIDNIGHT MURDERER

For who wou'd leave, unbrib'd, Hibernia's land,
Or change the rocks of Scotland for the Strand?
There none are swept by sudden fate away,
But all whom hunger spares, with age decay:
Here malice, rapine, accident, conspire,
And now a rabble rages, now a fire;
Their ambush here relentless ruffians lay,
And here the fell attorney prowls for prey;
Here falling houses thunder on your head,
And here a female atheist talks you dead.
While Thales waits the wherry that contains
Of dissipated wealth the small remains,

On Thames's banks, in silent thought we stood,
Where Greenwich smiles upon the silver flood;
Struck with the feat that gave Eliza birth,
We kneel, and kiss the consecrated earth;
In pleasing dreams the blissful age renew,
And call Britannia's glories back to view;
Behold her cross triumphant on the main,
The guard of commerce, and the dread of Spain,
Ere masquerades debauch'd, excise oppress'd,
Or English honour grew a standing jest.

    A transient calm the happy scenes bestow,
And for a moment lull the sense of woe.
At length awaking, with contemptuous frown,
Indignant Thales eyes the neighb'ring town.

    Since worth, he cries, in these degen'rate days
Wants ev'n the cheap reward of empty praise;
In those curs'd walls, devote to vice and gain,
Since unrewarded science toils in vain;
Since hope but soothes to double my distress,
And ev'ry moment leaves my little less;
While yet my steady steps no staff sustains,
And life still vig'rous revels in my veins;
Grant me, kind Heaven, to find some happier place,
Where honesty and sense are no disgrace;
Some pleasing bank where verdant osiers play,
Some peaceful vale with nature's paintings gay;
Where once the harass'd Briton found repose,
And safe in poverty defi'd his foes:
Some secret cell, ye pow'rs indulgent, give,
Let —— live here, for —— has learn'd to live.
Here let those reign, whom pensions can incite
To vote a patriot black, a courtier white;
Explain their country's dear-bought rights away,
And plead for pirates in the face of day;
With slavish tenets taint our poison'd youth,
And lend a lie the confidence of truth. . . .

    Could'st thou resign the park and play content,
For the fair banks of Severn or of Trent;

There might'st thou find some elegant retreat,
Some hireling senator's deserted seat;
And stretch thy prospects o'er the smiling land,
For less than rent the dungeons of the Strand;
There prune thy walks, support thy drooping flow'rs,
Direct thy rivulets, and twine thy bow'rs;
And, while thy grounds a cheap repast afford,
Despise the dainties of a venal lord:
There ev'ry bush with Nature's music rings,
There ev'ry breeze bears health upon its wings;
On all thy hours security shall smile,
And bless thine evening walk and morning toil.

   Prepare for death if here at night you roam,
And sign your will before you sup from home.
Some fiery fop, with new commission vain,
Who sleeps on brambles till he kills his man;
Some frolic drunkard, reeling from a feast,
Provokes a broil, and stabs you for a jest.
Yet ev'n these heroes, mischievously gay,
Lords of the street, and terrors of the way,
Flush'd as they are with folly, youth, and wine,
Their prudent insults to the poor confine;
Afar they mark the flambeau's bright approach,
And shun the shining train and golden coach.

   In vain these dangers past, your doors you close,
And hope the balmy blessings of repose:
Cruel with guilt, and daring with despair,
The midnight murd'rer bursts the faithless bar;
Invades the sacred hour of silent rest,
And leaves unseen a dagger in your breast.

  Scarce can our fields, such crowds at Tyburn die,
With hemp the Gallows and the Fleet supply.
Propose your schemes, ye senatorian band,
Whose ways and means support the sinking land,
Lest ropes be wanting in the tempting spring,
To rig another convoy for the King.

   A single gaol in Alfred's golden reign
Could half the nation's criminals contain;

Fair Justice then, without constraint ador'd,
Held high the steady scale, but sheath'd the sword;
No spies were paid, no special juries known,
Blest age! but ah! how diff'rent from our own!
    Much could I add,—but see the boat at hand,
The tide retiring calls me from the land:
Farewell!—When youth, and health, and fortune spent,
Thou fli'st for refuge to the wilds of Kent;
And, tir'd like me with follies and with crimes,
In angry numbers warn'st succeeding times,
Then shall thy friend, nor thou refuse his aid,
Still foe to vice, forsake his Cambrian shade;
In virtue's cause once more exert his rage,
Thy satire point, and animate thy page.

Samuel Johnson, from 'London', 1738

A DESCRIPTION OF THE SPRING IN LONDON

Now new-vamped silks the mercer's window shows,
And his spruce 'prentice wears his Sunday clothes;
His annual suit with nicest taste renewed,
The reigning cut and colour still pursued.
    The barrow now, with oranges a score,
Driv'n by at once a gamester and a whore,
No longer gulls the stripling of his pence,
Who learns that poverty is nurse to sense.
Much-injured trader whom the law pursues,
The law which winked and beckoned to the Jews,
Why should the beadle drive thee from the street?
To sell is always a pretence to cheat.
    'Large stewing-oysters!', in a deep'ning groan,
No more resounds, nor 'Mussels!' shriller tone;
Sev'n days to labour now is held no crime,
And Moll 'New mack'rel!' screams in sermon-time.
    In ruddy bunches radishes are spread,
And Nan with choice-picked salad loads her head.
    Now, in the suburb window, Christmas green,

The bays and holly are no longer seen,
But sprigs of garden-mint in vials grow,
And gathered laylocks perish as they blow.   *lilacs*
     The truant schoolboy now at eve we meet,
Fatigued and sweating through the crowded street,
His shoes embrowned at once with dust and clay,
With whitethorn loaded, which he takes for May:
Round his flapped hat in rings the cowslips twine,
Or in cleft osiers form a golden line.
     On milk-pail reared the borrowed salvers glare,
Topped with a tankard which two porters bear;
Reeking, they slowly toil o'er rugged stones,
And joyless beldams dance with aching bones.
More blithe the powdered, tie-wigged sons of soot
Trip to their shovel with a shoeless foot.
In gay Vauxhall now saunter beaux and belles,
And happier cits resort to Sadler's Wells.

                                        ANON., 1754

'THE NOISY AND EXPENSIVE SCENE'

Of the two years (May 1758–May 1760) between my return to England
and the embodying the Hampshire militia, I passed about nine months
in London and the remainder in the country. The metropolis affords
many amusements which are open to all; it is itself an astonishing and
perpetual spectacle to the curious eye; and each taste, each sense, may be
gratified by the variety of objects that will occur in the long circuit of
a morning walk. I assiduously frequented the Theatres at a very prosperous æra of the stage, when a constellation of excellent actors, both in
tragedy and comedy, was eclipsed by the meridian brightness of Garrick,
in the maturity of his judgement and vigour of his performance. The
pleasures of a town life, the daily round from the tavern to the play, from
the play to the coffee-house, from the coffee-house to the —— are within
the reach of every man who is regardless of his health, his money, and
his company. By the contagion of example I was sometimes seduced; but
the better habits which I had formed at Lausanne induced me to seek
a more elegant and rational society; and if my search was less easy and

successful than I might have hoped, I shall at present impute the failure to the disadvantages of my situation and character. Had the rank and fortune of my parents given them an annual establishment in London, their own house would have introduced me to a numerous and polite circle of acquaintance. But my father's taste had always preferred the highest and the lowest company, for which he was equally qualified; and after a twelve years' retirement he was no longer in the memory of the great with whom he had associated. I found myself a stranger in the midst of a vast and unknown city, and at my entrance into life I was reduced to some dull family parties, and some scattered connections which were not such as I should have chosen for myself. The most useful friends of my father were the Mallets: they received me with civility and kindness, at first on his account, and afterwards on my own; and (if I may use Lord Chesterfield's word) I was soon *domesticated* in their house. Mr Mallet, a name among the English poets, is praised by an unforgiving enemy for the ease and elegance of his conversation, and whatsoever might be the defects of his wife, she was not destitute of wit or learning. By his assistance I was introduced to Lady Hervey, the mother of the present Earl of Bristol: her age and infirmities confined her at home; her dinners were select; in the evening her house was open to the best company of both sexes and all nations; nor was I displeased at her preference and even affectation of the manners, the language, and the litterature of France. But my progress in the English World was in general left to my own efforts, and those efforts were languid and slow. I had not been endowed by art or Nature with those happy gifts of confidence and address which unlock every door and every bosom; nor would it be reasonable to complain of the just consequences of my sickly childhood, foreign education, and reserved temper. While coaches were rattling through Bond Street, I have passed many a solitary evening in my lodging with my books: my studies were sometimes interrupted by a sigh which I breathed towards Lausanne; and on the approach of spring I withdrew without reluctance from the noisy and expensive scene of crowds without company, and dissipation without pleasure. In each of the twenty-five years of my acquaintance with London (1758–1783) the prospect gradually brightened; and this unfavourable picture most properly belongs to the first period after my return from Switzerland.

EDWARD GIBBON (1737–94), *Autobiography*, 1796

A RICH MAN'S MONUMENT

I am just returned from Westminster-abbey, the place of sepulture for the philosophers, heroes, and kings of England. What a gloom do monumental inscriptions and all the venerable remains of deceased merit inspire! Imagine a temple marked with the hand of antiquity, solemn as religious awe, adorned with all the magnificence of barbarous profusion, dim windows, fretted pillars, long colonades, and dark cielings. Think then, what were my sensations at being introduced to such a scene. I stood in the midst of the temple, and threw my eyes round on the walls filled with the statues, the inscriptions, and the monuments of the dead.

Alas, I said to myself, how does pride attend the puny child of dust even to the grave! Even humble as I am, I possess more consequence in the present scene than the greatest hero of them all; they have toiled for an hour to gain a transient immortality, and are at length retired to the grave, where they have no attendant but the worm, none to flatter but the epitaph.

As I was indulging such reflections, a gentleman dressed in black, perceiving me to be a stranger came up, entered into conversation, and politely offered to be my instructor and guide through the temple. If any monument, said he, should particularly excite your curiosity, I shall endeavour to satisfy your demands. I accepted with thanks the gentleman's offer, adding, that 'I was come to observe the policy, the wisdom, and the justice of the English, in conferring rewards upon deceased merit. If adulation like this, continued I, be properly conducted, as it can no way injure those who are flattered, so it may be a glorious incentive to those who are now capable of enjoying it. It is the duty of every good government to turn this monumental pride to its own advantage, to become strong in the aggregate from the weakness of the individual. If none but the truly great have a place in this awful repository, a temple like this will give the finest lessons of morality, and be a strong incentive to true ambition. I am told, that none have a place here but characters of the most distinguished merit.' The man in black seemed impatient at my observations, so I discontinued my remarks, and we walked on together to take a view of every particular monument in order as it lay.

As the eye is naturally caught by the finest objects, I could not avoid being particularly curious about one monument, which appeared more beautiful than the rest; that, said I to my guide, I take to be the tomb of some very great man. By the peculiar excellence of the workmanship, and the magnificence of the design, this must be a trophy raised to the memory of some king who has saved his country from ruin, or law-giver, who has reduced his fellow-citizens from anarchy into just subjection. It is not requisite, replied my companion smiling, to have such qualifications in order to have a very fine monument here. More humble abilities will suffice. *What, I suppose then the gaining two or three battles, or the taking half a score towns, is thought a sufficient qualification?* Gaining battles, or taking towns replied the man in black, may be of service; but a gentleman may have a very fine monument here without ever seeing a battle or a siege. *This then is the monument of some poet, I presume, of one whose wit has gained him immortality?* No, sir, replied my guide, the gentleman who lies here never made verses; and as for wit, he despised it in others, because he had none himself. *Pray tell me then in a word, said I peevishly, what is the great man who lies here particularly remarkable for?* Remarkable, sir! said my companion; why, sir, the gentleman that lies here is remarkable, very remarkable—for a tomb in Westminster-abbey. *But, head of my Ancestors! how has he got here; I fancy he could never bribe the guardians of the temple to give him a place? Should he not be ashamed to be seen among company, where even moderate merit would look like infamy?* I suppose, replied the man in black, the gentleman was rich, and his friends, as is usual in such a case, told him he was great. He readily believed them; the guardians of the temple, as they got by the self delusion, were ready to believe him too; so he paid his money for a fine monument; and the workman, as you see, has made him one of the most beautiful.

OLIVER GOLDSMITH, The Citizen of the World, 1762

BOSWELL RETURNS TO LONDON

Friday, 19 November 1762

It was very cold. Stewart was as effeminate as I. I asked him how he, who shivered if a pane of glass was broke in a post-chaise, could bear the severe hardship of a sea life. He gave me to understand that necessity made anything be endured. Indeed this is very true. For when the mind knows that it cannot help itself by struggling, it quietly and patiently submits to whatever load is laid upon it. When we came upon Highgate hill and had a view of London, I was all life and joy. I repeated Cato's soliloquy on the immortality of the soul, and my soul bounded forth to a certain prospect of happy futurity. I sung all manner of songs, and began to make one about an amorous meeting with a pretty girl, the burthen of which was as follows:

> She gave me *this*, I gave her *that*;
> And tell me, had she not tit for tat?

I gave three huzzas, and we went briskly in.

I got from Digges a list of the best houses on the road, and also a direction to a good inn at London. I therefore made the boy drive me to Mr Hayward's, at the Black Lion, Water Lane, Fleet Street. The noise, the crowd, the glare of shops and signs agreeably confused me. I was rather more wildly struck than when I first came to London. My companion could not understand my feelings. He considered London just as a place where he was to receive orders from the East India Company. We now parted, with saying that we had agreed well and been happy, and that we should keep up the acquaintance. I then had a bit of dinner, got myself shaved and cleaned, and had my landlord, a civil jolly man, to take a glass of wine with me. I was all in a flutter at having at last got to the place which I was so madly fond of, and being restrained, had formed so many wild schemes to get back to. I had recourse to philosophy, and so rendered myself calm.

I immediately went to my friend Douglas's, surgeon in Pall Mall, a kind-hearted, plain, sensible man, where I was cordially received. His wife is a good-humoured woman, and is that sort of character which is often met with in England: very lively without much wit. Her fault is speaking too much, which often tires people. He was my great adviser as to everything; and in the mean time insisted that I should have a bed in his house till I got a lodging to my mind. I agreed to come there next day. I went to Covent Garden—*Every Man in His Humour*. Woodward played Bobadil finely. He entertained me much. It was fine after the fatigues of my journey to find myself snug in a theatre, my body warm and my mind elegantly amused. I went to my inn, had some negus, and went comfortably to bed.

'A LARGE FAT BEEFSTEAK'

Wednesday, 15 December 1762
The enemies of the people of England who would have them considered
in the worst light represent them as selfish, beef-eaters, and cruel. In this
view I resolved today to be a true-born Old Englishman. I went into the
City to Dolly's Steak-house in Paternoster Row and swallowed my dinner
by myself to fulfill the charge of selfishness; I had a large fat beefsteak
to fulfil the charge of beef-eating; and I went at five o'clock to the Royal
Cockpit in St James's Park and saw cock-fighting for about five hours to
fulfill the charge of cruelty.

A beefsteak-house is a most excellent place to dine at. You come in
there to a warm, comfortable, large room, where a number of people are
sitting at table. You take whatever place you find empty; call for what
you like, which you get well and cleverly dressed. You may either chat
or not as you like. Nobody minds you, and you pay very reasonably. My
dinner (beef, bread and beer and waiter) was only a shilling. The waiters
make a great deal of money by these pennies. Indeed, I admire the English for attending to small sums, as many smalls make a great, according
to the proverb.

At five I filled my pockets with gingerbread and apples (quite the
method), put on my old clothes and laced hat, laid by my watch, purse,
and pocket-book, and with oaken stick in my hand sallied to the pit. I
was too soon there. So I went into a low inn, sat down amongst a parcel
of arrant blackguards, and drank some beer. The sentry near the house
had been very civil in showing me the way. It was very cold. I bethought
myself of the poor fellow, so I carried out a pint of beer myself to him.
He was very thankful and drank my health cordially. He told me his
name was Hobard, that he was a watch-maker but in distress for debt,
and enlisted that his creditors might not touch him.

I then went to the Cockpit, which is a circular room in the middle of
which the cocks fight. It is seated round with rows gradually rising. The
pit and the seats are all covered with mat. The cocks, nicely cut and
dressed and armed with silver heels, are set down and fight with amazing
bitterness and resolution. Some of them were quickly dispatched. One
pair fought three quarters of an hour. The uproar and noise of betting is
prodigious. A great deal of money made a very quick circulation from
hand to hand. There was a number of professed gamblers there. An old

cunning dog whose face I had seen at Newmarket sat by me a while. I told him I knew nothing of the matter. 'Sir,' said he, 'you have as good a chance as anybody.' He thought I would be a good subject for him. I was young-like. But he found himself balked. I was shocked to see the distraction and anxiety of the betters. I was sorry for the poor cocks. I looked round to see if any of the spectators pitied them when mangled and torn in a most cruel manner, but I could not observe the smallest relenting sign in any countenance. I was therefore not ill pleased to see them endure mental torment. Thus did I complete my true English day, and came home pretty much fatigued and pretty much confounded at the strange turn of this people.

CHEER AND SORROW

Wednesday, 19 January 1763
This was a day eagerly expected by Dempster, Erskine, and I, as it was fixed as the period of our gratifying a whim proposed by me: which was that on the first day of the new tragedy called *Elvira's* being acted, we three should walk from the one end of London to the other, dine at Dolly's, and be in the theatre at night; and as the play would probably be bad, and as Mr David Malloch, the author, who has changed his name to David Mallet, Esq., was an arrant puppy, we determined to exert ourselves in damning it. I this morning felt stronger symptoms of the sad distemper, yet I was unwilling to imagine such a thing. However, the severe exercise of today, joined with hearty eating and drinking, I was sure would confirm or remove my suspicions.

We walked up to Hyde Park Corner, from whence we set out at ten. Our spirits were high with the notion of the adventure, and the variety that we met with as we went along is amazing. As the Spectator observes, one end of London is like a different country from the other in look and in manners. We eat an excellent breakfast at the Somerset Coffee-house. We turned down Gracechurch Street and went upon the top of London Bridge, from whence we viewed with a pleasing horror the rude and terrible appearance of the river, partly froze up, partly covered with enormous shoals of floating ice which often crashed against each other. Dempster said of this excursion from the road that our Epic Poem would be somewhat dull if it were not enlivened by such episodes. As we went along, I felt the symptoms increase, which was very confounding and very distressing to me. I thought the best thing I could do was not to keep it secret, which would be difficult and troublesome, but fairly to own it to Dempster and Erskine and ask their advice and sympathy. They really sympathized, and yet they could not help smiling a little at my catching a tartar so very unexpectedly, when I imagined myself quite safe, and had been vaunting most heroically of my felicity in having the possession of a fine woman, to whom I ascribed so many endearing qualities that they really doubted of her existence, and used to call her my *ideal lady*. We went half a mile beyond the turnpike at Whitechapel, which completed our course, and went into a little public house and drank some warm white wine with aromatic spices, pepper and cinnamon. We were pleased with the neat houses upon the road.

We met a coach loaded with passengers both within and without. Said I, 'I defy all the philosophers in the world to tell me why this is.' 'Because,' said Erskine, 'the people wanted a quick carriage from one place to another.' So very easily are the most of the speculations which I often perplex myself with refuted. And yet if some such clever answerer is not at hand, I may puzzle and confound my brain for a good time upon many occasions. To be sure this instance is too ludicrous. But surely, I and many more speculative men have been thrown into deep and serious thought about matters very little more serious. Yet the mind will take its own way, do what we will. So that we may be rendered uneasy by such cloudy reveries when we have no intention to be in such a humour. The best relief in such a case is mirth and gentle amusement.

We had a room to ourselves, and a jolly profusion of smoking juicy beefsteaks. I eat like a very Turk, or rather indeed like a very John Bull, whose supreme joy is good beef. We had some port, and drank damnation to the play and eternal remorse to the author. We then went to the Bedford Coffee-house and had coffee and tea; and just as the doors opened at four o'clock, we sallied into the house, planted ourselves in the middle of the pit, and with oaken cudgels in our hands and shrill-sounding catcalls in our pockets, sat ready prepared, with a generous resentment in our breasts against dullness and impudence, to be the swift ministers of vengeance. About five the house began to be pretty well filled. As is usual on first nights, some of us called to the music to play *Roast Beef*. But they did not comply with our request and we were not numerous enough to turn that request into a command, which in a London theatre is quite a different sort of public speech. This was but a bad omen for

our party. It resembled a party's being worsted in the choice of praeses
and clerk, at an election in a Scotch county.

However, we kept a good spirit, and hoped the best. The prologue was
politically stupid. We hissed it and had several to join us. That we might
not be known, we went by borrowed names. Dempster was Clarke; Erskine,
Smith; and I, Johnston. We did what we could during the first act, but
found that the audience had lost their original fire and spirit and were
disposed to let it pass. Our project was therefore disconcerted, our im-
petuosity damped. As we knew it would be needless to oppose that
furious many-headed monster, the multitude, as it has been very well
painted, we were obliged to lay aside our laudable undertaking in the
cause of genius and the cause of modesty.

After the play we went to Lady Betty's, and as they were not disposed
to eat and we were very hungry after our fatigues, we were set down in
the parlour by ourselves to an excellent warm supper. We were in high
glee, and after supper threw out so many excellent sallies of humour and
wit and satire on Malloch and his play that we determined to have a joint
sixpenny cut, and fixed next day for throwing our sallies into order. The
evening was passed most cheerfully. When I got home, though, then
came sorrow. Too, too plain was Signor Gonorrhoea. Yet I could scarce
believe it, and determined to go to friend Douglas next day.

JAMES BOSWELL, *London Journal 1762–1763*, ed. Frederick A. Pottle,
1950

*In 1764 Leopold Mozart brought his son, Wolfgang Amadeus, and family to
London. Wolfgang performed for King George III and Queen Charlotte.*

THE MOZARTS IN LONDON

On April 27th we were with the King and Queen in the Queen's Palace
in St James's Park; so that by the fifth day after our arrival we were
already at court. The present was only twenty-four guineas, which we
received immediately on leaving the King's apartment, but the graciousness with which both His Majesty the King and Her Majesty the Queen
received us cannot be described. In short, their easy manner and friendly
ways made us forget that they were the King and Queen of England. At
all courts up to the present we have been received with extraordinary
courtesy. But the welcome which we have been given here exceeds all

others. A week later we were walking in St James's Park. The King came along driving with the Queen and, although we had on different clothes, they recognized us nevertheless and not only greeted us, but the King opened the window, leaned out and saluted us and especially our Master Wolfgang, nodding to us and waving his hand.

I must tell you that in England there is a kind of native complaint, which is called a '*cold*'. That is why you hardly ever see people wearing summer clothes. They all wear cloth garments. This so-called '*cold*' in the case of people who are not constitutionally sound, becomes so dangerous that in many cases it develops into a '*consumption*' as they call it here; but I call it '*febrem lentam*'; and the wisest course for such people to adopt is to leave England and cross the sea; and many instances can be found of people recovering their health on leaving this country. I caught this '*cold*' unexpectedly and in the following way. On July 8th at six in the evening we were to go to Mylord Thanet's. Before six I sent out to the stand where carriages are to be found, but not one was to be had. It was Sunday, so all had been hired. It was an exceedingly fine and very hot day. I sent for a sedan-chair, put my two children into it and walked behind, as the weather was unusually lovely. But I had forgotten how fast the bearers stride along here; and I soon had a taste of it. I can walk fairly quickly, as you know, and my stoutness does not prevent me from doing so. But, before we arrived at Mylord Thanet's I often thought that I should have to give up; for London is not like Salzburg. And I perspired as profusely as it is possible for a man to do. I had only a silk waistcoat on, though I was wearing a cloth coat, which I buttoned up immediately on arriving at Mylord Thanet's. But it was to no purpose. The evening was cool and all the windows were open. We stayed until eleven o'clock and I at once fell ill and engaged a second sedan-chair to take me home. Yet until the 14th, although I did not feel well, I went about and tried to cure myself by perspiring, which is the remedy generally adopted here. But it was no good.

My wife and children send their greetings. My wife has had a great deal to do lately on account of my illness, and, as you may imagine, she has had a great many anxieties. In Chelsea we had our food sent to us at first from an eating-house; but as it was so poor, my wife began to do our cooking and we are now in such good trim that when we return to town next week we shall continue to do our own housekeeping. Perhaps too my wife, who has become very thin, will get a little fatter.

> LEOPOLD MOZART, letters to Lorenz Hagenauer, 28 May and 13 September 1764, from *The Letters of Mozart and his Family*, trans. and ed. Emily Anderson, 1966

'AN ABSOLUTE HELL UPON EARTH'

At the customary hour, being brimful of wine, we sallied forth, went the old Bow Street rounds, from whence I was led into an absolute hell upon earth. The first impression on my mind upon entering those diabolical regions never will be effaced from my memory. This den was distinguished by the name of Wetherby's, situate in the narrowest part of Little Russell Street, Drury Lane. Upon ringing at a door, strongly secured with knobs of iron, a cut-throat-looking rascal opened a small wicket, which was also secured with narrow iron bars, who in a hoarse and ferocious voice asked, 'Who's there?' Being answered 'Friends,' we were cautiously admitted one at a time, and when the last had entered, the door was instantly closed and secured, not only by an immense lock and key, but a massy iron bolt and chain.

I had then never been within the walls of a prison; yet this struck me like entering one of the most horrible kind. My companions conducted me into a room where such a scene was exhibiting that I involuntarily shrunk back with disgust and dismay, and would have retreated from the apartment, but that I found my surprise and alarm were so visible in my countenance as to have attracted the attention of several persons who came up, and good-naturedly enough encouraged me, observing that I was a young hand but should soon be familiarized and enjoy the fun. At this time the whole room was in an uproar, men and women promiscuously mounted upon chairs, tables, and benches, in order to see a sort of general conflict carrying on upon the floor. Two she-devils, for they scarce had a human appearance, were engaged in a scratching and boxing match, their faces entirely covered with blood, bosoms bare, and the clothes nearly torn from their bodies. For several minutes not a creature interfered between them, or seemed to care a straw what mischief they might do each other, and the contest went on with unabated fury.

In another corner of the same room, an uncommonly athletic young man of about twenty-five seemed to be the object of universal attack. No less than three Amazonian tigresses were pummelling him with all their might, and it appeared to me that some of the males at times dealt him blows with their sticks. He, however, made a capital defence, not sparing the women a bit more than the men, but knocking each down as opportunity occurred. As fresh hands continued pouring in upon him, he must at last have been miserably beaten, had not two of the gentlemen who went with me, (both very stout fellows) offended at the shameful odds used against a single person, interfered, and after a few knock-me-down arguments, succeeded in putting an end to the unequal conflict. This, to me, unusual riot, had a similar effect with Othello's sudden and unexpected appearance before his inebriated officer, Michael Cassio, for it produced an immediate restoration of my senses, the effect of which was an eager wish to get away; for which purpose I, in the confusion, slunk out of the room into the passage, and had just began fumbling at the street door, hoping to be able to liberate myself, when the same fierce and brutal Cerberus that had admitted my party coming up, roughly seized me by the collar exclaiming: 'Hulloa, what the devil have you been about here?'

To which I answered meekly: 'Nothing, but not being well I am desirous of going home.'

'Oh you are, are you! I think you came in not long since, and with a party. What! Do you want to tip us a bilk? Have you paid your reckoning, eh? No, no, youngster, no tricks upon travellers. No exit here until you have passed muster, my chick.'

More shocked than ever, I was compelled to return to the infuriate monsters, the ferocious door-keeper following me and addressing one of my companions whom he knew, said:

'So the young'un there wanted to be off, but I said as how I knew a trick worth two of that, too much experience to be taken in by such a sucker, told him not to expect to catch old birds with chaff, didn't I, young'un, hey?'

In this dreadful hole I was therefore obliged to stay until my friends chose to depart; and truly rejoiced did I feel at once more finding myself safe in the street. I expressed in strong terms my disgust at which I had just witnessed, declaring my determination never to subject myself to the like again. This only excited the laughter of my companions, who, notwithstanding all my remonstrances and resistance, dragged me with them to another scene of nocturnal dissoluteness, situate in the same street, but on the opposite side. This was called 'Murphy's,' where, although there was no actual personal hostilities going on when we entered, the war of words raged to the utmost extent; and such outré phrases never before encountered my ears, though certainly until that night I had considered myself a tolerable proficient in blackguardism. I found that it was the custom at Wetherby's never to serve any liquor after the clock struck three, so that those jolly blades whose bottles or bowls were empty when that hour arrived then adjourned to Murphy's, which at the end of that year changed its name to 'Marjoram's'; and here also the time for serving liquors was limited, the hour being five in the morning.

From this latter nest of pickpockets, and lowest description of prostitutes, we got away about half-past four, I inwardly wishing every mishap might attend me if ever I again crossed the threshold of either of the Russell Street houses during the remainder of my life. I continued to frequent the club as Slaughters, but rigidly adhered to my resolution not to accompany them to Wetherby's. In the early part of May, however, having dined with my brother Henry, and a party of his convivial associates, at the Shakespear, someone at a late hour proposed a visit to Wetherby's, when I instantly entered my negative. The company, surprised, asked the reason, and I related what had occurred to me, which excited much mirth. They, however, told me that I had been unlucky in encountering such a riot. Tethrington and my brother then said they would escort me, and I should find it a very different thing. Thus encouraged and being fortified with an ample dose of claret, I made no further objection, and was agreeably disappointed.

At the sound of Tethrington's voice, the door was opened wide. Upon entering the former place of action, all was not perfect peace, where three or four small parties of both sexes were drinking in high mirth and good humour. The women jumped up and ran to us, vociferously enquiring of my brother and Tethrington what they had been doing with themselves for an age past; then directing their attention towards me, they asked, 'And who is this nice youth, pray?' Being informed I was a brother of Henry's, half a dozen of them assailed me, and I thought would have stifled me with their endearments. One of them was particularly lavish of her kindnesses, in whom, to my utter astonishment, I recognized one of the ferocious combatants of the former night, whose name I now learnt was Burgess.

Our party adjourned from the public room to a private one in the rear of the house, where I at once discovered my brother and Tethrington to be quite at home. Burgess sung a number of admirable songs, and was very entertaining, as was another sad profligate girl, who had justly acquired the name of Blasted Bet Wilkinson. Burgess and I became very sociable, and I asked her how it happened that she could have been a principal in such a horrid broil as I have witnessed; to which she replied, that both herself and her antagonist were exceedingly intoxicated, having drank an unusual quantity of spirits, and in their cups had quarrelled; that the other battle royal, of which I was also a spectator, arose from the man (who was a notorious woman's bully) having basely robbed the two who attacked him; that the rest concerned were the friends of one party or the other, and acted accordingly. This Miss Burgess lived for several years afterwards with Dibdin, the actor, who had just at the above period commenced his theatrical career, in the character of Hodge in the comic opera of *The Maid of the Mill*.

After spending a couple of hours with great glee at Wetherby's, we all crossed the street to Marjoram's, which we found well stowed, a large crowd being collected round the famous and popular Ned Shuter, who, although immoderately drunk, was entertaining the circle of bystanders, with all sorts of buffoonery and tricks. Here, too, my companions seemed to be as well known and in as high favour as at Wetherby's; for, upon our approach, an opening was voluntarily made and chairs placed for us close to the facetious comedian, who, for above an hour, by his drollery kept us in a continued roar of laughter, when he suddenly fell from his seat as if he had been shot, and I really feared was dead; until those better acquainted than myself observed, if he was, it was only dead drunk, a finale nightly repeated. He was then lifted up and carried off like a hog to his lodgings, which were in the neighbourhood, and we departed to our beds, I being as much pleased with the night's amusement, as I had on the former been disgusted.

THE LORD MAYOR'S BANQUET, 1768

The 9th being the Lord Mayor's day, I arrayed myself in my full suit of velvet. Alderman Woolridge called at my father's and conveyed me in his chariot to Guildhall at half-past four o'clock; about half an hour after which the procession arrived from Westminster. At six, we sat down to a profusion of turtle and venison, followed by all the etceteras of French cookery, with splendid dessert of pines, grapes, and other fruits. I was seated between Mrs Healy, sister to Wilkes, and Lord Lewisham, eldest son of the Earl of Dartmouth. Mrs Healy almost enveloped me in her immense hoop, but was vastly attentive to me, whom she perceived to be a stranger, ordering one of her servants to wait upon me, and naming to me the different persons who sat at the same table, amongst whom were most of the great officers of state, the Lord Chancellor, judges, and Master of the Rolls. The heat from the crowd assembled and immense number of lights was disagreeable to all, to many quite oppressive and distressing.

The Lord Mayor's table, at which I was, and nearly opposite his Lordship, was less so than other parts of the hall, from being considerably elevated above the rest. The wines were excellent, and the dinner the same, served, too, with as much regularity and decorum as if we had been in a private house; but far different was the scene in the body of the hall, where, in five minutes after the guests took their stations at the tables, the dishes were entirely cleared of their contents, twenty hands seizing the same joint or bird, and literally tearing it to pieces. A more determined scramble could not be; the roaring and noise was deafening and hideous, which increased as the liquor operated, bottles and glasses flying across from side to side without intermission. Such a bear garden altogether I never beheld, except my first visit to Wetherby's, which it brought very forcibly to my recollection.

This abominable and disgusting scene continued till near ten o'clock, when the Lord Mayor, Sheriffs, the nobility, etc., adjourned to the ball and card rooms, and the dancing commenced. Here the heat was no way inferior to that of the hall, and the crowd so great there was scarce a possibility of moving. Rejoiced, therefore, was I upon Alderman Woolridge's saying he would take me home whenever I wished it; I eagerly answered, 'This moment, if you please.' He thereupon took me through some private apartments and down a flight of stairs to a door opening into a back lane where his carriage was ready, into which we stepped without the smallest difficulty or impediment, and were driven home. Completely exhausted, I retired to bed, perfectly satisfied with having once partaken of a Lord Mayor of London's feast.

WILLIAM HICKEY (?1749–1830), *Memoirs*, ed. Peter Quenell, 1960

HUMPHRY CLINKER TASTES LONDON WATER AND
EATS LONDON BREAD

I am pent up in frowsy lodgings, where there is not room enough to
swing a cat, and I breathe the steams of endless putrefaction; and these
would, undoubtedly, produce a pestilence, if they were not qualified by
the gross acid of sea-coal, which is itself a pernicious nuisance to lungs
of any delicacy of texture. But even this boasted corrector cannot prevent
those languid sallow looks that distinguish the inhabitants of London
from those ruddy swains that lead a country life. I go to bed after midnight, jaded and restless from the dissipations of the day. I start every
hour from my sleep, at the horrid noise of the watchmen bawling the
hour through every street, and thundering at every door; a set of useless
fellows, who serve no other purpose but that of disturbing the repose of
the inhabitants; and, by five o'clock, I start out of bed, in consequence
of the still more dreadful alarm made by the country carts, and noisy
rustics bellowing green peas under my window. If I would drink water,
I must quaff the mawkish contents of an open aqueduct, exposed to all
manner of defilement, or swallow that which comes from the river Thames,
impregnated with all the filth of London and Westminster. Human ex-
crement is the least offensive part of the concrete, which is composed of
all the drugs, minerals, and poisons used in mechanics and manufactures,
enriched with the putrefying carcases of beasts and men, and mixed with
the scourings of all the wash-tubs, kennels, and common sewers within
the bills of mortality.

This is the agreeable potation extolled by the Londoners as the finest
water in the universe. As to the intoxicating potion sold for wine, it is
a vile, unpalatable, and pernicious sophistication, balderdashed with
cider, corn spirit, and the juice of sloes. In an action at law, laid against
a carman for having staved a cask of port, it appeared, from the evidence
of the cooper, that there were not above five gallons of real wine in the
whole pipe, which held above a hundred, and even that had been brewed
and adulterated by the merchant at Oporto. The bread I eat in London
is a deleterious paste, mixed up with chalk, alum, and bone-ashes, in-
sipid to the taste, and destructive to the constitution. The good people
are not ignorant of this adulteration; but they prefer it to wholesome
bread, because it is whiter than the meal of corn. Thus they sacrifice their
taste and their health, and the lives of their tender infants, to a most

absurd gratification of a misjudging eye; and the miller or the baker is obliged to poison them and their families, in order to live by his profession. The same monstrous depravity appears in their veal, which is bleached by repeated bleedings, and other villanous arts, till there is not a drop of juice left in the body, and the poor animal is paralytic before it dies; so void of all taste, nourishment, and savour, that a man might dine as comfortably on a white fricassee of kidskin gloves, or chip hats from Leghorn.

TOBIAS SMOLLETT, The Expedition of Humphry Clinker, 1771

FRUIT-PICKERS AND PRESS-GANGS

There was another seasonal migration to London, that of the women who came on foot chiefly from Shropshire and North Wales to work in the market-gardens round London and returned in the autumn. They were employed in picking fruit, gathering peas (hence the old name of codder), weeding, haymaking and especially in carrying loads of fruit to Covent Garden. Their earnings at the end of the century were only five or seven shillings a week as compared with ten or twelve paid to men for the same work. But they slept in barns and outhouses and lived chiefly on garden produce allowed them by their employers, so that they returned to their homes with a little fund for the winter. They would carry a heavy load of fruit from Ealing or Brentford to Covent Garden, about nine miles, and would sometimes make the double journey twice a day. Londoners admired their gay, healthy appearance and neat clothes. There was a corresponding exodus from London of men and women who spent the winter in the workhouse and went out in the summer for tramping or harvesting, but it is difficult to see how these could compete with the Irish and the sturdy country people who worked so hard for such small pay.

This constant flow to London tended to make it always overcrowded. The outlets for an ever-redundant population (in spite of a general shortage of many kinds of labour) were the Army and the Navy (enlistment under the pressure of starvation being reinforced by the press-gang and the crimp as well as the penal system); indentured emigration to the colonies, and removal under the poor law and the Vagrant Act. Pressgangs directed their energies not only against seamen, but against those whom their officers chose to consider idle fellows, the attempt on Tom Jones being a case in point; 'neither law nor conscience forbid this project', said Lady Bellaston, 'for the fellow, I promise you, however well drest, is but a vagabond, and as proper as any fellow in the streets to be pressed into the service'. Magistrates encouraged the application of this principle. In 1776, for instance, the Lord Mayor refused to back the press warrants for the impressment of men in the City but ordered the City Marshals to go in force to search the public-houses and take into custody all 'loose and disorderly men' and bring them before him. Those who, like Goldsmith's private centinel, could not give a satisfactory account of themselves, were sent by the Lord Mayor on board the tender for service in the Navy. 'By this judicious step,' says a contemporary annalist, 'many idle persons were obtained, and the more industrious escaped being illegally forced from their friends and families.' The magistrates of Westminster took similar steps, great numbers, it is said, were obtained in this way, 'the principal part of whom were persons who had not any visible method of livelihood'.

M. Dorothy George, London Life in the Eighteenth Century, 2nd edn., 1966

THE GORDON RIOTS, 1780

'General Alarm'

When darkness broke away and morning began to dawn, the town wore a strange aspect indeed.

Sleep had hardly been thought of all night. The general alarm was so apparent in the faces of the inhabitants, and its expression was so aggravated by want of rest (few persons, with any property to lose, having dared go to bed since Monday), that a stranger coming into the streets would have supposed some mortal pest or plague to have been raging. In place of the usual cheerfulness and animation of morning, everything was dead and silent. The shops remained unclosed, offices and warehouses were shut, the coach and chair stands were deserted, no carts or waggons rumbled through the slowly waking streets, the early cries were all hushed; a universal gloom prevailed. Great numbers of people were out, even at daybreak, but they flitted to and fro as though they shrank from the sound of their own footsteps; the public ways were haunted rather than frequented; and round the smoking ruins people stood apart from one another and in silence, not venturing to condemn the rioters, or to be supposed to do so, even in whispers.

At the Lord President's in Piccadilly, at Lambeth Palace, at the Lord Chancellor's in Great Ormond Street, in the Royal Exchange, the Bank, the Guildhall, the Inns of Court, the Courts of Law, and every chamber fronting the streets near Westminster Hall and the Houses of Parliament, parties of soldiers were posted before daylight. A body of Horse Guards paraded Palace-yard; an encampment was formed in the Park, where fifteen hundred men and five battalions of Militia were under arms; the Tower was fortified, the drawbridges were raised, the cannon loaded and pointed, and two regiments of artillery busied in strengthening the fortress and preparing it for defence. A numerous detachment of soldiers were stationed to keep guard at the New River Head, which the people had threatened to attack, and where, it was said, they meant to cut off the main-pipes, so that there might be no water for the extinction of the flames. In the Poultry, and on Cornhill, and at several other leading points, iron chains were drawn across the street; parties of soldiers were distributed in some of the old city churches while it was yet dark; and in several private houses (among them, Lord Rockingham's in Grosvenor Square); which were blockaded as though to sustain a siege, and had guns pointed from the windows. When the sun rose, it shone into handsome apartments filled with armed men; the furniture hastily heaped away in corners, and made of little or no account, in the terror of the time—on arms glittering in city chambers, among desks and stools, and dusty books—into little smoky churchyards in odd lanes and by-ways, with soldiers lying down among the tombs, or lounging under the shade of the one old tree, and their pile of muskets sparkling in the light—on solitary sentries pacing up and down in court-yards, silent now, but yesterday resounding with the din and hum of business— everywhere on guard-rooms, garrisons, and threatening preparations.

As the day crept on, still more unusual sights were witnessed in the streets. The gates of the King's Bench and Fleet Prisons being opened at the usual hour, were found to have notices affixed to them, announcing that the rioters would come that night to burn them down. The wardens, too well knowing the likelihood there was of this promise being fulfilled, were fain to set their prisoners at liberty, and give them leave to move their goods; so, all day, such of them as had any furniture were occupied in conveying it, some to this place, some to that, and not a few to the brokers' shops, where they gladly sold it, for any wretched price those gentry chose to give. There were some broken men among these debtors who had been in jail so long, and were so miserable and destitute of friends, so dead to the world, and utterly forgotten and uncared for, that they implored their jailers not to set them free, and to send them, if need were, to some other place of custody. But they, refusing to comply, lest they should incur the anger of the mob, turned them into the streets, where they wandered up and down hardly remembering the ways untrodden by their feet so long, and crying—such abject things those rotten-hearted jails had made them—as they slunk off in their rags, and dragged their slipshod feet along the pavement.

Even of the three hundred prisoners who had escaped from Newgate, there were some—a few, but there were some—who sought their jailers out and delivered themselves up: preferring imprisonment and punishment to the horrors of such another night as the last. Many of the convicts, drawn back to their old place of captivity by some indescribable attraction, or by a desire to exult over it in its downfall and glut their revenge by seeing it in ashes, actually went back in broad noon, and loitered about the cells. Fifty were retaken at one time on this next day, within the prison walls; but their fate did not deter others, for there they went in spite of everything, and there they were taken in twos and threes, twice or thrice a day, all through the week. Of the fifty just mentioned, some were occupied in endeavouring to rekindle the fire; but in general they seemed to have no object in view but to prowl and lounge about the old place: being often found asleep in the ruins, or sitting talking there, or even eating and drinking, as in a choice retreat.

Besides the notices on the gates of the Fleet and the King's Bench, many similar announcements were left, before one o'clock at noon, at the houses of private individuals! and further, the mob proclaimed their intention of seizing on the Bank, the Mint, the Arsenal at Woolwich, and the Royal Palaces. The notices were seldom delivered by more than one man, who, if it were at a shop, went in, and laid it, with a bloody threat perhaps, upon the counter; or if it were at a private house, knocked at the door, and thrust it in the servant's hand. Notwithstanding the presence of the military in every quarter of the town, and the great force in the Park, these messengers did their errands with impunity all through the day. So did two boys who went down Holborn alone, armed with bars taken from the railings of Lord Mansfield's house, and demanded money for the rioters. So did a tall man on horseback who made a collection for the same purpose in Fleet-street, and refused to take anything but gold.

A rumour had now got into circulation, too, which diffused a greater dread all through London, even than these publicly announced intentions of the rioters, though all men knew that if they were successfully effected, there must ensue a national bankruptcy and general ruin. It was said that they meant to throw the gates of Bedlam open, and let all the madmen loose. This suggested such dreadful images to the people's minds, and was indeed an act so fraught with new and unimaginable horrors in the contemplation, that it beset them more than any loss or cruelty of which they could foresee the worst, and drove many sane men nearly mad themselves.

So the day passed on: the prisoners moving their goods; people running to and fro in the streets, carrying away their property; groups standing in silence round the ruins; all business suspended; and the soldiers disposed as has been already mentioned, remaining quite inactive. So the day passed on, and dreaded night drew near again.

At last, at seven o'clock in the evening, the Privy Council issued a solemn proclamation that it was now necessary to employ the military, and that the officers had most direct and effectual orders, by an immediate exertion of their utmost force, to repress the disturbances; and warning all good subjects of the King to keep themselves, their servants, and apprentices, within doors that night. There was then delivered out to every soldier on duty, thirty-six rounds of powder and ball; the drums beat; and the whole force was under arms at sunset.

'The Rabble's Rage'

The vintner's house with half-a-dozen others near at hand, was one great, glowing blaze. All night, no one had essayed to quench the flames, or stop their progress; but now a body of soldiers were actively engaged in pulling down two old wooden houses, which were every moment in danger of taking fire, and which could scarcely fail, if they were left to burn, to extend the conflagration immensely. The tumbling down of nodding walls and heavy blocks of wood, the hooting and the execrations of the crowd, the distant firing of other military detachments, the distracted looks and cries of those whose habitations were in danger, the hurrying to and fro of frightened people with their goods; the reflections in every quarter of the sky, of deep, red, soaring flames, as though the last day had come and the whole universe were burning; the dust, and smoke, and drift of fiery particles, scorching and kindling all it fell upon; the hot unwholesome vapour, the blight on everything; the stars, and moon, and very sky, obliterated;—made up such a sum of dreariness and ruin, that it seemed as if the face of Heaven were blotted out, and night, in its rest and quiet, and softened light, never could look upon the earth again.

But there was a worse spectacle than this—worse by far than fire and smoke, or even the rabble's unappeasable and maniac rage. The gutters of the street, and every crack and fissure in the stones, ran with scorching spirit, which being dammed up by busy hands, overflowed the road and pavement, and formed a great pool, into which the people dropped down dead by dozens. They lay in heaps all round this fearful pond, husbands and wives, fathers and sons, mothers and daughters, women with children in their arms and babies at their breasts, and drank until they died. While some stooped with their lips to the brink and never raised their heads again, others sprang up from their fiery draught, and danced, half in a mad triumph, and half in the agony of suffocation, until they fell, and steeped their corpses in the liquor that had killed them. Nor was even this the worst or most appalling kind of death that happened on this fatal night. From the burning cellars, where they drank out of hats, pails, buckets, tubs, and shoes, some men were drawn, alive, but all alight from head to foot; who, in their unendurable anguish and suffering, making for anything that had the look of water, rolled, hissing, in this hideous lake, and splashed up liquid fire which lapped in all it met with as it ran along the surface, and neither spared the living nor the dead. On this last night of the great riots—for the last night it was—the wretched victims of a senseless outcry, became themselves the dust and ashes of the flames they had kindled, and strewed the public streets of London.

CHARLES DICKENS, *Barnaby Rudge*, 1841

LONDON SUBURBS

Suburban villas, highway-side retreats,
That dread th'encroachment of our growing streets,
Tight boxes, neatly sash'd, and in a blaze

With all a July sun's collected rays,
Delight the citizen, who, gasping there,
Breathes clouds of dust, and calls it country air.
Oh sweet retirement, who would balk the thought,
That could afford retirement, or could not?
'Tis such an easy walk, so smooth and straight,
The second milestone fronts the garden gate;
A step if fair, and if a shower approach,
You find safe shelter in the next stage-coach.
There, prison'd in a parlour snug and small,
Like bottled wasps upon a southern wall,
The man of bus'ness and his friends compress'd,
Forget their labours, and yet find no rest;
But still 'tis rural—trees are to be seen
From ev'ry window, and the fields are green;
Ducks paddle in the pond before the door,
And what could a remoter scene show more?

WILLIAM COWPER (1731–1800), from 'Retirement'

THE JOLLY YOUNG WATERMAN

And did you not hear of a jolly young waterman,
    Who at Blackfriars Bridge used for to ply?
And he feathered his oars with such skill and dexterity,
    Winning each heart, and delighting each eye;
He looked so neat, and rowed so steadily,
The maidens all flocked in his boat so readily,
And he eyed the young rogues with so charming an air,
That this waterman ne'er was in want of a fare.

What sights of fine folks he oft rowed in his wherry,
    'Twas cleaned out so nice, and so painted withal;
He was always first oars when the fine city ladies
    In a party to Ranelagh went or Vauxhall.
And oftentimes would they be giggling and leering,
But 'twas all one to Tom, their gibing and jeering,
For loving or liking he little did care,
For this waterman ne'er was in want of a fare.

And yet but to see how strangely things happen,
  As he rowed along, thinking of nothing at all,
He was plied by a damsel so lovely and charming,
  That she smiled and so straightway in love he did fall;
And would this young damsel but banish his sorrow,
He'd wed her tonight before tomorrow:
And how should this waterman ever know care,
When he's married and never in want of a fare?

CHARLES DIBDIN, 1774

A LONDON RAMBLE

One night when Beauclerk and Langton had supped at a tavern in London, and sat till about three in the morning, it came into their heads to go and knock up Johnson, and see if they could prevail on him to join them in a ramble. They rapped violently at the door of his chambers in the Temple, till at last he appeared in his shirt, with his little black wig on the top of his head, instead of a nightcap, and a poker in his hand, imagining, probably, that some ruffians were coming to attack him. When he discovered who they were, and was told their errand, he smiled, and with great good humour agreed to their proposal: 'What, is it you, you dogs! I'll have a frisk with you.' He was soon drest, and they sallied forth together into Covent-Garden, where the greengrocers and fruiterers were beginning to arrange their hampers, just come in from the country. Johnson made some attempts to help them; but the honest gardeners stared so at his figure and manner, and odd interference, that he soon saw his services were not relished. They then repaired to one of the neighbouring taverns, and made a bowl of that liquor called *Bishop*, which Johnson had always liked; while in joyous contempt of sleep, from which he had been roused, he repeated the festive lines,

  'Short, O short then be thy reign,
  And give us to the world again!'

They did not stay long, but walked down to the Thames, took a boat, and rowed to Billingsgate. Beauclerk and Johnson were so well pleased with their amusement, that they resolved to persevere in dissipation for the rest of the day: but Langton deserted them, being engaged to breakfast with some young Ladies. Johnson scolded him for 'leaving his social friends, to go and sit with a set of wretched *un-idea'd* girls'. Garrick being told of this ramble, said to him smartly, 'I heard of your frolick t'other night. You'll be in the Chronicle.' Upon which Johnson afterwards observed, '*He* durst not do such a thing. His *wife* would not *let* him!'

JAMES BOSWELL, The Life of Samuel Johnson, 1791

POTTED TONGUE

To my mind this is the best and most subtle of all English potted meat inventions. My recipe is adapted from John Farley's *The London Art of Cookery* published in 1783. Farley was master of the London Tavern, and an unusually lucid writer. One deduces that the cold table at the London Tavern must have been exceptionally good, for all Farley's sideboard dishes, cold pies, hams, spiced beef joints and potted meats are thought out with much care, are set down in detail and show a delicate and educated taste.

Ingredients and proportions for potted tongue are ½ lb. each of cooked, brined and/or smoked ox tongue and clarified butter, a salt-spoonful of ground mace, a turn or two of black or white pepper from the mill.

Chop the tongue and, with 5 oz. (weighed after clarifying) of the butter, reduce it to a paste in the blender or liquidizer, season it, pack it tightly down into a pot or pots, smooth over the top, cover, and leave in the refrigerator until very firm. Melt the remaining 3 oz. of clarified butter and pour it, tepid, over the tongue paste, so that it sets in a sealing layer about one eighth of an inch thick. When completely cold, cover the pot with foil or greaseproof paper. The amount given will fill one ³/₄ to 1 pint shallow soufflé dish, although I prefer to pack my potted tongue in two or three smaller containers. Venison can be potted in the same way as tongue, and makes one of the best of all sandwich fillings. Salt beef makes another excellent potted meat.

ELIZABETH DAVID, An Omelette and a Glass of Wine, 1984

LONDON

I wander thro' each charter'd street,
Near where the charter'd Thames does flow,
And mark in every face I meet
Marks of weakness, marks of woe.

In every cry of every Man,
In every Infant's cry of fear,
In every voice, in every ban,
The mind-forg'd manacles I hear.

How the Chimney-sweeper's cry
Every black'ning Church appalls;
And the hapless Soldier's sigh
Runs in blood down Palace walls.

But most thro' midnight streets I hear
How the youthful Harlot's curse
Blasts the new born Infant's tear,
And blights with plagues the Marriage hearse.

WILLIAM BLAKE, *Songs of Experience*, 1794

RESIDENCE IN LONDON

O, wond'rous power of words, by simple faith
Licensed to take the meaning that we love!
Vauxhall and Ranelagh! I then had heard
Of your green groves, and wilderness of lamps
Dimming the stars, and fireworks magical,
And gorgeous ladies, under splendid domes,
Floating in dance, or warbling high in air
The songs of spirits! Nor had Fancy fed
With less delight upon that other class
Of marvels, broad-day wonders permanent:
The River proudly bridged; the dizzy top
And Whispering Gallery of St Paul's; the tombs
Of Westminster; the Giants of Guildhall;
Bedlam, and those carved maniacs at the gates,
Perpetually recumbent; Statues—man,
And the horse under him—in gilded pomp
Adorning flowery gardens, 'mid vast squares;
The Monument, and that Chamber of the Tower
Where England's sovereigns sit in long array,
Their steeds bestriding,—every mimic shape

Cased in the gleaming mail the monarch wore,
Whether for gorgeous tournament addressed,
Or life or death upon the battle-field.
Those bold imaginations in due time
Had vanished, leaving others in their stead:
And now I looked upon the living scene;
Familiarly perused it; oftentimes,
In spite of strongest disappointment, pleased
Through courteous self-submission, as a tax
Paid to the object by prescriptive right.

Rise up, thou monstrous ant-hill on the plain
Of a too busy world! Before me flow,
Thou endless stream of men and moving things!
Thy every-day appearance, as it strikes—
With wonder heightened, or sublimed by awe—
On strangers, of all ages; the quick dance
Of colours, lights, and forms; the deafening din;
The comers and the goers face to face,
Face after face; the string of dazzling wares,
Shop after shop, with symbols, blazoned names,
And all the tradesman's honours overhead:
Here, fronts of houses, like a title-page,
With letters huge inscribed from top to toe;
Stationed above the door, like guardian saints,
There, allegoric shapes, female or male,
Or physiognomies of real men.
Land-warriors, kings, or admirals of the sea,
Boyle, Shakspeare, Newton, or the attractive head
Of some quack-doctor, famous in his day.

Meanwhile the roar continues, till at length,
Escaped as from an enemy, we turn
Abruptly into some sequestered nook,
Still as a sheltered place when winds blow loud!
At leisure, thence, through tracts of thin resort,
And sights and sounds that come at intervals,
We take our way. A raree-show is here,
With children gathered round; another street

Presents a company of dancing dogs,
Or dromedary, with an antic pair
Of monkeys on his back; a minstrel band
Of Savoyards; or, single and alone,
An English ballad-singer. Private courts,
Gloomy as coffins, and unsightly lanes
Thrilled by some female vendor's scream, belike
The very shrillest of all London cries,
May then entangle our impatient steps;
Conducted through those labyrinths, unawares,
To privileged regions and inviolate,
Where from their airy lodges studious lawyers
Look out on waters, walks, and gardens green.

Thence back into the throng, until we reach,
Following the tide that slackens by degrees,
Some half-frequented scene, where wider streets
Bring straggling breezes of suburban air.
Here files of ballads dangle from dead walls;
Advertisements, of giant-size, from high
Press forward, in all colours, on the sight;
These, bold in conscious merit, lower down;
That, fronted with a most imposing word,
Is, peradventure, one in masquerade.
As on the broadening causeway we advance,
Behold, turned upwards, a face hard and strong
In lineaments, and red with over-toil.
'Tis one encountered here and everywhere;
A travelling cripple, by the trunk cut short,
And stumping on his arms. In sailor's garb
Another lies at length, beside a range
Of well-formed characters, with chalk inscribed
Upon the smooth flat stones: the Nurse is here,
The Bachelor, that loves to sun himself,
The military Idler, and the Dame,
That field-ward takes her walk with decent steps.

Now homeward through the thickening hubbub, where
See, among less distinguishable shapes,

The begging scavenger, with hat in hand;
The Italian, as he thrids his way with care,
Steadying, far-seen, a frame of images
Upon his head; with basket at his breast
The Jew; the stately and slow-moving Turk,
With freight of slippers piled beneath his arm!

Enough;—the mighty concourse I surveyed
With no unthinking mind, well pleased to note
Among the crowd all specimens of man,
Through all the colours which the sun bestows,
And every character of form and face:
The Swede, the Russian; from the genial south,
The Frenchman and the Spaniard; from remote
America, the Hunter-Indian; Moors,
Malays, Lascars, the Tartar, the Chinese,
And Negro Ladies in white muslin gowns.

WILLIAM WORDSWORTH, *The Prelude*, book vii, 1850

HAYDN ARRIVES IN LONDON

My arrival caused a great sensation throughout the whole city, and I
went the round of all the newspapers for 3 successive days. Everyone
wants to know me. I had to dine out 6 times up to now, and if I wanted,
I could dine out every day; but first I must consider my health, and 2nd
my work. Except for the nobility, I admit no callers till 2 o'clock in the
afternoon, and 4 o'clock I dine at home with *Mon.* Salomon. I have nice
and comfortable, but expensive, lodgings. My landlord is Italian, and
also a cook, and serves me 4 very respectable meals; we each pay 1 fl. 30
kr. a day excluding wine and beer, but everything is terribly expensive
here. Yesterday I was invited to á grand amateur concert, but I arrived
a bit late, and when I showed my ticket they wouldn't let me in but led
me to an antichamber, where I had to wait till the piece which was then
being played in the hall was over. Then they opened the door, and I was
conducted, on the arm of the *entrepreneur*, up the centre of the hall to the
front of the orchestra, amid universal applause, and there I was stared at
and greeted by a great number of English compliments. I was assured
that such honours had not been conferred on anyone for 50 years. After

the concert I was taken to a handsome adjoining room, where a table for 200 persons, with many places set, was prepared for all the amateurs; I was supposed to be seated at the head of the table, but since I had dined out on that day and had eaten more than usual, I declined this honour, with the excuse that I was not feeling very well, but despite this I had to drink the harmonious health, in Burgundy, of all the gentlemen present; they all returned the toast, and then allowed me to be taken home. All this, my gracious lady, was very flattering to me, and yet I wished I could fly for a time to Vienna, to have more quiet in which to work, for the noise that the common people make as they sell their wares in the street is intolerable.

> JOSEPH HAYDN, letter to Maria Anna von Grenzinger, 8 January 1791, from *Collected Correspondence and London Notebooks of Joseph Haydn*, ed. H. C. Robbins, 1959

COLERIDGE MEETS A LAND AGENT

Every night since my arrival I have spent at an Ale-house, by courtesy called a Coffee-house: the 'Salutation and Cat' in Newgate St—We have a comfortable Room to ourselves, and drink Porter and *Punch* round a good fire. My motive for all this is that every night I meet a most intelligent young man who has spent the last five years of his life in America—and is lately come from thence as an Agent to sell Land. He was of our School—I had been kind to him—he remembered it—and comes regularly every evening to 'benefit by conversation' he says. He says two thousand pound will do—that he doubts not we can contract for our Passage under £400—that we shall buy this Land a great deal cheaper when we arrive at America, than we could do in England—or why (adds he) am I sent over here? That twelve men can *easily* clear *three hundred* Acres in 4 or 5 months—and that for six hundred Dollars a thousand Acres may be cleared, and houses built upon them. He recommends the Susquehannah from its excessive Beauty, and its security from hostile Indians—Every possible assistance will be given us. We may get credit for the Land for ten years or more as we settle upon it—That literary characters make *money* there, that &c., &c. He never saw a Byson in his life, but has heard of them. They are quite backwards. The Mosquitos are not so bad as our Gnats—and after you have been there a little while,

they don't trouble you much. He says the Women's *teeth* are bad there—
but not the men's—at least not nearly so much—attributes it to neglect—
to particular foods—is by no means convinced it is the necessary effect
of Climate.

> SAMUEL TAYLOR COLERIDGE, letter to Robert Southey, postmarked
> 6 September 1794, in *Collected Letters*

THE CHIMNEY-SWEEPER

When my mother died I was very young,
And my father sold me while yet my tongue
Could scarcely cry *'weep 'weep, 'weep 'weep*!
So your chimneys I sweep, and in soot I sleep.

There's little Tom Dacre, who cried when his head,
That curled like a lamb's back, was shaved; so I said,
'Hush Tom, never mind it, for when your head's bare,
You know that the soot cannot spoil your white hair.'

And so he was quiet, and that very night,
As Tom was a-sleeping he had such a sight,
That thousands of sweepers, Dick, Joe, Ned, and Jack,
Were all of them locked up in coffins of black;

And by came an angel, who had a bright key,
And he opened the coffins and set them all free;
Then down a green plain leaping, laughing they run,
And wash in a river and shine in the sun.

Then naked and white, all their bags left behind,
They rise upon clouds and sport in the wind.
And the angel told Tom, if he'd be a good boy,
He'd have God for his father and never want joy.

And so Tom awoke, and we rose in the dark,
And got with our bags and our brushes to work.
Though the morning was cold, Tom was happy and warm;
So if all do their duty, they need not fear harm.

> WILLIAM BLAKE, *Songs of Innocence*, 1789

THE IMPROVEMENT OF THE CAPITAL

At the beginning of the century, London's street-lighting, paving and sanitation were of the most primitive kind. Lighting was regulated by an Act of William and Mary which provided for lamps to be hung out during six months of the year—from Michaelmas to Lady Day—and then only from dark till midnight. But even this modest aim was not achieved. The City had its own regulations, governed by an Act of the Common Council of 1716, which obliged citizens, on a penalty of 1*s*., to hang out candle-lights in the six winter months from 6 to 11 p.m. on 'dark nights' by the calendar, or on eighteen nights in each moon. Thus the City was plunged into total darkness an hour before midnight; and Maitland claimed that London had, until the 1730s, the unenviable reputation of being the worst lit of the great cities of Europe. It was also notorious that streets remained unpaved and unnumbered and that, outside the major thoroughfares, filth and refuse lay stacked almost shoulder-high at street corners and against the buildings. On the approaches to the City, Lincoln's Inn Fields, then unenclosed, had long become a public receptacle for rubbish; while the City itself endured the filthy open sewer of the Fleet, which stretched from Fleet Bridge to Holborn Bridge and was a constant threat to the health and survival of its inhabitants; even in 1748, a London newspaper wrote of the City's streets as 'a Hotch-Potch of half-moon and serpentine narrow streets, close, dismal, long Lanes, stinking Alleys, dark, gloomy Courts and suffocating Yards'. The condition of Westminster was little better; and Lord Tyrconnel, speaking in the House of Lords in 1741, referred to the 'neglect of cleanliness of which, perhaps, no part of the world affords more proof than the streets of London, a city famous for wealth, commerce, and plenty, and for every other kind of civility and politeness; but which abounds with such heaps of filth, as a savage would look on with amazement'. And he added that 'the present neglect of cleansing and paving the streets is such as ought not to be borne . . . and that this great grievance is without a remedy, is a sufficient proof that no magistrate has, at present, power to remove it'. And in 1750 John Gwynn listed in his *Essay on Improvements* some of the most notorious of the 'nuisances' which he believed could (unlike the greater evils of which Lord Tyrconnel spoke) be remedied without further statutory provision. These were: ordure left lying in the streets (he notes, as particular black-spots, the posterns of the City and the area to the north of the Royal Exchange); open cellar doors or stone steps projecting into the street; broken pavements; delapidated houses; streets blocked with sheds and stalls; the projections of newly built houses into the streets; the cluttering of the streets with mad dogs, beggars and bullock-carts; the 'deluge of profanity'; and the total absence of street lighting from such precincts as St Martin's le Grand, Cloth Fair and St Bartholomew the Great.

Some steps had, of course, already been taken to remedy this depressing state of affairs. The Great Fire itself had helped to thin out the densely packed medieval city; and only about 9,000 of the 13,000 houses destroyed had been rebuilt. New brick houses had begun to replace the old buildings of lath and plaster, and the inhabitants of London's newly built squares had taken steps to secure them against the threat of becoming refuse-dumps by seeking powers to 'enclose, adorn and beautify' them: these were the first steps towards a long succession of Improvement Acts. The City's nocturnal gloom began to be dispelled by an Act of 1736 which gave powers to rate the inhabitants to hang out lights throughout the year; and a similar Act was applied to Christchurch, Spitalfields, two years later. Lincoln's Inn Fields was enclosed by an Act of 1735, and the Fleet Ditch was filled, by order of the Common Council, in 1747. The Thames was embanked from the Fleet to London Bridge; and the building of Westminster and Blackfriars Bridges (completed, respectively, in 1750 and 1756) entailed the clearing away of old delapidated buildings and the opening of new thoroughfares on both sides of the river. The New Road through Marylebone and Islington opened up new building prospects to the north. And in 1760 the City embarked on a bold plan to widen its thoroughfares, a task that was carried out (though admittedly, without much speed) by the Committee of the City Lands. Far more decisive was the step taken in 1787, when all London roads south of the Thames were placed under a single authority. (Those north of the river had to wait for the Metropolitan Road Board of 1826.)

But the real turning-point in the improvement of the capital was marked by the first Westminster Paving Act of 1762; it was quickly followed by other Acts applied to the City of London and other parts of the metropolis. Previous to these Acts, all measures relating to paving had depended, for their realization, on the civic duty of the householder to keep the street in front of his own door in good repair; the old methods of enforcement were cumbersome, slow and uncertain. Now paving commissioners were appointed with paid staffs at their disposal, and infringements of the Acts brought summary punishment by the magistrates. Moreover, gutters were built on each side of the road, and in the principal streets flat Purbeck stone replaced the old rounded pebbles. The Acts also provided for regular scavenging and cleansing and for the removal of the numerous obstructions—the stalls, the show-boards, unprotected coal-shoots, uncovered cellars and projecting balconies— that held up traffic and endangered lives. Further, houses began to be numbered, many of the old shop signs that shut out the light in narrow streets were taken down, sewers and drains were deepened, and the water spouting from rooftop gutters was channelled through pipes. In consequence, the old city began to acquire a neat and spruce appearance, and, twenty-five years after the first of the Paving Acts was passed, a commentator proudly described the whole enterprise as 'an undertaking which has introduced a degree of elegance and symmetry into the streets of the metropolis, that is the admiration of all Europe and far exceeds anything of the kind in the modern world'.

Street-lighting, too, had kept pace with paving. Since the first of the improved Lighting Acts of 1736 and 1738, a long succession of such Acts had been passed, many of them linked with the Paving Acts, so that paving and lighting powers were often vested in the same body of trustees or commissioners. Turnpike trustees also obtained powers to light and watch the highways into the city. The result was that the new oil-lamps of London, covered by crystal globes and hung on posts short intervals apart, became as much an object of admiration by foreign visitors as her pavements; Archenholtz, on his visit to the capital in the 1780s, wrote enthusiastically: 'In Oxford Road alone there are more lamps than in all the city of Paris. Even the great roads, for seven or eight miles round, are crowded with them, which makes the effect exceedingly grand.' Such a judgment would, of course, seem a little ingenuous when, only a generation later, gas-lighting made its first appearance in the streets of London. Gas was first used for lighting in Beech and Whitecross Streets in the City in August 1807; a year later, Winsor, a German Chemist, proved his point that it could be used for the general illumination of the capital by setting up a row of gas-lamps in Pall Mall. But, at the time that Archenholtz was writing, his claim that London's oil-lamps were more than a match for Paris was amply justified.

Thus London, by the end of the century, could claim to be a pioneer among the world's great cities in her paving, her street-lighting and her public sanitation; possibly, too, in the excellence of her water supply, her fire-plugs and her sewers. This was a solid achievement to which Parliament, the City Corporation, the justices of Middlesex and Surrey, and the city's innumerable vestries, and the initiative of their inhabitants, had made their varied contribution. But there were other matters to which the Paving, Lighting and Improvement Acts and hosts of Local Acts had not extended, or which they had barely touched. These had affected, above all, the more fashionable streets and squares, the central commercial districts, and the city's main thoroughfares; they had largely neglected the old courts and alleys, the markets, slaughter-houses and burial grounds, and (most notorious of all) the old slums and rookeries of Holborn and St Giles in the Fields. These were left as a legacy of filth, squalor and disease for the next century to deal with.

There was also the continuing, festering and corroding problem of London's poor for whom the old Poor Law of 1601 was still (with minor alterations) intended to provide. The Elizabethan Statute had entrusted the care of the poor to the churchwardens and overseers of the parish, authorized them to raise a poor rate, and instructed them to relieve the old and impotent, to train pauper children to follow a trade, and to provide the able-bodied unemployed with work. It had been the product of a largely rural society with a national population of at most four millions. Yet, with all the social and economic changes that had taken place and the great rise in population, especially in London, the law remained basically the same in the eighteenth century as it had been in the days of Elizabeth and James. Above all, the usual unit of administration was still the parish, and the parish had by now, in large urban communities at least, become quite unsuited for the job. In the City of London the wards levied and collected the poor rate, but the parish disbursed it; while, in Westminster and the out-parishes, the overseers were nominally responsible to the justices of the peace, but these latter had become increasingly reluctant to interfere, and in the course of the eighteenth century rarely did so except in matters in which public expenditure (as in litigation over 'settlements') and public 'morality' appeared to be involved. This was all the more unfortunate, as the parish officers held their posts for only a year, were unpaid and overworked, and consequently discharged their duties without enthusiasm. Moreover, there were poor parishes like Spitalfields and the dockside parishes of East London, which had a disproportionate number of persons requiring relief and where, in consequence, the rate levied on the local householders was quite insufficient to meet the needs of the poor. In Middlesex the justices had realized the problem, and late in the previous century had considered a number of remedies, including the creation of an overall corporate authority. But the discussions had come to nothing, and in the Hanoverian period the matter was allowed to rest until Gilbert's Bill of 1782 attempted to find a more rational solution.

There were other problems besides. The fact that the work of the overseers was unpaid and uncongenial, and that their accounts were not subject to a proper inspection, frequently led to dishonesty and corruption. They might take the relatively innocent form of diverting a proportion of the monies collected for the poor into banquets and carousals in the local pubs: this was a frequent complaint of ratepayers in City parishes. A more serious form might be to add fictitious names or the names of persons deceased to the lists of those in receipt of 'casual' relief, or it might be to give lucrative contracts to parish officers or to their friends and relations: both these abuses came to light when an enquiry was held, in 1714, into the management of the poor rates in St Martin in the Fields, which had, up to then, enjoyed a reputation for honest and efficient administration.

GEORGE RUDÉ, *History of London: Hanoverian London, 1714–1808*, 1971

COUNTRY AND TOWN

In London I never know what to be at,
Enraptured with this and enchanted with that!
I'm wild with the sweets of variety's plan,
And life seems a blessing too happy for man.

But the country, Lord help us, sets all matters right,
So calm and composing from morning till night;
O, it settles the spirits when nothing is seen
But an ass on a common or goose on a green.

In town if it rains, why it damps not our hope,
The eye has its range and the fancy her scope;

Still the same, though it pour all night and all day,
It spoils not our prospects, it stops not our way.

In the country how blessed, when it rains in the fields,
To feast upon transports that shuttlecock yields,
Or go crawling from window to window to see
A hog on a dunghill or crow on a tree.

In London how easy we visit and meet,
Gay pleasure the theme and sweet smiles are our treat;
Our morning's a round of good-humoured delight,
And we rattle in comfort and pleasure all night.

In the country how charming our visits to make
Through ten miles of mud for formality's sake,
With the coachman in drink and the moon in a fog,
And no thought in our head but a ditch and a bog.

In London if folks ill together are put,
A bore may be dropped or a quiz may be cut;
We change without end and, if happy or ill,
Our wants are at hand and our wishes at will.

In the country you're nailed, like a pale in your park,
To some stick of a neighbour, crammed into the ark;
Or if you are sick or in fits tumble down,
You reach death ere the doctor can reach you from town.

I have heard how that love in a cottage is sweet,
When two hearts in one link of soft sympathy meet;
I know nothing of that, for alas! I'm a swain
Who requires, I own it, more links to my chain.

You jays and your magpies may chatter on trees,
And whisper soft nonsense in groves if they please;
But a house is much more to my mind than a tree,
And for groves, O! a fine grove of chimneys for me.

Then in town let me live and in town let me die,
For in truth I can't relish the country, not I.
If one must have a villa in summer to dwell,
O give me the sweet shady side of Pall Mall.

CHARLES MORRIS, *c.*1797

PART II

THE NINETEENTH CENTURY

THE VAST CAPITAL

It was a most heavenly day in May of this year (1800) when I first beheld and first entered this mighty wilderness, the city—no! not the city, but the nation—of London. Often since then, at distances of two and three hundred miles or more from this colossal emporium of men, wealth, arts, and intellectual power, have I felt the sublime expression of her enormous magnitude in one simple form of ordinary occurrence—viz., in the vast droves of cattle, suppose upon the great north roads, all with their heads directed to London, and expounding the size of the attracting body, together with the force of its attractive power, by the never-ending succession of these droves, and the remoteness from the capital of the lines upon which they were moving. A suction so powerful, felt along radii so vast, and a consciousness, at the same time, that upon other radii still more vast, both by land and by sea, the same suction is operating, night and day, summer and winter, and hurrying for ever into one centre the infinite means needed for her infinite purposes, and the endless tributes to the skill or to the luxury of her endless population, crowds the imagination with a pomp to which there is nothing corresponding upon this planet, either amongst the things that have been, or the things that are. Or, if any exception there is, it must be sought in ancient Rome. We, upon this occasion, were in an open carriage, and, chiefly (as I imagine) to avoid the dust, we approached London by rural lanes, where any such could be found, or, at least, along by-roads, quiet and shady, collateral to the main roads. In that mode of approach, we missed some features of the sublimity belonging to any of the common approaches upon a main road; we missed the whirl and the uproar, the tumult and the agitation, which continually thicken and thicken throughout the last dozen miles before you reach the suburbs. Already at three stages' distance (say, forty miles from London), upon some of the greatest roads, the dim presentiment of some vast capital reaches you obscurely, and like a misgiving. This blind sympathy with a mighty but unseen object, some vast magnetic range of Alps, in your neighbourhood, continues to increase, you know not how. Arrived at the last station for changing horses—Barnet, suppose, on one of the north roads, or Hounslow on the western—you no longer think (as in all other places) of naming the next stage; nobody says, on pulling up, 'Horses on to London'; that would sound ridiculous; one mighty idea broods over all minds, making it impossible to suppose any other destination. Launched upon this final stage, you soon begin to feel yourself entering the stream as it were of a Norwegian *mælstrom*; and the stream at length becomes the rush of a cataract. Finally, for miles before you reach a suburb of London such as Islington, for instance, a last great sign and augury of the immensity which belongs to the coming metropolis forces itself upon the dullest observer, in the growing sense of his own utter insignificance. Everywhere else in England, you yourself, horses, carriage, attendants (if you travel with any), are regarded with attention, perhaps even curiosity: at all events you are seen. But, after passing the final post-house on every avenue to London, for the latter ten or twelve miles, you become aware that you are no longer noticed: nobody sees you; nobody hears you; nobody regards you; you do not even regard yourself. In fact, how should you at the moment of first ascertaining your own total unimportance in the sum of things—a poor shivering unit in the aggregate of human life? Now, for the first time, whatever manner of man you were or seemed to be at starting, squire or 'squireen,' lord or lordling, and however related to that city, hamlet, or solitary house, from which yesterday or today you slipped your cable—beyond disguise you find yourself but one wave in a total Atlantic, one plant (and a parasitical plant besides, needing alien props) in a forest of America.

These are feelings which do not belong by preference to thoughtful people—far less to people merely sentimental. No man ever was left to himself for the first time in the streets, as yet unknown, of London, but he must have been saddened and mortified, perhaps terrified, by the sense of desertion and utter loneliness which belong to his situation. No loneliness can be like that which weighs upon the heart in the centre of faces never-ending, without voice or utterance for him; eyes innumerable, that have 'no speculation' in their orbs which *he* can understand; and hurrying figures of men and women weaving to and fro, with no apparent purposes intelligible to a stranger, seeming like a mask of maniacs, or, oftentimes, like a pageant of phantoms. The great length of the streets in many quarters of London; the continual opening of transient glimpses into other vistas equally far-stretching, going off at right angles to the one which you are traversing; and the murky atmosphere which, settling upon the remoter end of every long avenue, wraps its termination in gloom and uncertainty; all these are circumstances aiding that sense of vastness and illimitable proportions which for ever brood over the aspect of London in its interior. Much of the feeling which belongs to the outside of London, in its approaches for the last few miles, I had lost, in consequence of the stealthy route of by-roads, lying near Uxbridge and Watford, through which we crept into the suburbs. But, for that reason, the more abrupt and startling had been the effect of emerging somewhere into the Edgeware Road, and soon afterwards into the very streets of London itself—though *what* streets, or even what quarter of London, is now totally obliterated from my mind, having perhaps never been comprehended. All that I remember is one monotonous awe and blind sense of mysterious grandeur and Babylonian confusion, which seemed to pursue and to invest the whole equipage of human life, as we moved for nearly two hours through streets; sometimes brought to anchor for ten minutes or more, by what is technically called a 'lock'—that is, a line of carriages of every description inextricably massed and obstructing each other, far as the eye could stretch; and then, as if under an enchanter's rod, the 'lock' seemed to thaw; motion spread with the fluent race of light or sound through the whole icebound mass, until the subtle influence reached *us* also; who were again absorbed into the great rush of flying carriages; or, at times, we turned off into some less tumultuous street, but of the same mile-long character; and finally, drawing up about noon, we alighted at some place, which is as little within my distinct remembrance as the route by which we reached it.

THOMAS DE QUINCEY (1785–1859), 'The Nation of London', 1834

In 1801 Charles Lamb responded to an invitation from William and Dorothy Wordsworth to visit them in Cumberland with the following magnificent letter, which constitutes the most heartfelt appreciation of London's varied beauty in English literature.

'TEARS IN THE MOTLEY STRAND'

I ought before this to have reply'd to your very kind invitation into Cumberland. With you and your sister I could gang any where. But I am afraid whether I shall ever be able to afford so desperate a Journey. Separate from the pleasure of your company, I dont much care if I never see a mountain in my life. I have passed all my days in London, until I have formed as many and intense local attachments, as any of your mountaineers can have done with dead nature. The Lighted shops of the Strand and Fleet Street, the innumerable trades, tradesmen and customers, coaches, waggons, playhouses, all the bustle and wickedness round about Covent Garden, the very women of the Town, the watchmen, drunken scenes, rattles,—life awake, if you awake, at all hours of the night, the impossibility of being dull in Fleet Street, the crowds, the very dirt and mud, the Sun shining upon houses and pavements, the print shops, the old book stalls, parsons cheap'ning books, coffee houses, steams of soup from kitchens, the pantomimes, London itself a pantomime and a masquerade,—all these things work themselves into my mind and feed me without a power of satiating me. The wonder of these sights impells me into nightwalks about the crowded streets, and I often shed tears in the motley Strand from fulness of joy at so much Life.— All these emotions must be strange to you. So are your rural emotions to me. But consider, what must I have been doing all my life, not to have lent great portions of my heart with usury to such scenes?—

My attachments are local, purely local. I have no passion (or have had none since I was in love, and then it was the spurious engendering of poetry and books) to groves and vallies. The rooms where I was born, the furniture which has been before my eyes all my life, a book case which has followed me about (like a faithful dog, only exceeding him in knowledge) wherever I have moved, old tables, streets, squares, where I have sunned myself, my old school,—these are my mistresses. Have I not enough, without your mountains? I do not envy you. I should pity you, did I not know, that the Mind will make friends of any thing. Your sun and moon and skies and hills and lakes affect me no more, or scarcely come to me in more venerable characters, than as a gilded room with tapestry and tapers, where I live with handsome visible objects. I consider the clouds above me but as a roof, beautifully painted, but unable to satisfy the mind, and at last, like the pictures of the apartment of a connoisseur, unable to afford him any longer a pleasure. So fading upon me, from disuse, have been the Beauties of Nature, as they have been constantly called; so ever fresh and green and warm are all the inventions of men in this great city.

CHARLES LAMB, letter to William Wordsworth, 30 January 1801, in *Collected Letters*

CROSSING WESTMINSTER BRIDGE

Tuesday, 26 July 1802
On Thursday morning, 29th, we arrived in London. Wm left me at the Inn—I went to bed. Etc. etc. After various troubles and disasters we left London on Saturday morning at ½ past 5 or 6, the 31st of July (I have forgot which). We mounted the Dover Coach at Charing Cross. It was a beautiful morning. The City, St Paul's, with the River and a multitude of little Boats, made a most beautiful sight as we crossed Westminster Bridge. The houses were not overhung by their cloud of smoke and they were spread out endlessly, yet the sun shone so brightly with such a pure light that there was even something like the purity of one of nature's own grand spectacles.

DOROTHY WORDSWORTH, *Journals*, ed. Mary Moorman, 2nd edn., 1971

COMPOSED UPON WESTMINSTER BRIDGE

Earth has not anything to show more fair:
Dull would he be of soul who could pass by
A sight so touching in its majesty:
This City now doth, like a garment, wear
The beauty of the morning; silent, bare,
Ships, towers, domes, theatres, and temples lie
Open unto the fields, and to the sky;
All bright and glistening in the smokeless air.

Never did sun more beautifully steep
In his first splendour valley, rock, or hill;
Ne'er saw I, never felt, a calm so deep!
The river glideth at his own sweet will:
Dear God! the very houses seem asleep;
And all that mighty heart is lying still!

WILLIAM WORDSWORTH, 3 September 1802

PILLARS OF GOLD

The fields from Islington to Marybone,
To Primrose Hill and Saint John's Wood,
    Were builded over with pillars of gold,
And there Jerusalem's pillars stood.

Her Little-ones ran on the fields,
The Lamb of God among them seen,
    And fair Jerusalem his Bride,
Among the little meadows green.

Pancrass & Kentish-town repose
Among her golden pillars high,
    Among her golden arches which
Shine upon the starry sky.

The Jew's-harp-house & the Green Man,
The Ponds where Boys to bathe delight,
    The fields of Cows by Willan's farm,
Shine in Jerusalem's pleasant sight.

She walks upon our meadows green,
The Lamb of God walks by her side,
    And every English Child is seen
Children of Jesus & his Bride.

WILLIAM BLAKE, from 'Jerusalem', 1804–20

'A GRAND FRAGMENT'

These dim eyes have in vain explored for some months past a well-known
figure, or part of the figure, of a man, who used to glide his comely upper
half over the pavements of London, wheeling along with most ingenious

celerity upon a machine of wood; a spectacle to natives, to foreigners, and to children. He was of a robust make, with a florid sailor-like complexion, and his head was bare to the storm and sunshine. He was a natural curiosity, a speculation to the scientific, a prodigy to the simple. The infant would stare at the mighty man brought down to his own level. The common cripple would despise his own pusillanimity, viewing the hale stoutness, and hearty heart, of this half-limbed giant. Few but must have noticed him; for the accident, which brought him low, took place during the riots of 1780, and he has been a groundling so long. He seemed earth-born, an Antæus, and to suck in fresh vigour from the soil which he neighboured. He was a grand fragment; as good as an Elgin marble. The nature, which should have recruited his reft legs and thighs, was not lost, but only retired into his upper parts, and he was half a Hercules. I heard a tremendous voice thundering and growling, as before an earthquake, and casting down my eyes, it was this mandrake reviling a steed that had started at his portentous appearance. He seemed to want but his just stature to have rent the offending quadruped in shivers. He was as the man-part of a Centaur, from which the horse-half had been cloven in some dire Lapithan controversy. He moved on, as if he could have made shift with yet half of the body-portion which was left him. The *os sublime* was not wanting; and he threw out yet a jolly countenance upon the heavens. Forty-and-two years had he driven this out of door trade, and now that his hair is grizzled in the service, but his good spirits no way impaired, because he is not content to exchange his free air and exercise for the restraints of a poor-house, he is expiating his contumacy in one of those houses (ironically christened) of Correction.

Was a daily spectacle like this to be deemed a nuisance, which called for legal interference to remove? or not rather a salutary and a touching object, to the passers-by in a great city? Among her shows, her museums, and supplies for ever-gaping curiosity (and what else but an accumulation of sights—endless sights—*is* a great city; or for what else is it desirable?) was there not room for one *Lusus* (not *Naturæ*, indeed, but) *Accidentium*? What if in forty-and-two years' going about, the man had scraped together enough to give a portion to his child (as the rumour ran) of a few hundreds—whom had he injured?—whom had he imposed upon? The contributors had enjoyed their *sight* for their pennies. What if after being exposed all day to the heats, the rains, and the frosts of heaven—shuffling his ungainly trunk along in an elaborate and painful motion—he was enabled to retire at night to enjoy himself at a club of his fellow cripples over a dish of hot meat and vegetables, as the charge was gravely brought against him by a clergyman deposing before a House of Commons' Committee—was *this*, or was his truly paternal consideration, which (if a fact) deserved a statue rather than a whipping-post, and is inconsistent at least with the exaggeration of nocturnal orgies which he has been slandered with—a reason that he should be deprived of his chosen, harmless, nay edifying, way of life, and be committed in hoary age for a sturdy vagabond?—

There was a Yorick once, whom it would not have shamed to have sate down at the cripples' feast, and to have thrown in his benediction, ay, and his mite too, for a companionable symbol. 'Age, thou hast lost thy breed.'

CHARLES LAMB, *Essays of Elia*, 1820–3

A LOVE LETTER

My dear Girl,

I have been hurried to Town by a Letter from my brother George; it is not of the brightest intelligence. Am I mad or not? I came by the Friday night coach and have not yet been to Hampstead. Upon my soul it is not my fault. I cannot resolve to mix any pleasure with my days: they go one like another undistinguishable. If I were to see you to day it would destroy the half comfortable sullenness I enjoy at present into downright perplexities. I love you too much to venture to Hampstead, I feel it is not paying a visit, but venturing into a fire. Que feraije? as the french novel writers say in fun, and I in earnest: really what can I do? Knowing well that my life must be passed in fatigue and trouble, I have been endeavouring to wean myself from you: for to myself alone what can be much of a misery? As far as they regard myself I can despise all events: But I cannot cease to love you. This morning I scarcely know what I am doing. I am going to Walthamstow. I shall return to Winchester tomorrow; whence you shall hear from me in a few days. I am a Coward, I cannot bear the pain of being happy: 'tis out of the question: I must admit no thought of it.

Yours ever affectionately

John Keats

JOHN KEATS, letter to Fanny Brawne, 13 September 1819, in *Collected Letters*

LINES ON THE MERMAID TAVERN

Souls of Poets dead and gone,
What Elysium have ye known,
Happy field or mossy cavern,
Choicer than the Mermaid Tavern?
Have ye tippled drink more fine
Than mine host's Canary wine?
Or are fruits of Paradise
Sweeter than those dainty pies
Of venison? O generous food!
Drest as though bold Robin Hood
Would, with his maid Marian,
Sup and bowse from horn and can.

I have heard that on a day
Mine host's sign-board flew away,
Nobody knew whither, till
An astrologer's old quill
To a sheepskin gave the story,
Said he saw you in your glory,
Underneath a new old sign
Sipping beverage divine,
And pledging with contented smack
The Mermaid in the Zodiac.

Souls of Poets dead and gone,
What Elysium have ye known,
Happy field or mossy cavern,
Choicer than the Mermaid Tavern?

JOHN KEATS, 1820

In his Mémoires d'outre-tombe, *written in the 1840s, Chateaubriand remembers his time in London, when he was his country's ambassador at the court of
King George IV.*

FASHIONABLE LONDON IN 1822

The arrival of the King, the re-opening of Parliament, the commence-
ment of the Season blended duty, business and pleasure: one could meet
the ministers only at Court, at balls, or in Parliament. To celebrate His
Majesty's birthday, I dined with Lord Londonderry; I dined on the Lord
Mayor's galley, which went up to Richmond: I prefer the miniature
Bucentaur in the arsenal at Venice, which no longer bears more than the
memory of the Doges and a Virgilian name. In the old days, as an
Emigrant, lean and half-naked, I had amused myself, without being
Scipio, by throwing stones into the water along that bank now hugged
by the Lord Mayor's plump and well-lined barge.

I also dined in the East End of the town with Mr Rothschild of
London, of the younger branch of Salomon: where did I not dine? The
roast-beef equalled that of the Tower of London in stateliness; the fish
were so long that one could not see their tails; ladies, whom I met there
and nowhere else, sang like Abigail. I quaffed tokay not far from the
place which had seen me toss off water by the pitcherful and almost die
of hunger; reclining against the silk-squabbed back of my well-padded
carriage, I saw that same Westminster where I had spent a night locked
in the Abbey, and around which I had strolled, covered with mud, with
Hingant and Fontanes. My house, the rent of which cost me twelve
hundred pounds a year, was opposite the garret inhabited by my cousin
de La Boüétardais what time, in a red robe, he used to play the guitar
on a borrowed truckle-bed to which I had offered shelter beside my own.

There was no longer a question of those Emigrant hops at which we
used to dance to the tune of the violin of a counsellor to the Breton
Parliament; it was Almack's, conducted by Collinet, that provided my
delight: a public ball under the patronage of the great ladies of the West
End. There the old and the young dandies met. Among the old, shone
the victor of Waterloo, who aired his glory like a snare for women
stretched across the quadrilles; at the head of the young, stood out Lord
Clanwilliam, said to be the son of the Duke of Richmond. He did wonderful things: he galloped out to Richmond and returned to Almack's after
twice falling from his horse. He had a certain manner of utterance, after

the fashion of Alcibiades, which was thought enchanting. The fashions in words, the affectations of language and pronunciation changing, as they do, in almost every parliamentary session in high society in London, an honest man is wonder-struck at no longer knowing English, which he believed himself to know perfectly six months before. In 1822, the duty of the man of fashion was, at the first glance, to present an unhappy and ailing figure; he was expected to have something neglected about his person: long nails; beard worn neither full nor shaved, but seeming to have sprouted at a given moment by surprise, through forgetfulness, amid the preoccupations of despair; a waving lock of hair; a profound, sublime, wandering and fatal glance; lips contracted in scorn of the human race; a heart bored, Byronian, drowned in the disgust and mystery of existence.

To-day it is no longer so: the dandy must have a conquering, thought-less, insolent air; he must attend to his dress, wear mustachios or a beard cut round like Queen Elizabeth's ruff or the radiant disk of the sun; he reveals the lofty independence of his character by keeping his hat on his head, by lolling on the sofa, stretching out his boots before the noses of the ladies seated in admiration on chairs before him; he rides with a cane which he carries like a wax-taper, indifferent to the horse which chances to be between his legs. His health must be perfect and his soul always at the height of five or six felicities. A few Radical dandies, those most advanced towards the future, possess a pipe.

But, no doubt, all these things are changed in the very time which I am taking to describe them. They say that the dandy of the present moment must no longer know if he exists, if the world is there, if there are women, and if he ought to salute his neighbour. Is it not curious to find the original of the dandy under Henry III?

FRANÇOIS RENÉ CHATEAUBRIAND, *Memoirs*, 1849–50

THE SHIPS' INSTRUMENT-MAKER'S SHOP

Though the offices of Dombey and Son were within the liberties of the City of London, and within hearing of Bow Bells, when their clashing voices were not drowned by the uproar in the streets, yet were there hints of adventurous and romantic story to be observed in some of the adjacent objects. Gog and Magog held their state within ten minutes' walk; the Royal Exchange was close at hand; the Bank of England, with its vaults of gold and silver 'down among the dead men' underground, was their magnificent neighbour. Just round the corner stood the rich East India House, teeming with suggestions of precious stuffs and stones, tigers, elephants, howdahs, hookahs, umbrellas, palm trees, palanquins, and gorgeous princes of a brown complexion sitting on carpets, with their slippers very much turned up at the toes. Anywhere in the immediate vicinity there might be seen pictures of ships speeding away full sail to all parts of the world; outfitting warehouses ready to pack off anybody anywhere, fully equipped in half an hour; and little timber midshipmen in obsolete naval uniforms, eternally employed outside the shop doors of nautical instrument-makers in taking observations of the hackney coaches.

Sole master and proprietor of one of these effigies—of that which might be called, familiarly, the woodenest—of that which thrust itself out above the pavement, right leg foremost, with a suavity the least endurable, and had the shoe buckles and flapped waistcoat the least reconcileable to human reason, and bore at its right eye the most offensively disproportionate piece of machinery—sole master and proprietor of that midshipman, and proud of him too, an elderly gentleman in a Welsh wig had paid house-rent, taxes, and dues, for more years than many a full-grown midshipman of flesh and blood has numbered in his life; and midshipmen who have attained a pretty green old age, have not been wanting in the English navy.

The stock-in-trade of this old gentleman comprised chronometers, barometers, telescopes, compasses, charts, maps, sextants, quadrants, and specimens of every kind of instrument used in the working of a ship's course, or the keeping of a ship's reckoning, or the prosecuting of a ship's discoveries. Objects in brass and glass were in his drawers and on his shelves, which none but the initiated could have found the top of, or guessed the use of, or having once examined, could have ever got back again into their mahogany nests without assistance. Everything was jammed into the tightest cases, fitted into the narrowest corners, fenced up behind the most impertinent cushions, and screwed into the acutest angles, to prevent its philosophical composure from being disturbed by the rolling of the sea. Such extraordinary precautions were taken in every instance to save room, and keep the thing compact; and so much practical navigation was fitted, and cushioned, and screwed into every box (whether the box was a mere slab, as some were, or something between a cocked hat and a star-fish, as others were, and those quite mild and modest boxes as compared with others); that the shop itself, partaking of the general infection, seemed almost to become a snug, sea-going, ship-shape concern, wanting only good sea-room, in the event of an unexpected launch, to work its way securely to any desert island in the world.

Many minor incidents in the household life of the Ships' Instrument-maker who was proud of his little midshipman, assisted and bore out this fancy. His acquaintance lying chiefly among ship-chandlers and so forth, he had always plenty of the veritable ships' biscuit on his table. It was familiar with dried meats and tongues, possessing an extraordinary flavour of rope yarn. Pickles were produced upon it, in great wholesale jars, with 'dealer in all kinds of Ships' Provisions' on the label; spirits were set forth in case bottles with no throats. Old prints of ships with alphabetical references to their various mysteries, hung in frames upon the walls; the Tartar Frigate under weigh, was on the plates; outlandish shells, seaweeds, and mosses, decorated the chimney-piece; the little wainscotted back parlour was lighted by a sky-light, like a cabin.

CHARLES DICKENS, *Dombey and Son*, 1848

NAPOLEON DEIFIED

The day was thus distributed in London: at six o'clock in the morning, one hastened to a party of pleasure, consisting of a breakfast in the country; one returned to lunch in London; one changed one's dress to walk in Bond Street or Hyde Park; one dressed again to dine at half-past seven; one dressed again for the Opera; at midnight, one dressed once more for an evening party or rout. What a life of enchantment! I should a hundred times have preferred the galleys: The supreme height of fashion was to be unable to make one's way into the small rooms of a private ball, to remain on the stair-case blocked by the crowd, and to find one's self nose to nose with the Duke of Somerset; a state of beatitude to which I once attained. The English of the new breed are infinitely more frivolous than we; their heads are turned for a 'show:' if the Paris executioner were to go to London, all England would run after him. Did not Marshal Soult enrapture the ladies, like Blücher, whose mustachios they kissed? Our marshal, who is not Antipater, nor Antigonus, nor Seleucus, nor Antiochus, nor Ptolemy, nor any of the captain-kings of Alexander, is a distinguished soldier, who pillaged Spain while getting beaten, and with whom Capuchins redeemed their lives with pictures. But it is true that, in March 1814, he published a furious proclamation against Bonaparte, whom he received in triumph a few days later: he has since done his Easter duty at Saint-Thomas-d'Aquin. They show his old boots in London for a shilling.

All reputations are quickly made on the banks of the Thames and as quickly lost. In 1822, I found that great city immersed in the recollection of Bonaparte; the people had passed from the vilification of 'Nick' to a stupid enthusiasm. Memoirs of Bonaparte swarmed; his bust adorned every chimney-piece; his engravings shone in the windows of all the picture-dealers; his colossal statue, by Canova, decorated the Duke of Wellington's stair-case. Could they not have consecrated another sanctuary to Mars enchained? This deification seems rather the work of the vanity of a door-porter than of the honour of a warrior. General, you did not defeat Napoleon at Waterloo: you only forced the last link of a destiny already shattered.

FRANÇOIS RENÉ CHATEAUBRIAND, *Memoirs*, 1849–50

LONDON BRIDGE AT MIDNIGHT

The church clocks chimed three quarters past eleven, as two figures emerged on London Bridge. One, which advanced with a swift and rapid step, was that of a woman who looked eagerly about her as though in quest of some expected object; the other figure was that of a man, who slunk along in the deepest shadow he could find, and, at some distance, accommodated his pace to hers: stopping when she stopped: and as she moved again, creeping stealthily on: but never allowing himself, in the ardour of his pursuit, to gain upon her footsteps. Thus, they crossed the bridge, from the Middlesex to the Surrey shore, when the woman, apparently disappointed in her anxious scrutiny of the foot-passengers, turned back. The movement was sudden; but he who watched her was not thrown off his guard by it; for, shrinking into one of the recesses which surmount the piers of the bridge, and leaning over the parapet the better to conceal his figure, he suffered her to pass on the opposite pavement. When she was about the same distance in advance as she had been before, he slipped quietly down, and followed her again. At nearly the centre of the bridge, she stopped. The man stopped too.

It was a very dark night. The day had been unfavourable, and at that hour and place there were few people stirring. Such as there were, hurried quickly past: very possibly without seeing, but certainly without noticing, either the woman, or the man who kept her in view. Their appearance was not calculated to attract the importunate regards of such of London's destitute population, as chanced to take their way over the bridge that night in search of some cold arch or doorless hovel wherein to lay their heads; they stood there in silence: neither speaking nor spoken to, by any one who passed.

A mist hung over the river, deepening the red glare of the fires that burnt upon the small craft moored off the different wharfs, and rendering darker and more indistinct the mirky buildings on the banks. The old smoke-stained storehouses on either side, rose heavy and dull from the dense mass of roofs and gables, and frowned sternly upon water too black to reflect even their lumbering shapes. The tower of old Saint Saviour's Church, and the spire of Saint Magnus, so long the giant-warders of the ancient bridge, were visible in the gloom; but the forest of shipping below bridge, and the thickly scattered spires of churches above, were nearly all hidden from the sight.

The girl had taken a few restless turns to and fro—closely watched meanwhile by her hidden observer—when the heavy bell of St Paul's tolled for the death of another day. Midnight had come upon the crowded city. The palace, the night-cellar, the jail, the madhouse: the chambers of birth and death, of health and sickness, the rigid face of the corpse and the calm sleep of the child: midnight was upon them all.

CHARLES DICKENS, *Oliver Twist*, 1837

A WARNING OF CHOLERA, AND THE AFTERMATH

The remorseless spread of cholera through the north was causing growing concern in London during the early weeks of 1832. Foreign capitals like St Petersburg and Berlin had suffered severely from the disease and London offered at least as attractive a target. It had not yet entirely thrown off its rural past. It was still surrounded by fields, it still contained pigsties and market gardens, and it still obtained much of its milk from 'cow-keepers', whose animals were tethered behind the shop in the very heart of the built-up areas. But it was far the largest and the most densely populated place in the whole of the British Isles. 'Within the bills', the area covered by the weekly Bills of Mortality which were the index of the capital's health, were crammed almost a million people, while half a million more lived in adjacent districts such as Paddington, Chelsea and Kensington.

On 25th January a warning went out to every local Board of Health in London drawing attention to 'the uninterrupted and steady' advance of cholera 'in defiance of Winter' and urging preparations to meet an outbreak in the capital. Many public-spirited citizens, however, were not content to leave the protection of London to the authorities and a flood of 'open letters' to public personages recommending a variety of ingenious precautions was soon pouring from the presses. One elderly Fellow of the Royal Society wrote to the Home Secretary recommending that buildings be commandeered to house the very poor, whose own unhealthy dwellings could be demolished; and that doors and windows should be compulsorily removed from many houses, to improve ventilation, along with the skylights of closed-in shopping streets like Burlington Arcade. Where these measures were insufficient to clear the atmosphere, for example in 'back-kitchens, closets, cellars, dust-holes, back houses, etc.', small quantities of gunpowder should be exploded. Inside such houses as were left unaffected by all this activity, the author recommended a remedy he had learned as a student fifty years before—placing in every room saucers full of chemicals to produce chlorine. His former neighbours, he claimed, could vouch for the efficacy of this type of disinfectant because, twenty years earlier, he had 'received the body of a huge elephant for dissection . . . in the hot month of August . . . but by the use of the above-mentioned chemical preparation the air was immediately purified'.

The same writer was much troubled by the danger which, he believed, lurked in old clothes. He pointed out 'the absolute necessity for the immediate change of the tattered vestments of the destitute', which could be accomplished by 'disburthening the wardrobes of the rich of their superfluous articles of dress', which, instead of being given 'to valets or to favourite footmen' were to be handed over for distribution to the poor. 'Previously to receiving them each pauper should receive a thorough ablution with soap and warm water in the bath of the Infirmary; the hair cut close or the heads shaved'. As for food, 'Bones of all kinds, being chopped and crushed, with scraps of meat, poultry, etc., might be made into excellent soup. . . . All waste bread might be soaked in milk and with pieces of suet or fat cut small, some coarse sugar or treacle, with a little powdered pimento or ginger, may be converted into puddings . . . thus forming a nutritious food for children'. These measures might even be made self-financing: 'Some of the extensive and unoccupied warehouses in the City, might be appropriated to the salutary purposes of clothes bazaars' and stocked up with 'the immense accumulation of worn clothes deposited in various receptacles in Rosemary Lane, Holywell Street (Strand), Monmouth Street and elsewhere, kept almost exclusively by Jew merchants. . . . The torn and defective coverings of the poor, with all spoiled beddings, curtains, etc., should be immersed in the Thames (a part being hurdled off for the purpose) and after being macerated there about a month, when washed and dried, might be sold for the purpose of paper manufacture'. The author also favoured lowering the duty on soap and beer, raising the duty on gin and forcing public houses to close at 11 p.m.

*

There was indeed little excuse for anyone who refused to admit the existence of cholera in London for the facts were reported in many of the 80 newspapers and magazines then published in the capital and were set out in great detail in the government's own publication, the *Cholera Gazette*, of which six issues, each of about 40 pages, appeared between mid-January and early April. Many of the London cases were also of a virulence which made diagnosis easy. The lightning speed with which the disease struck was noticed in Southwark, where the first warning of one case was 'a heavy noise in Mrs Taylor's apartment'. A neighbour, going to investigate, 'found that the poor creature had been seized with the disease while standing by the fireplace and had actually been struck down so unexpectedly that she fell into the fire'. The tendency of the disease to leave the patient discoloured was also noticed in several areas. In the West End a doctor called to a small boy noticed that 'His nails looked as if they had been stained with ink'; in Whitechapel a nurse commented that her patient seemed to have 'been rubbed with a washerwoman's blue rag'; while in Brentford Dr Melin examined a man who 'from his lips to his toes was more deeply blue than . . . in any case I saw in the north'. Despite such evidence, given great prominence in the medical journals, the allegation that there was no epidemic persisted. An anonymous ballad writer commented cynically:

Some people say it was a puff,
It was done to raise the doctor's stuff,
And there has now been near enough,
About the cholera morbus.

The belief that cholera was not really present in London had serious consequences. The Board of Health representative, Dr Anderson, reported from Southwark how he had been summoned too late to save one man. 'I left his unhappy family expressing in the bitterest terms their unavailing regret that they had been prevented from calling in medical aid at an early period of the attack by the idea . . . that cholera existed only in the imagination of interested persons'. John Melin, surgeon of the 9th Queens Royal Lancers, was confronted with a similar situation at Brentford, in Middlesex, on the outskirts of London. He reported in a hurried despatch to the Central Board of Health ('Excuse this hasty detail: the sergeant is waiting to take it to the post') how, 'as in all other places, there are numbers of obstinate persons who deny its existence in the parish and are endeavouring to raise an outcry against the medical men, who have honestly come forward to acknowledge this . . . fact'. It was even rumoured that the Board of Health's medical officers were stirring up alarm about the epidemic because they received a fee of twenty guineas a day while it lasted. The actual sum, Poulett Thomson disclosed in the House of Commons, was seven and sixpence.

NORMAN LONGMATE, *King Cholera*, 1966

FOG

London. Michaelmas Term lately over, and the Lord Chancellor sitting in Lincoln's Inn Hall. Implacable November weather. As much mud in the streets, as if the waters had but newly retired from the face of the earth, and it would not be wonderful to meet a Megalosaurus, forty feet long or so, waddling like an elephantine lizard up Holborn Hill. Smoke lowering down from chimney-pots, making a soft black drizzle, with flakes of soot in it as big as full-grown snowflakes—gone into mourning, one might imagine, for the death of the sun. Dogs, undistinguishable in mire. Horses, scarcely better; splashed to their very blinkers. Foot passengers, jostling one another's umbrellas, in a general infection of ill-temper, and losing their foot-hold at street-corners, where tens of thousands of other foot passengers have been slipping and sliding since the day broke (if this day ever broke), adding new deposits to the crust upon crust of mud, sticking at those points tenaciously to the pavement, and accumulating at compound interest.

Fog everywhere. Fog up the river, where it flows among green aits and meadows; fog down the river, where it rolls defiled among the tiers of shipping, and the waterside pollutions of a great (and dirty) city. Fog on the Essex marshes, fog on the Kentish heights. Fog creeping into the cabooses of collier-brigs; fog lying out on the yards, and hovering in the rigging of great ships; fog drooping on the gunwales of barges and small boats. Fog in the eyes and throats of ancient Greenwich pensioners, wheezing by the firesides of their wards; fog in the stem and bowl of the afternoon pipe of the wrathful skipper, down in his close cabin; fog cruelly pinching the toes and fingers of his shivering little prentice boy on deck. Chance people on the bridges peeping over the parapets into a nether sky of fog, with fog all round them, as if they were up in a balloon, and hanging in the misty clouds.

Gas looming through the fog in divers places in the streets, much as the sun may, from the spongy fields, be seen to loom by husbandman and ploughboy. Most of the shops lighted two hours before their time—as the gas seems to know, for it has a haggard and unwilling look.

The raw afternoon is rawest, and the dense fog is densest, and the muddy streets are muddiest, near that leaden-headed old obstruction, appropriate ornament for the threshold of a leaden-headed old corporation: Temple Bar. And hard by Temple Bar, in Lincoln's Inn Hall, at the very heart of the fog, sits the Lord High Chancellor in his High Court of Chancery.

Never can there come fog too thick, never can there come mud and mire too deep, to assort with the groping and floundering condition which this High Court of Chancery, most pestilent of hoary sinners, holds, this day, in the sight of heaven and earth.

CHARLES DICKENS, *Bleak House*, 1852–3

'AS BROWN AS UMBER'

It was by this time about nine in the morning, and the first fog of the season. A great chocolate-coloured pall lowered over heaven, but the wind was continually charging and routing these embattled vapours; so that as the cab crawled from street to street, Mr Utterson beheld a marvellous number of degrees and hues of twilight; for here it would be dark like the back-end of evening; and there would be a glow of a rich, lurid brown, like the light of some strange conflagration; and here, for a moment, the fog would be quite broken up, and a haggard shaft of daylight would glance in between the swirling wreaths. The dismal quarter of Soho seen under these changing glimpses, with its muddy ways, and slatternly passengers, and its lamps, which had never been extinguished or had been kindled afresh to combat this mournful re-invasion of darkness, seemed, in the lawyer's eyes, like a district of some city in a nightmare.

The thoughts of his mind, besides, were of the gloomiest dye; and when he glanced at the companion of his drive, he was conscious of some touch of that terror of the law and the law's officers which may at times assail the most honest.

As the cab drew up before the address indicated, the fog lifted a little, and showed him a dingy street, a gin-palace, a low French eating-house, a shop for the retail of penny numbers and twopenny salads, many ragged children huddled in the doorways, and many women of many different nationalities passing out, key in hand, to have a morning glass; and the next moment the fog settled down again upon that part, as brown as umber, and cut him off from his blackguardly surroundings.

ROBERT LOUIS STEVENSON, *The Strange Case of Dr Jekyll and Mr Hyde*, 1886

LONDON IN JUNE 1846

The stored-up heat of the houses caused many fires in London, and there were other disagreeable effects of town life in the heat. On this 19th June 'a correspondent requests us to call the attention of the authorities to the offensive condition of the sewers, the effluvia from which, in this hot weather, is most offensive' announced the *Daily News*, the paper which Dickens had founded a few months earlier. The rapid development of London in recent years had overstrained the sewers, as everyone could now perceive. 'The Heat has been so savage that not only we Italians, but the East Indians, have suffered much from it. I never knew hot nights so oppressive and hot days so little agreeable' wrote Milnes to a friend, while his future wife Annabel Crewe, whose spelling was not always perfectly reliable, recorded in her diary on 19th June 'Heat of weather quite unparralled in England'.

The only pleasant thing to contemplate was ice. A ship called the *Ilizaide* came into St Katharine's Docks with 664 tons of ice in large blocks; little boys hung all day round the depots of the Wenham Lake ice, as though the mere sight of the great white blocks would cool them; sherry coblers with ice (and no doubt quantities of typhoid germs) in them were a favourite drink. But it was impossible to keep cool, or look as if you were cool. 'This hot weather puts us all into Falstaff's state' wrote Wordsworth to Crabb Robinson, conjuring up an unlikely vision of the stately old poet 'larding the lean earth' with his sweat as he pottered about Rydal Mount. The papers were full of advertisements for clothes to keep cool in. 'The Delightful Coolness of the Golden Flax Cravat Collar, together with its perfect fit, however loosely tied on, recommend it especially during this weather'. For the women 'dresses of the most aerial textures, tulles, barèges, muslinés, organdies, tarlatans, and Chinese Batiste were alone wearable during the late insupportable heat'. If you had lost a relation within the year, you could go to Jay's, or The London General Mourning Warehouse as it was then called, and get 'Muslin Dresses for Half-Mourning. The extreme heat of the season has given an extraordinary impetus to the sale of PRINTED MUSLINS'. In a world without refrigerators, it was also useful to be told of Carson's Meat Preservers, by which meat could be cured in twelve or fifteen minutes and 'all taints avoided, even in the hottest weather', or of 'Lemon and Kali, a cooling beverage' advertised by a chemist in Cornhill as 'of inestimable value to those whose duties oblige them to perambulate the crowded streets of large towns in hot weather'.

But crowds, even out of doors, were a thing to avoid. An article in the *Illustrated London News* describes the 'languid limbs, and lazy lounging gait of people who passed . . . in the street, or crowded to the Serpentine'. Indoors it was far worse; evening parties were too hot to attend, even though the doors were taken right off their hinges, and morning concerts were a sea of waving fans, an undulation of fainting ladies.

The theatres were half empty. Macready's season at the Princess Theatre, where he had been playing *King Lear* and a new play called *The King of the Commons*, finished on this Friday 19th June. 'Acted King James better than usual, wishing my last night at the Princess's to leave a pleasing impression—as I think it did. Called for and very warmly received' he noted in his diary, adding a sarcastic note about the poor receipts at the Haymarket and Drury Lane that week. If the theatres were empty, the open-air pleasure gardens, Vauxhall, Surrey Gardens and Cremorne, were crowded every night with people watching the fireworks and the balloons which floated about in the night sky. The river steamers, cutting their way up and down the crowded Thames, were packed with people trying to get some cool breezes.

Those who had the money and the time even for these modest diversions were the best off. It was a grim time for those who had to work indoors. At Wolverhampton, where on the 18th the temperature was 96° in the shade, the works had to be stopped because the workmen could not support the unprecedented heat. In London, work went languidly on in stifling warehouses, and those with business in the City felt the pavements burning through the soles of their boots as they went to and fro, and were thankful when a passing water-cart gave an illusion of freshness to the dusty street.

> ALETHEA HAYTER, *A Sultry Month: Scenes of Literary London Life in 1846*, 1965

SWANS AT RICHMOND

How beautiful did Old Father Thames look yesterday—it was prettily scattered about with swans above Richmond—and when they flew over the water, the clapping of their wings was very loud indeed.

> JOHN CONSTABLE, letter to C. R. Leslie, RA, 8 September 1834, written in his house in Charlotte Street

THE SAWING WIND

Mr Mortimer Lightwood and Mr Eugene Wrayburn took a coffee-house dinner together in Mr Lightwood's office. They had newly agreed to set up a joint establishment together. They had taken a bachelor cottage near Hampton, on the brink of the Thames, with a lawn, and a boat-house, and all things fitting, and were to float with the stream through the summer and the Long Vacation.

It was not summer yet, but spring; and it was not gentle spring ethereally mild, as in Thomson's Seasons, but nipping spring with an easterly wind, as in Johnson's, Jackson's, Dickson's, Smith's, and Jones's Seasons. The grating wind sawed rather than blew; and as it sawed, the sawdust whirled about the sawpit. Every street was a sawpit, and there were no top-sawyers; every passenger was an under-sawyer, with the sawdust blinding him and choking him.

That mysterious paper currency which circulates in London when the wind blows, gyrated here and there and everywhere. Whence can it come, whither can it go? It hangs on every bush, flutters in every tree, is caught flying by the electric wires, haunts every enclosure, drinks at every pump, cowers at every grating, shudders upon every plot of grass, seeks rest in vain behind the legions of iron rails. In Paris, where nothing is wasted, costly and luxurious city though it be, but where wonderful human ants creep out of holes and pick up every scrap, there is no such thing. There, it blows nothing but dust. There, sharp eyes and sharp stomachs reap even the east wind, and get something out of it.

The wind sawed, and the sawdust whirled. The shrubs wrung their many hands, bemoaning that they had been over-persuaded by the sun to bud; the young leaves pined; the sparrows repented of their early marriages, like men and women; the colours of the rainbow were discernible, not in floral spring, but in the faces of the people whom it nibbled and pinched. And ever the wind sawed, and the sawdust whirled.

CHARLES DICKENS, *Our Mutual Friend*, 1864–5

IN EPPING FOREST

How beautiful this hill of fern swells on!
So beautiful the chapel peeps between
The hornbeams—with its simple bell. Alone
I wander here, hid in a palace green.
Mary is absent—but the forest queen,
Nature, is with me. Morning, noon and gloaming,
I write my poems in these paths unseen;
And when among these brakes and beeches roaming,
I sigh for truth, and home, and love and woman.

I sigh for one and two—and still I sigh,
For many are the whispers I have heard
From beauty's lips. Love's soul in many an eye

Hath pierced my heart with such intense regard,
I looked for joy and pain was the reward.
I think of them I love, each girl and boy,
Babes of two mothers,—on this velvet sward,
And Nature thinks—in her so sweet employ,
While dews fall on each blossom, weeping joy.

Here is the chapel yard enclosed with pales,
And oak trees nearly top its little bell.
Here is the little bridge with guiding rail
That leads me on to many a pleasant dell.
The fern owl chitters like a startled knell
To nature—yet 'tis sweet at evening still.
A pleasant road curves round the gentle swell,
Where Nature seems to have her own sweet will,
Planting her beech and thorn about the sweet fern hill

JOHN CLARE (1793–1864)

BEAUTY IN MODEST CORNERS

Georges says Epping is not very beautiful. But then beautiful things can
be made with so little and motifs which have too much beauty can look
theatrical—look at Switzerland. Didn't old Corot make beautiful little
pictures in Gisors out of a couple of willow trees, and a tiny stream, and
a bridge, like that picture of his at the Exposition Universelle? What a
masterpiece that was! Happy the people who can see beauty in a modest
corner where others can't see a thing. Everything is beautiful, the secret
is putting it across. And from the way you describe it, Epping must be
very interesting at least.

CAMILLE PISSARRO, letter to Lucien Pissarro, 1895, from *Camille Pissarro:
Letters to his Son Lucien*, trans. John Rewald, 1943

MR DOMBEY'S HOUSE

Mr Dombey's house was a large one, on the shady side of a tall, dark,
dreadfully genteel street in the region between Portland Place and
Bryanstone Square. It was a corner house, with great wide areas containing

cellars frowned upon by barred windows, and leered at by crooked-eyed doors leading to dustbins. It was a house of dismal state, with a circular back to it, containing a whole suit of drawing-rooms looking upon a gravelled yard, where two gaunt trees, with blackened trunks and branches, rattled rather than rustled, their leaves were so smoke-dried. The summer sun was never on the street, but in the morning about breakfast-time, when it came with the water-carts and the old-clothes men, and the people with geraniums, and the umbrella-mender, and the man who trilled the little bell of the Dutch clock as he went along. It was soon gone again to return no more that day; and the bands of music and the straggling Punch's shows going after it, left it a prey to the most dismal of organs, and white mice; with now and then a porcupine, to vary the entertainments; until the butlers whose families were dining out, began to stand at the house-doors in the twilight, and the lamplighter made his nightly failure in attempting to brighten up the street with gas.

CHARLES DICKENS, Dombey and Son, 1848

ALONE AND UNHAPPY IN LONDON

When I reached London no mode of life was prepared for me,—no advice ever given to me. I went into lodgings, and then had to dispose of my time. I belonged to no club, and knew very few friends who would receive me into their houses. In such a condition of life a young man should no doubt go home after his work, and spend the long hours of the evening in reading good books and drinking tea. A lad brought up by strict parents, and without having had even a view of gayer things, might perhaps do so. I had passed all my life at public schools, where I had seen gay things, but had never enjoyed them. Towards the good books and tea no training had been given me. There was no house in which I could habitually see a lady's face and hear a lady's voice. No allurements to decent respectability came in my way. It seems to me that in such circumstances the temptations of loose life will almost certainly prevail with a young man. Of course if the mind be strong enough, and the general stuff knitted together of sufficiently stern material, the temptations will not prevail. But such minds and such material are, I think, uncommon. The temptation at any rate prevailed with me.

I wonder how many young men fall utterly to pieces from being turned loose into London after the same fashion. Mine, I think, was of all phases of such life the most dangerous. The lad who is sent to mechanical work has longer hours, during which he is kept from danger, and has not generally been taught in his boyhood to anticipate pleasure. He looks for hard work and grinding circumstances. I certainly had enjoyed but little pleasure, but I had been among those who did enjoy it and were taught to expect it. And I had filled my mind with the ideas of such joys. And now, except during official hours, I was entirely without control,—without the influences of any decent household around me. I have said something of the comedy of such a life, but it certainly had its tragic aspect. Turning it all over in my own mind, as I have constantly done in after years, the tragedy has always been uppermost. And so it was as the time was passing. Could there be any escape from such dirt? I would ask myself; and I always answered that there was no escape. The mode of life was itself wretched. I hated the office. I hated my work. More than all I hated my idleness. I had often told myself since I left school that the only career in life within my reach was that of an author, and the only mode of authorship open to me that of a writer of novels. In the journal which I read and destroyed a few years since, I found the matter argued out before I had been in the Post Office two years. Parliament was out of the question. I had not means to go to the Bar. In official life, such as that to which I had been introduced, there did not seem to be any opening for real success. Pens and paper I could command. Poetry I did not believe to be within my grasp. The drama, too, which I would fain have chosen, I believed to be above me. For history, biography, or essay writing I had not sufficient erudition. But I thought it possible that I might write a novel. I had resolved very early that in that shape must the attempt be made. But the months and years ran on, and no attempt was made. And yet no day was passed without thoughts of attempting, and a mental acknowledgment of the disgrace of postponing it. What reader will not understand the agony of remorse produced by such a condition of mind? The gentleman from Mecklenburgh Square was always with me in the morning,—always angering me by his hateful presence,—but when the evening came I could make no struggle towards getting rid of him.

In those days I read a little, and did learn to read French and Latin. I made myself very familiar with Horace, and became acquainted with the works of our own greatest poets. I had my strong enthusiasms, and remember throwing out of the window in Northumberland Street, where

I lived, a volume of Johnson's *Lives of the Poets*, because he spoke sneeringly of *Lycidas*. That was Northumberland Street by the Marylebone Workhouse, on to the back-door of which establishment my room looked out—a most dreary abode, at which I fancy I must have almost ruined the good-natured lodging-house keeper by my continued inability to pay her what I owed.

How I got my daily bread I can hardly remember. But I do remember that I was often unable to get myself a dinner. Young men generally now have their meals provided for them. I kept house, as it were. Every day I had to find myself with the day's food. For my breakfast I could get some credit at the lodgings, though that credit would frequently come to an end. But for all that I had after breakfast I had to pay day by day; and at your eating-house credit is not given. I had no friends on whom I could sponge regularly. Out on the Fulham Road I had an uncle, but his house was four miles from the Post Office, and almost as far from my own lodgings. Then there came borrowings of money, sometimes absolute want, and almost constant misery.

> ANTHONY TROLLOPE, *Autobiography*, 1883; the 'gentleman from
> Mecklenburgh Square' was Col. Maberly, his boss at the Post Office.

MRS CARLYLE SETTLES IN LONDON

Well! is it not very strange that I am here; sitting in my own hired house by the side of the Thames, as if nothing had happened; with fragments of Haddington, of Comely Bank, of Craigenputtoch interweaved with *cockneyalities* into a very habitable whole? Is it not strange that I should have an everlasting sound in my ears, of men, women, children, omnibuses, carriages, glass coaches, street coaches, waggons, carts, dog-carts, steeple bells, door bells, gentlemen-raps, twopenny post-raps, footmen-showers-of-raps, of the whole devil to pay, as if plague, pestilence, famine, battle, murder, sudden death, and wee, Eppie Daidle were broken loose to make me diversion? And where is the stillness, the eternal sameness, of the last six years? Echo answers, at Craigenputtoch! There let them 'dwell with Melancholy' and old Nancy Macqueen; for this stirring life is more to my mind, and has besides a beneficial effect on my bowels. Seriously I have almost entirely discontinued drugs, and look twenty per cent. better, every one says, and 'what every one says must be true.' This being the case, you may infer that I am tolerably content in my new position; indeed—, I am more and more persuaded that there is no complete misery in the world that does not emanate from the bowels.

We have got an excellent lodgment, of most antique physiognomy, quite to our humour; all wainscoated, carved, and queer looking, roomy, substantial, commodious, with closets to satisfy any Bluebeard, a china-closet in particular that would hold our whole worldly substance converted into china! Two weeks ago there was a row of ancient trees in front, but some crazy-headed Cockneys have uprooted them. Behind we have a garden (so called in the language of flattery) in the worst order, but boasting of two vines which produced two bunches of grapes in the season, which 'might be eaten,' and a walnut-tree from which I have gathered almost sixpence worth of walnuts. This large and comfortable tenement we have, without bugs, for some two or three pounds more rent than we paid for the pepper-box at Comely Bank. This comes of our noble contempt for fashion, Chelsea being highly unfashionable. The only practical disadvantage in this circumstance is that we are far from most of our acquaintances—a disadvantage which I endeavour to obviate by learning to walk. My success is already considerable. I have several times walked ten miles without being laid up. Besides, we are not wholly isolated. Leigh Hunt lives a few doors off. The celebrated Mrs Somerville is at Chelsea Hospital, within five minutes' walk, and Mrs Austin is coming to introduce me to her to-morrow; and within a mile I have a *circle* of acquaintances. One of these who lives in prodigious *shine* with wife and family, you may happen to recollect something about—a grave, handsome man, who has been here repeatedly, and treats me with infinite respect, and takes immensely to my Husband—a sort of person with whom one talks about 'the condition of art' in this country, and suchlike topics of general interest, and studies to support the reputation of a rather intellectual and excessively reasonable woman. Can you divine who I mean? Impossible. George Rennie! How has it happened? Quite simply. I am one of the most amiable women living, tho', like your Uncle, 'my virtues are unknown.'

JANE WELSH CARLYLE, letter to Miss Stodart, 1843

HOW TO LIVE WELL ON NOTHING A YEAR

And so, Colonel and Mrs Crawley came to London: and it is at their house in Curzon Street, Mayfair, that they really showed the skill which must be possessed by those who would live on the resources above named.

In the first place, and as a matter of the greatest necessity, we are bound to describe how a house may be got for nothing a year. These mansions are to be had either unfurnished, where, if you have credit with Messrs Gillows or Bantings, you can get them splendidly *montées* and decorated entirely according to your own fancy; or they are to be let furnished; a less troublesome and complicated arrangement to most parties. It was so that Crawley and his wife preferred to hire their house.

Before Mr Bowls came to preside over Miss Crawley's house and cellar in Park Lane, that lady had had for a butler a Mr Raggles, who was born on the family estate of Queen's Crawley, and indeed was a younger son of a gardener there. By good conduct, a handsome person and calves, and a grave demeanour, Raggles rose from the knifeboard to the footboard of the carriage; from the footboard to the butler's pantry. When he had been a certain number of years at the head of Miss Crawley's establishment, where he had had good wages, fat perquisites, and plenty of opportunities of saving, he announced that he was about to contract a matrimonial alliance with a late cook of Miss Crawley's, who had subsisted in an honourable manner by the exercise of a mangle, and the keeping of a small greengrocer's shop in the neighbourhood. The truth is, that the ceremony had been clandestinely performed some years back; although the news of Mr Raggles' marriage was first brought to Miss Crawley by a little boy and girl of seven and eight years of age, whose continual presence in the kitchen had attracted the attention of Miss Briggs.

Mr Raggles then retired and personally undertook the superintendence of the small shop and the greens. He added milk and cream, eggs, and country-fed pork to his stores, contenting himself, whilst other retired butlers were vending spirits in public-houses, by dealing in the simplest country produce. And having a good connection amongst the butlers in the neighbourhood, and a snug back parlour where he and Mrs Raggles received them, his milk, cream, and eggs got to be adopted by many of the fraternity, and his profits increased every year. Year after year he quietly and modestly amassed money and when at length that snug and

complete bachelor's residence at No. 201 Curzon Street, Mayfair, lately
the residence of the Honourable Frederic Deuceace, gone abroad, with its
rich and appropriate furniture by the first makers, was brought to the
hammer, who should go in and purchase the lease and furniture of the
house but Charles Raggles? A part of the money he borrowed, it is true,
and at rather a high interest, from a brother butler, but the chief part he
paid down, and it was with no small pride that Mrs Raggles found
herself sleeping in a bed of carved mahogany, with silk curtains, with a
prodigious cheval glass opposite to her, and a wardrobe which would
contain her, and Raggles, and all the family.

Of course, they did not intend to occupy permanently an apartment
so splendid. It was in order to let the house again that Raggles purchased
it. As soon as a tenant was found, he subsided into the greengrocer's shop
once more; but a happy thing it was for him to walk out of that tenement and into Curzon Street, and there survey his house—his own house—
with geraniums in the window and a carved bronze knocker. The footman
occasionally lounging at the area railing, treated him with respect; the
cook took her green stuff at his house, and called him Mr Landlord; and
there was not one thing the tenant did, or one dish which they had for
dinner, that Raggles might not know of, if he liked.

He was a good man; good and happy. The house brought him in so
handsome a yearly income, that he was determined to send his children
to good schools, and accordingly, regardless of expense, Charles was sent
to boarding at Dr Swishtail's, Sugarcane Lodge, and little Matilda to
Miss Peckover's, Laurentinum House, Clapham.

Raggles loved and adored the Crawley family as the author of all his
prosperity in life. He had a *silhouette* of his mistress in his back shop,
and a drawing of the Porter's Lodge at Queen's Crawley, done by that
spinster herself in India ink—and the only addition he made to the
decorations of the Curzon Street house was a print of Queen's Crawley
in Hampshire, the seat of Sir Walpole Crawley, Baronet, who was represented in a gilded car drawn by six white horses, and passing by a lake
covered with swans, and barges containing ladies in hoops, and musicians
with flags and periwigs. Indeed, Raggles thought there was no such
palace in all the world, and no such august family.

As luck would have it, Raggles' house in Curzon Street was to let
when Rawdon and his wife returned to London. The Colonel knew it and
its owner quite well; the latter's connection with the Crawley family had

been kept up constantly, for Raggles helped Mr Bowls whenever Miss Crawley received friends. And the old man not only let his house to the Colonel, but officiated as his butler whenever he had company; Mrs Raggles operating in the kitchen below, and sending up dinners of which old Miss Crawley herself might have approved. This was the way, then, Crawley got his house for nothing; for though Raggles had to pay taxes and rates, and the interest of the mortgage to the brother butler; and the insurance of his life; and the charges for his children at school; and the value of the meat and drink which his own family—and for a time that of Colonel Crawley too—consumed; and though the poor wretch was utterly ruined by the transaction, his children being flung on the streets, and himself driven into the Fleet Prison: yet somebody must pay even for gentlemen who live for nothing a year—and so it was this unlucky Raggles was made the representative of Colonel Crawley's defective capital.

I wonder how many families are driven to roguery and to ruin by great practitioners in Crawley's way?—how many great noblemen rob their petty tradesmen, condescend to swindle their poor retainers out of wretched little sums, and cheat for a few shillings? When we read that a nobleman has left for the Continent, or that another noble nobleman has an execution in his house—and that one or other owes six or seven millions, the defeat seems glorious even, and we respect the victim in the vastness of his ruin. But who pities a poor barber who can't get his money for powdering the footmen's heads; or a poor carpenter who has ruined himself by fixing up ornaments and pavilions for my ladies' *déjeuner*; or the poor devil of a tailor whom the steward patronises, and who has pledged all he is worth and more, to get the liveries ready, which my lord has done him the honour to bespeak?—When the great house tumbles down, these miserable wretches fall under it unnoticed: as they say in the old legends, before a man goes to the devil himself, he sends plenty of other souls thither.

Rawdon and his wife generously gave their patronage to all such of Miss Crawley's tradesmen and purveyors as chose to serve them. Some were willing enough, especially the poor ones. It was wonderful to see the pertinacity with which the washerwoman from Tooting brought the cart every Saturday, and her bills week after week. Mr Raggles himself had to supply the greengroceries. The bill for servants' porter at the Fortune of War public-house is a curiosity in the chronicles of beer.

Every servant also was owed the greater part of his wages, and thus kept up perforce an interest in the house. Nobody in fact was paid. Not the blacksmith who opened the lock; nor the glazier who mended the pane; nor the jobber who let the carriage; nor the groom who drove it; nor the butcher who provided the leg of mutton; nor the coals which roasted it; nor the cook who basted it; nor the servants who ate it: and this I am given to understand is not unfrequently the way in which people live elegantly on nothing a year.

In a little town such things cannot be done without remark. We know there the quantity of milk our neighbour takes, and espy the joint or the fowls which are going in for his dinner. So, probably, 200 and 202 in Curzon Street might know what was going on in the house between them, the servants communicating through the area-railings; but Crawley and his wife and his friends did not know 200 and 202. When you came to 201 there was a hearty welcome, a kind smile, a good dinner, and a jolly shake of the hand from the host and hostess there, just for all the world as if they had been undisputed masters of three or four thousand a year—and so they were, not in money, but in produce and labour—if they did not pay for the mutton, they had it; if they did not give bullion in exchange for their wine, how should we know? Never was better claret at any man's table than at honest Rawdon's; dinners more gay and neatly served. His drawing-rooms were the prettiest little modest salons conceivable: they were decorated with the greatest taste, and a thousand nicknacks from Paris, by Rebecca; and when she sate at her piano trilling songs with a lightsome heart, the stranger voted himself in a little paradise of domestic comfort, and agreed that, if the husband was rather stupid, the wife was charming, and the dinners the pleasantest in the world.

W. M. THACKERAY, *Vanity Fair*, 1847

THE POOTER RESIDENCE

My dear wife Carrie and I have just been a week in our new house 'The Laurels', Brickfield Terrace, Holloway—a nice six-roomed residence, not counting basement, with a front breakfast-parlour. We have a little front garden; and then is a flight of ten steps up to the front door, which, by-the-by, we keep locked with the chain up. Cummings, Gowing, and our other intimate friends always come to the little side entrance, which saves the servant the trouble of going up to the front door, thereby taking her from her work. We have a nice little back garden which runs down to the railway.

GEORGE AND WEEDON GROSSMITH, *The Diary of a Nobody*, 1892

LINES WRITTEN IN KENSINGTON GARDENS

In this lone, open glade I lie,
Screened by deep boughs on either hand;
And at its end, to stay the eye,
Those black-crowned, red-boled pine-trees stand!

Birds here make song, each bird has his,
Across the girdling city's hum.
How green under the boughs it is!
How thick the tremulous sheep-cries come!

Sometimes a child will cross the glade
To take his nurse his broken toy;
Sometimes a thrush flit overhead
Deep in her unknown day's employ.

Here at my feet what wonders pass,
What endless, active life is here!
What blowing daisies, fragrant grass!
An air-stirred forest, fresh and clear.

Scarce fresher is the mountain-sod
Where the tired angler lies, stretched out,
And, eased of basket and of rod,
Counts his day's spoil, the spotted trout.

In the huge world, which roars hard by,
Be others happy if they can!
But in my helpless cradle I
Was breathed on by the rural Pan.

I, on men's impious uproar hurled,
Think often, as I hear them rave,

That peace has left the upper world
And now keeps only in the grave.

Yet here is peace for ever new!
When I who watch them am away,
Still all things in this glade go through
The changes of their quiet day.

Then to their happy rest they pass!
The flowers upclose, the birds are fed,
The night comes down upon the grass,
The child sleeps warmly in his bed.

Calm soul of all things! make it mine
To feel, amid the city's jar,
That there abides a peace of thine,
Man did not make, and cannot mar.

MATTHEW ARNOLD (1822–88)

PIP TAKES A WALK IN THE CITY

When I told the clerk that I would take a turn in the air while I waited,
he advised me to go round the corner and I should come into Smithfield.
So, I came into Smithfield; and the shameful place, being all asmear with
filth and fat and blood and foam, seemed to stick to me. So I rubbed it
off with all possible speed by turning into a street where I saw the great
black dome of Saint Paul's bulging at me from behind a grim stone
building which a bystander said was Newgate Prison. Following the wall
of the jail, I found the roadway covered with straw to deaden the noise
of passing vehicles; and from this, and from the quantity of people standing about, smelling strongly of spirits and beer, I inferred that the trials
were on.

While I looked about me here, an exceedingly dirty and partially
drunk minister of justice asked me if I would like to step in and hear
a trial or so: informing me that he could give me a front place for half-
a-crown, whence I should command a full view of the Lord Chief Justice
in his wig and robes—mentioning that awful personage like waxwork,
and presently offering him at the reduced price of eighteenpence. As
I declined the proposal on the plea of an appointment, he was so good

as to take me into a yard and show me where the gallows was kept, and also where people were publicly whipped, and then he showed me the Debtors' Door, out of which culprits came to be hanged; heightening the interest of that dreadful portal by giving me to understand that 'four on 'em' would come out at that door the day after to-morrow at eight in the morning to be killed in a row. This was horrible, and gave me a sickening idea of London: the more so as the Lord Chief Justice's proprietor wore (from his hat down to his boots and up again to his pocket-handkerchief inclusive) mildewed clothes, which had evidently not belonged to him originally, and which, I took it into my head, he had bought cheap of the executioner. Under these circumstances I thought myself well rid of him for a shilling.

CHARLES DICKENS, Great Expectations, 1860–1

TOM THUMB

In April 1846, soon after his return from his visit to Edinburgh, [the painter Benjamin Haydon] decided to exhibit *Aristides* and *Nero*, with some portraits and drawings, at a one-man show at the Egyptian Hall. The startling façade of this vanished exhibition hall, squeezed between the sober Georgian houses of Piccadilly, was a fitting drop-curtain for the ludicrous tragedy that was now played behind it. A menacing cornice and three monumental first-floor windows, crowded with giant statues and sphinxes, scarabs and hawks' wings and lotus capitals, weighted down a low ground floor, with an entrance fit for the entombment scene in *Aida*.

Haydon's pictures were installed on the first floor of the Egyptian Hall, to the right. He sent out four hundred invitations to the Private View, which was on 4th April. It poured with rain all that day, and only four people came. *The Times* and the *Herald* gave good notices to Haydon's pictures; he himself wrote and published a flamboyant advertisement of it; but day after day the attendance was wretched, the receipts almost nothing.

Meanwhile in the same building a very different exhibition was in progress. The American circus proprietor Barnum was showing 'General Tom Thumb, the midget', actually an eight-year-old boy called Stratton, only thirty-one inches tall. Tom Thumb was no novelty to London—he had appeared at the Egyptian Hall two years earlier, and had put on an act of 'Napoleon Musing at St Helena' for the benefit of the Duke of Wellington, who went to see him. Haydon, who had painted a well-known series of pictures with the title of *Napoleon Musing at St Helena*, had prophetically noted in his diary at the time 'I do not like this'. Novelty or not, Tom Thumb was an immense attraction when he re-appeared at the Egyptian Hall in 1846, to everyone up to Queen Victoria, who sent for him three times to the Palace, thus enabling Barnum to put a notice on the door of the Egyptian Hall each time saying 'Closed this evening, General Tom Thumb being at Buckingham Palace by the command of Her Majesty'. The Tom Thumb show at the Egyptian Hall ran from 20th March to 20th July 1846, and such were the crowds that came to see him that Barnum made up to 500 dollars a day out of it. 'They rush by thousands to see Thumb. They push, they fight, they scream, they faint, they cry help and murder, and oh and ah. They see my bills, my boards, my caravans, and don't read them. Their eyes are open but their sense is shut. It is an insanity, a Rabies, a madness, a Furor, a dream. I would not have believed it of the English people!' wrote Haydon in his journal. It was not only the mob who went to see Tom Thumb. On 2nd May a group of men, most of them acquaintances of Haydon's— Charles Dickens, Samuel Rogers, the painters Landseer and Stanfield, the actor Macready, the barrister and dramatist Talfourd—met at the opening day of the Royal Academy. Dickens persuaded them to go and see General Tom Thumb, but Macready, who records this in his diary, makes no mention of their going to see Haydon's pictures in the same building. The American writer Bayard Taylor, on his way to see Tom Thumb, saw Haydon standing outside the door of his exhibition room. 'He was stout, broad-shouldered . . . rather shabbily dressed, with a general air of dilapidated power. There was something fierce and bitter in the expression of his face, as he glanced across to the groups hurrying to see Tom Thumb'. In one week 12,000 people went to see Tom Thumb; in the same week 133 adults and a little girl went to see Haydon's pictures. On 18th May he closed his exhibition; it had been a disastrous failure and he had lost £111 by it. It was a month later, on 18th June, when no more money had come in and his creditors were besieging him, that he sent his journals and pictures to Elizabeth Barrett for safe keeping.

ALETHEA HAYTER, *A Sultry Month*, 1965

THE WESTWARD GROWTH

On this Saturday morning Elizabeth Barrett drove with her sister Arabel to pay a call in St John's Wood. The Marylebone and Paddington area across which she drove was now solidly built up. By 1846 the district north of Oxford Street, south and south-west of Regent's Park, was covered with handsome new terraces and squares for the prosperous professional class who now preferred this part of London to any other. It contained pockets of slum—there was one just off Portman Square. The sewers under Cavendish, Manchester and Bryanston Squares were in a very shaky state, clogged and collapsing. The streets, not yet all paved, were full of dust in this hot dry June. But it looked a glossy prosperous district, full of shining carriages, and in it lived many of the most successful writers and painters of the day. The Procters lived in Harley Street, the painter Turner in a gloomy dilapidated house in Queen Anne Street, Miss Barrett herself in Wimpole Street, her cousin John Kenyon in York Place, as the northern half of Baker Street was then called. Dickens had a charming roomy house, with two triple-windowed bays running up two stories, and a spacious garden behind a high brick wall, in the angle of Devonshire Terrace and the New Road, as the Marylebone Road then was. The painter John Martin lived in Allsop Terrace, just the other side of the New Road, and a little further west Macready had a fine Regency house, behind a free-standing screen of Ionic pillars, in Clarence Terrace. It alone, of these houses, is still there—but for how long? In 1964 it stands empty and derelict-looking. A bank has replaced Turner's house, a block of flats Miss Barrett's, an office Charles Dickens'.

In 1846 lawyers like Serjeant Talfourd, editors like Forster, were still apt to live a little further east, nearer the scene of their labours. Talfourd had a house in Russell Square, Forster lived in the handsome pilastered house in Lincoln's Inn Fields whose dark roomy staircases and antechambers Dickens described as Mr Tulkinghorn's in *Bleak House*. This, like Macready's house, still stands.

But the growth of London in the 1840's was westward. By 1846 Bayswater was wholly built up as far as Stanhope Gate, though there were still some open fields west of there and north of the Bayswater Road, then the Uxbridge Road. All this newly built area drained into the Serpentine, and such was the effect that people still could catch a lethal fever if they took an evening stroll by its waters. . . .

West of the new Bayswater terraces, Notting Hill was still fields, with just a fringe of houses along the north side of the Uxbridge Road and along Moscow Road. Then you came to leafy Campden Hill, and Holland House with its great green oblong of park, and so south to the village of Kensington, at whose western end Leigh Hunt lived in a pretty but sadly smelly house in Edwardes Square, while at its eastern end Thackeray had just moved into a bow-windowed little house in Young Street. South from there were fields and lanes and market gardens, and a few new streets and terraces in Brompton and the King's Private Road, until you reached the village of Chelsea, and the Carlyles' house in Great Cheyne Row, and Turner's secret and poorly-furnished hide-out in Cremorne Road. If you wanted to get from the Carlyles' to New Cross, where Browning lived, you would have to take a river boat from the Cadogan Steam Boat Pier a few yards east from the Carlyles' house along Cheyne Walk, or have a long ride or drive, due east, crossing the river at Vauxhall Bridge, through built-up Kennington and Walworth to where the fringes of the Rotherhithe and Deptford dockland faded out into open fields. Except for Mrs Jameson, far away to the westward in the distant village of Ealing, Browning lived the furthest from the centre of London of any of this group of friends and acquaintances. Only the rich banker Samuel Rogers and the well-to-do Member of Parliament Monckton Milnes had houses right in the centre, in St James's Place and Pall Mall, which in 1846 was still where the Establishment lived.

'HEAPS OF BRICKS AND STREAKS OF LIME'

North of Regent's Park the way to Golders Hill was almost all through open fields, with a few scattered farms and large houses, such as Belsize House in its great park. West across the fields ran the new Birmingham Railway from Euston. This was the area, beginning to be devastated by the railway and its accompanying streets and warehouses, that Dickens was just about to start describing so vividly in *Dombey and Son*, the first words of which were written at Lausanne six days after this hot Sunday morning. The tentacles of Camden Town were stretching out along the railway into the fields, which were rutted with cart-wheel tracks and defaced with heaps of bricks and streaks of lime. Cow-houses, and summer-houses, and the foundations of new little streets of dwellings for the railway workers, were all jumbled together on the edge of the open country.

ALETHEA HAYTER, *A Sultry Month*, 1965

THE COMING OF THE RAILWAY

There was no such place as Staggs's Gardens. It had vanished from the earth. Where the old rotten summer-houses once had stood, palaces now reared their heads, and granite columns of gigantic girth opened a vista to the railway world beyond. The miserable waste ground, where the refuse-matter had been heaped of yore, was swallowed up and gone; and in its frowsy stead were tiers of warehouses, crammed with rich goods and costly merchandise. The old by-streets now swarmed with passengers and vehicles of every kind: the new streets that had stopped disheartened in the mud and waggon-ruts, formed towns within themselves, originating wholesome comforts and conveniences belonging to themselves, and never tried nor thought of until they sprung into existence. Bridges that had led to nothing, led to villas, gardens, churches, healthy public walks. The carcasses of houses, and beginnings of new thoroughfares, had started off upon the line at steam's own speed, and shot away into the country in a monster train.

As to the neighbourhood which had hesitated to acknowledge the railroad in its straggling days, that had grown wise and penitent, as any Christian might in such a case, and now boasted of its powerful and prosperous relation. There were railway patterns in its drapers' shops, and railway journals in the windows of its newsmen. There were railway hotels, office-houses, lodging-houses, boarding-houses; railway plans, maps, views, wrappers, bottles, sandwich-boxes, and timetables; railway hackney-coach and cabstands; railway omnibuses, railway streets and buildings, railway hangers-on and parasites, and flatterers out of all calculation. There was even railway time observed in clocks, as if the sun itself had given in. Among the vanquished was the master chimney-sweeper, whilome incredulous at Staggs's Gardens, who now lived in a stuccoed house three stories high, and gave himself out, with golden flourishes upon a varnished board, as contractor for the cleansing of railway chimneys by machinery.

To and from the heart of this great change, all day and night, throbbing currents rushed and returned incessantly like its life's blood. Crowds of people and mountains of goods, departing and arriving scores upon scores of times in every four-and-twenty hours, produced a fermentation in the place that was always in action. The very houses seemed disposed to pack up and take trips. Wonderful Members of Parliament, who, little more than twenty years before, had made themselves merry with the wild railroad theories of engineers, and given them the liveliest rubs in cross-examination, went down into the north with their watches in their hands, and sent on messages before by the electric telegraph, to say that they were coming. Night and day the conquering engines rumbled at their distant work, or, advancing smoothly to their journey's end, and gliding like tame dragons into the allotted corners grooved out to the inch for their reception, stood bubbling and trembling there, making the walls quake, as if they were dilating with the secret knowledge of great powers yet unsuspected in them, and strong purposes not yet achieved.

But Staggs's Gardens had been cut up root and branch. Oh woe the day when 'not a rood of English ground'—laid out in Staggs's Gardens—is secure!

CHARLES DICKENS, *Dombey and Son*, 1848

CHARLOTTE BRONTË VISITS LONDON

The impression Miss Brontë made upon those with whom she first became acquainted during this visit to London, was of a person with clear judgment and fine sense; and though reserved, possessing unconsciously the power of drawing out others in conversation. She never expressed an opinion without assigning a reason for it; she never put a question without a definite purpose; and yet people felt at their ease in talking with her. All conversation with her was genuine and stimulating; and when she launched forth in praise or reprobation of books, or deeds, or works of art, her eloquence was indeed burning. She was thorough in all that she said or did; yet so open and fair in dealing with a subject, or contending with an opponent, that instead of rousing resentment, she merely convinced her hearers of her earnest zeal for the truth and right.

Not the least singular part of their proceedings was the place at which the sisters had chosen to stay.

Paternoster Row was for many years sacred to publishers. It is a narrow flagged street, lying under the shadow of St Paul's; at each end there are posts placed, so as to prevent the passage of carriages, and thus preserve a solemn silence for the deliberations of the 'Fathers of the Row.' The dull warehouses on each side are mostly occupied at present by wholesale stationers; if they be publishers' shops, they show no attractive front to the dark and narrow street. Half-way up, on the left-hand side, is the Chapter Coffee-house. I visited it last June. It was then unoccupied. It had the appearance of a dwelling-house, two hundred years old or so, such as one sometimes sees in ancient country towns; the ceilings of the small rooms were low, and had heavy beams running across them; the walls were wainscotted breast high; the staircase was shallow, broad, and dark, taking up much space in the centre of the house. This then was the Chapter Coffee-house, which, a century ago, was the resort of all the booksellers and publishers; and where the literary hacks, the critics, and even the wits, used to go in search of ideas or employment. This was the place about which Chatterton wrote, in those delusive letters he sent to his mother at Bristol, while he was starving in London. 'I am quite familiar at the Chapter Coffee-house, and know all the geniuses there.' Here he heard of chances of employment; here his letters were to be left.

Years later, it became the tavern frequented by university men and country clergymen, who were up in London for a few days, and, having no private friends or access into society, were glad to learn what was going on in the world of letters, from the conversation which they were sure to hear in the Coffee-room. In Mr Brontë's few and brief visits to town, during his residence at Cambridge, and the period of his curacy in Essex, he had stayed at this house; hither he had brought his daughters, when he was convoying them to Brussels; and here they came now, from very ignorance where else to go. It was a place solely frequented by men; I believe there was but one female servant in the house. Few people slept there; some of the stated meetings of the Trade were held in it, as they had been for more than a century; and, occasionally country booksellers, with now and then a clergyman, resorted to it; but it was a strange desolate place for the Miss Brontës to have gone to, from its purely business and masculine aspect. The old 'grey-haired elderly man,' who officiated as waiter, seems to have been touched from the very first with the quiet simplicity of the two ladies, and he tried to make them feel comfortable and at home in the long, low, dingy room up-stairs, where the meetings of the Trade were held. The high narrow windows looked into the gloomy Row; the sisters, clinging together on the most remote window-seat, (as Mr Smith tells me he found them, when he came, that Saturday evening, to take them to the Opera,) could see nothing of motion, or of change, in the grim, dark houses opposite, so near and close, although the whole breadth of the Row was between. The mighty roar of London was round them, like the sound of an unseen ocean, yet every footfall on the pavement below might be heard distinctly, in that unfrequented street. Such as it was, they preferred remaining at the Chapter Coffee-house, to accepting the invitation which Mr Smith and his mother urged upon them; and, in after years, Charlotte says:—

'Since those days, I have seen the West End, the parks, the fine squares; but I love the City far better. The City seems so much more in earnest; its business, its rush, its roar, are such serious things, sights, sounds. The City is getting its living—the West End but enjoying its pleasure. At the West End you may be amused; but in the City you are deeply excited.' (*Villette*, vol. i. p. 89.)

Their wish had been to hear Dr Croly on the Sunday morning, and Mr Williams escorted them to St Stephen's, Walbrook; but they were disappointed, as Dr Croly did not preach. Mr Williams also took them (as Miss Brontë has mentioned) to drink tea at his house. On the way thither, they had to pass through Kensington Gardens, and Miss Brontë was much 'struck with the beauty of the scene, the fresh verdure of the turf, and the soft rich masses of foliage.' From remarks on the different character of the landscape in the South to what it was in the North, she was led to speak of the softness and varied intonation of the voices of those with whom she conversed in London, which seem to have made a strong impression on both sisters. All this time those who came in contact with the 'Miss Browns' (another pseudonym, also beginning with B), seem only to have regarded them as shy and reserved little country-women, with not much to say. Mr Williams tells me that on the night when he accompanied the party to the Opera, as Charlotte ascended the flight of stairs leading from the grand entrance up to the lobby of the first tier of boxes, she was so much struck with the architectural effect of the splendid decorations of that vestibule and saloon, that involuntarily she slightly pressed his arm, and whispered, 'You know I am not accustomed to this sort of thing.' Indeed, it must have formed a vivid contrast to what they were doing and seeing an hour or two earlier the night before, when they were trudging along, with beating hearts and high-strung courage, on the road between Haworth and Keighley, hardly thinking of the thunderstorm that beat about their heads, for the thoughts which filled them of how they would go straight away to London, and prove that they were really two people, and not one imposter. It was no wonder that they returned to Haworth utterly fagged and worn out, after the fatigue and excitement of this visit.

ELIZABETH GASKELL, *The Life of Charlotte Brontë*, 1857

'MILK!'

During the summer months milk is sold in Smithfield, Billingsgate, and other markets, and on Sundays in Battersea-fields, Clapham-common, Camberwell-green, Hampstead-heath, and similar places. About twenty men are engaged in this sale. They usually wear a smock frock, and have the cans and yoke used by the regular milk-sellers; they are not itinerant. The skim milk—for they sell none else—is purchased at the dairies at 1½*d*. a quart, and even the skim milk is also further watered by the street-sellers. Their cry is 'Half-penny half-pint! Milk!' The tin measure however in which the milk-and-water is served is generally a 'slang', and contains but half of the quantity proclaimed. The purchasers are chiefly boys and children; rarely men, and never costermongers, I was told, 'for they reckon milk sickly'.

HENRY MAYHEW, *London Labour and the London Poor*, 1851–2

STARVELINGS AND URCHINS

It is notorious that the taste of the period included an extraordinary relish for literary scenes in which a good-looking, fatally ill child, often of humble status, is released from suffering by an edifying death. However, Little Nell, the Little Match Girl, and all the countless others were ideal creations: between the prosperous bourgeois and the actual wild, verminous starveling in the gutter there was a gulf that inhibited any immediate warmth and charity. If he was moved to action, the obvious course for a level-headed citizen was to send a guinea to the Mendicity Society. But nothing could be better calculated to touch a sluggish imagination and evoke a pre-conditioned response than a tranquil, wanly-pretty beggar child, wasted with misery yet as neat and almost as nicely dressed as one brought down to the drawing room from a respectable nursery.

This was known and traded on. Skilful manipulators of child beggars got them up with care in clean pinafores and collars and well-combed locks. Sometimes false ringlets were added, and where the child's face was not sufficiently spiritual-looking and suggestive of mortality, the eyes could be shadowed, or made to look hollower by a spotless bandage about the forehead. Several children might be stationed within a short walking distance of each other; they could then be conveniently intimidated into staying put and their takings could be regularly collected by a supervisor. It seems to have been quite a profitable style of begging even with very mediocre stands. Near Pentonville Hill, which was by no means an affluent place, four girls aged from five to twelve were reported to have kept an unmarried couple in idleness. (Two were claimed by the man as his own children, two by the woman.) Even in the savage mid-winter frost of 1853–4 when canals were ice-bound, these four little wretches were callously sent out and 'nearly frozen to death'—though one may question whether they were much better off when they were later shut up in the St Giles Union.

To profit from begging children, it was not necessary to breed them up from babyhood. Small boys and girls could be hired for a copper or two a day (though perhaps not very accomplished ones) and sometimes they changed hands permanently for a few shillings. No doubt it was partly by such trading that the master beggars who made a regular speciality of training and organising youngsters got hold of their human material. Their method of instruction remains obscure, but plainly some of them were exceedingly adept at teaching their pupils how best to exploit their childish pathos, for according to a contemporary report, children so schooled 'when turned out of hand by their tutors are generally the most successful impostors in the metropolis on account of their age'.

In 1853 the Mendicity Society's records showed that children accounted for eleven per cent of registered cases, many of them being the sole subsistence of people 'of the worst description'. This figure is almost certainly an underestimate. The Society was chiefly concerned with confirmed professional beggars in London (especially in the respectable districts where they were most obvious to the Society's subscribers) so its interest was in the children regularly trained and manipulated by professionals. But in fact parts of every large commercial town were alive with half-savage brats scratching a living by every means under the sun. To them cadging—like pilfering—was simply a matter of opportunity, and as natural as breathing. If they are included, child beggars probably outnumbered adults.

The police, hard put to it to keep juvenile thieving in bounds, were more or less defeated by the incessant street-arab mendicancy. Many urchins who lived by begging put up some sort of camouflage. Perhaps, like the tiny wretches who swarmed around King's Cross, they flourished a few damp lucifers under pretence of sale; or those who were a little older hung about by the gutter and rushed forward in squads offering to hold the horse's head whenever a carriage showed signs of stopping. The little make-believe roadsweeper who could 'only splash the mud from side to side with the stump of an old broom,' like the boy who turned cartwheels among the traffic or 'curled up his tiny body as closely as a woodlouse' and trundled himself along the pavement 'wabbling like an egg', was looked on by the public with a kind of favour: at least he was trying to earn a living rather than steal one. In the eyes of the law it might aggravate the offence to hawk without a licence or obstruct the highway; but a six foot officer cut a poor figure chivvying a half-starved urchin and hauling him off to the tune of the crowd's ironical congratulations. Moreover he was likely to get no thanks for producing his capture. Magistrates were simply at a loss how to deal with these children, and unless one of them had already been before them on a more serious charge they were apt to let him go with a futile warning. In general the only place they could rationally send them to was the workhouse, which was where children usually were consigned when their parents were imprisoned for setting them to beg or when there was no one who would take responsibility for them. But parish authorities were often almost as reluctant to take in children as the children were to be taken, and many city poorhouses would certainly have been flooded out if every loose beggar child had been admitted. All the same, terror of the workhouse must have kept many an exploited little beggar—like many a little pickpocket—loyal to his master.

KELLOW CHESNEY, *The Victorian Underworld*, 1970

NARRATIVE OF A LONDON SNEAK, OR COMMON THIEF

The following narrative was given us by a convicted thief, who has for years wandered over the streets of London as a ballad singer, and has resided in the low lodging-houses scattered over its lowest districts. He was a poor wretched creature, degraded in condition, of feeble intellect, and worthless character, we picked up in a low lodging house in Drury Lane. He was shabbily dressed in a pair of old corduroy trousers, old brown coat, black shabby vest, faded grey neckerchief, an old dark cap and peak, and unwashed shirt. For a few shillings he was very ready to tell us the sad story of his miserable life.

'I was born at Abingdon, near Oxford, where my father was a brick-layer, and kept the N———n public-house. He died when I was fourteen years of age; I was sent to school and was taught to read, but not to write. At this time I was a steady, well-conducted boy. At fourteen years of age I went to work with my uncle, a basket-maker and rag merchant in Abingdon, and lived with my mother. I wrought there for three years, making baskets and cutting willows for them. I left my uncle then, as he had not got any more work for me to do, and was living idle with my mother. At this time I went with a Cheap John to the fairs, and travelled with him the whole of that season. He was a Lancashire man, between fifty and sixty years of age, and had a woman who travelled the country with him, but I do not think they were married. He was a tall, dark-complexioned man, and was a "duffer," very unprincipled in his dealings. He sold cutlery, books, stationery, and hardware.

'When we were going from one fair to another, we would stop on the road and make a fire, and steal fowls and potatoes, or any green-stuff that was in season. We sometimes travelled along with gipsies, occasionally to the number of fifty or sixty in a gang. The gipsies are a curious sort of people, and would not let you connect with any of them unless they saw you were to remain among them.

'I assisted Cheap John in the markets when selling his goods, and handed them to the purchasers.

'The first thing I ever pilfered was a pair of boots and a handkerchief from a drunken man who lay asleep at a fair in Reading, in Berks. He was lying at the back of a booth and no one near him. This was about dusk in September. I pawned the boots at Windsor on the day of a fair for 3s., and sold the handkerchief for 1s.

'I was about seventeen years of age when I went with Cheap John, and remained with him about thirteen weeks, when I left, on account of a row I had with him. I liked this employment very well, got 2*s*. in the pound for my trouble, and sometimes had from £1 to 25*s*. a week. But the fairs were only occasional, and the money I earned was very precarious.

'I left Cheap John at Windsor, and came to Slough with a horse-dealer, where I left him. He gave me 2*s*. for assisting him. I then came up to London, where I have lived ever since in the lodging-houses in the different localities. I remember on coming to this great city I was much astonished at its wonders, and every street appeared to me like a fair. On coming to London I had no money, and had not any friend to assist me. I went to Kensington workhouse and got a night's lodging, and lived for about a fortnight at different workhouses in London. They used to give the lodgers a piece of bread at night, and another in the morning, and a night's lodging on straw and boards.

'I then went out singing ballads in the streets of London, and could get at an average from 2*s*. to 2*s*. 6*d*. a night, but when the evenings were wet, I could not get anything. In the winter I sang in the daytime, and in summer I went out in the evening. I have wandered in this way over many of the streets and thoroughfares of London. I sing in Marylebone, Somers Town, Camden Town, Paddington, Whitecross Street, City, Hammersmith, Commercial Road, and Whitechapel, and live at different lodgings, and make them my home as I move along. I sing different kinds of songs, sentimental and comic; my favourites are "Gentle Annie," "She's reckoned a good hand at it," "The Dandy Husband," "The Week's Matrimony," "The Old Woman's Sayings," and "John Bull and the Taxes." I often sing "The Dark-eyed Sailor," and "The Female Cabin Boy." For many years now I have lived by singing in the public street, sometimes by myself, at other times with a mate. I occasionally beg in Regent Street and Bond Street on the "fly," that is, follow people passing along, and sometimes in Oxford Street and Holborn. Sometimes I get a little job to do from people at various kinds of handiwork, such as turning the wheel to polish steel, and irons, etc., and do other kinds of job work. When hard up I pick pockets of handkerchiefs, by myself or with one or two mates. [In the course of our interview we saw he was very clumsy at picking pockets.] I sometimes go out with the dark-complexioned lad you saw down stairs, who is very clever at pocket picking, and has been often convicted before the criminal courts.

'I have spent many years living in the low lodging-houses of London. The worst I ever saw was in Keat Street, Whitechapel, about nine years ago, before they were reformed and changed. Numbers were then crowded into the different rooms, and the floors were littered with naked people of all ages, and of both sexes, men and women, and boys and girls sleeping alongside indiscriminately. It was very common to see young boys and girls sleeping together. The conversations that passed between them, and the scenes that were transacted, were enough to contaminate the morals of the young.

'In the morning they used to go to their different haunts over the city, some begging, and others thieving.

'On Sunday evenings the only books read were such as "Jack Sheppard," "Dick Turpin," and the "Newgate Calendar," they got out of the neighbouring libraries by depositing 1s. These were read with much interest; the lodgers would sooner have these than any other books. I never saw any of them go to church on Sundays. Sometimes one or two would go to the ragged-school, such as the one in Field Lane near Smithfield.

'It often happened a man left his wife, and she came to the lodging-house and got a livelihood by begging. Some days she would glean 2s. or 3s., and at other times would not get a half-penny.

'The thieves were seldom in the lodging-house, except to meals and at bedtime. They lived on better fare than the beggars. The pickpocket lives better than the sneaking thief, and the pickpocket is thought more of in the lodging-houses and prisons than the beggar.

'The lowest pickpockets often lived in these low lodging-houses, some of them young lads, and others middle-aged men. The young pickpockets, if clever, soon leave the lodging-houses and take a room in some locality, as at Somers Town, Marylebone, the Burgh, Whitechapel, or Westminster. The pickpockets in lodging-houses, for the most part, are stock-buzzers, i.e., stealers of handkerchiefs.

'I have often seen the boys picking each others' pockets for diversion in the lodging-house, many of them from ten to eleven years of age.

'There are a great number of sneaks in the lodging-houses. Two of them go out together to the streets, one of them keeps a look-out while the other steals some article, shoes, vest, or coat, etc., from the shop or stall. I sometimes go out with a mate and take a pair of boots at a shop-door and sell them to the pawnbroker, or to a labouring man passing in the street.

'Sometimes I have known the lodgers make up a packet of sawdust and put in a little piece of tobacco to cover an opening, leaving only the tobacco to be seen looking through, and sell it to persons passing by in the street as a packet of tobacco.

'When I am hard up I have gone out and stolen a loaf at a baker's shop, or chandler's shop, and taken it to my lodging. I have often stolen handkerchiefs, silk and cambric, from gentlemen's pockets.

'I once stole a silver snuff-box from a man's coat-pocket, and on one occasion took a pocket-book with a lot of papers and postage-stamps. I burnt the papers and sold the stamps for about 1s. 6d.

'I never had clothes respectable enough to try purses and watches, and did not have nerve for it. I have seen young thieves encouraged by people who kept the lodging-houses, such as at Keat Street, Whitechapel, and at the Mint. They would ask the boys if they had anything, and wish them to sell it to them, which was generally done at an under-price. In these lodging-houses some lived very well, and others were starving. Some had steaks and pickles, and plenty of drink, porter and ale, eggs and bacon, and cigars to smoke. Some of the poorest go out and get a pennyworth of bread, halfpennyworth of tea, halfpennyworth of butter, and halfpennyworth of sugar, and perhaps not have a halfpenny left to pay for their lodging at night. When they do get money they often go out and spend it in drink, and perhaps the next night are starving again.

'I have been tried for stealing a quart pot and a handkerchief, at Bagnigge Wells police station, and was taken to Vine Street police station for stealing 2s. 6d. from a drunken woman respectably dressed. I took it out of her hand, and was seen by a policeman, who ran after me and overtook me, but the woman refused to prosecute me, and I was discharged. I was also brought before Marylebone police-court for begging.

'In my present lodging I am pretty comfortable. We spend our evenings telling tales and conversing to each other on our wanderings, and playing at games, such as "hunt the slipper." I have often been in great want, and have been driven to steal to get a livelihood.'

HENRY MAYHEW, *London Labour and the London Poor*, 1851–2

The great revolutionary thinker Alexander Herzen arrived in London from France in 1851. 'He and his children wandered from home to home,' to quote Isaiah Berlin. Following the death of Tsar Nicholas I, Herzen's friend Nicholas Ogarëv was allowed to leave Russia, and joined the Herzen family in the English capital. They set up a printing press, and published the periodical Pole Star, *in Russian. Herzen began work on his autobiography at the same time.*

A RUSSIAN THINKER IN EXILE

London life was very favourable for such a break. There is no town in the world which is more adapted for training one away from people and training one into solitude than London. The manner of life, the distances, the climate, the very multitude of the population in which personality vanishes, all this together with the absence of Continental diversions conduces to the same effect. One who knows how to live alone has nothing to fear from the tedium of London. The life here, like the air here, is bad for the weak, for the frail, for one who seeks a prop outside himself, for one who seeks welcome, sympathy, attention; the moral lungs here must be as strong as the physical lungs, whose task it is to separate oxygen from the smoky fog. The masses are saved by battling for their daily bread, the commercial classes by their absorption in heaping up wealth, and all by the bustle of business; but nervous and romantic temperaments, fond of living among people, fond of intellectual sloth and of idly luxuriating in emotion, are bored to death here and fall into despair.

Wandering lonely about London, through its stony lanes and stifling passages, sometimes not seeing a step before me for the thick, opaline fog, and colliding with shadows running—I lived through a great deal.

In the evening, when my son had gone to bed, I usually went out for a walk; I scarcely ever went to see anyone; I read the newspapers and stared in taverns at the alien race, and lingered on the bridges across the Thames.

On one side the stalactites of the Houses of Parliament would loom through the darkness, ready to vanish again; on the other, the inverted bowl of St Paul's . . . and street-lamps . . . street-lamps . . . street-lamps without end in both directions. One city, full-fed, went to sleep: the other, hungry, was not yet awake—the streets were empty and nothing could be heard but the measured tread of the policeman with his lantern. I used to sit and look, and my soul would grow quieter and more peaceful. And so for all this I came to love this fearful ant-heap, where every night a hundred thousand men know not where they will lay their heads, and the police often find women and children dead of hunger beside hotels where one cannot dine for less than two pounds.

But this kind of transition, however quickly it approaches, is not achieved all at once, especially at forty. A long time passed while I was coming to terms with my new ideas. Though I had made up my mind to work, for a long time I did nothing, or did not do what I wanted to do.

The idea with which I had come to London, to seek the tribunal of my own people, was a sound and right one. I repeat this even now, with full, considered conviction. To whom, in fact, are we to appeal for judgment, for the re-establishment of the truth, for the unmasking of falsehood?

It is not for us to litigate in the court of our enemies, who judge by other principles, by laws which we do not recognise.

One can settle one's quarrels for oneself; no doubt one can. To take the law in one's own hands is to snatch back by force what has been taken by force, and so restore the balance; vengeance is just as sound and simple a human feeling as gratitude; but neither revenge nor taking the law into one's own hands explains anything. It may happen that a clear explanation is what matters most to a man. The re-establishment of the truth may be dearer to him than revenge. My own error lay not in the main proposition but in the underlying assumption; in order that there may be a tribunal of one's own people one must first of all have one's own people. Where were mine . . .?

I had had my own people once in Russia. But I was so completely cut off in a foreign land; I had at all costs to get into communication with my own people; I wanted to tell them of the weight that lay on my heart. Letters were not allowed in, but books would get through of themselves; writing letters was impossible: I would print; and little by little I set to work upon *My Past and Thoughts*, and upon setting up a Russian printing-press.

ALEXANDER HERZEN, *My Past and Thoughts*, 1885, trans. Constance Garnett, rev. edn., 1968

COSTERS' DONKEYS

The costermongers almost universally treat their donkeys with kindness. Many a costermonger will resent the ill-treatment of a donkey, as he would a personal indignity. These animals are often not only favourites, but pets, having their share of the costermonger's dinner when bread forms a portion of it, or pudding, or anything suited to the palate of the brute. Those well-used, manifest fondness for their masters, and are easily manageable; it is, however, difficult to get an ass, whose master goes regular rounds, away from its stable for any second labour during the day, unless it has fed and slept in the interval. The usual fare of a donkey is a peck of chaff, which costs 1*d*., a quart of oats and a quart of beans, each averaging 1½*d*., and sometimes a pennyworth of hay, being an expenditure of 4*d*. or 5*d*. a day; but some give double this quantity in a prosperous time. Only one meal a day is given. Many costermongers told me, that their donkeys lived well when they themselves lived well.

'It's all nonsense to call donkeys stupid,' said one costermonger to me; 'them's stupid that calls them so: they're sensible. Not long since I worked Guildford with my donkey-cart and a boy. Jack (the donkey) was slow and heavy in coming back, until we got in sight of the lights at Vauxhall-gate, and then he trotted on like one o'clock, he did indeed! just as if he smelt it was London besides seeing it, and knew he was at home. He had a famous appetite in the country, and the fresh grass did him good. I gave a country lad 2*d*. to mind him in a green lane there. I wanted my own boy to do so, but he said, 'I'll see you further first.' A London boy hates being by himself in a lone country part. He's afraid of being burked; he is indeed. One can't quarrel with a lad when he's away with one in the country; he's very useful. I feed my donkey well. I sometimes give him a carrot for a luxury, but carrots are dear now. He's fond of mashed potatoes, and has many a good mash when I can buy them at 4 lb a penny.'

HENRY MAYHEW, *London Labour and the London Poor*, 1851–2

MACREADY'S VIGOROUS LEAR

Anyone living in London and going to the theatre in the 1820's and 1830's was bound to feel a special revived impact from *King Lear*. All through the long years of George III's insanity it had been banned from the stage; plays about mad kings were too near the bone. When George III died in 1820 and it became possible to revive the play, Drury Lane and Covent Garden raced to put it on first. Covent Garden won, with a cast which had Junius Brutus Booth as Lear and the twenty-six-year-old

Macready as Edmund. This was still the Nahum Tate version of *King Lear* with Edgar marrying Cordelia at the end. Thirteen years later Macready was playing Lear himself, and he played it at intervals all through the 'thirties, restoring the proper text including the part of the Fool which was normally cut then. In February 1839 he played it at Covent Garden before Queen Victoria and, republican that he was, hurled Lear's prayer for the 'poor naked wretches', the 'houseless heads and unfed sides' straight at the Royal Box with meaning emphasis. The Hungry Forties were beginning, and Lear's voice seemed to echo through them. 'O Do-nothing Pomp; quit thy down-cushions; expose thyself to learn what wretches feel, and how to cure it' thundered Carlyle in *Past and Present*, scarcely remembering that he was quoting.

In this June 1846, Macready was acting Lear again at the Princess Theatre, but 'very languidly and not at all possessed with the character', he thought. His conception of Lear was a vigorous one; he thought Garrick, Kemble and Kean all concentrated on the feebleness instead of the vigour of old age when playing Lear. He himself saw Lear as a strong energetic old man, able to ride, hunt, rush about in a storm, kill the man who was hanging Cordelia; hearty and blithe in his good moments, vast in imagination and range of thought, huge in grief, no trembling tottering old dotard.

ALETHEA HAYTER, *A Sultry Month*, 1965

BLOOD-AND-THUNDER AT THE 'VIC'

There is a transpontine theatre, situated laterally towards the Waterloo Road, and having a northern front towards an anomalous thoroughfare that runs from Lambeth to Blackfriars, for which I have had, during a long period of years, a great esteem and affection. This is the Royal Victoria Theatre . . . Come with me, and sit on the coarse deal benches in the coarsely and tawdrily-decorated cheap theatre, and listen to the sorrily-dressed actors and actresses—periwigged-pated fellows and slatternly wenches, if you like—tearing their passion to tatters, mouthing and ranting, and splitting the ears of the groundlings. But in what description of pieces? In dramas, I declare and maintain, in which, for all the jargon, silliness, and buffoonery, the immutable principles of right and justice are asserted; in which virtue, in the end, is always triumphant, and vice is punished; in which cowardice and falsehood are hissed . . . in which, were we to sift away the bad grammar, and the extravagant action, we should find the dictates of the purest and highest morality. These poor people can't help misplacing their h's . . . They haven't been to the university of Cambridge; they can't compete for the middle-class examinations; they don't subscribe to the *Saturday Review*; they have never taken dancing lessons . . . they can't even afford to purchase a *Shilling Handbook of Etiquette*. Which is best? That they should gamble in low coffee-shops, break each other's heads with pewter pots in public-houses, fight and wrangle at street corners, or lie in wait in doorways and blind alleys to rob and murder, or that they should pay their threepence for admission to the gallery of the 'Vic.'?

GEORGE A. SALA, *Twice Round the Clock*, 1859

LONDON SONGBIRDS

The *Goldfinch* is also in demand by street customers, and is a favourite from its liveliness, beauty, and sometimes sagacity. It is, moreover, the longest lived of our caged small birds, and will frequently live to the age of fifteen or sixteen years. A goldfinch has been known to exist twenty-three years in a cage. Small birds, generally, rarely live more than nine years. This finch is also in demand because it most readily of any bird pairs with the canary, the produce being known as a 'mule', which, from its prettiness and powers of song, is often highly valued.

Goldfinches are sold in the streets at from 6*d.* to 1*s.* each, and when there is an extra catch, and they are nearly all caught about London, and the shops are fully stocked, at 3*d.* and 4*d.* each. The yearly catch is about the same as that of the linnet, or 70,000, the mortality being perhaps 30 per cent. If any one casts his eye over the stock of hopping, chirping little creatures in the window of a bird-shop, or in the close array of small cages hung outside, or at the stock of a street-seller, he will be struck by the preponderating number of goldfinches. No doubt the dealer, like any other shopkeeper, dresses his window to the best advantage, putting forward his smartest and prettiest birds. The demand for the goldfinch, especially among women, is steady and regular. The street-sale is a tenth of the whole.

The *Chaffinch* is in less request than either of its congeners, the bull-finch or the goldfinch, but the catch is about half that of the bullfinch, and with the same rate of mortality. The prices are also the same.

Greenfinches (called *green birds*, or sometimes *green linnets*, in the streets) are in still smaller request than are chaffinches, and that to about one-half. Even this smaller stock is little saleable, as the bird is regarded as 'only a middling singer'. They are sold in the open air, at 2*d.* and 3*d.* each, but a good 'green bird' is worth 2*s.* 6*d.*

Larks are of good sale and regular supply, being perhaps more readily caught than other birds, as in winter they congregate in large quantities. It may be thought, to witness the restless throwing up of the head of the caged sky-lark, as if he were longing for a soar in the air, that he was very impatient of restraint. This does not appear to be so much the fact, as the lark adapts himself to the poor confines of his prison—poor indeed for a bird who soars higher and longer than any of his class—more rapidly than other wild birds, like the linnet, &c. The mortality of larks, however, approaches one-third.

The yearly 'take' of larks is 60,000. This includes sky-larks, wood-larks, tit-larks, and mud-larks. The sky-lark is in far better demand than any of the others for his 'stoutness of song', but some prefer the tit-lark, from the very absence of such stoutness. 'Fresh-catched' larks are vended in the streets at 6*d.* and 8*d.*, but a seasoned bird is worth 2*s.* 6*d.* One-tenth is the street-sale.

The larks for the supply of fashionable tables are never provided by the London bird-catchers, who catch only 'singing larks', for the shop and street-traffic. The edible larks used to be highly esteemed in pies, but they are now generally roasted for consumption. They are principally the produce of Cambridgeshire, with some from Bedfordshire, and are sent direct (killed) to Leadenhall-market, where about 215,000 are sold yearly, being nearly two-thirds of the gross London consumption.

It is only within these twelve or fifteen years that the London dealers have cared to trade to any extent in *Nightingales*, but they are now a part of the stock of every bird-shop of the more flourishing class. Before that they were merely exceptional as cage-birds. As it is, the 'domestication', if the word be allowable with reference to the nightingale, is but partial. Like all migratory birds, when the season for migration approaches, the caged nightingale shows symptoms of great uneasiness, dashing himself against the wires of his cage or his aviary, and sometimes dying in a few days.

HENRY MAYHEW, *London Labour and the London Poor*, 1851–2

A HERON

Saturday, 19 March 1864
Walked to Edgware from Hampstead and home by Hendon, stopping at Kingsbury water a quarter of an hour or so. Saw what was probably a heron: it settled on a distant elm, was driven away by two rooks, settled on a still more distant, the same thing happened, the rooks pursuing it. It then flew across the water, circled about, and flew Hampsteadwards away.

                              The sparky air
             Leaps up before my vision,—thou art gone.

GERARD MANLEY HOPKINS, *The Journals and Papers of Gerard Manley Hopkins*, ed. Humphrey House, 1959

DOSTOEVSKY IN THE HAYMARKET

In London the masses can be seen on a scale and in conditions not to be seen anywhere else in the world.

I have been told, for example, that on Saturday nights half a million working men and women and their children spread like the ocean all over town, clustering particularly in certain districts, and celebrate their sabbath all night long until five o'clock in the morning, in other words guzzle and drink like beasts to make up for a whole week. They bring with them their weekly savings, all that was earned by hard work and with many a curse. Great jets of gas burn in meat and food shops, brightly lighting up the streets. It is as if a grand reception were being held for those white negroes. Crowds throng the open taverns and the streets. There they eat and drink. The beer houses are decorated like palaces. Everyone is drunk, but drunk joylessly, gloomily and heavily, and everyone is somehow strangely silent. Only curses and bloody brawls occasionally break that suspicious and oppressively sad silence. . . .

Everyone is in a hurry to drink himself into insensibility . . . wives in no way lag behind their husbands and all get drunk together, while children crawl and run about among them.

One such night—it was getting on for two o'clock in the morning—I lost my way and for a long time trudged the streets in the midst of a vast crowd of gloomy people, asking my way almost by gestures, because I do not know a word of English. I found my way, but the impression of what I had seen tormented me for three days afterwards. The populace is much the same anywhere, but there all was so vast, so vivid that you almost physically felt things which up till then you had only imagined. In London you no longer see the populace. Instead, you see a loss of sensibility, systematic, resigned and encouraged. And you feel, as you look at all those social pariahs, that it will be a long time before the prophecy is fulfilled for them, a long time before they are given palm branches and white robes, and that for a long time yet they will continue to appeal to the Throne of the Almighty, crying: 'How long, oh Lord?' And they know it themselves and in the meantime take their revenge on society by producing all kinds of underground mormons, shakers, tramps . . . We are surprised at the stupidity which leads people to become shakers and tramps, and fail to understand that what we have here is a repudiation of our social formula, an obstinate and unconscious repudiation; an instinctive repudiation at any cost, in order to achieve salvation, a horrified and disgusted repudiation of the rest of us. Those millions of people, abandoned and driven away from the feast of humanity, push and crush each other in the underground darkness into which they have been cast by their elder brethren, they grope around seeking a door at which to knock and look for an exit lest they be smothered to death in that dark cellar. This is the last desperate attempt to huddle together and form one's own heap, one's own mass and to repudiate everything, the very image of man if need be, only to be oneself, only not to be with us . . .

I saw in London another and similar 'mass', such as you would never see on a like scale anywhere else. An unusual spectacle it certainly was. Anyone who has ever visited London must have been at least once in the Haymarket at night. It is a district in certain streets of which prostitutes swarm by night in their thousands. Streets are lit by jets of gas—something completely unknown in our own country. At every step you come across magnificent public houses, all mirrors and gilt. They serve as meeting places as well as shelters. It is a terrifying experience to find oneself in that crowd. And, what an odd amalgam it is. You will find old women there and beautiful women at the sight of whom you stop in amazement. There are no women in the world as beautiful as the English.

The streets can hardly accommodate the dense, seething crowd. The mob has not enough room on the pavements and swamps the whole street. All this mass of humanity craves for booty and hurls itself at the first comer with shameless cynicism. Glistening, expensive clothes and semi-rags and sharp differences in age—they are all there. A drunken tramp shuffling along in this terrible crowd is jostled by the rich and titled. You hear curses, quarrels, solicitations and the quiet, whispered invitation of some still bashful beauty. And how beautiful they some-times are with their keepsake faces! I remember once I went into a 'casino'. The music was blaring, people were dancing, a huge crowd was milling round. The place was magnificently decorated. But gloom never forsakes the English even in the midst of gaiety; even when they dance they look serious, not to say sullen, making hardly any steps and then only as if in execution of some duty. Upstairs, in the gallery I saw a girl and stopped in amazement. She was sitting at a little table together with an apparently rich and respectable young man who, by all the signs, was an unaccustomed visitor to the casino. Perhaps he had been looking for her and they had at last found each other and arranged to meet there. He spoke to her little and only in short, jerky phrases as if he was not talking about what really interested him. Their conversation was punctuated by long and frequent silences. She, too, looked sad. Her face was delicate and fine, and there was something deep-hidden and sad, something thoughtful and melancholy in the proud expression of her eyes. I should say she had consumption. Mentally and morally she was, she could not fail to be, above the whole crowd of those wretched women; otherwise, what meaning would there be in a human face? All the same, however, she was then and there drinking gin, paid for by the young man. At last he got up, shook hands with her and went away. He left the casino, while she, her pale cheeks now flushed deep with drink, was soon lost in the crowd of women trading in their bodies.

In the Haymarket I noticed mothers who brought their little daugh-ters to make them ply that same trade. Little girls, aged about twelve, seize you by the arm and beg you to come with them. I remember once amidst the crowd of people in the street I saw a little girl, not older than six, all in rags, dirty, bare-foot and hollow-cheeked; she had been severely beaten, and her body, which showed through the rags, was covered with bruises. She was walking along, as if oblivious of everybody and everything, in no hurry to get anywhere, and Heaven knows why loafing about in that crowd; perhaps she was hungry. Nobody was paying any attention to her. But what struck me most was the look of such distress, such hopeless despair on her face that to see that tiny bit of humanity already bearing the imprint of all that evil and despair was somehow unnatural and terribly painful. She kept on shaking her tousled head as if arguing about something, gesticulated and spread her little hands and then suddenly clasped them together and pressed them to her little bare breast. I went back and gave her sixpence. She took the small silver coin, gave me a wild look full of frightened surprise, and suddenly ran off as fast as her legs could carry her, as if afraid that I should take the money away from her. Jolly scenes, altogether. . . .

And then one night in the midst of a crowd of loose women and debauchees I was stopped by a woman making her way hurriedly through it. She was dressed all in black and her hat almost concealed her face; in fact I had hardly time to make it out, I only remember the steady gaze of her eyes. She said something in broken French which I failed to understand, thrust a piece of paper into my hand and hurried on. I examined the paper at the light of a café window: it was a small square slip. One side bore the words 'Crois-tu cela?' printed on it. The other, also in French: 'I am the Resurrection and the Life' . . . , etc.—the well-known text. This too, you must admit, is rather bizarre. It was explained to me afterwards that that was Catholic propaganda ferreting round everywhere, persistent and tireless. Sometimes they distribute these bits of paper in the streets, sometimes booklets containing extracts from the New Testament and the Bible. They distribute them free, thrust them into people's hands, press them on people. It is ingenious and cunning propaganda. A Catholic priest would search out and insinuate himself into a poor workman's family. He would find, for example, a sick man lying in his rags on a damp floor, surrounded by children crazy from cold and hunger, with a wife famished and often drunk. He would feed them all, provide clothes and warmth for them, give treatment to the sick man, buy medicine for him, become the friend of the family and finally convert them all to the Catholic faith. Sometimes, however, after the sick man has been restored to health, the priest is driven out with curses and kicks.

He does not despair and goes off to someone else. He is chucked out again, but puts up with everything and catches someone in the end.

But an Anglican minister would never visit a poor man. The poor are not even allowed inside a church because they have not the money to pay for a seat.

FYODOR DOSTOEVSKY, *Winter Notes on Summer Impressions*, 1863, trans. Kyril Fitzlyon, 1986

ELMS, AND A PAIR OF ASHES

22 August 1867

Bright.—Walked to Finchley and turned down a lane to a field where I sketched an appletree. Their sprays against the sky are gracefully curved and the leaves looping over edge them, as it looks, with rows of scales. In something the same way I saw some tall young slender wych-elms of thin growth the leaves of which enclosed the light in successive eyebrows. From the spot where I sketched—under an oak, beyond a brook, and reached by the above green lane between a park-ground and a pretty field—there was a charming view, the field, lying then on the right of the lane, being a close-shaven smoothly-rounded shield of bright green ended near the high road by a row of viol-headed or flask-shaped elms— not rounded merely but squared—of much beauty—dense leafing, rich dark colour, ribs and spandrils of timber garlanded with leaf between tree and tree. But what most struck me was a pair of ashes in going up the lane again. The further one was the finer—a globeish just-sided head with one launching-out member on the right; the nearer one was more naked and horny. By taking a few steps one could pass the further behind the nearer or make the stems close, either coincidingly, so far as disagreeing outlines will coincide, or allowing a slit on either side, or again on either side making a broader stem than either would make alone. It was this which was so beautiful—making a noble shaft and base to the double tree, which was crested by the horns of the nearer ash and shaped on the right by the bosom of the hinder one with its springing bough. The outline of the double stem was beautiful to whichever of the two sides you slid the hinder tree—in one (not, I think, in both) shaft-like and narrowing at the ground. Besides I saw how great the richness and subtlety is of the curves in the clusters, both in the forward bow mentioned before and in some most graceful hangers on the other side: it combines somewhat-slanted outward strokes with rounding, but I cannot very well characterise it now.—Elm-leaves:—they shine much in the sun—bright green when near from underneath but higher up they look olive: their shapelessness in the flat is from their being made, διά τὸ πεφυκέυα ['flashes of forked lightning'; Aeschylus, *Prometheus*], to be dimpled and dog's-eared: their leaf-growth is in this point more rudimentary than that of oak, ash, beech, etc that the leaves lie in long rows and do not subdivide or have central knots but tooth or cog their woody twigs.

> GERARD MANLEY HOPKINS, *The Journals and Papers of Gerard Manley Hopkins*, ed. Humphrey House, 1959

IN THE BRITISH MUSEUM

'What do you see in that time-touched stone,
    When nothing is there
But ashen blankness, although you give it
    A rigid stare?

'You look not quite as if you saw,
    But as if you heard,
Parting your lips, and treading softly
    As mouse or bird.

'It is only the base of a pillar, they'll tell you,
    That came to us
From a far old hill men used to name
    Areopagus.'

—'I know no art, and I only view
    A stone from a wall,
But I am thinking that stone has echoed
    The voice of Paul;

'Paul as he stood and preached beside it
    Facing the crowd,
A small gaunt figure with wasted features,
    Calling out loud

'Words that in all their intimate accents
  Pattered upon
That marble front, and were wide reflected,
  And then were gone.

'I'm a labouring man, and know but little,
  Or nothing at all;
But I can't help thinking that stone once echoed
  The voice of Paul.'

THOMAS HARDY, *Satires of Circumstance*, 1914

IMPRESSIONISTS IN LONDON

In 1870 I found myself in London with Monet, and we met Daubigny and Bonvin. Monet and I were very enthusiastic over the London landscapes. Monet worked in the parks, whilst I, living at Lower Norwood, at that time a charming suburb, studied the effects of fog, snow, and springtime: We worked from Nature, and later on Monet painted in London some superb studies of mist. We also visited the museums. The water-colours and paintings of Turner and of Constable, the canvases of Old Crome, have certainly had influence upon us. We admired Gainsborough, Lawrence, Reynolds, etc., but we were struck chiefly by the landscape painters, who shared more in our aim with regard to *plein air*, light, and fugitive effects. Watts, Rossetti, strongly interested us amongst the modern men. About this time we had the idea of sending our studies to the exhibitions of the Royal Academy. Naturally we were rejected.

CAMILLE PISSARRO, letter to Wynford Dewhurst, from *Impressionist Painting*, 1904

'NO ONE EVER TALKS'

Verlaine and Rimbaud remained two months in Brussels, wandering about the country from there, but finally, in September, they crossed over from Ostend to Dover.

On their arrival in London they first went to their fellow countryman, the artist Régamey, who has given us a picture of the dishevelled appearance of the two poets which did not, as it happened, strike a discordant note in the bohemian atmosphere of Continental Soho. With the exiles from the Commune—politicians, journalists, writers and agitators—there was more true bohemianism in Soho than there was, at that time, in the literary world in Paris. Régamey helped the two Frenchmen to find lodgings and they first rented the room which had once been occupied by Vermersch at 35 Howland Street, an eighteenth-century house in the style of Adam—off the Tottenham Court Road.

At first the two friends felt lonely and home-sick. 'A flat black bug, that is London,' wrote Verlaine to Lepelletier. They missed the light stimulating air of Paris, the welcoming cafés on the boulevards with their tables set out on the pavement; they missed above all the friendly waiters, with their cheeky humour and their skill at pouring the icy water on the green absinthe, drop by drop, to turn it into a snowy liqueur. Verlaine described with disgust the small and narrow English public-houses, where standing at the counter, you hastily swallow drink after drink. You enter by a heavy door that is held ajar by a thick leather strap, and the door treats you in a most unfriendly and unwelcoming manner, striking you in the back as you go in and often knocking off your hat. The interior is dingy and mean, there are no tables to be seen, only a zinc-topped counter in front of which men stand, silently and solemnly drinking. In these bars, says Verlaine, 'Oh! lamentable infériorité des Anglo-Saxons,' no one ever talks. There is none of the bright, intelligent and literary conversation which makes an hour in a French café an education as well as a pleasure. Behind the counter stand the bar-tenders, in their shirt sleeves, and sometimes blowsy barmaids, richly dressed in the worst of style.

Like all Continental visitors to London, Verlaine and Rimbaud were deeply impressed and depressed by the dreariness of the Anglo-Saxon Sunday, which in these far-off Victorian days must have been even more dreary than now. It was Sunday morning when they had arrived and they had found it almost impossible to discover a place open that would give them some sort of a meal. Until one o'clock everywhere was closed; from one o'clock until three a few public-houses and restaurants opened their doors, under the vigilant eye of a policeman, who stood, watch in hand, to see that the time limit was not exceeded; the same comedy was enacted again from six until ten. Even the shoeblacks did not work on Sundays; one of these had dared ply his trade on the day of the Lord and he had been severely reprimanded by a passing 'copper.' There were no theatres or places of amusement open and the sole recreation available to the citizens of the biggest city in the world was the open-air preachers in Hyde Park and the dismal music of the Salvation Army Band.

By degrees Verlaine and Rimbaud sank into the French atmosphere of the Soho quarter. There were there, at that time, many Parisian refugees who, after the Commune, had fled from France under penalty of death, or fearing reprisals, from the new and reactionary government; men like Andrieu and Vermersch, the latter of whom had been condemned, in absence, to death for the part he had played in the publication of that revolutionary paper *Père Duchesne*. These refugees lived in dingy lodgings round Leicester and Soho Squares, or in sordid rooms in the streets off the Tottenham Court Road. They used all to forgather at the *Cercles d'Études Sociales* in Francis Street and in a few public-houses in which they managed to create a certain Continental atmosphere. There was the Duke of York, near Gray's Inn Road, the *Café de la Sablonnière et de Provence* off Leicester Square and particularly the bar at 5 Old Compton Street. It was there that Vermersch delivered a lecture on Blanqui and read the poem written by Verlaine in honour of the revolt: O *Cloître de Saint-Merry*.

The lot of these refugees was wretched in the extreme for they found it almost impossible to obtain work. There was, at that time, a very close co-operation between the London and the Paris police, the former keeping the latter well informed of all the activities of French nationals and, on the request of Paris, putting all obstacles in the way of their earning a livelihood. England, then as now, had a horror of violence and revolt and these unfortunate men were considered dangerous anarchists and revolutionary agents, and not upholders and martyrs of liberty; they were consequently submitted constantly to the most irritating and humiliating surveillance. Amongst these poor wretches Verlaine and Rimbaud with their dishevelled and disreputable appearance seemed in their element. After they had settled down to a more or less regular life Verlaine was completely happy in London and wished that this existence could continue for ever; he was able then to finish his lovely collection of poems, *Romances sans Paroles*. 'Here I devote myself entirely to poetry,' he wrote to Lepelletier, 'to intellectual considerations, to purely artistic and serious conversations amongst a small circle of artists and literary men.'

It is said that in London Verlaine and Rimbaud met members of the English literary movement—writers such as Rossetti and Swinburne.

But the acquaintanceship, if indeed acquaintanceship there was, cannot have been very deep, for on neither side—English or French—have we any mention of it. In a letter to Émile Blémont Verlaine says that he is soon to make the acquaintance of Swinburne, but we hear no more about it, and we can only surmise that they must have met, for later, from prison in Belgium, he requested Lepelletier to send a copy of his recently published work, *Romances sans Paroles*, to Swinburne.

ENID STARKIE, Arthur Rimbaud, 2nd edn., 1947

A GERMAIN NOUVEAU

Ce fut à Londres, ville où l'Anglaise domine,
Que nous nous sommes vus pour la première fois,
Et, dans King's Cross mêlant ferrailles, pas et voix,
Reconnus dès l'abord sur notre bonne mine.

Puis, la soif nous creusant à fond comme une mine,
De nous précipiter, dès libres des convois,
Vers des bars attractifs comme les vieilles fois,
Où de longues misses plus blanches que l'hermine

Font couler l'ale et le bitter dans l'étain clair
Et le cristal chanteur et léger comme l'air,
—Et de boire sans soif à l'amitié future!

Notre toast a tenu sa promesse. Voici
Que vieillis quelque peu depuis cette aventure,
Nous n'avons ni le cœur ni le coude transi.

PAUL VERLAINE (1844–96)

'TYRE AND CARTHAGE ALL ROLLED INTO ONE'

As soon as Verlaine's health was restored the two friends took up once more their life of pub-crawling and debauch which Verlaine was later to call 'our shameful life in London in 1873.' In between times they used to wander on foot through the town in order to get to know it thoroughly. 'Every day we take enormous walks in the suburbs and in the country round London,' wrote Verlaine to Blémont. 'We've seen Kew, Woolwich and many other places, for London is by now well known to us. Drury Lane, Whitechapel, Pimlico, the City, Hyde Park, all these have no longer any mystery for us.' Rimbaud used to drag Verlaine away to visit the Docks. 'The docks are impossible to describe,' wrote Verlaine, the city dweller who had rarely left Paris. 'They are unbelievable! Tyre and Carthage all rolled into one!' In the docks they saw all types of humanity swarming from all the four quarters of the world, black, brown and yellow faces; coarse, bestial and beautiful faces, beneath their multi-coloured and variously shaped headgear. They saw, piled up in rich profusion, crates, boxes and baskets of goods from the furthest ends of the earth; they heard strange languages spoken, and saw printed on the bales of goods mysterious signs they could not read. Rimbaud spent in the docks more and more time, examining the various types of goods and talking, when he could make himself understood, to the sailors whom he met, making them describe what they had seen in their far-flung wandering, trying to understand and penetrate the mystery of their restless and nomadic life.

This was his first experience of big ships and they brought back to him, with a new poignancy, the dreams of his childhood—before he had embarked on his spiritual mission—when, in his imagination, he had travelled to the ends of the earth, and had only needed his mother's rolls of linen cloth to feel that he was on his *bateau ivre*. Now the same dreams began to crowd into his mind once more, the same longings. Perhaps it was then that he began to wonder whether a life of action might not be, after all, preferable and more worth living than a life of contemplation and mystical experience. He had begun by being an adventurer of the worldly regions before he became an adventurer of the beyond and he was to return finally to his first manner. Jean Aubry says that it was in London that Rimbaud formed a connection amongst sailors who came from all quarters of the globe, that he discovered from them what were the commercial possibilities in those distant lands, and what lay before those who ventured there.

Verlaine and Rimbaud used to wander as well through the poorer districts, through Whitechapel and Poplar, and Verlaine in his correspondence describes the picturesque, leprous little hovels on which hung signs written in Hebrew, and the Jews, whom he saw wandering amongst the dark lanes and who seemed to him figures from a picture by

Rembrandt, with their livid yellow skin, their drawn and haggard features, their straggling beards and their skeleton-like claws.

ENID STARKIE, *Arthur Rimbaud*, 2nd edn., 1947

Vincent van Gogh was employed as a master in a small school for boys—Holme Court in Isleworth—run by the Revd Mr Jones, when he wrote this letter to his brother Theo. He had previously worked in another school, run by a Mr Stokes.

SCENTED VIOLETS

Dear Theo,

It is Saturday again and I am writing once more. How I long to see you again. Oh! my longing is sometimes so strong. Drop me a line soon, telling how you are.

Last Wednesday we took a long walk to a village an hour from here. The road led through meadows and fields, along hedges of hawthorn, full of blackberries and traveler's joy, and an occasional large elm tree. It was so beautiful when the sun set behind the gray clouds and the shadows were long. By chance we came upon Mr Stokes's school; several of the boys I knew are still there. The clouds stayed red long after the sun had set and the dusk had settled over the fields; and in the distance we saw the lamps lit in the village.

While I was writing to you, I was called to Mr Jones, who asked if I would walk to London to collect some money for him. And when I came home in the evening, hurrah! there was a letter from Father with news of you. How I should like to be with you both, my boy. And thank God there is some improvement, though you are still weak. And you will be longing to see Mother, and now that I hear that you are going home with her, I think of Conscience's words . . .

Now I am going to tell you about my walk to London. I left here at twelve o'clock in the morning and reached my destination between five and six. When I came into the part of town where most of the picture galleries are, around the Strand, I met many acquaintances: it was dinnertime, so many were in the street, leaving the office or going back there. First I met a young clergyman with whom I became acquainted when he preached here once. After that, Mr Wallis's employee and then one of the Messrs Wallis, whose house I visited occasionally; now he has two children. Then I met Mr Reid and Mr Richardson, who are already old friends. Last year about this time Mr Richardson was in Paris and we walked together to Père Lachaise.

After that I went to Van Wisselingh, where I saw sketches for two church windows. In the middle of one window was a portrait of a middle-aged lady—oh, such a noble face—with the words 'Thy will be done' over it; and in the other window, a portrait of her daughter with the words, 'Faith is the substance of things hoped for, the evidence of things not seen.' There, and in Messrs Goupil & Co.'s gallery, I saw beautiful pictures and drawings. It is such an intense delight to be so often reminded of Holland by art.

In the City I went to see Mr Gladwell and to St Paul's Church, and then from the City to the other end of London, where I visited a boy who had left Mr Stokes's school because of illness; I found him quite well, playing in the street. Then to the place where I had to collect the money for Mr Jones. The suburbs of London have a peculiar charm; between the little houses and gardens there are open spots covered with grass and generally with a church or school or workhouse in the middle among the trees and shrubs. It can be so beautiful there when the sun is setting red in the thin evening mist.

Yesterday evening it was like that, and afterward I wished you could have seen those London streets when the twilight began to fall and the lamps were lit and everybody went home. Everything showed that it was Saturday night, and in all that bustle there was peace, one felt the need of and the excitement at the approaching Sunday. Oh, those Sundays and all that is done and accomplished on those Sundays, it is such a comfort for those poor districts and crowded streets.

In the City it was dark, but it was a beautiful walk along the row of churches one has to pass. Near the Strand I caught a bus which took me quite a long way; it was already pretty late. I passed Mr Jones's little church and saw another one in the distance, with a light still burning at that hour; I entered and found it to be a very beautiful little Catholic church where a few women were praying. Then I came to that dark park which I have already written you about; from it I saw far away the lights of Isleworth and the church with the ivy, and the churchyard with the weeping willows on the banks of the Thames.

Tomorrow for the second time I shall get some small salary for my new work, and with it buy a pair of new boots and a new hat. And then, God willing, I shall gird myself up again.

Everywhere in the London streets they sell scented violets, which bloom here twice a year. I bought some for Mrs Jones to make her forget the pipe I smoke now and then, especially late in the evening in the playground, but the tobacco here is rather a gloomy weed.

Well, Theo, try to get well soon and read this letter when Mother is sitting with you, because I should like to be with you both in thought. I cannot tell you how glad I am that Mr Jones has promised to give me work in his parish, so that I shall find by and by what I want. I am longing so much for you. A handshake for yourself and one for Mother when she is sitting beside you. Many regards to the Roos family and to everyone I know, especially to Mr Tersteeg. Tell Mother it was delightful to put on a pair of socks knitted by her after that long walk to London.

This morning the sun rose so beautifully again; I see it every morning when I wake the boys. à Dieu.

Your loving brother,
Vincent

VINCENT VAN GOGH, letter to his brother Theo, 7 October 1876, from *The Complete Letters of Vincent van Gogh*, 1958

'IT IS ONLY MAGNIFICENT'

The history of the five years I have spent in London—a pledge, I suppose, of many future years—is too long, and too full to write. I can only glance at it here. I took a lodging at 3 Bolton St., Piccadilly; and there I have remained till today—there I have left my few earthly possessions, to await my return. I have *lived* much there, felt much, thought much, learned much, produced much; the little shabby furnished apartment ought to be sacred to me. I came to London as a complete stranger, and today I know much too many people. *J'y suis absolument comme chez moi.* Such an experience is an education—it fortifies the character and embellishes the mind. It is difficult to speak adequately or justly of London. It is not a pleasant place; it is not agreeable, or cheerful, or easy, or exempt from reproach. It is only magnificent. You can draw up a tremendous list of reasons why it should be insupportable. The fogs, the smoke, the dirt, the darkness, the wet, the distances, the ugliness, the brutal size of the place, the horrible numerosity of society, the manner in which this senseless bigness is fatal to amenity, to convenience, to conversation, to good manners—all this and much more you may expatiate upon. You may call it dreary, heavy, stupid, dull, inhuman, vulgar at heart and tiresome in form. I have felt these things at times so strongly that I have said—'Ah London, you too then are impossible?' But these are occasional moods; and for one who takes it as I take it, London is on the whole the most possible form of life. I take it as an artist and as a bachelor; as one who has the passion of observation and whose business is the study of human life. It is the biggest aggregation of human life—the most complete compendium of the world. The human race is better represented there than anywhere else, and if you learn to know your London you learn a great many things. I felt all this in that autumn of 1876, when I first took up my abode in Bolton St. I had very few friends, the season was of the darkest and wettest; but I was in a state of deep delight. I had complete liberty, and the prospect of profitable work; I used to take long walks in the rain. I took possession of London; I felt it to be the right place. I could get English books: I used to read in the evenings, before an English fire. I can hardly say how it was, but little by little I came to know people, to dine out, etc. I did, I was able to do, nothing at all to bring this state of things about; it came rather of itself. I had very few letters—I was afraid of letters. Three or four from Henry Adams, three or four from Mrs Wister, of which I only, as I think, presented one (to George Howard). Poor Motley, who died a few months later, and on whom I had no claim of *any* kind, sent me an invitation to the Athenaeum, which was renewed for several months, and which proved an unspeakable blessing. When once one starts in the London world (and one cares enough about it, as I did, to make one's self agreeable, as I did) *cela va de soi*; it goes with constantly increasing velocity. I remained in London all the following summer—till Sept. 1st—and then went abroad and spent some six weeks in Paris, which was rather empty and very lovely, and went a good deal to the theatre. Then I went to Italy, spending almost all my time in Rome (I had a little apartment flooded with sun, in the Capo le Case). I came back to England before Xmas and spent the following nine months or so in Bolton St. The club question had become serious and difficult; a club was indispensable, but I had of course none of my own. I went through Gaskell's (and I think Locker's) kindness for some time to the Travellers'; then after that for a good while to the St James's, where I could pay a monthly fee. At last, I forget exactly when, I was elected to the Reform; I think it was about April, 1878. (F. H. Hill had proposed, and C. H. Roberts had seconded, me:

or vice versa.) This was an excellent piece of good fortune, and the Club has ever since been, to me, a convenience of the first order. I could not have remained in London without it, and I have become extremely fond of it; a deep local attachment. I can now only briefly enumerate the landmarks of the rest of my residence in London. In the autumn of 1878 I went to Scotland, chiefly to stay at Tillypronie.

> Henry James, *Notebooks*, ed. F. O. Matthiessen and Kenneth B. Murdoch, 1947

In 1878 the American painter James Abbott McNeill Whistler brought a libel action against the critic John Ruskin over Ruskin's doubting that a Nocturne by Whistler was a correct representation of Battersea Bridge.

WHISTLER, THE JUDGE, AND BATTERSEA BRIDGE

The picture called the nocturne in blue and silver was now produced in Court.

'That is Mr Grahame's picture. It represents Battersea Bridge by moonlight.'

Baron Huddleston: Which part of the picture is the bridge? (*Laughter.*)

His Lordship earnestly rebuked those who laughed.

And witness [i.e. Whistler] explained to his Lordship the composition of the picture.

'Do you say that this is a correct representation of Battersea Bridge?'

'I did not intend it to be a "correct" portrait of the bridge. It is only a moonlight scene, and the pier in the centre of the picture may not be like the piers of Battersea Bridge as you know them in broad daylight. As to what the picture represents, that depends upon who looks at it. To some persons it may represent all that is intended; to others it may represent nothing.'

'The prevailing colour is blue?'

'Perhaps.'

'Are those figures on the top of the bridge intended for people?'

'They are just what you like.'

'Is that a barge beneath?'

'Yes. I am very much encouraged at your perceiving that. My whole scheme was only to bring about a certain harmony of colour.'

'What is that gold-coloured mark on the right of the picture like a cascade?'

'The "cascade of gold" is a firework.'

A second nocturne in blue and silver was then produced.

WITNESS: That represents another moonlight scene on the Thames looking up Battersea Reach.

POETRY OF THE THAMES

Nature contains the elements, in colour and form, of all pictures, as the keyboard contains the notes of all music.

But the artist is born to pick, and choose, and group with science, these elements, that the result may be beautiful—as the musician gathers his notes, and forms his chords, until he bring forth from chaos glorious harmony.

To say to the painter, that Nature is to be taken as she is, is to say to the player, that he may sit on the piano.

That Nature is always right, is an assertion, artistically, as untrue, as it is one whose truth is universally taken for granted. Nature is very rarely right, to such an extent even, that it might almost be said that Nature is usually wrong: that is to say, the condition of things that shall bring about the perfection of harmony worthy a picture is rare, and not common at all.

This would seem, to even the most intelligent, a doctrine almost blasphemous. So incorporated with our education has the supposed aphorism become, that its belief is held to be part of our moral being, and the words themselves have, in our ear, the ring of religion. Still, seldom does Nature succeed in producing a picture.

The sun blares, the wind blows from the east, the sky is bereft of cloud, and without, all is of iron. The windows of the Crystal Palace are seen from all points of London. The holiday-maker rejoices in the glorious day, and the painter turns aside to shut his eyes.

How little this is understood, and how dutifully the casual in Nature is accepted as sublime, may be gathered from the unlimited admiration daily produced by a very foolish sunset.

The dignity of the snow-capped mountain is lost in distinctness, but the joy of the tourist is to recognise the traveller on the top. The desire to see, for the sake of seeing it, is, with the mass, alone the one to be gratified, hence the delight in detail.

And when the evening mist clothes the riverside with poetry, as with a veil, and the poor buildings lose themselves in the dim sky, and the tall chimneys become campanili, and the warehouses are palaces in the night, and the whole city hangs in the heavens, and fairy-land is before us—then the wayfarer hastens home; the working man and the cultured one, the wise man and the one of pleasure, cease to understand, as they have ceased to see, and Nature, who, for once, has sung in tune, sings her exquisite song to the artist alone, her son and her master—her son in that he loves her, her master in that he knows her.

To him her secrets are unfolded, to him her lessons have become gradually clear. He looks at her flower, not with the enlarging lens, that he may gather facts for the botanist, but with the light of the one who sees in her choice selection of brilliant tones and delicate tints, suggestions of future harmonies.

> JAMES MCNEILL WHISTLER, 'The Ten O'Clock Lecture', in *The Gentle Art of Making Enemies*, 1890

The young Walter Greaves was a disciple of Whistler, who encouraged him to paint views of Chelsea and Battersea. In his old age, he talked to the critic and curator John Rothenstein about his time by the Thames.

WATCHING THE RED-SAILED BARGES

I still draw. In fact, I couldn't pass the time without it. I think I could draw all old Chelsea by heart. I don't suppose I'd get it extraordinarily exact, but I can *see* the place all right as I do it.

I never seemed to have any ideas about painting—the river just *made* me do it. You see, you have to have them if you paint in a studio; but if you are outside all day, as I was, by the river, all you've got to do is to watch the red-sailed barges passing. And then there was the bridge—I suppose Battersea Bridge got a bit on the brain of all of us.

> WALTER GREAVES, in G. Grigson, *Britain Observed*, 1975

THE YOUNG KIPLING IN KENSINGTON

Then we went to London and stayed for some weeks in a tiny lodging-house in the semi-rural Brompton Road, kept by an ivory-faced, lordly-whiskered ex-butler and his patient wife. Here, for the first time, it happened that the night got into my head. I rose up and wandered about that still house till daybreak, when I slipped out into the little brick-walled garden and saw the dawn break. All would have been well but for Pluto, a pet toad brought back from Epping Forest, who lived mostly in one of my pockets. It struck me that he might be thirsty, and I stole into my Mother's room and would have given him drink from a water-jug. But it slipped and broke and very much was said. The ex-butler could not understand why I had stayed awake all night. I did not know then that such night-wakings would be laid upon me through my life; or that my fortunate hour would be on the turn of sunrise, with a sou'-west breeze afoot.

The sorely tried Mother got my sister and me season-tickets for the old South Kensington Museum which was only across the road. (No need in those days to caution us against the traffic.) Very shortly we two, on account of our regular attendance (for the weather had turned wet), owned that place and one policeman in special. When we came with any grown-ups he saluted us magnificently. From the big Buddha with the little door in his back, to the towering dull-gilt ancient coaches and carven chariots in long dark corridors—even the places marked 'private' where fresh treasures were always being unpacked—we roved at will, and divided the treasures child-fashion. There were instruments of music inlaid with lapis, beryl and ivories; glorious gold-fretted spinets and clavi-chords; the bowels of the great Glastonbury clock; mechanical models; steel- and silver-butted pistols, daggers and arquebusses—the labels alone were an education; a collection of precious stones and rings—we quarrelled over those—and a big bluish book which was the manuscript of one of Dickens' novels. That man seemed to me to have written very carelessly; leaving out lots which he had to squeeze in between the lines afterwards.

These experiences were a soaking in colour and design with, above all, the proper Museum smell; and it stayed with me. By the end of that long holiday I understood that my Mother had written verses, that my Father 'wrote things' also; that books and pictures were among the most important affairs in the world; that I could read as much as I chose and ask the meaning of things from any one I met. I had found out, too, that one could take pen and set down what one thought, and that nobody accused one of 'showing off' by so doing. I read a good deal; *Sidonia the Sorceress*; Emerson's poems; and Bret Harte's stories; and I learned all sorts of verses for the pleasure of repeating them to myself in bed.

RUDYARD KIPLING, Something of Myself, 1937

IN THE NATIONAL GALLERY

Wednesday, 26 November 1884

Went on to the National Gallery and enjoyed myself exceedingly. How large it is! I was rather surprised at the selection of pictures which I had remembered. I wonder what governs a child's perception? I remembered more of the Turners than any others. Clearest of all the *Building of Carthage*, of which I am sure I have seen no engraving.

Swarms of young ladies painting, frightfully for the most part, O dear, if I was a boy and had courage! We did not see a single really good copy. They are as flat and smooth as ditch-water. The drawing as a rule seems pretty good, but they cannot have the slightest eye for colour. I always think I do not manage my paint in that respect, but what I have seen today gives me courage, in spite of depression caused by the sight of the wonderful pictures.

What I am troubled by is the inability to control my medium, but these copyists, content to work greasily with camel hair brushes, paint with the greatest facility, and yet can't colour in the least. If I could govern my paint I'd go better. Age imparts to pictures a peculiar glow and mellowness, varying in different pictures from green or yellow to orange, the first being the commonest, but, the stronger the green tint of age, the more persistedly do these young ladies apply a kind of sickly chocolate which they seem to have caught from one another. Their works certainly would be the better for going up the chimney a bit. I cannot understand it, and they have such perfect self reliance, uncertainty always makes the colours muddy.

What marvellous pictures the Turners are! I think *Ulysses and Polyphemus* is the most wonderful in the gallery. Well might Turner despise fame and wealth with such a world in his brain, and yet his end was hastened by drink. What a mixture of height and depth!

Mr Gladstone's health and vigour is said to be owing to his chewing every mouthful thirty-two times, but Mr Millais who has been staying there says they eat faster than he, which is saying a good deal. Disraeli, looking at Mr Gladstone's portrait by Millais in the Academy, remarked there was just one thing in the face which Millais had not caught, that was the vindictiveness.

> BEATRIX POTTER, *Journals*, transcribed from her code writing by Leslie Linder, 1966

HERE'S LONDON

The name Vivian came in useful on our return journey, for our luggage was all labelled with it. At Paddington in those days all bags and trunks were arranged on the arrival platform under the letters of the alphabet. To find your belongings all you had to do was to go to the right initial. Since few people's names began with 'V', our baggage was to be seen in lonely state. It seems to me a good plan, for friends could also meet you at the initial. There we would find my father with cab engaged and all ready for us.

None but an old Londoner can understand the curious attraction of the town. After the music of the words 'London only' at Reading, we gave ourselves up to the *nil admirari* spirit. The size and importance of the terminus might alarm a timid fellow passenger, but were nothing to us. The wet streets (for it invariably seemed to rain on our return), the reflections from the street-lamps and the shops, the utter indifference of everybody to us and our concerns—why was it fascinating even to a child? I suppose we took on that feeling of superiority to all the world, the idea of finality, that London gives. No sign-posts to other towns are to be seen. Here's London. Here you are. We were almost of the same mind as the old Cornish farm-labourer who could not be made to believe that there was anything *beyond* London.

> M. V. HUGHES, *A London Child of the Seventies*, 1934

EAST END CHEVRAS

The Jewish settlement at the East End. . . . stands outside the communal life, so far as voting power is concerned—partly on account of its extreme poverty, and partly because of the foreign habits and customs of the vast majority of East End Jews.

For the East End Jews of the working class rarely attend the larger synagogues (except on the Day of Atonement), and most assuredly they are not seat-holders. For the most part the religious-minded form themselves into associations (Chevras), which combine the functions of a benefit club for death, sickness, and the solemn rites of mourning with that of public worship and the study of the Talmud. Thirty or forty of these Chevras are scattered throughout the Jewish quarters; they are of varying size as congregations, of different degrees of solvency as friendly societies, and of doubtful comfort and sanitation as places of public worship. Usually each Chevras is named after the town or district in Russia or Poland from which the majority of its members have emigrated: it is, in fact, from old associations—from ties of relationship or friendship, or, at least, from the memory of a common home—that the new association springs.

Here, early in the morning, or late at night, the devout members meet to recite the morning and evening prayers, or to decipher the sacred books of the Talmud. And it is a curious and touching sight to enter one of the poorer and more wretched of these places on a Sabbath morning. Probably the one you choose will be situated in a small alley or narrow court, or it may be built out in a back yard. To reach the entrance you stumble over broken pavement and household débris; possibly you pick your way over the rickety bridge connecting it with the cottage property fronting the street. From the outside it appears a long wooden building surmounted by a skylight, very similar in construction to the ordinary sweater's workshop. You enter; the heat and odour convince you that the skylight is not used for ventilation. From behind the trellis of the 'ladies' gallery' you see at the far end of the room the richly curtained Ark of the Covenant, wherein are laid, attired in gorgeous vestments, the sacred scrolls of the Law. Slightly elevated on a platform in the midst of the congregation, stands the reader or minister, surrounded by the seven who are called up to the reading of the Law from among the congregation. Scarves of white cashmere or silk, softly bordered and fringed, are thrown across the shoulders of the men, and relieve the dusty hue and disguise the Western cut of the clothes they wear. A low, monotonous, but musical-toned recital of Hebrew prayers, each man praying for himself to the God of his fathers, rises from the congregation, whilst the reader intones, with a somewhat louder voice, the recognized portion of the Pentateuch. Add to this rhythmical cadence of numerous voices, the swaying to and fro of the bodies of the worshippers—expressive of the words of personal adoration: 'All my bones exclaim, Oh! Lord, who is like unto Thee!'—and you may imagine yourself in a far-off Eastern land. But you are roused from your dreams. Your eye wanders from the men, who form the congregation, to the small body of women who watch behind the trellis. Here, certainly, you have the Western world, in the bright-coloured ostrich feathers, large bustles, and tight-fitting coats of cotton velvet or brocaded satinette. At last you step out, stifled by the heat and dazed by the strange contrast of the old-world memories of a majestic religion and the squalid vulgarity of an East End slum.

And, perchance, if it were permissible to stay after Divine service is over, and if you could follow the quick-spoken Jüdisch, you would be still more bewildered by these 'destitute foreigners,' whose condition, according to Mr Arnold White, 'resembles that of animals.' The women have left; the men are scattered over the benches (maybe there are several who are still muttering their prayers), or they are gathered together in knots, sharpening their intellects with the ingenious points and subtle logic of the Talmudical argument, refreshing their minds from the rich stores of Talmudical wit, or listening with ready helpfulness to the tale of distress of a new-comer from the foreign home.

> CHARLES BOOTH, *Life and Labour of the People in London*, 1889; the chapter 'Jews in London', from which this is taken, was written by the researcher Beatrice Potter

THE RISE OF THE MUSIC HALLS

Although Music Hall soon spread from London to the provinces, and although provincial (and Irish and Scottish) artists were soon to become stars, the whole art began in London, and the bulk of the greatest artists remained Londoners.

The 'music halls' began round about the 1840s simply as adjuncts to public houses when the landlords discovered that a song encouraged customers to drink. These rapidly grew in size—the 'hall' becoming larger than the adjoining pub itself—but until the 'seventies and 'eighties, most Music Halls remained attached to a local tavern. In those days the audience sat not in rows of seats, but at chairs beside tables where drink and food (pease puddings and pigs' trotters were favourite dishes) were sold by waiters like 'Brush' Wood, Marie Lloyd's father. The entertainment was presided over by a Chairman, a man of voluble authority and strong local popularity, who sat at a table at the foot of the stage, introduced the numbers, rebuked interrupters, encouraged further orders from the waiters, and courteously accepted drinks from admiring clients. The Chairman called for order with a hammer, and also used this, after his preparatory spiel ('Ladies and gentlemen, I give you the one and only etc etc'), to assure a rousing reception to each new artist.

Throughout the 'eighties and 'nineties, larger Halls were built as theatres proper, and the Chairmen, presiding over a smaller gathering of some two to three hundred people, gradually disappeared, though Chairmen were still functioning in the 'nineties at Gatti's, Westminster bridge, and Collins' in Islington. The most legendary of the early Music Hall impresarios was Charles Morton, who built the Palace (still standing) in the 'nineties. He'd begun at the Canterbury Arms in Westminster Bridge road which he started in 1849, and in addition to Music Hall turns, he'd put on opera and exhibitions of painting so that his theatre became known as the 'Academy over the water'. He rose as the Halls did, launching, as we shall soon see, many new talents, and by the time he built the Palace in Shaftesbury avenue, was a figure of some substance in the theatrical and even social world. Seeing a well-dressed client stub out his cigar on the sumptuous carpet of his new theatre, he told the man to leave: 'I would not do that in your house, sir. You shall not do it in mine.' Many of the new theatres became known as Palaces of Variety, and an attempt was made by theatrical entrepreneurs to attract a wider, less proletarian public, and to enforce seemly behaviour inside the Halls. The wire netting stretched over the orchestra pit to protect the musicians from missiles hurled from the gallery at the performers was no longer deemed necessary, nor were the bottles still chained, as they used to be, to the waiters' trays. The 'Gallery Boys' were tamed, if not altogether subdued, though in the North they continued to fling iron rivets at inept performers.

Those who can remember the Queen's Poplar, or the Metropolitan Edgware road, could form an idea of what the hundreds of smaller local

Halls were like. In both of these Halls, there was the agreeable architectural situation that you could watch the show through a wide glass panel from the inside of the main stalls bar—indeed, the Queen's later wired this for sound, so that there was no need to leave the bar at all if you didn't want to. The Metropolitan, like the Bedford Camden Town—both of which Sickert frequented and recorded—were exceedingly pretty, being adorned with ornate statuary in a pop art rococo that has now completely vanished. As for the Granville Walham Green, it was tiled throughout in decorated faïence, so that one had rather the impression of being in a vast swimming pool.

Towards the turn of the century, big theatrical business moved into the Halls, in the persons, principally, of Oswald Stoll and Maurice de Freece (who became the husband of Vesta Tilley). The old single-act programmes running without a break from 6.30 p.m. to midnight were replaced by 'twice nightly' performances—one of the many causes of the Music Hall strike of 1907 in which the artists, led by Marie Lloyd—and to the immense delight of the populace—picketed the chief theatres in central London. Stoll built Empires throughout the provinces, and joining with Moss, founded Moss Empires who erected vast palaces like the Hippodrome (now Talk of the Town) and the Coliseum. In these huge barns intimacy and direct contact with the audience were of course impossible, and though the stars grew even richer (as did their promoters), the art was already in decline.

Perhaps the most famous London Hall was the Old Mogul, or Old Mo, in Drury Lane. Originally the Old Mogul tavern, this started as a modest Hall, was rebuilt more lavishly in 1872, and in 1891 was once again refurbished and transformed more decorously into the Middlesex. With the fading of the Halls it underwent a further metamorphosis into the Winter Garden theatre, and as such lingered on until quite recently. A playbill of a gala evening at the Middlesex on 20th March, 1902, in honour of 'the Popular and Only Marie Lloyd', shows that no less than one hundred and four turns appeared (at prices ranging from sixpence to five shillings), and among them more than a dozen stars. Also advertised on this bill was the 'Edisonograph', more usually known as the 'bioscope'—a gadget which was shown at the end of the programme, when everyone was getting up to leave; for few foresaw that the 'Edisonograph' would, within two decades, invade almost all of the old Halls and expel the live artists entirely.

Down the road from the Old Mo (or Middlesex) there stood, of course, the Theatre Royal Drury Lane. And in the late 'eighties this came under the management of Sir Augustus ('Druriolanus') Harris, whose tenancy is commemorated by a portrait bust at the entrance to the theatre, where he now stares at patrons of *Hello Dolly* (or whatever it may be) with a contorted expression remarkably resembling that of Edward VII—whom, indeed, so many eminent men at the turn of the century contrived to look like. In the late 'eighties, Harris hit upon the brilliant plan of reviving the pantomimes so popular in Grimaldi's day and, to give them a contemporary twist and attract multitudinous clients, to invite selected stars from the Halls to take part. This invitation came as something of a surprise to the Music Hall artists who thought the Lane altogether too grand for them, yet they accepted. Accordingly, some of the greatest stars migrated from the Halls to the Lane at Christmas time, and Dan Leno, Little Tich, Marie Lloyd, Vesta Tilley, Herbert Campbell, Johnny Danvers, Harry Randall and Harry Fragson all appeared there. I . . . would mention that Harry Fragson, like Little Tich, was one of the rare English artists who was as popular in Paris as in London. Song sheets of the 'Répertoire Fragson' appeared in France throughout the Edwardian era, and Fragson's Cockney accent when speaking French in Paris was apparently as hilarious as his device of speaking English with a Parisian accent when in London.

COLIN MACINNES, *Sweet Saturday Night*, 1967

This enchanting song, written for Gus Elen (music by George Le Brunn, lyric by Edgar Bateman), perfectly catches the coster's nostalgia for the countryside. The singer tends his little garden in a London that is growing larger every day, with houses multiplying fast. One verse ends

> If you climbed up on a chimbley
> You could see right out to Wembley
> If it wasn't for the 'ouses in between.

and another

> If yer eyesight didn't fail yer
> Yer could see right to Australia
> If it wasn't for the 'ouses in between.

IF IT WASN'T FOR THE 'OUSES IN BETWEEN

If you saw my little back yard, 'Wot a pretty spot!' you'd cry—
It's a picture on a sunny summer day;
Wiv the turnip tops and cabbages wot people doesn't buy
I makes it on a Sunday look all gay.
The neighbours finks I grows 'em and you'd fancy you're in Kent,
Or at Epsom if you gaze into the mews—
It's a wonder as the landlord doesn't want to raise the rent,
Because we've got such nobby distant views.

Oh! it really is a werry pretty garden,
And Chingford to the eastward could be seen;
Wiv a ladder and some glasses,
You could see to 'Ackney marshes,
If it wasn't for the 'ouses in between.

EDGAR BATEMAN (1860–1946)

'A CENTURY OF COMFORT'

Comforters, dispensing balm—in jokes and ballads, in sketches and songs, in novelty acts as grotesque as they were macabre. Comforters with lived-in faces, singing of brutal or feckless husbands, charm-encrusted biga-mists, gin-guzzling doctors, shifty clerics, hard-hearted rent collectors—a vast assortment of everyday scoundrels. Comforters, lightening the pain of the here-and-now with mockery—for they were veterans when it came to distress. Their comforting art had been nurtured on an abundance of indignities. Plaster cherubs, some plumper than others, beamed down on Cockney vestal virgins knocked off their plinths by dashing young cads who knocked them up as a consequence before deserting them for ever; on ferocious mothers-in-law, rolling-pins at the ready, waiting for the objects of their misguided daughters' affections to stagger home drunk from the pub on pay day; on *lions comiques*, those upstarts from the back streets who transformed themselves into Champagne Charlies and break-ers of foreign banks—on such familiar scenes, on such vital people, those wise little angels of the second order beamed down for a century of comfort, in a thousand Alhambras and Empires . . .

PAUL BAILEY, *Gabriel's Lament*, 1986

A DANCING HARE

Monday, 22 October 1883

Left Woodfield Friday, Oct. 12, '83. Mr Mallock died Tuesday 16th. aged 78, having caught cold the previous Friday. There will be none of the old faces left soon.

Time goes so fast I cannot keep up with it.

Went along Knightsbridge the other evening, passed a happy family. As we were passing the man took a hare out of a bag, and setting it on the table before a tambourine, the creature apparently not at all frightened, began to dance on it. I think it is a trick hares and rabbits, particularly the former, have. I have seen the blue hares dance with their fore feet.

Have been painting some plovers.

Crossing-sweeper died Sunday 14th. Another appeared on 22nd.

Papa and mamma went to Stalybridge, the Bazaar is 24th.

'I stand,' said a stupid orator, 'on the broad platform of the principles of 1776.' 'You stand on nothing of the sort,' shouted a little shoemaker in the crowd, 'you stand on my boots that you've never paid for, and I want the money!'

> BEATRIX POTTER, *Journals*, transcribed from her code writing by Leslie Linder, 1966

THE ELEVATION MISSION

But the Missionaries were few, and the subscribers to the Elevation Mission were many. Most had been convinced, by what they had been told, by what they had read in charity appeals, and perhaps by what they had seen in the police-court and inquest reports, that the whole East End was a wilderness of slums: slums packed with starving human organisms without minds and without morals, preying on each other alive. These subscribers visited the Institute by twos and threes, on occasions of particular festivity among the neat clerks, and were astonished at the wonderful effects of Pansophic Elevation on the degraded classes, their aspect and their habits. Perhaps it was a concert where nobody was drunk: perhaps a little dance where nobody howled a chorus, nor wore his hat, nor punched his partner in the eye. It was a great marvel, whereunto the observers testified: so that more subscriptions came, and the new wing was built.

The afternoon was bright, and all was promising. A small crowd of idlers hung about the main door of the Institute, and stared at a string of flags. Away to the left stood the new wing, a face of fair, clean brick; the ornamentation of approved earnestness, in terra-cotta squares at regular intervals. Within sat many friends and relations of the shopmen and superior mechanics, and waited for the Bishop; the Eminences of the Elevation Mission sitting apart on the platform. Without, among the idlers, waited Dicky Perrott. His notions of what was going on were indistinct, but he had a belief, imbibed through rumour and tradition, that all celebrations at such large buildings were accompanied by the consumption, in the innermost recesses, of cake and tea. Even to be near cake was something. In Shoreditch High Street was a shop where cake stood in the window in great slabs, one slab over another, to an incalculable value. At this window—against it, as near as possible, his face flattened white—Dicky would stand till the shopkeeper drove him off: till he had but to shut his eyes to see once more, in the shifting black, the rich yellow sections with their myriad raisins. Once a careless errand-boy, who had bought a slice, took so clumsy a bite as he emerged that near a third of the whole piece broke and fell; and this Dicky had snatched from the paving and bolted with, ere the owner quite saw his loss. This was a superior sort of cake, at a penny. But once he had managed to buy himself a slice of an inferior sort for a halfpenny, in Meakin Street.

Dicky Perrott, these blessed memories in his brain, stood unobtrusively near the door, with the big jacket buttoned over as decently as might be, full of a desperate design: which was to get inside by whatsoever manner of trick or opportunity he might, and so, if it were humanly possible, to the cake.

The tickets were being taken at the door by an ardent young Elevator—one of the missionaries. Him, and all such washed and well-dressed people, Dicky had learnt to hold in serene contempt when the business in hand was dodging. There was no hurry: the Elevator might waste his vigilance on the ticket-holders for some time yet. And Dicky knew better than to betray the smallest sign of a desire for entrance while his enemy's attention was awake.

Carriages drew up, and yielded more Eminences: toward the end the

Bishop himself, whom Dicky observed but as a pleasant-looking old gentleman in uncommon clothes; and on whom he bestowed no more thought than a passing wonder at what might be the accident to his hat which had necessitated its repair with string.

But at the spikes of the Bishop's carriage came another; and out of that there got three ladies, friends of the ticket-receiver, on whom they closed, greeting and shaking hands; and in a flash Dicky Perrott was beyond the lobby and moving obscurely along the walls of the inner hall, behind pillars and in shadow, seeking cake.

The Choral Society sang their lustiest, and there were speeches. Eminences expressed their surprise and delight at finding the people of the East End, gathered in the Institute building, so respectable and clean, thanks to persistent, indefatigable, unselfish Elevation.

The good Bishop, amid clapping of hands and fluttering of hand-kerchiefs, piped cherubically of everything. He rejoiced to see that day, whereon the helping hand of the West was so unmistakably made apparent in the East. He rejoiced also to find himself in the midst of so admirably typical an assemblage—so representative, if he might say so, of that great East End of London, thirsting and crying out for—for Elevation: for that—ah—Elevation which the fortunately circumstanced denizens of—of other places, had so munificently—laid on. The people of the East End had been sadly misrepresented—in popular periodicals and in—in other ways. The East End, he was convinced, was not so black as it was painted. (Applause.) He had but to look about him. *Etcetera, etcetera.* He questioned whether so well-conducted, morally-given, and respectable a gathering could be brought together in any West End parish with which he was acquainted. It was his most pleasant duty on this occasion—and so on and so forth.

Dicky Perrott had found the cake. It was in a much smaller room at the back of the hall, wherein it was expected that the Bishop and certain Eminences of the platform would refresh themselves with tea after the ceremony. There were heavy, drooping curtains at the door of this room, and deep from the largest folds the ratling from the Jago watched. The table was guarded by a sour-faced man—just such a man as drove him from the window of the cake shop in Shoreditch High Street. Nobody else was there yet, and plainly the sour-faced man must be absent or busy ere the cake could be got at.

There was a burst of applause in the hall: the new wing had been

declared open. Then there was more singing, and after that much shuffling and tramping, for everybody was free to survey the new rooms on
the way out; and the Importances from the platform came to find the tea.

Filling the room and standing about in little groups; chatting, munch-
ing, and sipping, while the sour-faced man distractedly floundered amid
crockery: not a soul of them all perceived an inconsiderable small boy,
ducking and dodging vaguely among legs and round skirts, making,
from time to time, a silent snatch at a plate on the table: and presently
he vanished altogether. Then the amiable Bishop, beaming over the tea-
cup six inches from his chin, at two courtiers of the clergy, bethought
him of a dinner engagement, and passed his hand downward over the
rotundity of his waistcoat.

'Dear, dear,' said the Bishop, glancing down suddenly, 'why—what's
become of my watch?'

There hung three inches of black ribbon, with a cut end. The Bishop
looked blankly at the Elevators about him.

Three streets off, Dicky Perrott, with his shut fist deep in his breeches
pocket, and a gold watch in the fist, ran full drive for the Old Jago.

> ARTHUR MORRISON, *A Child of the Jago*, 1969; the 'Jago' is the fictional
> name Morrison gave to the area of the East End known as Old Nichol.

HAUNTED HOUSES

Wednesday, 2 July 1884
Lord Selborne has taken the haunted house in Berkeley Square. It is now
in the hands of the builders. It has been empty a long time. About the
last who braved its horrors were a party of gentlemen who went there
with their collie dogs. It is said that they gave the ghost a sound thrash-
ing, but the difficulty is that no one seems to know what the said ghost
is. Anyway, the house has a notoriously bad name.

19, Queens Gate is another house which is no canny. Nearly twenty
years sȳne a gentleman about to marry took it, but the bride died a few
hours before the wedding-time, suddenly. The gentleman would not live
there, and they say that to this day the untouched breakfast is on the
table.

Then the low red house second from the bottom of Palace Gardens has
always been unlucky. Thackeray died there, then it was the home of three

notorious braves. The next owner's son, running down stairs at a club, could not stop himself, and went over the banisters. I believe yet another owner died suddenly.

> BEATRIX POTTER, *Journals*, transcribed from her code writing by Leslie Linder, 1966

LONDON TOWN

Let others chaunt a country praise,
Fair river walks and meadow ways;
Dearer to me my sounding days
    In *London Town*:
To me the tumult of the street
Is no less music, than the sweet
Surge of the wind among the wheat,
    By dale or down.

Three names mine heart with rapture hails,
With homage: *Ireland, Cornwall, Wales*:
Lands of lone moor, and mountain gales,
    And stormy coast:
Yet *London's* voice upon the air
Pleads at mine heart, and enters there;
Sometimes I wellnigh love and care
    For *London* most.

Listen upon the ancient hills:
All silence! save the lark, who trills
Through sunlight, save the rippling rills:
    There peace may be.
But listen to great *London!* loud,
As thunder from the purple cloud,
Comes the deep thunder of the crowd,
    And heartens me.

O gray, O gloomy skies! What then?
Here is a marvellous world of men;
More wonderful than *Rome* was, when
    The world was *Rome!*

See the great stream of life flow by!
Here thronging myriads laugh and sigh,
Here rise and fall, here live and die:
    In this vast home.

In long array they march toward death,
Armies, with proud or piteous breath:
Forward! the spirit in them saith,
    Spirit of life:
Here the triumphant trumpets blow;
Here mourning music sorrows low;
Victors and vanquished, still they go
    Forward in strife.

Who will not heed so great a sight?
Greater than marshalled stars of night,
That move to music and with light:
    For these are men!
These move to music of the soul;
Passions, that madden or control:
These hunger for a distant goal,
    Seen now and then.

Is mine too tragical a strain,
Chaunting a burden full of pain,
And labour, that seems all in vain?
    I sing but truth.
Still, many a merry pleasure yet,
To many a merry measure set,
Is ours, who need not to forget
    Summer and youth.

Do *London* birds forget to sing?
Do *London* trees refuse the spring?
Is *London* May no pleasant thing?
    Let country fields,
To milking maid and shepherd boy,
Give flowers, and song, and bright employ:
Her children also can enjoy,
    What *London* yields.

Gleaming with sunlight, each soft lawn
Lies fragrant beneath dew of dawn;
The spires and towers rise, far withdrawn,
    Through golden mist:
At sunset, linger beside *Thames:*
See now, what radiant lights and flames!
That ruby burns: that purple shames
    The amethyst.

Winter was long, and dark, and cold:
Chill rains! grim fogs, black fold on fold,
Round street, and square, and river rolled!
    Ah, let it be:
Winter is gone! Soon comes July,
With wafts from hayfields by-and-by:
While in the dingiest courts you spy
    Flowers fair to see.

Take heart of grace: and let each hour
Break gently into bloom and flower:
Winter and sorrow have no power
    To blight all bloom.
One day, perchance, the sun will see
London's entire felicity:
And all her loyal children be
    Clear of all gloom.

A dream? Dreams often dreamed come true:
Our world would seem a world made new
To those, beneath the churchyard yew
    Laid long ago!
When we beneath like shadows bide,
Fair *London*, throned upon *Thames'* side,
May be our children's children's pride:
    And we shall know.

LIONEL JOHNSON (1867–1902)

On Thursday, 27 September 1888, the Central News Agency, with offices in Fleet Street, received this letter, written in red ink and postmarked London East Central. This was the first time the sobriquet was used. The journalist Donald McCormick, author of The Identity of Jack the Ripper, *wrote, 'without this nickname, in all probability the crimes he committed would long ago have been forgotten'.*

A LETTER TO THE PRESS

Dear Boss,

I keep on hearing the police have caught me, but they won't fix me just yet. I have laughed when they look so clever and talk about being on the right track. The joke about Leather Apron gave me real fits.

I am down on whores and I shan't quit ripping them till I do get buckled. Grand work, the last job was. I gave the lady no time to squeal. How can they catch me now? I love my work and want to start again. You will soon hear of me and my funny little games.

I saved some of the proper red stuff in a ginger beer bottle over the last job, to write with, but it went thick like glue and I can't use it. Red ink is fit enough, I hope. Ha! Ha!

The next job I do I shall clip the lady's ears off and send them to the police, just for jolly, wouldn't you? Keep this letter back until I do a bit more work, then give it out straight. My knife's so nice and sharp, I want to get to work right away if I get a chance. Good luck,

Yours truly,

JACK THE RIPPER

Don't mind me giving the trade name. Wasn't good enough to post this before I got all the red ink off my hands; curse it. No luck yet. They say I am a doctor now. Ha! Ha!

This postcard, addressed to the Central News Agency, bearing a large, bloody thumbprint, was posted in the East End on Sunday, 30 September 1888. Nothing had then appeared in the press about the double murder.

AND A POSTCARD

I was not codding, dear old Boss, when I gave you the tip. You'll hear about Saucy Jack's work tomorrow. Double event this time. Number

One squealed a bit. Couldn't finish straight off. Had no time to get ears for police. Thanks for keeping last letter back till I got to work again.— JACK THE RIPPER

> Tom Cullen, *Autumn of Terror*, 1960

A CLOUD OVER LONDON

Mother and I were invited to go north again, to spend the Christmas with Tom. We were glad to get away for a week or two, not only to escape from the decorum of the boarding-house, but also from London itself. For a cloud had been hanging over the town—a mental one in addition to the customary fogs. After the lapse of over forty years Jack the Ripper has become as legendary as Dick Turpin, and to many he is almost a joke. No one can now believe how terrified and unbalanced we all were by his murders. A thriller in a book is quite different from a thriller round the corner. It seemed to be round the corner, although it all happened in the East End, and we were in the West; but even so, I was afraid to go out after dark, if only to post a letter. Just as dusk came on we used to hear down our quiet and ultra-respectable Edith Road the cries of newspaper-boys, in tones made as alarming as they could: 'Another 'orrible murder! . . . Whitechapel! . . . Murder! . . . Disgustin' details. . . . Murder!' One can only dimly imagine what the terror must have been in those acres of narrow streets, where the inhabitants knew the murderer to be lurking. John Tenniel departed from his usual political subjects for *Punch* in order to stir public opinion by blood-curdling cartoons of 'murder stalking the slums', and by jeers at the inefficiency of the police. From all the suburban districts police were hurried to the East End, and yet we would read of a murder committed within a few moments of the passing by of a policeman. Naturally, I suppose, the murderer knew the time of the policeman's beat, and waited till he had passed. Some sensible fellow thought of making the police more stealthy by putting india-rubber on their heels; and it was this that started the widespread use of rubber-heels by the public at large. Another strange by-product of the crimes was the disuse of black-bags for the ordinary professional or business man. A suspect had been described as 'carrying a black bag', and no one cared to be seen with one, not from fear of arrest, but simply from the ugly association—a curious instance of the whimsical way in which trade can suffer from a sudden drop in demand.

The press was full of theories about the murderer. One idea was that he must be a sailor, because he could join his ship and get away quickly; another was that he must be a madman, because he hid so cunningly (though why this ability should be a sign of mental derangement I could never see); another strong suspicion was that he must be a doctor, because of the skill and rapidity with which the mutilations were performed, and also because of the uncanny disappearance of the man in a few seconds after the deed, for a doctor carrying a black bag of instruments was a familiar figure anywhere at all hours, and might easily masquerade as a passer-by and natural first-aider. Horrible though the murders themselves were, I think it was more the mysterious disappearances that affected people's minds, giving a quality of the supernatural to the work—declared, of course, by some to be a judgement on vice. The murders stopped completely after one of surpassing savagery, looking as if an avenger had been seeking a special victim and had found her at last.

M. V. HUGHES, *A London Girl of the Eighties*, 1936

ON THE DEATH OF 'DARK ANNIE' CHAPMAN

'Dark Annie's' spirit still walks Whitechapel, unavenged by Justice . . . And yet even this forlorn, despised citizeness of London cannot be said to have suffered in vain. On the contrary, she has effected more by her death than many long speeches in Parliament and countless columns of letters to the newspapers could have brought about. She has forced innumerable people who never gave a serious thought before to the subject to realize how it is and where it is that our vast floating population—the waifs and strays of our thoroughfares—live and sleep at night and what sort of accommodation our rich and enlightened capital provides for them, after so many Acts of Parliament passed to improve the dwellings of the poor, and so many millions spent by our Board of Works, our vestries . . . 'Dark Annie' will effect in one way what fifty Secretaries of State could never accomplish . . .

Some mention was made at the inquest upon Annie Chapman of a wild proposal to photograph her glazed eyes, and so try if the dying retina would present any image of the cruel monster who killed her and mutilated her. Better have listened with ear of imagination at her poor swollen lips, for, without much fancy, a Home Secretary or Chairman of the Metropolitan Board of Works might have heard them murmuring: 'We, your murdered sisters, are what the dreadful homes where we live have made us. Behind your fine squares and handsome streets you continue to leave our wild-beast lairs unchanged and uncleansed. The slums kill us, body and soul, with filth and shame and spread fever and death among your gentry also, while they are spawning beds for crime and social discontent. When it is possible for the poor of London to live and sleep in decency you will not pick up from backyards so many corpses like mine.'

Editorial in the Daily Telegraph, 1888

SYMPHONY IN YELLOW

An omnibus across the bridge
  Crawls like a yellow butterfly,
  And, here and there, a passer-by
Shows like a little restless midge.

Big barges full of yellow hay
  Are moored against the shadowy wharf,
  And, like a yellow silken scarf,
The thick fog hangs along the quay.

The yellow leaves begin to fade
  And flutter from the Temple elms,
  And at my feet the pale green Thames
Lies like a rod of rippled jade.

OSCAR WILDE, 1889

PAINTING AT KEW

I am now very busy at Kew Gardens where I have found a series of splendid motifs which I am trying to render as well as I can. The weather helps—it's quite exceptional, it seems. But the difficulty! More than ever I feel how weak I am when faced with such a hard job.

*

I try to do the best I can here despite the continual change of weather.
Kew Gardens are marvellous and the surroundings are superb. But time
is so short and the work takes so long that I'm driven to despair at last!

> CAMILLE PISSARRO, letters to Durand-Ruel, his dealer, June and July
> 1892, from *Les Archives de l'Impressionisme*, 1939

A LONDON STREET

This street is in the East End. There is no need to say in the East End
of what. The East End is a vast city, as famous in its way as any the hand
of man has made. But who knows the East End? It is down through
Cornhill and out beyond Leadenhall Street and Aldgate Pump, one will
say: a shocking place, where he once went with a curate; an evil plexus
of slums that hide human creeping things; where filthy men and women
live on penn'orths of gin, where collars and clean shirts are decencies
unknown, where every citizen wears a black eye, and none ever combs his
hair. The East End is a place, says another, which is given over to the
Unemployed. And the Unemployed is a race whose token is a clay pipe,
and whose enemy is soap: now and again it migrates bodily to Hyde Park
with banners, and furnishes adjacent police courts with disorderly drunks.
Still another knows the East End only as the place whence begging
letters come; there are coal and blanket funds there, all perennially
insolvent, and everybody always wants a day in the country. Many and
misty are the people's notions of the East End; and each is commonly but
the distorted shadow of a minor feature. Foul slums there are in the East
End, of course, as there are in the West; want and misery there are, as
wherever a host is gathered together to fight for food. But they are not
often spectacular in kind.

Of this street there are about one hundred and fifty yards—on the
same pattern all. It is not pretty to look at. A dingy little brick house
twenty feet high, with three square holes to carry the windows, and an
oblong hole to carry the door, is not a pleasing object; and each side of
this street is formed by two or three score of such houses in a row, with
one front wall in common. And the effect is as of stables.

Round the corner there are a baker's, a chandler's and a beer-shop.
They are not included in the view from any of the rectangular holes; but

they are well known to every denizen, and the chandler goes to church on Sunday and pays for his seat. At the opposite end, turnings lead to streets less rigidly respectable: some where 'Mangling done here' stares from windows, and where doors are left carelessly open; others where squalid women sit on doorsteps, and girls go to factories in white aprons. Many such turnings, of as many grades of decency, are set between this and the nearest slum.

They are not a very noisy or obtrusive lot in this street. They do not go to Hyde Park with banners, and they seldom fight. It is just possible that one or two among them, at some point in a life of ups and downs, may have been indebted to a coal and blanket fund; but whosoever these may be, they would rather die than publish the disgrace, and it is probable that they very nearly did so ere submitting to it.

Some who inhabit this street are in the docks, some in the gasworks, some in one or other of the few shipbuilding yards that yet survive on the Thames. Two families in a house is the general rule, for there are six rooms behind each set of holes: this, unless 'young men lodgers' are taken in, or there are grown sons paying for bed and board. As for the grown daughters, they marry as soon as may be. Domestic service is a social descent, and little under millinery and dressmaking is compatible with self-respect. The general servant may be caught young among the turnings at the end where mangling is done; and the factory girls live still further off, in places skirting slums.

Every morning at half-past five there is a curious demonstration. The street resounds with thunderous knockings, repeated upon door after door, and acknowledged ever by a muffled shout from within. These signals are the work of the night-watchman or the early policeman, or both, and they summon the sleepers to go forth to the docks, the gasworks, and the ship-yards. To be awakened in this wise costs fourpence a week, and for this fourpence a fierce rivalry rages between night-watchmen and policemen. The night-watchmen—a sort of by-blow of the ancient 'Charley,' and himself a fast vanishing quantity—is the real professional performer; but he goes to the wall, because a large connection must be worked if the pursuit is to pay at fourpence a knocker. Now, it is not easy to bang at two knockers three-quarters of a mile apart, and a hundred others lying between, all punctually at half-past five. Wherefore the policeman, to whom the fourpence is but a perquisite, and who is content with a smaller round, is rapidly supplanting the night-watchman, whose cry of 'Past nine o'clock,' as he collects orders in the evening, is now seldom heard.

The knocking and the shouting pass, and there comes the noise of opening and shutting of doors, and a clattering away to the docks, the gasworks and the ship-yards. Later more door-shutting is heard, and then the trotting of sorrow-laden little feet along the grim street to the grim Board School three grim streets off. Then silence, save for a subdued sound of scrubbing here and there, and the puny squall of croupy infants. After this, a new trotting of little feet to docks, gasworks, and ship-yards with father's dinner in a basin and a red handkerchief, and so to the Board School again. More muffled scrubbing and more squalling, and perhaps a feeble attempt or two at decorating the blankness of a square hole here and there by pouring water into a grimy flower-pot full of dirt. Then comes the trot of little feet toward the oblong holes, heralding the slower tread of sooty artisans; a smell of bloater up and down; nightfall; the fighting of boys in the street, perhaps of men at the corner near the beer-shop; sleep. And this is the record of a day in this street; and every day is hopelessly the same.

Every day, that is, but Sunday. On Sunday morning a smell of cooking floats round the corner from the half-shut baker's, and the little feet trot down the street under steaming burdens of beef, potatoes, and batter pudding—the lucky little feet these, with Sunday boots on them, when father is in good work and has brought home all his money; not the poor little feet in worn shoes, carrying little bodies in the thread-bare clothes of all the week, when father is out of work, or ill, or drunk, and the Sunday cooking may very easily be done at home—if any there be to do.

On Sunday morning one or two heads of families appear in wonderful black suits, with unnumbered creases and wrinklings at the seams. At their sides and about their heels trot the unresting little feet, and from under painful little velvet caps and straw hats stare solemn little faces towelled to a polish. Thus disposed and arrayed, they fare gravely through the grim little streets to a grim Little Bethel where are gathered together others in like garb and attendance; and for two hours they endure the frantic menace of hell-fire.

Most of the men, however, lie in shirt and trousers on their beds and read the Sunday paper; while some are driven forth—for they hinder the housework—to loaf, and await the opening of the beer-shop round the corner. Thus goes Sunday in this street, and every Sunday is the same as every other Sunday, so that one monotony is broken with another. For the women, however, Sunday is much as other days, except that there is rather more work for them. The break in their round of the week is washing day.

ARTHUR MORRISON, *Tales of Mean Streets*, 1894

Edwin Reardon, the protagonist of George Gissing's New Grub Street, *is a man who, like his creator, tries to live by his writing. Here he is, in one of his various London addresses, attempting to work on the book he hopes will make his name and his fortune.*

'CHAPTER III'

Eight flights of stairs, consisting alternately of eight and nine steps. Amy had made the calculation, and wondered what was the cause of this arrangement. The ascent was trying, but then no one could contest the respectability of the abode. In the flat immediately beneath resided a successful musician, whose carriage and pair came at a regular hour each afternoon to take him and his wife for a most respectable drive. In this special building no one else seemed at present to keep a carriage, but all the tenants were gentlefolk.

And as to living up at the very top, why, there were distinct advantages—as so many people of moderate income are nowadays hastening to discover. The noise from the street was diminished at this height; no possible tramplers could establish themselves above your head; the air was bound to be purer than that of inferior strata; finally, one had the flat roof whereon to sit or expatiate in sunny weather. True that a gentle rain of soot was wont to interfere with one's comfort out there in the open, but such minutiæ are easily forgotten in the fervour of domestic description. It was undeniable that on a fine day one enjoyed extensive views. The green ridge from Hampstead to Highgate, with Primrose Hill and the foliage of Regent's Park in the foreground; the suburban spaces of St John's Wood, Maida Vale, Kilburn; Westminster Abbey and the Houses of Parliament, lying low by the side of the hidden river, and a glassy gleam on far-off hills which meant the Crystal Palace; then the clouded majesty of eastern London, crowned by St Paul's dome. These things one's friends were expected to admire. Sunset often afforded rich effects, but they were for solitary musing.

A sitting-room, a bedroom, a kitchen. But the kitchen was called dining-room, or even parlour at need; for the cooking-range lent itself to concealment behind an ornamental screen, the walls displayed pictures and bookcases, and a tiny scullery which lay apart sufficed for the coarser domestic operations. This was Amy's territory during the hours when her husband was working, or endeavouring to work. Of necessity, Edwin Reardon used the front room as his study. His writing-table stood against the window; each wall had its shelves of serried literature; vases, busts, engravings (all of the inexpensive kind) served for ornaments.

A maid-servant, recently emancipated from the Board school, came at half-past seven each morning, and remained until two o'clock, by which time the Reardons had dined; on special occasions, her services were enlisted for later hours. But it was Reardon's habit to begin the serious work of the day at about three o'clock, and to continue with brief inter-ruptions until ten or eleven; in many respects an awkward arrangement, but enforced by the man's temperament and his poverty.

One evening he sat at his desk with a slip of manuscript paper before him. It was the hour of sunset. His outlook was upon the backs of certain large houses skirting Regent's Park, and lights had begun to show here and there in the windows: in one room a man was discoverable dress-ing for dinner, he had not thought it worth while to lower the blind; in another, some people were playing billiards. The higher windows reflected a rich glow from the western sky.

For two or three hours Reardon had been seated in much the same attitude. Occasionally he dipped his pen into the ink, and seemed about to write: but each time the effort was abortive. At the head of the paper was inscribed 'Chapter III.,' but that was all. And now the sky was dusking over; darkness would soon fall.

GEORGE GISSING, *New Grub Street*, 1891

AN EXCURSION TO PUTNEY

I left my house on a bicycle about 12.0. and rushed up town after an unsatisfactory morning of odds and ends. I had been received by Mr Watts-Dunton with a great amount of epistolary ceremony, many courteous letters arranging my visit, written by a secretary. The day was dark and gloomy. I got to Putney about 1.15 and walked into the street; I asked my way to the house expecting it to stand high up. I was standing in a very common suburban street, with omnibuses and cabs, and two rows of semi-detached houses going up the gentle acclivity of the hill. I suddenly saw I was standing opposite the house, a perfectly commonplace bow-windowed yellow-brick house, with a few shrubs in the tiny garden. I went up to the door, and was at once taken in by a maid. The house was redolent of cooking, dark, not very clean-looking, but comfortable enough—the walls crowded everywhere with pictures, mostly Rossetti's designs in pen and ink or chalk. I was taken into a dining-room on the right looking out at the back. To the left the tall backs of yellow-brick houses; the gardens full of orchard trees in bloom. A little garden lay beneath with a small yew hedge and a statue of a nymph, rather smoke-stained, some tall elms in the background.

Mr Watts-Dunton came out and greeted me with great cordiality. He seemed surprised at my size, as I was similarly surprised at his—and had not remembered he was so small. He was oddly dressed in waistcoat and trousers of some greenish cloth and with a large heavy blue frock-coat, too big for him with long cuffs. He was rather bald, with his hair grown rather thick and long and a huge moustache which concealed a small chin. He had lost his teeth since I saw him and looked an old man, though healthily bronzed and with firm small hands. After a compliment or two he took me upstairs. There lay a pair of elastic-sided boots outside a door, the passage thickly carpeted and pictures everywhere. He went quickly in, the room being over the dining-room.

There stood before me a little pale, rather don-like man, quite bald, with a huge head and domelike forehead, a ragged red beard in odd whisks, a small aquiline red nose. He looked supremely shy but received me with a distinguished courtesy, drumming on the ground with his foot and uttering strange little whistling noises. He seemed very deaf. The room was crammed with books; bookcases all about—a great sofa entirely filled with stacked books—books on the table. He bowed me to a chair, 'Will you sit?' On the fender was a pair of brown socks. W.D. said to me 'he has just come in from one of his long walks', took up the socks and put them behind a coal scuttle. 'Stay!' said Swinburne, and took them out carefully holding them in his hand, 'they are drying.' W.D. murmured something to me about his fearing they would get scorched, and we sate down. Swinburne sate down concealing his feet behind a chair and proceeded with strange motions to put the socks on out of sight. 'He seems to be changing them' said W.D. Swinburne said nothing but continued to whistle and drum.

Then he rose and bowed me down to lunch, throwing the window open. We went down and solemnly seated ourselves, W.D. at the head, back to light; Swinburne opposite to me. We had soup, chickens, many sweets, plovers' eggs. Swinburne had a bottle of beer which he drank. He was rather tremulous with his hands and clumsy. At first he said nothing, but gazed at intervals out of the window with a mild blue eye, and a happy sort of look. Watts-D. and I talked gravely, W.D. mumbling his food with difficulty. When he thought that Swinburne was sufficiently refreshed he drew him gracefully into the conversation. I *could* not make Swinburne hear, but W.D. did so without difficulty. He began to talk about Hawthorne; he said that *The Scarlet Letter* was a great book, but that any book *must* be a bathos after such a first chapter. 'I want more catastrophe for my money.' He smiled at me. Then he went on to speak of *The House with Seven Gables,* and then of certain dramas which were names to me—*Le Tourneur* etc. He waxed very enthusiastic over Elizabeth Arden(?), which he said was as great as Shakespeare, greater than Romeo and Juliet or the early plays. He said it was published in 1598(?) and that if it was *not* by Shakespeare there was the extraordinary fact of a dramatist living at the same time as Shakespeare who could create and embody a perfectly natural supreme woman.

He seemed content to be silent, and I was struck with his great courtesy, esp. to W.D. This was very touching. W.D. made some criticism on Scott (Swinburne having said the *Bride of Lammermuir* was a *perfect* story) about the necessity when Scott became bookish of translating him into patois. 'Very beautiful and just' said Swinburne, looking affectionately and gratefully at W.D. 'I have never heard that before and it is just. You must put that down.' W.D. smiled and bowed. Later on W.D. attributed some opinion to Rossetti—'Gabriel thought etc.' Swinburne smiled and said 'I have often heard you say that, but' (he turned smiling to me) 'Mr Benson, there is no truth in it. Rossetti had no opinions when I first knew him on Chatterton and many other subjects—and our friend here had merely to say a thing to him and it was absolutely adopted and fixed in the firmament.' W.D. stroked Swinburne's small pink hand which lay on the table and Swinburne gave a pleased schoolboy smile.

Lunch being over, Swinburne looked revived, and talked away merrily. He bowed me out of the room with ceremony. W.D. seemed to wish me to stay and Swinburne looked concerned, drew nearer to him and said 'Mr Benson must come and sit a little in my room'—so we went up. Swinburne began pulling down book after book and showed them to me, talking delightfully. As he became more assured he talked rhetorically. He has a full firm beautiful pronunciation, and talks like one of his books. Occasionally his voice went into a little squeak. He suddenly rose and went and drank some medicine in a corner. He had on an odd black tail-coat, a greenish waistcoat and slippers; low white collar, made-up tie—very shabby indeed. There was an odd bitter bookish scent about the room, which hung I noticed about him too.

He talked a little about Eton and Warre, saying 'he sate next me many a half and he was a good friend of mine'. Then W.D. proposed that I should go, when Swinburne said, half timidly, 'I hope there is time just to show Mr Benson one of these scenes.'—'Well, one scene', said W.D., 'but we have a lot of business to talk. You read it to him.' he took the book I was holding—the Arden play—and read very finely and dramatic-ally, with splendid inflections, a fine scene; his little feet kicked spas-modically under his chair and he drummed on the table. He was pleased at my pleasure; and then took up some miracle plays, and told me a long story of the Annunciation of the Nativity in it—the sheep-stealer, called Mack, who steals a sheep and puts it into the child's cradle; the shep-herds come to find it and laugh; then the angel appears. 'Do you think Mr Benson will be shocked if I show him what Cain says?', he said, and showed me giggling a piece of ancient schoolboy coarseness. W.D. smiled indulgently.

Then at last W.D. took me away. Swinburne shook hands with great cordiality, and a winning shy kind of smile lighting up his pale eyes. I was haunted by a dim resemblance to William Sidgwick. W.D. led me off, saying 'I like him to get a good siesta. He is such an excitable fellow. He is like a schoolboy—unfailing animal spirits, always pleased with everything; but he has to take care.' He was much amused at Swinburne asking me if I was his contemporary at Eton.

I was somehow tremendously touched by these two old fellows living together (Swinburne must be 66 and W.D. about 72?), and paying each other these romantic compliments and displaying distinguished con-sideration; as though the world was young. I imagine that the secret of W.D.'s influence is that he is ready to take all the trouble off the shoulders of these eminent men; that he is very sedulous, complimentary, gentle—and that he is at the same time just enough of an egotist to require and draw out some sympathy.

He is certainly a *great* egotist, and not, in any technical sense, a gentleman. He drops his h's; he pronounces 'prowl' *'proal'*, 'cloud' *'clowd'*, 'round' *'roaned'* etc. He leads the talk back and back to himself. I will give some instances of this first. He kept on saying that he didn't say and didn't do this or that. 'Good God, the world's a great whispering gallery' and he seemed to have quite a disproportionate sense of the place he occupied in the world's eye. Here is this kind old gentleman, living in the glow of the embers of two great literary friendships, in a comfortable frowsy kind of house at Putney, and thinking that he is a kind of pivot on which the world turns. But then he has excuses. His absurd book (*Aylwin*) flies into a twentieth edition. Rossetti tells him that the figure of 'Rosabell' in *The Coming of Love* is the most living breathing vital thing since Shakespeare. *I* should believe myself a great and inspired poet on much less. And after all, what harm does it do? To take oneself seriously is the great happiness of life.

W.D. kept—all through our long talk (we sate from 2.30 to 5.0)— reverting to himself: how *he* was the only man not dominated by Rossetti; how dogs wouldn't bite him; how as a boy at school, *he* dominated all the school, so that no boy ever got a hamper without bringing it to W.D. for him to choose what he liked best (he called it a very big fashionable private school) and would have carried him about all day on their shoulders if he had desired it; and how no edict of the masters would have availed, if he had given contrary orders.

He sighed heavily at one time and said that he had himself not done what he ought to have done in literature. At this I poured in a good deal of rather rancid oil and ginger-wine. He smiled indulgently and deprecatingly, and then said that the charge of Rossetti had been very anxious—the stratagems to reduce chloral, the dancing attendance on his whims. But he said: 'In his friendship and the friendship of Swinburne I find my consolation.' This I did not think sincerely said.

'Swinburne', he said several times over, 'is a mere boy still—and must be treated like one—a simple schoolboy, full of hasty impulses and generous thought—like April showers.' He added 'his mental power grows stronger every year—everybody's does—he is now a pure and simple improvisatore.'

W.D. sipped a little whisky and water and smoked a cigarette. He sometimes reclined in an armchair; sometimes came and sate near me. I sate in a great carved chair of Rossetti's (very fine—Indian) facing the light. There were fine pictures everywhere: a *most* interesting one of Rossetti reading poetry to Watts-Dunton in the Green Room at 16 Cheyne Walk, by Dunn. He gave me a reproduction of this; a Shakespeare in a heavy frame; beautiful witches of Rossetti, in crayons, pale red, peeping out of great gold frames. Outside [were] the white orchard blooms and trees—and I arranged myself so that I could see no house-backs, and we might have been at Kelmscott.

I now transcribe as accurately as I can what he told me about Rossetti, in answer to many questions.

Rossetti was *not* a hard worker. He had *no* permanent quarrel with Morris. Mackail's book, he said, was a mere *joke*. Morris had a peculiar dislike to Mackail, and it was as Burne Jones's friend that Mackail did it. It was not what Rossetti *did* that impressed you. It was what he *was*. His work was nothing. It came streaming out irrepressibly as heat from radium. He had an extraordinary effect on everyone (except W.D.) and dominated them. 'Look at Swinburne's poetry. Swinburne has no animal nature at all—a mere bookman and a schoolboy. *The feminine and sensuous element in Swinburne's poetry was entirely under Rossetti's influence.*'

Mystical passion, he said, was the root idea of Rossetti's life. 'That was his life—yes, that was his life', he said very gravely and impressively. He was *very* susceptible to female charm; and women fell wildly in love with him. W.D. had refused to introduce a lady-friend of his to Rossetti. She kept on asking why. 'Because you are a married woman—a beautiful woman—and if he falls in love with you, I won't answer for the consequences.' He had no *conscience* in the matter, though superstitious and in other ways much troubled by conscience. The odd Holman Hunt quarrel was this: Holman Hunt had a young model, Annie Miller, a simple pretty girl, to whom he was engaged. When he went out to the East, he committed her to Rossetti's charge. 'Good God', said W.D., 'the folly of committing such a girl to so susceptible and so dominant a man!' However, Rossetti did *not* fall in love with her (and when W.D. once questioned him as to whether he had in any way played Holman Hunt false about it, he answered very angrily that he would not have behaved so to H.H., and moreover that he had never any temptation to act otherwise). But he saw a great deal of the girl; took her about to restaurants and music-halls. Holman Hunt heard of all this, when he came back; was very angry, broke off with the girl and married someone else and broke with Rossetti—'very unfairly', said Watt-Dunton.

Rossetti's engagement to Miss Siddal was too long protracted (ten years—I found I knew all the dates better than W.D.). She was *sewing* in a back shop when Deverell saw her. She was indescribably lovely, but not very clever (tho' Swinburne thought so), but about 55? Rossetti fell in love with Mrs Morris, then a girl, daughter of an Oxford tradesman (W.D. would not mention her name, but said 'a dear friend of mine' represented 'in that picture behind you'—afterwards saying 'that is Mrs Morris'). But Morris was also in love; and Rossetti, between friendship to Morris and loyalty to Miss Siddal, gave her up. Miss Siddal was fiercely in love with Rossetti. Rossetti was good and kind to her, but neglected her a good deal. Mrs Rossetti was very unhappy.

He went on to talk of his humour—not *delicate*, but *fancy in rapid evolution*. He was never tolerant of any subject he did not feel interested in and used to put it indignantly or contemptuously away. He would talk of art, poetry, people, life, character; loathed politics.

He did not re-touch his poems much; but was a great corrector *in print*. Like Tennyson, he did not seem to realise what a poem was, until he saw it in print.

These really interesting things were sandwiched in with a lot of rot—about a girls' school at New York and a girl of Caribbean origin etc. He said to me very gravely, 'I shall *not* write the life of Gabriel. I cannot. I knew him *too well*. He told me too much about himself—day after day, year after year.'

I had intended to go earlier but we talked on. Occasionally he went to his secretaries. Before I went, we had some tea; and then he brought in two little framed pictures (Rossetti in Green Room and Kelmscott), prepared for his illustrated *Aylwin*—and the illustrated edition of *Aylwin* itself, and gave them to me, with many expressions of kindness and cordial offers of help. '*Come* and see me', he said. 'Don't write. My correspondence is a simple curse. I have thirty letters a post' (I wonder what about?).

He wrote my name in the book. He talked a good deal about Lord de Tabley, or rather a good deal of the influence he had over de Tabley! I can't understand this enigma—how this egotistical, ill-bred, little man can have established such relations with Rossetti and Swinburne. There must be something fine about him, and his extraordinary kindness is perhaps the reason. But his talk, his personal habits (dripping moustache etc) and his egotism would grate on me at every hour of the day. And yet 'he is a hero of friendship' said Rossetti.

I went out with my precious parcel; back by train in driving rain to Windsor.

> A. C. BENSON, *Edwardian Excursions*, from *The Diaries of A. C. Benson 1898–1909*, ed. David Newsome, 1981

OSCAR WILDE AT CLAPHAM JUNCTION

Everything about my tragedy has been hideous, mean, repellent, lacking in style; our very dress makes us grotesque. We are the zanies of sorrow. We are clowns whose hearts are broken. We are specially designed to appeal to the sense of humour. On November 13th, 1895, I was brought down here from London. From two o'clock till half-past two on that day I had to stand on the centre platform of Clapham Junction in convict dress, and handcuffed, for the world to look at. I had been taken out of the hospital ward without a moment's notice being given to me. Of all possible objects I was the most grotesque. When people saw me they laughed. Each train as it came up swelled the audience. Nothing could exceed their amusement. That was, of course, before they knew who I was. As soon as they had been informed they laughed still more. For half an hour I stood there in the grey November rain surrounded by a jeering mob.

For a year after that was done to me I wept every day at the same hour and for the same space of time. That is not such a tragic thing as possibly it sounds to you. To those who are in prison tears are a part of every day's experience. A day in prison on which one does not weep is a day on which one's heart is hard, not a day on which one's heart is happy.

> OSCAR WILDE, *De Profundis*, wr. 1895

The 'Louise' referred to in this extract was one of Charles Chaplin Senior's mistresses. Chaplin's biographer, David Robinson, was unable to trace her second name.

'NARCISSUS, MISS!'

The Three Stags in the Kennington Road was not a place my father frequented, yet as I passed it one evening an urge prompted me to peek inside to see if he was there. I opened the saloon door just a few inches, and there he was, sitting in the corner! I was about to leave, but his face lit up and he beckoned me to him. I was surprised at such a welcome, for he was never demonstrative. He looked very ill; his eyes were sunken, and his body had swollen to an enormous size. He rested one hand, Napoleon-like, in his waistcoat as if to ease his difficult breathing. That evening he was most solicitous, enquiring after Mother and Sydney, and before I left took me in his arms and for the first time kissed me. That was the last time I saw him alive.

Three weeks later, he was taken to St Thomas's Hospital. They had to get him drunk to get him there. When he realised where he was, he fought wildly—but he was a dying man. Though still very young, only thirty-seven, he was dying of dropsy. They tapped sixteen quarts of liquid from his knee.

Mother went several times to see him and was always saddened by the visit. She said he spoke of wanting to go back to her and start life anew in Africa. When I brightened at such a prospect, Mother shook her head, for she knew better. 'He was saying that only to be nice,' she said.

One day she came home from the hospital indignant over what the Reverend John McNeil, Evangelist, had said when he paid Father a visit: 'Well, Charlie, when I look at you, I can only think of the old proverb: "Whatsoever a man soweth, that shall he also reap".'

'Nice words to console a dying man,' said Mother. A few days later Father was dead.

The hospital wanted to know who would bury him. Mother, not having a penny, suggested the Variety Artists' Benevolent Fund, a theatrical charity organisation. This caused an uproar with the Chaplin side of the family—the humiliation of being buried by charity was repugnant to them. An Uncle Albert from Africa, my father's youngest brother, was in London at the time and said he would pay for the burial.

The day of the funeral we were to meet at St Thomas's Hospital, where we were to join the rest of the Chaplins and from there drive out to Tooting Cemetery. Sydney could not come, as he was working. Mother and I arrived at the hospital a couple of hours before the allotted time because she wanted to see Father before he was enclosed.

The coffin was enshrouded in white satin and around the edge of it, framing Father's face, were little white daisies. Mother thought they looked so simple and touching and asked who had placed them there. The attendant told her that a lady had called early that morning with a little boy. It was Louise.

In the first carriage were Mother, Uncle Albert and me. The drive to Tooting was a strain, for she had never met Uncle Albert before. He was somewhat of a dandy and spoke with a cultured accent; although polite, his attitude was icy. He was reputed to be rich; he had large horse ranches in the Transvaal and had provided the British Government with horses during the Boer War.

It poured with rain during the service; the grave-diggers threw down clods of earth on the coffin which resounded with a brutal thud. It was macabre and horrifying and I began to weep. Then the relatives threw in their wreaths and flowers. Mother, having nothing to throw in, took my precious black-bordered handkerchief. 'Here, sonny,' she whispered, 'this will do for both of us.' Afterwards the Chaplins stopped off at one of their pubs for lunch, and before leaving asked us politely where we desired to be dropped. So we were driven home.

When we returned there was not a particle of food in the cupboard except a saucer of beef dripping, and Mother had not a penny, for she had given Sydney her last twopence for his lunch money. Since Father's illness she had done little work, and now, near the end of the week, Sydney's wages of seven shillings as a telegraph boy had already run out. After the funeral we were hungry. Luckily the rag-and-bone man was passing outside and we had an old oil stove, so reluctantly she sold it for a halfpenny and bought a halfpenny worth of bread to go with the dripping.

Mother, being the legal widow of my father, was told the next day to call at the hospital for his belongings, which consisted of a black suit spotted with blood, underwear, a shirt, a black tie, an old dressing-gown, and some plaid house slippers with oranges stuffed in the toes. When she took the oranges out, a half sovereign fell out of the slippers on to the bed. This was a godsend!

For weeks I wore crêpe on my arm. These insignia of grief became profitable when I went into business on a Saturday afternoon, selling flowers. I had persuaded Mother to loan me a shilling, and went to the flower market and purchased two bundles of narcissus, and after school busied myself making them into penny bundles. All sold, I could make a hundred per cent profit.

I would go into the saloons, looking wistful, and whisper: 'Narcissus, miss!' 'Narcissus, madame!' The women always responded: 'Who is it, son?' And I would lower my voice to a whisper: 'My father,' and they would give me tips. Mother was amazed when I came home in the evening with more than five shillings for an afternoon's work. One day she bumped into me as I came out of a pub, and that put an end to my flower-selling; that her boy was peddling flowers in bar-rooms offended her Christian scruples. 'Drink killed your father, and money from such a source will only bring us bad luck,' she said. However, she kept the proceeds, though she never allowed me to sell flowers again.

CHARLES CHAPLIN, *My Autobiography*, 1964

SHERLOCK HOLMES AT WORK AND PLAY

We travelled by the Underground as far as Aldersgate; and a short walk took us to Saxe-Coburg-square, the scene of the singular story which we had listened to in the morning. It was a pokey, little, shabby-genteel place, where four lines of dingy two-storied brick houses looked out into a small railed-in enclosure, where a lawn of weedy grass, and a few clumps of faded laurel bushes made a hard fight against a smoke-laden and uncongenial atmosphere. Three gilt balls and a brown board with 'JABEZ WILSON' in white letters, upon a corner house, announced the place where our red-headed client carried on his business. Sherlock Holmes stopped in front of it with his head on one side and looked it all over, with his eyes shining brightly between puckered lids. Then he walked slowly up the street and then down again to the corner, still looking keenly at the houses. Finally he returned to the pawnbroker's, and, having thumped vigorously upon the pavement with his stick two or three times, he went up to the door and knocked. It was instantly opened by a bright-looking, clean-shaven young fellow, who asked him to step in.

'Thank you,' said Holmes, 'I only wished to ask you how you would go from here to the Strand.'

'Third right, fourth left,' answered the assistant promptly, closing the door.

'Smart fellow, that,' observed Holmes as we walked away. 'He is, in my judgment, the fourth smartest man in London, and for daring I am not sure that he has not a claim to be third. I have known something of him before.'

'Evidently,' said I, 'Mr Wilson's assistant counts for a good deal in this mystery of the Red-headed League. I am sure that you inquired your way merely in order that you might see him.'

'Not him.'

'What then?'

'The knees of his trousers.'

'And what did you see?'

'What I expected to see.'

'Why did you beat the pavement?'

'My dear Doctor, this is a time for observation, not for talk. We are spies in an enemy's country. We know something of Saxe-Coburg-square. Let us now explore the paths which lie behind it.'

The road in which we found ourselves as we turned round the corner from the retired Saxe-Coburg-square presented as great a contrast to it as the front of a picture does to the back. It was one of the main arteries which convey the traffic of the City to the north and west. The roadway was blocked with the immense stream of commerce flowing in a double tide inwards and outwards, while the footpaths were black with the hurrying swarm of pedestrians. It was difficult to realise as we looked at the line of fine shops and stately business premises that they really abutted on the other side upon the faded and stagnant square which we had just quitted.

'Let me see,' said Holmes, standing at the corner, and glancing along the line, 'I should like just to remember the order of the houses here. It is a hobby of mine to have an exact knowledge of London. There is Mortimer's, the tobacconist, the little newspaper shop, the Coburg branch of the City and Suburban Bank, the Vegetarian Restaurant, and McFarlane's carriage-building depôt. That carries us right on to the other block. And now, Doctor, we've done our work, so it's time we had some play. A sandwich, and a cup of coffee, and then off to violin-land, where all is sweetness, and delicacy, and harmony, and there are no red-headed clients to vex us with their conundrums.'

My friend was an enthusiastic musician, being himself not only a very capable performer, but a composer of no ordinary merit. All the afternoon he sat in the stalls wrapped in the most perfect happiness, gently waving his long thin fingers in time to the music, while his gently smiling face and his languid dreamy eyes were as unlike those of Holmes the sleuth-hound, Holmes the relentless, keen-witted, ready-handed criminal agent, as it was possible to conceive. In his singular character the dual nature alternately asserted itself, and his extreme exactness and astuteness represented, as I have often thought, the reaction against the poetic and contemplative mood which occasionally predominated in him. The swing of his nature took him from extreme languor to devouring energy; and, as I knew well, he was never so truly formidable as when, for days on end, he had been lounging in his armchair amid his improvisations and his black-letter editions. Then it was that the lust of the chase would suddenly come upon him, and that his brilliant reasoning power would rise to the level of intuition, until those who were unacquainted with his methods would look askance at him as on a man whose knowledge was not that of other mortals. When I saw him that afternoon so enwrapped in the music at St James's Hall I felt that an evil time might be coming upon those whom he had set himself to hunt down.

'You want to go home, no doubt, Doctor,' he remarked, as we emerged.

'Yes, it would be as well.'

'And I have some business to do which will take some hours. This business at Coburg-square is serious.'

'Why serious?'

'A considerable crime is in contemplation. I have every reason to believe that we shall be in time to stop it.'

'But to-day being Saturday rather complicates matters. I shall want your help to-night.'

'At what time?'

'Ten will be early enough.'

'I shall be at Baker-street at ten.'

'Very well. And, I say, Doctor! there may be some little danger, so kindly put your army revolver in your pocket.' He waved his hand, turned on his heel, and disappeared in an instant among the crowd.

ARTHUR CONAN DOYLE, 'The Adventure of the Red-Headed League', in *The Adventures of Sherlock Holmes*, 1892

A QUAINT CITY

Wednesday, 6 October 1897

At times, and in some fortunate aspects, London will look as quaint, picturesque, and mediaeval, as any old-world continental city. But it must be regarded with a 'fresh' eye, an eye unprejudiced by custom and associations. When I catch the town in such an aspect, I understand how the inhabitants of these old-world continental cities can be oblivious to the attractiveness which surrounds them, as they certainly are, and I suddenly see eye to eye with the appreciative foreigner in London.

This morning, as I walked through the Green Park in an October mist, it occurred to me that the sheep grazing there, and the soldiers practising flag-signals, would, if seen by me in an unfamiliar city, have constituted for me a memorable picture of pure quaintness. Then, walking in the Strand as the sun overpowered the fog, what mellow picturesque was there in the vista of churches, backed by the roofs of the Law Courts and further away a tower for all the world like the Beffroi at Bruges. Observed five hundred miles away, a scene less striking than this would be one to talk about and grow enthusiastic over, one to buy photographs of . . . But it happens to be in London.

ARNOLD BENNETT, *Journals*, 1932

PART III

THE TWENTIETH CENTURY

THE AQUARIUM

It was the first of January, 1900: New Year's Day; New Century's Day. But that portentous fact was of no interest to two little boys walking with extreme care and anxiety across Battersea Bridge at half-past three in the afternoon.

Their concern was immediate, for the elder brother, a small fellow of eleven, with a large nose, brown eyes, and a sallow skin that gave him a Spanish cast, was carrying an aquarium.

This task so occupied him that his follower, the brother who shadowed his life, and for whom he usually felt solemnly responsible, was for the moment forgotten.

This did not disturb the junior, for he too was as anxious, and as signally concentrated, as his brother. Though only seven years old, he carried the burden of life with gravity. His nose was smaller than his brother's, and it was somewhat pinched, the nostrils white and enlarged. This made the red cheeks all the more noticeable: and it may have added to the fiery light of his eyes, which were also brown.

Rather short of breath, from excitement and not from haste, he trotted along close to his brother, from time to time putting out a worried hand and grasping the elder's coat-tail, only to be shrugged off with a muttered exclamation of 'Stop it! You'll make me drop it!'

He appeared to understand this abruptness, for his brother, always sardonic even in affection, was inclined to be sharply irritable in moments of stress.

And how tense, how critical, was this particular moment! It marked a stage, a peak-point, in their lives. Both had longed, through childhood's infinity of time, for a goldfish. Their father, however, was so boyishly concerned with his own enthusiasms that he had ignored this longing. Their mother was by experience and temperament so generally apprehensive that she hesitated before committing herself, or her children, to the caring for livestock. There was already a cat in the house, and she had made this excuse for banning the buying of a goldfish. She said that the cat would hook it out of the bowl and eat it, thus adding to the general redness and toothiness of nature, under whose menace she was convinced that her two boys were doomed to fulfil their fragile destinies.

This timid philosophy, however, had been shaken by a touch of kindness; and kindness from a humble quarter. One of the father's many colleagues in the South-West District Post Office had been prematurely pensioned after having his wits permanently addled by a blow on the head from the lid of a post-van. The poor man, semi-speechless and existing in a mental vacuum, fortunately possessed a sensible wife who happened to be handsome in a pre-Raphaelite way. She got a job as caretaker in the house of the American artist Abbey, in Tite Street, Chelsea, where she lived in the spacious basement with her little daughter and her now wholly innocent husband.

The boys' father still befriended this man, for he had a strong *esprit de corps*, and appeared to be personally intimate with several hundred of his fellow mail-sorters in the red-brick building behind Victoria Street, adjoining the site where the Byzantine cathedral of Westminster was at that time being built.

Regular visits were paid to the retired comrade in the comfortable basement in Tite Street, and on occasion the two boys were taken along too, the father having a sentimental pride in his youngsters.

So it was that the craving for a goldfish became known to the wife of the stricken man. She may have spoken to her employer about it, for a message at Christmas had said that if the boys came over the river to Tite Street one afternoon, she would have a surprise for them.

That younger brother being myself, I can now recall, with envy, the shudder of excitement with which I crossed the river that day, chattering to my silent brother, who even at that time was something of an enigma, and an oracle, to me. My attitude was not unusual, for a child's world, while being timeless and spaceless, is also closely hedged-in by fear, brevity of attention, lack of association of ideas and experience, and all the rest of the unattempted potentials of the infant consciousness. . . .

Finally, our measured procedure brought us across the river to Chelsea, where at once we were in so foreign a land that I shrank closer to the side of my familiar Virgil, even daring to grasp his hand and cling to it, as we turned a little way along the Embankment, passing what seemed to me at that time the vast mansions whose inhabitants were beings so fabulous that my mind did not attempt to envisage them. I did not even think of them as rich, or high-born, for those categories had not yet reached me.

But I was not intimidated; merely nervous at the remoteness, the *difference* of this tall and silent district from the cosy, working-class streets of houses so far away across the river, my native land. Indeed, I felt some half-sense of recognition, as though a self beyond myself welcomed these huge doorways, these noble windows, recalling them as familiar to a way of life impossible to a Battersea-born child, but which I must have known.

I was half-conscious of this while we made our way to Tite Street, I still clinging to my brother's hand, though my fears were assuaged by this other sensation; dim enough, but before the afternoon ended, to be unforgettably brought forward to the front of my mind, and kept there for deeper cogitation when, later on, life brought some possible evidence to explain its genesis.

We were met at the area door by Mrs Langton, the caretaker. . . .

We walked along the basement passage, past several closed doors, and one that stood open upon a boiler-room where I could see a faint glow round the door of the furnace. The oilcloth, with a plain blue border (so different from the Greek key-pattern of the stair-covering at home), was continued up the flight of dark stairs which led to a landing, facing a door covered in green baize.

Mrs Langton pushed open this door, and ushered us on under her outstretched arm. We entered another world, like Gulliver entering the land of the giants. A vast hall soared above us, with a correspondingly vast front door at the end of it. I drew in my breath sharply. I must have given a gasp that Mrs Langton misconstrued as fear, for she bent down and kissed me, and took me by the hand, leaving my silent brother to follow us.

She approached a tall, wide door on the left, opened it by turning first the key and then the china knob, and led us into the studio.

Here was something still more gargantuan. I stopped, and Mrs Langton was forced to stop with me, so forceful was my reaction. Jack trod on my heel, and impatiently pushed me in the back. But I did not move. I stared. I stared up, into the vault, a height such as I had never seen before. I stared at the huge north-light, that sloped over part of the vaulting and then came down straight almost to floor level. A black blind was drawn *up* from the floor to about the height of my head, but a tear in it revealed the glass behind.

The sun shone on a naked tree outside, with a golden light that struck back into the studio; but it did not warm the great space, or fill the emptiness. Yet I was neither chilled nor repelled by this austerity. Looking up into the shadowy height, I felt that I was *returning* to something just right, a place where I could breathe and move without restraint.

'Oh!' I cried, in a hollow, round voice; and I flung up my arm in a gesture of magnificence that made Mrs Langton study me with surprise and amusement. She gave me a playful hug.

'What? You like it?' she said. 'This bare old place; dusty, and cold as charity?'

I didn't know what she meant by 'cold as charity', but I could see the dust, a pallid mantle on the tops of stacks of picture-frames turned to the wall; on a huge easel on four wheels; on odd chairs and stools; on a piano loaded with piles of papers, books, portfolios; on a long sofa at the other end of the studio, raised on a dais. The only object free from this indoor frost was a life-size lay-figure in a velvet robe, with a cape of brown paper pinned round the shoulders.

Mrs Langton saw me studying this.

'Sharp eyes! Sharp eyes!' she said, and squeezed my small body again. 'They don't miss much, I'll lay! But I have to keep her clean. It wouldn't seem right!' . . .

This great room slumbered in semi-darkness, for venetian blinds were drawn down, with slats half-closed, so that we saw shapes of sheeted furniture, striped with shadow. My memory of this is equally vague, but I recall some statuary, and a carved fireplace flanked by two vases taller than myself. These great pots were understandably recognised, for in our parlour at home we had two vases, on a smaller scale, that stood exactly thus, one on each side of the fireplace, like two of the oil-jars in the story of Ali Baba. I used to peer into these, imagining strange contents conjured by the faint musty smell that hovered over those circular mouths, as a whiff of smoke hangs over a sleeping volcano.

We did not remain long, staring at this twilight splendour under a shroud. Taking Mrs Langton's 'Well now!' as a signal, we followed her down to the basement, where we ceremoniously said good-bye to Mr Langton and Gracie (rather a one-sided ritual) and were led by our hostess to the area door. On a shelf beside it, where tradesmen left their goods, stood the surprise which had been promised us; the aquarium.

What puzzles me now is that instantly we knew what it was; for we had never seen goldfish in anything but small glass bowls, in the window of a shop at a cross-roads called The Latchmere, a sinister junction that always filled me with dread, perhaps because one of the radiations from it led past a candle factory, where Mr Price made his world-famous night-lights. The ugly building with its ranks of inhuman windows, and the rancid smell that sank from them over the pavements, so that they appeared to be permanently greasy and cold, like dirty plates after a dinner of mutton, must have been offensive to my virgin eyes and nostrils. I shuddered whenever I approached The Latchmere and sniffed that dull, rank odour.

We stood spellbound by the area door. Neither of us dared believe in our hope, for gifts from the outside world seldom came our way. Indeed, nothing of much account came our way from beyond the four walls of home. We were a close community of four, on guard against some invisible peril, so that all our family happiness (and it was a constant feast) had something of the Syracusan banquet at which Damocles sat beneath a naked sword suspended by a single horsehair.

Somebody had to make a move, however. It was my brother who broke the spell. His taciturnity for once gave way under pressure of this long-nurtured passion. His dark, full eyes flashed, the long lashes flickered, and he spoke.

'It's an aquarium,' he whispered. And he repeated it; teaching me something.

'Is it any use to you?' asked Mrs Langton. Her question had the intended rhetorical effect, for my brother put on his cap, and I dragged on my tasselled tam-o'-shanter, while Mrs Langton opened the door. 'Now go steady,' she said, and gave me a final hug as I followed my brother, who had seized the aquarium in his bare hands, and was groping his way up the area steps, stubbing his toes on the risers because his attention was wholly concentrated upon the precious burden, the almost holy burden.

Once he stumbled and might have fallen backwards to disaster, but was saved by his own powerful infatuation, which gave him a sixth sense, and a superhuman authority over the laws of nature, especially that of gravity.

I was also there to steady him from beneath. Thus, an uneasy tandem, we reached street level, and did not even turn to wave good-bye to Mrs Langton, who had cried out in alarm at the near-disaster on the steps. We did not realise that we had failed to thank her, an omission that haunted us later when we got home, and Mother inquired, 'And what did Mrs Langton say when you thanked her?' It was always her habit to want to know what people said, and to be given verbatim the whole of a conversation in which she had not taken part because of her absence from that particular drama. . . .

Tite Street and Chelsea Embankment were empty, and the day was dying under a shroud of frost. Through this fawn-grey world we made our way, moving with spasmodic slowness, the spasms due to bursts of eager excitement, our desire to get home safely with the aquarium, tempered by fear of dropping it.

At the back of my mind lurked a greater fear. I knew that, once across the bridge, we were likely to encounter school-fellows, bands of marauding freebooters of the Battersea gutters, ripe for any action, so long as it was destructive. I knew that the sight of a large glass aquarium in the arms of a boy somewhat more warmly dressed than themselves would rouse their hunting gusto.

For a moment, however, I was sufficiently concerned with the immediate cares. I saw the signs of strain on my brother's face. His huge nose was blue, his eyes even more cavernous than usual. He had forgotten, in his excitement, to put on his gloves before leaving, and now was unable to do so, the idea of committing the aquarium to my hands, even for a moment, being quite unrealistic.

RICHARD CHURCH, *Over the Bridge*, 1956

'A LONDON SPECIALTY'

My dear MacAlister,

We do really start next Saturday. I meant to sail earlier but waited to finish some studies of what are called Family Hotels. They are a London specialty. God has not permitted them to exist elsewhere. They are ramshackle clubs which were dwellings at the time of the Heptarchy. Dover and Albemarle Streets are filled with them. The once spacious rooms are split up into coops which afford as much discomfort as can be had anywhere out of jail for any money. All the modern inconveniences are furnished, and some that have been obsolete for a century. The prices are astonishingly high for what you get. The bedrooms are hospitals for incurable furniture. I find it so in this one. They exist upon a tradition. They represent the vanishing home-like inn of fifty years ago, and are mistaken by foreigners for it. Some quite respectable Englishmen still frequent them through inherited habit and arrested development; many Americans also, through ignorance and superstition. The rooms are as interesting as the Tower of London, but older I think. Older and dearer. The lift was a gift of William the Conqueror. Some of the beds are pre-historic. They represent geological periods.

Mine is the oldest. It is formed in strata of Old Red Sandstone, vol-canic tufa, ignis fatuus, and bicarbonate of hornblende, superimposed upon argillaceous shale, and contains the prints of prehistoric man. It is in No. 149. Thousands of scientists come to see it. They consider it holy. They want to blast out the prints but cannot. Dynamite rebounds from it.

> MARK TWAIN, letter to J. Y. M. MacAlister, September 1900, from *Selected Letters of Mark Twain*, ed. C. Neider, 1982

'A VAST AND MALODOROUS SEA'

Nowhere in the streets of London may one escape the sight of abject poverty, while five minutes' walk from almost any point will bring one to a slum; but the region my hansom was now penetrating was one unending slum. The streets were filled with a new and different race of people, short of stature, and of wretched or beer-sodden appearance. We rolled along through miles of bricks and squalor, and from each cross street and alley flashed long vistas of bricks and misery. Here and there lurched a drunken man or woman, and the air was obscene with sounds of jangling and squabbling. At a market, tottery old men and women were searching in the garbage thrown in the mud for rotten potatoes, beans, and vegetables, while little children clustered like flies around a festering mass of fruit, thrusting their arms to the shoulders into the liquid corruption, and drawing forth morsels but partially decayed, which they devoured on the spot.

Not a hansom did I meet with in all my drive, while mine was like an apparition from another and better world, the way the children ran after it and alongside. And as far as I could see were the solid walls of brick, the slimy pavements, and the screaming streets; and for the first time in my life the fear of the crowd smote me. It was like the fear of the sea; and the miserable multitudes, street upon street, seemed so many waves of a vast and malodorous sea, lapping about me and threatening to well up and over me.

JACK LONDON, *The People of the Abyss*, 1903

THE CORONATION OF EDWARD VII

It is quite impossible to describe the scene [in Westminster Abbey] at all. The galleries were very steep, so that we could all see down into the nave. Opposite me in the galleries sate mostly girls and young women. In front rows, children—minor sons of peers—nice little boys in court suits. I noticed Clifton and Roos. One little boy played so much with his gold-hilted sword that his mother took it away. Our side was mainly men—diplomats all round me: Headlam, in a magnificent coat (he told me afterwards that it was borrowed and of much too high a grade) and next me a smart young Foreign Office man. I talked to him and he said he was a Westminster boy in 87. He began to talk about the Archbishop and his cope. I said: 'My father'—it is always better to do this, I think, in case people say awkward things. He looked at me, and then said 'Well—and how's Hugh, then? I was up at Trinity with him.' I disencumbered myself of cocked hat, tickets and sword by putting them into a curve of the vaulting close by me.

Down below the costumes were very magnificent: the Knights of Orders in full robes. The red of the Bath is fine, but the Michael and George— a dark blue—even finer. There were abundance of gorgeous uniforms and academic silks. Some judges came in, and I think that a judge *moving about* looks ridiculous—like a bogy. After a bit a procession came in of men in odd copelike robes, barred with gold who stood by the choir door. These were Cinque Port Barons. It was too dark for me to recognise much. The peers and peeresses kept arriving, looking very splendid in sweeping robes, and I could see them taking their places beyond. The centre space was carpeted with rich blue, and lights burning low. The time moved slowly on—the procession of choir etc. went down to the West. Then princesses with long trains began to arrive. People stood or sate and there was loud talking. I read my book philosophically, talked or looked about and the time was not long. The sight of long-trained flashing persons sweeping up the choir steps like peacocks was very beautiful. In fact it was all so rich that it looked theatrical, as if it could not be true.

Then the Prince and Princess of Wales arrived, he looked perky and common. Then the *Queen*—most beautiful, leaning on the Bishop of Oxford's hand, he oddly bowed over it, in a stiff cope.

The choir were on both sides just to my right. I saw Lloyd [Precentor of Eton], and several eminent musicians in Doctor's Hoods. Someone—Parratt? beat time in the screen centre, which was followed by a conductor on each side, so that the music was perfect; but I heard so much of the tenors where I was, that it was not very balanced. It is of no use recounting the service. The arrival of the King was the great excitement. It was preceded by a long pause—the clergy had passed—the Archbishop walking more strongly than I had hoped.

Everyone was very nervous about the Dean. He was quite dotty. He was for ever saying in a pause—'Might not I do this? I think I might do this?' whether there was anything to do or not. He feels acutely being allowed hardly to do anything. The Archbishop is very weak on his legs, very absent in mind, and so blind that the service has all been specially printed for him in huge black letters. . . .

The service I could hardly hear at all—except odd provincial and guttural vowels from the Archbishop—here and there a word—and the King was inaudible to me, except as a kind of hoarse grunting.

The Archbishop's homage was terrible. He had already made a fearful series of mistakes in the prayers: instead of telling the King to support widows, he said 'widowers' and so forth. He made long pauses and everyone was very anxious about him. When he went to do homage, the Bishop of Winchester said, he could not rise after kneeling. He made one or two attempts and fell half over backwards and sideways. The King caught his hands and tried to pull him up. Several people said that they thought he was kissing the Archbishop's hand (I believe he *did* kiss the Abp.'s hand). Then he said hurriedly to the bishops near him 'You had better help him, I think.' So they closed in and got him up, but his legs gave way under him like a doll's legs, and they had to carry him by main force to his chair. The Bishop of Winchester went and said 'Can I get you

anything? There is some sal volatile close at hand.' To which, in a loud
voice, the Archbishop said 'No! I don't want anything at all. Go away—
I'm all right'—and so he was. He said afterwards at tea that he was not
faint, but simply his legs failed him; age had attacked him there. He
added 'I had made up my mind to get up on my *right* leg, and they
pulled me over on to my left leg. It was kindly meant, but upset me.'

Further disasters were in store. The moment the ceremony was over
and the King withdrew into his Robing-room to divest himself of some
of the masses of drapery, the Archbishop was asked, at his command, to
come in to the ante-room and rest. 'I went in', said the Archbishop, 'and
took the only chair in the room. In a moment I smelt the steam of broth.
The King had sent me a cup of soup, which I drank. Then he came in
himself to ask me how I felt, and in getting out of the chair I nearly fell
down—and I could not stand.'

But the worst of all was in the Communion. He could not see where
the King was, and went to quite the wrong place to administer and
nearly put the bread on the carpet. He was guided right. The King
looked frightfully nervous at the Archbishop's movements.

The service slowly proceeded. The flare up of the light when the King
was crowned was very fine, but it made it feel more theatrical than ever.
Then came the processions away. As before, the Queen looked lovely and
the crown suited, not so the King. The crown looked too big and heavy.
He looked like one of the Kings in *Through the Looking-Glass.* My own
little contribution, the words to the Kaiser-march, was spoilt because the
Choir were so anxious to see the King depart that they did not attend
or sing, and the result was awfully feeble. . . .

I got out about 3.30 and went to Barton St, where they were at
lunch—very hungry and tired—but revived as soon as I had taken off my
tight robes and shoes. I went off to club to read and smoke. Coming back
down Whitehall it was pleasant to see the crowds. They were serious,
interested, not amused, no rowdiness, just silently parading. I was in a
hansom and we had to go at a fool's pace. There was a sea of heads with
a distant hansom wading through. But the order and gravity were very
nice; and there has been no disorder at all.

When I turned into Barton St, about a dozen *gamins* had made up a
game of cricket in the street, coats for wickets, and were gravely playing
as if there was nothing else to do and the street belonged to them. (I
could not make out how some of the people got in to the Coronation.

Just below me were two very bourgeois people in morning dress, like a tradesman and wife, who ate peppermints and looked horribly out of place. But I fancy that there were many vacant places and people were almost compelled to come in.)

A. C. BENSON, *Edwardian Excursions*, from *The Diaries of A. C. Benson 1898–1909*, ed. David Newsome, 1981

AN UNLUCKY WAGER

Thursday, 13 December 1917

I was told the following at dinner last night. Two working men were in the Tube and began arguing whether a certain peculiarly dressed person in the same carriage was or was not the Archbishop of Canterbury. They bet. To settle it one of them went up to the person and said, 'Please, sir, are you the Archbishop of Canterbury?' The reply was: 'What the bloody hell has that got to do with you?' The workman went back to his mate and said: 'No good, mate. The old cow won't give me a straight answer either way.'

ARNOLD BENNETT, *Journals*, 1932

LONDON SNOW

When men were all asleep the snow came flying,
In large white flakes falling on the city brown,
Stealthily and perpetually settling and loosely lying,
    Hushing the latest traffic of the drowsy town;
Deadening, muffling, stifling its murmurs failing;
Lazily and incessantly floating down and down:
    Silently sifting and veiling road, roof and railing;
Hiding difference, making unevenness even,
Into angles and crevices softly drifting and sailing.
    All night it fell, and when full inches seven
It lay in the depth of its uncompacted lightness,
The clouds blew off from a high and frosty heaven;
    And all woke earlier for the unaccustomed brightness
Of the winter dawning, the strange unheavenly glare:

The eye marvelled—marvelled at the dazzling whiteness;
    The ear hearkened to the stillness of the solemn air;
No sound of wheel rumbling nor of foot falling,
And the busy morning cries came thin and spare.
    Then boys I heard, as they went to school, calling,
They gathered up the crystal manna to freeze
Their tongues with tasting, their hands with snowballing;
    Or rioted in a drift, plunging up to the knees;
Or peering up from under the white-mossed wonder,
'O look at the trees!' they cried, 'O look at the trees!'
    With lessened load a few carts creak and blunder,
Following along the white deserted way,
A country company long dispersed asunder:
    When now already the sun, in pale display
Standing by Paul's high dome, spread forth below
His sparkling beams, and awoke the stir of the day.
    For now doors open, and war is waged with the snow;
And trains of sombre men, past tale of number,
Tread long brown paths, as toward their toil they go:
    But even for them awhile no cares encumber
Their minds diverted; the daily word is unspoken,
The daily thoughts of labour and sorrow slumber
At the sight of the beauty that greets them, for the charm
    they have broken.

ROBERT BRIDGES (1844–1930)

KIPPS LOSES HIS SOCIAL AMBITIONS

Kipps endured splendour at the Royal Grand Hotel for three nights and
days, and then he retreated in disorder. The Royal Grand defeated and
overcame and routed Kipps not of intention, but by sheer royal grandeur,
grandeur combined with an organization for his comfort carried to
excess. On his return he came upon a difficulty, he had lost his circular
piece of cardboard with the number of his room, and he drifted about the
hall and passages in a state of perplexity for some time, until he thought
all the porters and officials in gold lace caps must be watching him, and
jesting to one another about him. Finally, in a quiet corner down below

near the hairdresser's shop, he found a kindly-looking personage in bottle green, to whom he broached his difficulty. 'I say,' he said, with a pleasant smile, 'I can't find my room nohow.' The personage in bottle green, instead of laughing in a nasty way, as he might well have done, became extremely helpful, showed Kipps what to do, got his key, and conducted him by lift and passage to his chamber. Kipps tipped him half a crown.

Safe in his room, Kipps pulled himself together for dinner. He had learnt enough from young Walshingham to bring his dress clothes, and now he began to assume them. Unfortunately in the excitement of his flight from his Aunt and Uncle he had forgotten to put in his other boots, and he was some time deciding between his purple cloth slippers with a golden marigold and the prospect of cleaning the boots he was wearing with the towel, but finally, being a little footsore, he took the slippers.

Afterwards, when he saw the porters and waiters and the other guests catch sight of the slippers, he was sorry he had not chosen the boots. However, to make up for any want of style at that end, he had his crush hat under his arm.

He found the dining-room without excessive trouble. It was a vast and splendidly decorated place, and a number of people, evidently quite *au fait*, were dining there at little tables lit with electric red-shaded candles, gentlemen in evening dress, and ladies with dazzling astonishing necks. Kipps had never seen evening dress in full vigour before, and he doubted his eyes. And there were also people not in evening dress, who no doubt wondered what noble family Kipps represented. There was a band in a decorated recess, and the band looked collectively at the purple slippers, and so lost any chance they may have had of a donation so far as Kipps was concerned. The chief drawback to this magnificent place was the excessive space of floor that had to be crossed before you got your purple slippers hidden under a table.

He selected a little table—not the one where a rather impudent-looking waiter held a chair, but another—sat down, and, finding his gibus in his hand, decided after a moment of thought to rise slightly and sit on it. (It was discovered in his abandoned chair at a late hour by a supper-party and restored to him next day.)

He put the napkin carefully on one side, selected his soup without difficulty, 'Clear please,' but he was rather floored by the presentation of a quite splendidly bound wine-card. He turned it over, discovered a section devoted to whisky, and had a bright idea.

''Ere,' he said to the waiter, with an encouraging movement of the head; and then in a confidential manner, 'You 'aven't any Old Methuselah Three Stars, 'ave you?'

The waiter went away to inquire, and Kipps went on with his soup with an enhanced self-respect. Finally, Old Methuselah being unattainable, he ordered a claret from about the middle of the list. 'Let's 'ave some of this,' he said. He knew claret was a good sort of wine.

'A half bottle?' said the waiter.

'Right you are,' said Kipps.

He felt he was getting on. He leant back after his soup, a man of the world, and then slowly brought his eyes round to the ladies in evening dress on his right. . . .

He couldn't have thought it!

They were scorchers. Jest a bit of black velvet over the shoulders!

He looked again. One of them was laughing with a glass of wine half raised—wicked-looking woman she was; the other, the black velvet one, was eating bits of bread with nervous quickness and talking fast.

He wished old Buggins could see them.

He found a waiter regarding him and blushed deeply. He did not look again for some time, and became confused about his knife and fork over the fish. Presently he remarked a lady in pink to the left of him eating the fish with an entirely different implement.

It was over the *vol au vent* that he began to go to pieces. He took a knife to it; then saw the lady in pink was using a fork only, and hastily put down his knife, with a considerable amount of rich creaminess on the blade, upon the cloth. Then he found that a fork in his inexperienced hand was an instrument of chase rather than capture. His ears became violently red, and then he looked up to discover the lady in pink glancing at him, and then smiling, as she spoke to the man beside her.

He hated the lady in pink very much.

He stabbed a large piece of the *vol au vent* at last, and was too glad of his luck not to make a mouthful of it. But it was an extensive fragment, and pieces escaped him. Shirt-front! 'Desh it!' he said, and had resort to his spoon. His waiter went and spoke to two other waiters, no doubt jeering at him. He became very fierce suddenly. ''Ere!' he said, gesticulating; and then, 'Clear this away!'

The entire dinner-party on his right, the party of the ladies in advanced evening dress, looked at him. . . . He felt that every one was watching him and making fun of him, and the injustice of this angered him. After all, they had had every advantage he hadn't. And then, when they got him there doing his best, what must they do but glance and sneer and nudge one another. He tried to catch them at it, and then took refuge in a second glass of wine.

Suddenly and extraordinarily he found himself a Socialist. He did not care how close it was to the lean years when all these things would end.

Mutton came with peas. He arrested the hand of the waiter. 'No peas,' he said. He knew something of the danger and difficulty of eating peas. Then, when the peas went away, he was embittered again. . . . Echoes of Masterman's burning rhetoric began to reverberate in his mind. Nice lot of people these were to laugh at any one! Women half undressed—It was that made him so beastly uncomfortable. How could one eat one's dinner with people about him like that? Nice lot they were. He was glad he wasn't one of them anyhow. Yes, they might look. He resolved, if they looked at him again, he would ask one of the men who he was staring at. His perturbed and angry face would have concerned any one. The band, by an unfortunate accident, was playing truculent military music. The mental change Kipps underwent was, in its way, what psychologists call a conversion. In a few moments all Kipps' ideals were changed. He who had been 'practically a gentleman,' the sedulous pupil of Coote, the punctilious raiser of hats, was instantly a rebel, an outcast, the hater of everything 'stuck up,' the foe of Society and the social order of to-day. Here they were among the profits of their robbery, these people who might do anything with the world. . . .

'No thenks,' he said to a dish.

He addressed a scornful eye at the shoulders of the lady to his left.

Presently he was refusing another dish. He didn't like it—fussed-up food! Probably cooked by some foreigner. He finished up his wine and his bread. . . .

'No, thenks.'

'No, thenks.'. . . .

He discovered the eye of a diner fixed curiously upon his flushed face. He responded with a glare. Couldn't he go without things if he liked?

'What's this?' said Kipps, to a great green cone.

'Ice,' said the waiter.

'I'll 'ave some,' said Kipps.

He seized fork and spoon and assailed the bombe. It cut rather stiffly. 'Come up!' said Kipps, with concentrated bitterness, and the truncated summit of the bombe flew off suddenly, travelling eastward with remarkable velocity. Flop, it went upon the floor a yard away, and for a while time seemed empty.

At the adjacent table they were laughing altogether.

Shy the rest of the bombe at them?

Flight?

At any rate, a dignified withdrawal.

'No!' said Kipps, 'no more,' arresting the polite attempt of the waiter to serve him with another piece. He had a vague idea he might carry off the affair as though he meant the ice to go on the floor—not liking ice, for example, and being annoyed at the badness of his dinner. He put both hands on the table, thrust back his chair, disengaged a purple slipper from his napkin, and rose. He stepped carefully over the prostrate ice, kicked the napkin under the table, thrust his hands deep into his pockets, and marched out—shaking the dust of the place as it were from his feet. He left behind him a melting fragment of ice upon the floor, his gibus hat, warm and compressed in his chair, and, in addition, every social ambition he had ever entertained in the world.

H. G. WELLS, *Kipps*, 1905

A BALLAD OF LONDON

Ah, London! London! our delight,
Great flower that opens but at night,
Great City of the Midnight Sun,
Whose day begins when day is done.

Lamp after lamp against the sky
Opens a sudden beaming eye,
Leaping alight on either hand,
The iron lilies of the Strand.

Like dragonflies, the hansoms hover,
With jewelled eyes, to catch the lover;
The streets are full of lights and loves,
Soft gowns, and flutter of soiled doves.

The human moths about the light
Dash and cling close in dazed delight,
And burn and laugh, the world and wife,
For this is London, this is life!

Upon thy petals butterflies,
But at thy root, some say, there lies
A world of weeping trodden things,
Poor worms that have not eyes or wings.

From out corruption of their woe
Springs this bright flower that charms us so,
Men die and rot deep out of sight
To keep this jungle-flower bright.

Paris and London, World-Flowers twain
Wherewith the World-Tree blooms again,
Since Time hath gathered Babylon,
And withered Rome still withers on.

Sidon and Tyre were such as ye,
How bright they shone upon the Tree!
But Time hath gathered, both are gone,
And no man sails to Babylon.

Ah, London! London! our delight,
For thee, too, the eternal night,
And Circe Paris hath no charm
To stay Time's unrelenting arm.

Time and his moths shall eat up all.
Your chiming towers proud and tall
He shall most utterly abase,
And set a desert in their place.

RICHARD LE GALLIENNE (1866–1947)

Henry Irving was the first actor to be knighted, and thus to achieve complete social respectability. Max Beerbohm described his funeral in Westminster Abbey in a letter to the actress Florence Kahn, whom he later married.

IRVING'S FUNERAL

Very dear little friend,

How are you? I haven't heard from you since I wrote. Is Lady Macbeth stalking into the foreground of your thoughts? I have had a very theatrical morning—the most theatrical of my life: poor Irving's funeral in

Westminster Abbey. All the young and old actors and actresses there, and making such a show of suppressed emotion, with the sense that the whole Abbey's eyes were upon them, and comporting themselves with such terrific grace and seemliness. And outside the Abbey, hawkers innumerable selling penny-mementoes of 'the late Irving'—driving their own humbler trade over the tomb. And, as I jumped into a hansom, 'Don't forget the linkman today, sir. He's been *very* attentive.' Funerals ought not to be held in so commercial a place as London; and 'the histrionic temperament', moreover, mars them—what a blessing for you, dear, that you, with all your power for acting, haven't got what one calls 'the histrionic temperament' in private life. Write to me, please

MAX

MAX BEERBOHM, letter to Florence Kahn, 20 October 1905, from *The Letters of Max Beerbohm 1892–1956*, ed. Rupert Hart-Davis, 1988

A TOPOGRAPHICAL MYSTERY

Such was the house, the household, and the business Mr Verloc left behind him on his way westward at the hour of half past ten in the morning. It was unusually early for him; his whole person exhaled the charm of almost dewy freshness; he wore his blue cloth overcoat unbuttoned; his boots were shiny; his cheeks, freshly shaven, had a sort of gloss; and even his heavy-lidded eyes, refreshed by a night of peaceful slumber, sent out glances of comparative alertness. Through the park railings these glances beheld men and women riding in the Row, couples cantering past harmoniously, others advancing sedately at a walk, loitering groups of three or four, solitary horsemen looking unsociable, and solitary women followed at a long distance by a groom with a cockade to his hat and a leather belt over his tight-fitting coat. Carriages went bowling by, mostly two-horse broughams, with here and there a victoria with the skin of some wild beast inside and a woman's face and hat emerging above the folded hood. And a peculiarly London sun—against which nothing could be said except that it looked bloodshot—glorified all this by its stare. It hung at a moderate elevation above Hyde Park Corner with an air of punctual and benign vigilance. The very pavement under Mr Verloc's feet had an old-gold tinge in that diffused light, in which neither wall, nor tree, nor beast, nor man cast a shadow. Mr Verloc was going westward through a town without shadows in an atmosphere of powdered old gold. There were red, coppery gleams on the roofs of houses, on the corners of walls, on the panels of carriages, on the very coats of the horses, and on the broad back of Mr Verloc's overcoat, where they produced a dull effect of rustiness. But Mr Verloc was not in the least conscious of having got rusty. He surveyed through the park railings the evidences of the town's opulence and luxury with an approving eye. All these people had to be protected. Protection is the first necessity of opulence and luxury. They had to be protected; and their horses, carriages, houses, servants had to be protected; and the source of their wealth had to be protected in the heart of the city and the heart of the country; the whole social order favourable to their hygienic idleness had to be protected against the shallow enviousness of unhygienic labour. It had to—and Mr Verloc would have rubbed his hands with satisfaction had he not been constitutionally averse from every superfluous exertion. His idleness was not hygienic, but it suited him very well. He was in a manner devoted to it with a sort of inert fanaticism, or perhaps rather with a fanatical inertness. Born of industrious parents for a life of toil, he had embraced indolence from an impulse as profound as inexplicable and as imperious as the impulse which directs a man's preference for one particular woman in a given thousand. He was too lazy even for a mere demagogue, for a workman orator, for a leader of labour. It was too much trouble. He required a more perfect form of ease; or it might have been that he was the victim of a philosophical unbelief in the effectiveness of every human effort. Such a form of indolence requires, implies, a certain amount of intelligence. Mr Verloc was not devoid of intelligence—and at the notion of a menaced social order he would perhaps have winked to himself if there had not been an effort to make in that sign of scepticism. His big, prominent eyes were not well adapted to winking. They were rather of the sort that closes solemnly in slumber with majestic effect.

Undemonstrative and burly in a fat-pig style, Mr Verloc, without either rubbing his hands with satisfaction or winking sceptically at his thoughts, proceeded on his way. He trod the pavement heavily with his shiny boots, and his general get-up was that of a well-to-do mechanic in business for himself. He might have been anything from a picture-frame maker to a locksmith; an employer of labour in a small way. But there was also about him an indescribable air which no mechanic could have acquired in the practice of his handicraft however dishonestly exercised: the air common to men who live on the vices, the follies, or the baser fears of mankind; the air of moral nihilism common to keepers of gambling hells and disorderly houses; to private detectives and inquiry agents; to drink sellers and, I should say, to the sellers of invigorating electric belts and to the inventors of patent medicines. But of that last I am not sure, not having carried my investigations so far into the depths. For all I know, the expression of these last may be perfectly diabolic. I shouldn't be surprised. What I want to affirm is that Mr Verloc's expression was by no means diabolic.

Before reaching Knightsbridge, Mr Verloc took a turn to the left out of the busy main thoroughfare, uproarious with the traffic of swaying omnibuses and trotting vans, in the almost silent, swift flow of hansoms. Under his hat, worn with a slight backward tilt, his hair had been carefully brushed into respectful sleekness; for his business was with an embassy. And Mr Verloc, steady like a rock—a soft kind of rock— marched now along a street which could with every propriety be described as private. In its breadth, emptiness, and extent it had the majesty of inorganic nature, of matter that never dies. The only reminder of mortality was a doctor's brougham arrested in august solitude close to the kerbstone. The polished knockers of the doors gleamed as far as the eye could reach, the clean windows shone with a dark opaque lustre. And all was still. But a milk cart rattled noisily across the distant perspective; a butcher boy, driving with the noble recklessness of a charioteer at Olympic Games, dashed round the corner sitting high above a pair of red wheels. A guilty-looking cat issuing from under the stones ran for a while in front of Mr Verloc, then dived into another basement; and a thick police constable, looking a stranger to every emotion, as if he, too, were part of inorganic nature, surging apparently out of a lamp-post, took not the slightest notice of Mr Verloc. With a turn to the left Mr Verloc pursued his way along a narrow street by the side of a yellow wall which, for some inscrutable reason, had No. 1 Chesham Square written on it in black letters. Chesham Square was at least sixty yards away, and Mr Verloc, cosmopolitan enough not to be deceived by London's topographical mysteries, held on steadily, without a sign of surprise or indignation. At last, with business-like persistency, he reached the Square, and made diagonally for the number 10. This belonged to an imposing carriage gate in a high, clean wall between two houses, of which one rationally enough bore the number 9 and the other was numbered 37; but the fact that this last belonged to Porthill Street, a street well known in the neighbourhood, was proclaimed by an inscription placed above the ground-floor windows by whatever highly efficient authority is charged with the duty of keeping track of London's strayed houses. Why powers are not asked of Parliament (a short Act would do) for compelling those edifices to return where they belong is one of the mysteries of municipal administration. Mr Verloc did not trouble his head about it, his mission in life being the protection of the social mechanism, not its perfectionment or even its criticism.

JOSEPH CONRAD, *The Secret Agent*, 1907

The novelist Italo Svevo, whose real name was Ettore Schmitz, worked in his father-in-law's paint business, in which capacity—as a salesman—he lived and worked in London for a time. This letter, to his wife, is in the language he was briefly taught by James Joyce in his native Trieste.

'WHAT A REST DEAR ME!'

He came to like England and to be fascinated by it, but never got used to it. He continued to go about London, he said, in a state of astonishment, muttering 'Splendid!', 'Colossal!', 'Appalling!' It was a long while before he visited the West End at all, and when he did finally go to a matinée at the Coliseum and then made his way towards Piccadilly in search of his favourite 'Sultan' cigarettes, it was such a labour, and he had to ask the way of so many policemen, that he half decided never to try it again. He wrote a description, again in English, of a later expedition to the West End by horse-tram:

Charlton, 3 August 1908.

My dear own darling,

. . . On Saturday evening I went to the Colyseum. We coosed this theatre because it is quite closed to Charing Cross. No special or interesting things were performed there and before midnight we fell asleep in our beds at Carlton-Disjunction like I call it. On Sunday morning we were again busy in the factory with our engines. At three o'clock p.m. Nicoletto, his bride and me went to Greenwich by the usual horse-Tramway still existing from Church-Lane. I wanted to go through the Tunnel on the other side of the river to take there the electric Tramway and go to Westminster, a drive you already know. When we left the

Horse-Tramway, we found awaiting us an electric car going straightway to Charing Cross. Well, it was all I wanted. The drive is more pleasant than that through gloomy White Chapel and you stop on the Strand. It was the first time I had a drive through London. London externally has changed very much. I fear that some of her changed features will not agree with you. You liked especially to see such a big traffic well regulated; in such a noise and movement you felt your life sure protected by the police and by every driver himself. That is quite changed. The traffic—it appears to me—has been increased still. It was on a Sunday, the day of rest. What a rest dear me! You see one street filled with carriages and buses and one or two horses, poor beasts feeling quite lonely in the crowded street. The smell is terrible; they say it is healthier then the smell of horses but quite sure it is not very pleasant. What may not be very healthy is to be injured by a motor-car or a motor-bus. It seems that at every moment the drivers loose control of their engines and every day the coronee has to held an inquest on the body of some killed man. The Londoners—like always— grumble about such a state of things but they are so many, you know, that they think it is a better thing to improve the life of several millions of living persons than to save the life of a few hundreds. We took a Horse-Bus and went to Hide-Park to the Preachers-Corner where I have like alwais my little lesson of Cockney. Afterwards we took the Tube (three pennies tube) and went to Vienna-Coffee where Miss Nell and Nicoletto had a tea and I a cup of coffee. At Charing Cross we saw a motor-bus going to Lewisham and we took our seats at the topo of it. It is something like the crossing of the Channel when there are moderate breezes. I was almost seasick. When they stopo they are obliged like all buses to clear the middle part of the road and to approach the pavement always the lowest part of the street and you believe always to be smashed to the approaching houses. . . .

What amusements and social life they had were almost all local. Svevo became a fan of Charlton Athletic and he frequented the local cinema, where his deafening laugh made the rest of the audience giggle. He also formed a chamber trio with the Charlton postmistress, Miss Streeter, and her brother.

P. N. FURBANK, Italo Svevo: The Man and the Writer, 1966

ANDRÉ DERAIN

'I always associate with London much of my early happiness and the fun that I got out of life before the First World War.' He told us that he had spent many delightful hours wandering about London, popping into pubs and frequenting the music halls, which had evidently made a great impression on him. He had also discovered Wapping; there it didn't matter in the least if you were a foreigner, you always found sympathy and amusement. In the Pool of London, too, he had come across those gaily coloured steamers that appear in several of his Fauve paintings. He reminisced gently about meals at the Cheshire Cheese and related how on one occasion he had made Picasso eat so much steak and oyster pudding and toasted cheese that the latter fell ill and jokingly accused Derain of trying to poison him.

London had not only stimulated his imagination with its gusto and local colour; it was clear that the museums had meant much to him. He told us that in 1905 he had studied primitive art in the British Museum and began to be interested in negro sculpture; and this, he added, before any of the others. He still kept many examples of negro sculpture in his collection (and very fine ones they were, especially the Benin heads), but he was no longer interested in them now that they had ceased to stir by their emotional impact alone and had become a subject for classification. Yes, he continued, London presented a dazzling spectacle to the painter, and who could forget Hyde Park with its horsemen and nursemaids?

ANDRÉ DERAIN, conversation with Denys Sutton, from G. Grigson, *Britain Observed*, 1975

'MOULTING'

21 April 1911
London. Palace Theatre. Pavlova dancing the dying swan. Feather falls off her dress. Two silent Englishmen. One says, 'Moulting'. That is all they say.

ARNOLD BENNETT, *Journals*, 1932

LONDRES

Après avoir aimé des yeux dans Burlington Arcade,
Je redescends Piccadilly à pied, doucement.
O bouffées de printemps mêlées à des odeurs d'urine,
Entre les grilles du Green Park et la station des cabs,
Combien vous êtes émouvantes!

Puis, je suis Rotten Row, vers Kensington, plus calme,
Moins en poésie, moins sous le charme
De ces couleurs, de ces odeurs et de ce grondement de Londres.
(O Johnson, je comprends ton cœur, savant Docteur,
Ce cœur tout résonnant des bruits de la grand'ville:
L'horizon de Fleet Street suffisait à tes yeux.)

O jardins verts et bleus, brouillards blancs, voiles mauves!
Barrant l'eau de platine morne du Bassin,
Qui dort sous l'impalpable gaze d'une riche brume,
Le long sillage d'un oiseau d'eau couleur de rouille . . .
Il y a la Tamise, que Madame d'Aulnoy
Trouvait «un des plus beaux cours d'eau du monde».
Ses personnages historiques y naviguaient, l'été,
Au soir tombant, froissant le reflet blanc
Des premières étoiles;
Et les barges, tendues de soie, chargées de princes
Et de dames couchés sur les carreaux brodés,
Et Buckingham et les menines de la Reine,
S'avançaient doucement, comme un rêve, sur l'eau,
Ou comme notre cœur se bercerait longtemps
Aux beaux rythmes des vers royaux d'Albert Samain.
La rue luisante où tout se mire;
Le bus multicolore, le cab noir, la girl en rose
Et même un peu de soleil couchant, on dirait . . .
Les toits lavés, le square bleuâtre et tout fumant . . .
Les nuages de cuivre sali qui s'élèvent lentement . . .
Accalmie et tiédeur humide, et odeur de miel du tabac;
La dorure de ce livre
Devient plus claire à chaque instant: un essai de soleil sans doute.
(Trop tard, la nuit le prendra fatalement.)
Et voici qu'éclate l'orgue de Barbarie après l'averse.

                                    VALERY LARBAUD (1881–1957)

THE FLOWER-GIRL AND THE NOTE-TAKER

*Covent Garden at 11.15 p.m. Torrents of heavy summer rain. Cab whistles
blowing frantically in all directions. Pedestrians running for shelter into the
market and under the portico of St Paul's Church, where there are already several*

people, among them a lady and her daughter in evening dress. They are all peering out gloomily at the rain, except one man with his back turned to the rest, who seems wholly preoccupied with a notebook in which he is writing busily.

The church clock strikes the first quarter.

The Daughter [*in the space between the central pillars, close to the one on her left*]. I'm getting chilled to the bone. What can Freddy be doing all this time? Hes been gone twenty minutes.

The Mother [*on her daughter's right*]. Not so long. But he ought to have got us a cab by this.

A Bystander [*on the lady's right*]. He wont get no cab not until half-past eleven, missus, when they come back after dropping their theatre fares.

The Mother. But we must have a cab. We cant stand here until half-past eleven. It's too bad.

The Bystander. Well, it aint my fault, missus.

The Daughter. If Freddy had a bit of gumption, he would have got one at the theatre door.

The Mother. What could he have done, poor boy?

The Daughter. Other people got cabs. Why couldnt he? *Freddy rushes in out of the rain from the Southampton Street side, and comes between them closing a dripping umbrella. He is a young man of twenty, in evening dress, very wet round the ankles.*

The Daughter. Well, havnt you got a cab?

Freddy. Theres not one to be had for love or money.

The Mother. Oh, Freddy, there must be one. You cant have tried.

The Daughter. It's too tiresome. Do you expect us to go and get one ourselves?

Freddy. I tell you theyre all engaged. The rain was so sudden: nobody was prepared; and everybody had to take a cab. Ive been to Charing Cross one way and nearly to Ludgate Circus the other; and they were all engaged.

The Mother. Did you try Trafalgar Square?

Freddy. There wasnt one at Trafalgar Square.

The Daughter. Did you try?

Freddy. I tried as far as Charing Cross Station. Did you expect me to walk to Hammersmith?

The Daughter. You havnt tried at all.

The Mother. You really are very helpless, Freddy. Go again; and dont come back until you have found a cab.

Freddy. I shall simply get soaked for nothing.

The Daughter. And what about us? Are we to stay here all night in this draught, with next to nothing on. You selfish pig—

Freddy. Oh, very well: I'll go, I'll go. [*He opens his umbrella and dashes off Strandwards, but comes into collision with a flower girl, who is hurrying in for shelter, knocking her basket out of her hands. A blinding flash of lightning, followed instantly by a rattling peal of thunder, orchestrates the incident.*]

The Flower Girl. Nah then, Freddy: look wh' y' gowin, deah.

Freddy. Sorry [*he rushes off*].

The Flower Girl [*picking up her scattered flowers and replacing them in the basket*]. Theres menners f'yer! Te-oo banches o voylets trod into the mad. [*She sits down on the plinth of the column, sorting her flowers, on the lady's right. She is not at all an attractive person. She is perhaps eighteen, perhaps twenty, hardly older. She wears a little sailor hat of black straw that has long been exposed to the dust and soot of London and has seldom if ever been brushed. Her hair needs washing rather badly: its mousy color can hardly be natural. She wears a shoddy black coat that reaches nearly to her knees and is shaped to her waist. She has a brown skirt with a coarse apron. Her boots are much the worse for wear. She is no doubt as clean as she can afford to be; but compared to the ladies she is very dirty. Her features are no worse than theirs; but their condition leaves something to be desired; and she needs the services of a dentist.*]

The Mother. How do you know that my son's name is Freddy, pray?

The Flower Girl. Ow, eez ye-ooa san, is e? Wal, fewd dan y' de-ooty bawmz a mather should, eed now bettern to spawl a pore gel's flahrzn than ran awy athaht pyin. Will ye-oo py me f'them? [*Here, with apologies, this desperate attempt to represent her dialect without a phonetic alphabet must be abandoned as unintelligible outside London.*]

The Daughter. Do nothing of the sort, mother. The idea!

The Mother. Please allow me, Clara. Have you any pennies?

The Daughter. No. Ive nothing smaller than sixpence.

The Flower Girl [*hopefully*]. I can give you change for a tanner, kind lady.

The Mother [*to Clara*]. Give it to me. [*Clara parts reluctantly.*] Now [*to the girl*]. This is for your flowers.

The Flower Girl. Thank you kindly, lady.

The Daughter. Make her give you the change. These things are only a penny a bunch.

The Mother. Do hold your tongue, Clara. [*To the girl.*] You can keep the change.

The Flower Girl. Oh, thank you, lady.

The Mother. Now tell me how you know that young gentleman's name.

The Flower Girl. I didnt.

The Mother. I heard you call him by it. Dont try to deceive me.

The Flower Girl [*protesting*]. Whos trying to deceive you? I called him Freddy or Charlie same as you might yourself if you was talking to a stranger and wished to be pleasant. [*She sits down beside her basket.*]

The Daughter. Sixpence thrown away! Really, mamma, you might have spared Freddy that. [*She retreats in disgust behind the pillar.*]

    An elderly gentleman of the amiable military type rushes into shelter, and closes a dripping umbrella. He is in the same plight as Freddy, very wet about the ankles. He is in evening dress, with a light overcoat. He takes the place left vacant by the daughter's retirement.

The Gentleman. Phew!

The Mother [*to the gentleman*]. Oh, sir, is there any sign of its stopping?

The Gentleman. I'm afraid not. It started worse than ever about two minutes ago. [*He goes to the plinth beside the flower girl; puts up his foot on it; and stoops to turn down his trouser ends.*]

The Mother. Oh dear! [*She retires sadly and joins her daughter.*]

The Flower Girl [*taking advantage of the military gentleman's proximity to establish friendly relations with him*]. If it's worse, it's a sign it's nearly over. So cheer up, Captain; and buy a flower off a poor girl.

The Gentleman. I'm sorry. I havnt any change.

The Flower Girl. I can give you change, Captain.

The Gentleman. For a sovereign? Ive nothing less.

The Flower Girl. Garn! Oh do buy a flower off me, Captain. I can change half-a-crown. Take this for tuppence.

The Gentleman. Now dont be troublesome: theres a good girl. [*Trying his pockets.*] I really havnt any change—Stop: heres three hapence, if thats any use to you. [*He retreats to the other pillar.*]

The Flower Girl [*disappointed, but thinking three halfpence better than nothing*]. Thank you, sir.

The Bystander [*to the girl*]. You be careful: give him a flower for it. Theres a bloke here behind taking down every blessed word youre saying. [*All turn to the man who is taking notes.*]

The Flower Girl [*springing up terrified*]. I aint done nothing wrong by speaking to the gentleman. Ive a right to sell flowers if I keep off the kerb. [*Hysterically*] I'm a respectable girl: so help me, I never spoke to him except to ask him to buy a flower off me. [*General hubbub, mostly sympathetic to the flower girl, but deprecating her excessive sensibility. Cries of* Dont start hollerin. Whos hurting you? Nobody's going to touch you. Whats the good of fussing? Steady on. Easy easy, *etc., come from the elderly staid spectators, who pat her comfortingly. Less patient ones bid her shut her head, or ask her roughly what is wrong with her. A remoter group, not knowing what the matter is, crowd in and increase the noise with question and answer:* Whats the row? Whatshe do? Where is he? A tec taking her down. What! him? Yes: him over there: Took money off the gentleman, *etc. The flower girl, distraught and mobbed, breaks through them to the gentleman, crying wildly.*] Oh, sir, dont let him charge me. You dunno what it means to me. Theyll take away my character and drive me on the streets for speaking to gentlemen. They—

The Note Taker [*coming forward on her right, the rest crowding after him*]. There, there, there, there! whos hurting you, you silly girl? What do you take me for?

The Bystander. It's all right: hes a gentleman: look at his boots. [*Explaining to the note taker.*] She thought you was a copper's nark, sir.

The Note Taker [*with quick interest*]. Whats a copper's nark?

The Bystander [*inapt at definition*]. It's a—well, it's a copper's nark, as you might say. What else would you call it? A sort of informer.

The Flower Girl [*still hysterical*]. I take my Bible oath I never said a word—

The Note Taker [*overbearing but good-humored*]. Oh, shut up, shut up. Do I look like a policeman?

The Flower Girl [*far from reassured*]. Then what did you take down my words for? How do I know whether you took me down right? You just shew me what youve wrote about me. [*The note taker opens his book and holds it steadily under her nose, though the pressure of the mob trying to read it over his shoulders would upset a weaker man.*] Whats that? That aint proper writing. I cant read that.

The Note Taker. I can. [*Reads, reproducing her pronunciation exactly.*] 'Cheer ap, Keptin; n' baw ya flahr orf a pore gel.'

The Flower Girl [*much distressed*]. It's because I called him Captain. I meant no harm. [*To the gentleman.*] Oh, sir, dont let him lay a charge agen me for a word like that. You—

The Gentleman. Charge! I make no charge. [*To the note taker.*] Really, sir, if you are a detective, you need not begin protecting me against molestation by young women until I ask you. Anybody could see that the girl meant no harm.

The Bystanders Generally [*demonstrating against police espionage*]. Course they could. What business is it of yours? You mind your own affairs. He wants promotion, he does. Taking down people's words! Girl never said a word to him. What harm if she did? Nice thing a girl cant shelter from the rain without being insulted, etc., etc., etc. [*She is conducted by the more sympathetic demonstrators back to her plinth, where she resumes her seat and struggles with her emotion.*]

The Bystander. He aint a tec. Hes a blooming busybody: thats what he is. I tell you, look at his boots.

The Note Taker [*turning on him genially*]. And how are all your people down at Selsey?

The Bystander [*suspiciously*]. Who told you my people come from Selsey?

The Note Taker. Never you mind. They did. [*To the girl.*] How do you come to be up so far east? You were born in Lisson Grove.

The Flower Girl [*appalled*]. Oh, what harm is there in my leaving Lisson Grove? It wasnt fit for a pig to live in; and I had to pay four-and-six a week. [*In tears.*] Oh, boo—hoo—oo—

The Note Taker. Live where you like; but stop that noise.

The Gentleman [*to the girl*]. Come, come! he cant touch you: you have a right to live where you please.

A Sarcastic Bystander [*thrusting himself between the note taker and the gentleman*]. Park Lane, for instance. Id like to go into the Housing Question with you, I would.

The Flower Girl [*subsiding into a brooding melancholy over her basket, and talking very low-spiritedly to herself*]. I'm a good girl, I am.

The Sarcastic Bystander [*not attending to her*]. Do you know where *I* come from?

The Note Taker [*promptly*]. Hoxton.

Titterings. Popular interest in the note taker's performance increases.

The Sarcastic One [*amazed*]. Well, who said I didnt? Bly me! You know everything, you do.

The Flower Girl [*still nursing her sense of injury*]. Aint no call to meddle with me, he aint.

The Bystander [*to her*]. Of course he aint. Dont you stand it from him. [*To the note taker.*] See here: what call have you to know about people what never offered to meddle with you? Wheres your warrant?

Several Bystanders [*encouraged by this seeming point of law*]. Yes: wheres your warrant?

The Flower Girl. Let him say what he likes. I dont want to have no truck with him.

The Bystander. You take us for dirt under your feet, dont you? Catch you taking liberties with a gentleman!

The Sarcastic Bystander. Yes: tell him where he come from if you want to go fortune-telling.

The Note Taker. Cheltenham, Harrow, Cambridge, and India.

The Gentleman. Quite right. [*Great laughter. Reaction in the note taker's favor. Exclamations of* He knows all about it. Told him proper. Hear him tell the toff where he come from? etc.] May I ask, sir, do you do this for your living at a music hall?

The Note Taker. Ive thought of that. Perhaps I shall some day.

The rain has stopped; and the persons on the outside of the crowd begin to drop off.

The Flower Girl [*resenting the reaction*]. Hes no gentleman, he aint, to interfere with a poor girl.

The Daughter [*out of patience, pushing her way rudely to the front and displacing the gentleman, who politely retires to the other side of the pillar*]. What on earth is Freddy doing? I shall get pneumonia if I stay in this draught any longer.

The Note Taker [*to himself, hastily making a note of her pronunciation of 'monia'*]. Earlscourt.

The Daughter [*violently*]. Will you please keep your impertinent remarks to yourself.

The Note Taker. Did I say that out loud? I didnt mean to. I beg your pardon. Your mother's Epsom, unmistakeably.

The Mother [*advancing between her daughter and the note taker*]. How very curious! I was brought up in Largelady Park, near Epsom.

The Note Taker [*uproariously amused*]. Ha! ha! What a devil of a name! Excuse me. [*To the daughter.*] You want a cab, do you?

The Daughter. Dont dare speak to me.

The Mother. Oh please, please, Clara. [*Her daughter repudiates her with an angry shrug and retires haughtily.*] We should be so grateful to you, sir, if you found us a cab. [*The note taker produces a whistle.*] Oh, thank you. [*She joins her daughter.*]

The note taker blows a piercing blast.

The Sarcastic Bystander. There! I knowed he was a plain-clothes copper.

The Bystander. That aint a police whistle: thats a sporting whistle.

The Flower Girl [*still preoccupied with her wounded feelings*]. Hes no right to take away my character. My character is the same to me as any lady's.

The Note Taker. I dont know whether youve noticed it; but the rain stopped about two minutes ago.

The Bystander. So it has. Why didnt you say so before? and us losing our time listening to your silliness! [*He walks off towards the Strand.*]

The Sarcastic Bystander. I can tell where you come from. You come from Anwell. Go back there.

The Note Taker [*helpfully*]. Hanwell.

The Sarcastic Bystander [*affecting great distinction of speech*]. Thank you, teacher. Haw haw! So long [*he touches his hat with mock respect and strolls off*].

The Flower Girl. Frightening people like that! How would he like it himself?

The Mother. It's quite fine now, Clara. We can walk to a motor bus. Come. [*She gathers her skirts above her ankles and hurries off towards the Strand.*]

The Daughter. But the cab—[*her mother is out of hearing*]. Oh, how tiresome! [*She follows angrily.*]

   All the rest have gone except the note taker, the gentleman, and the flower girl, who sits arranging her basket, and still pitying herself in murmurs.

The Flower Girl. Poor girl! Hard enough for her to live without being worrited and chivied.

The Gentleman [*returning to his former place on the note taker's left*]. How do you do it, if I may ask?

The Note Taker. Simply phonetics. The science of speech. Thats my profession: also my hobby. Happy is the man who can make a living by his hobby! You can spot an Irishman or a Yorkshireman by his brogue. *I* can place any man within six miles. I can place him within two miles in London. Sometimes within two streets.

The Flower Girl. Ought to be ashamed of himself, unmanly coward!

The Gentleman. But is there a living in that?

The Note Taker. Oh yes. Quite a fat one. This is an age of upstarts. Men begin in Kentish Town with £80 a year, and end in Park Lane with a hundred thousand. They want to drop Kentish Town; but they give themselves away every time they open their mouths. Now I can teach them—

The Flower Girl. Let him mind his own business and leave a poor girl—

The Note Taker [*explosively*]. Woman: cease this detestable boohooing instantly; or else seek the shelter of some other place of worship.

The Flower Girl [*with feeble defiance*]. Ive a right to be here if I like, same as you.

The Note Taker. A woman who utters such depressing and disgusting sounds has no right to be anywhere—no right to live. Remember that you are a human being with a soul and the divine gift of articulate speech: that your native language is the language of Shakespear and Milton and The Bible; and dont sit there crooning like a bilious pigeon.

The Flower Girl [*quite overwhelmed, looking up at him in mingled wonder and deprecation without daring to raise her head*]. Ah-ah-ah-ow-ow-ow-oo!

The Note Taker [*whipping out his book*]. Heavens! what a sound! [*He writes; then holds out the book and reads, reproducing her vowels exactly.*] Ah-ah-ah-ow-ow-ow-oo!

The Flower Girl [*tickled by the performance, and laughing in spite of herself*]. Garn!

The Note Taker. You see this creature with her kerbstone English: the English that will keep her in the gutter to the end of her days. Well, sir, in three months I could pass that girl off as a duchess at an ambassador's garden party. I could even get her a place as lady's maid or shop assistant, which requires better English. Thats the sort of thing I do for commercial millionaires. And on the profits of it I do genuine scientific work in phonetics, and a little as a poet on Miltonic lines.

The Gentleman. I am myself a student of Indian dialects; and—

The Note Taker [*eagerly*]. Are you? Do you know Colonel Pickering, the author of Spoken Sanscrit?

The Gentleman. I am Colonel Pickering. Who are you?

The Note Taker. Henry Higgins, author of Higgins's Universal Alphabet.

Pickering [*with enthusiasm*]. I came from India to meet you.

Higgins. I was going to India to meet you.

Pickering. Where do you live?

Higgins. 27A Wimpole Street. Come and see me tomorrow.

Pickering. I'm at the Carlton. Come with me now and lets have a jaw over some supper.

Higgins. Right you are.

The Flower Girl [*to Pickering, as he passes her*]. Buy a flower, kind gentleman. I'm short for my lodging.

Pickering. I really havnt any change. I'm sorry [*he goes away*].

Higgins [*shocked at the girl's mendacity*]. Liar. You said you could change half-a-crown.

The Flower Girl [*rising in desperation*]. You ought to be stuffed with nails, you ought. [*Flinging the basket at his feet.*] Take the whole blooming basket for sixpence.

   The church clock strikes the second quarter.

Higgins [*hearing in it the voice of God, rebuking him for his Pharisaic want of charity to the poor girl*]. A reminder. [*He raises his hat solemnly; then throws a handful of money into the basket and follows Pickering.*]

The Flower Girl [*picking up a half-crown*]. Ah-ow-ooh! [*Picking up a couple of florins.*] Aaah-ow-ooh! [*Picking up several coins.*] Aaaaaah-ow-ooh! [*Picking up a half-sovereign.*] Aaaaaaaaaaaah-ow-ooh!!!

Freddy [*springing out of a taxicab*]. Got one at last. Hallo! [*To the girl.*] Where are the two ladies that were here?

The Flower Girl. They walked to the bus when the rain stopped.

Freddy. And left me with a cab on my hands! Damnation!

The Flower Girl [*with grandeur*]. Never you mind, young man. I'm going home in a taxi. [*She sails off to the cab. The driver puts his hand behind him and holds the door firmly shut against her. Quite understanding his mistrust, she shews him her handful of money.*] Eightpence aint no object to me, Charlie. [*He grins and opens the door.*] Angel Court, Drury Lane, round the corner of Micklejohn's oil shop. Lets see how fast you can make her hop it. [*She gets in and pulls the door to with a slam as the taxicab starts.*]

Freddy. Well, I'm dashed!

GEORGE BERNARD SHAW, *Pygmalion*, Act I, 1912

THE PORTER AND THE 'POET'

Fifty years ago, in the teens of the twentieth century, it was still the fashion for citizens to wear clothes indicative of their occupation: the farm-worker his smock, the navvy his buckled corduroy trousers, the carpenter his paper cap, the stockbroker and banker their silk toppers.

   The fish porters of Billingsgate had a picturesque uniform. Over their jackets they sported a long grey linen garment like a frock-coat, and on their heads they wore a wooden helmet with a platform top, for carrying heavy burdens. The pressure of a box full of mackerel would ram the helmet down, causing the flesh on the skull beneath to wrinkle, and pass on that wrinkling down the forehead and temples, giving the porter's face a distortion that resembled rage, incredible grief, or an imbecile mirth, according to the basic cast of the features it had to work upon.

Both overalls and helmets were saturated by fish-slime, a dreadful, glutinous fluid that pervaded the market, its buildings, its pavements, hanging in viscous skeins through the grids of its gutters, and from the edges of boxes being carried at a slow trot by the porters, whom it festooned in a hideous travesty of bridal veiling, the very reverse of aphrodisiac in its fœtid stench, which can only be likened to the odour of the lowest dregs of Davy Jones's locker.

I, too, was orthodox in my garments. Having found my *métier* as a poet, I wore my hair long, and sported a deep-green velvet coat, with a loose bow tie of wide black ribbon. This costume, suitable for the part of Rudolph in *La Bohème*, made its way that first morning, with me inside it as a nervous ghost, over London Bridge, down past the Monument, and through Billingsgate Market at the busiest hour.

From every doorway in the labyrinth of wholesalers' premises laden porters dashed, their heads thrown back to support the weight of their malodorous and dripping burdens of fish. Shouts, cries, imprecations, related to prices, enquiries as to the whereabouts of retailers' vans and barrows; jokes and blasphemous ribaldry; all filled the air, if so contaminated an atmosphere could be called air, with an almost solid confusion, bewildering and crushing to the nerves of an intruder.

I, the unwitting Rudolph, picked my way with half-apologetic disgust through this marine traffic, my eyes furtive in an effort to avoid collision with a weight-entranced porter, or contact with one of the myriad independently floating skeins of fish-slime. My nostrils, the long nostrils of the dedicated Apollonian or Dionysiac, quivered with revolt against the asafœtid air which they had so reluctantly to inhale. I was tempted to escape by exercising my secret faculty of rising from the ground and soaring above the contamination, but to do so I should have to breathe deeply; and that would make contamination worse contaminated, filth within as well as without. I was trapped. I had to walk on through the fishmarket as though I were an ordinary human being, risking the danger that threatened my singing robes.

So intent was I upon my self-protective advance down the slippery slope past the Monument that disaster was bound to overtake me.

Suddenly, out of a doorway, there burst a gigantic porter, balancing a barrel upright on his helmet. He was bawling the name of the retailer, linking it with ornaments of blasphemous design, to maintain the continuity of his enquiry. His bloated face was contused by pressure of blood from the top of his head, this sculpturing so affecting his features that his eyes protruded like headlamps of hate, and his mouth sagged open under the expulsion of his angry monologue. He was of the wretches writhing in one of the more repulsive lakes of Dante's *Inferno*.

This dreadful force coincided with my feather-weight in the middle of the treacherous pavement. I put out a hand and shut my eyes. I felt a mountainous, warm body, as though I were caressing Moby Dick. I heard a sliding sound, followed by a cry, a crash, and a long, slow rustle, as of shingle being lured back into the relapse of a sea-wave.

I opened my eyes, to see my hand still outstretched; beyond it, the porter sprawling in the gutter; beyond him, the barrel; out of the barrel, a gentle flow of winkles, whose semi-hollow shells were the source of this sweet, mermaid music which had followed the crash.

Then silence fell. Billingsgate Market came to a standstill, to watch, and to listen. It saw the fallen Goliath, and the oblation of winkles. It stared at the fairy-like figure, the figment from opera, in green velvet coat and flowing tie. It waited for the kill.

I too waited. I could do nothing else. I could not turn and run, for I was hemmed in by the army of porters and the floating bondage of fish-slime. Besides, I had to report, on my first morning, at 9 a.m. at the Government Laboratory, as instructed by J. L. le B. Hammond of the Civil Service Commission, and it has always been my oddity to have a dread of ever being late for an appointment . . .

Goliath sat for a moment or two. Then he straightened his helmet on his head, rose to his feet, contemplated the half-empty barrel and the long, oyster-coloured tongue of winkles protruding from it along the pavement and the gutter. Slowly, he turned to me, and looked me up and down. He scrutinised the velvet coat, the flowing tie, the bohemia of hair.

Billingsgate Market sighed. It knew what was coming: the raised sword of imprecation, long, heavy, sharp with every cruel and blasphemous invective that had ever been forged in ships and further whetted in Cockneydom.

One or two of the forefront spectators shuffled half a pace nearer, morbid to witness the annihilation of this ephemerid with the green body and the now helpless, invisible wings. The skeins of fish-slime, that had been streaming horizontally, now hung vertical during the moment-ary inaction. Gnarled hands supported the boxes on their heads, caryatid-fashion. My eyes saw all these elements in the glaucous auditorium with the vision of a martyr about to be executed.

Goliath's scrutiny at last settled on my face. He looked me in the eye, his great loose lips contorted, and he spoke.

'*Now* you've done it!' he said.

Billingsgate gasped, woke, and resumed its traffic. The cries redou-bled, the jog-trot took a quicker urge, the wisps of slime floated out to the horizontal once more. Shaken, and still incredulous, I muttered an apology, and resumed my way, with a few minutes to spare.

RICHARD CHURCH, *The Golden Sovereign*, 1957

LAMBETH IS HOME

The question is often asked why the people live where they do. Why do they not live in a district where rents are cheaper, and spend more on tram fares? The reason is that these over-burdened women have no know-ledge, no enterprise, no time, and no cash, to enable them to visit distant suburbs along the tram routes, even if, in their opinion, the saving of money in rent would be sufficient to pay the extra outlay on tram fares. Moreover—strange as it may seem to those whose bi-weekly visit to Lambeth is like a bi-weekly plunge into Hades—the people to whom Lambeth is home want to stay in Lambeth. They do not expect to be any better off elsewhere, and meantime they are in surroundings they know, and among people who know and respect them. Probably they have relatives near by who would not see them come to grief without making great efforts to help them. Should the man go into hospital or into the workhouse infirmary, extraordinary kindness to the wife and children will be shown by the most stand-off neighbours, in order to keep the little household together until he is well again. A family who have lived for years in one street are recognised up and down the length of that street as people to be helped in time of trouble. These respectable but very poor people live over a morass of such intolerable poverty that they unite instinctively to save those known to them from falling into it. A family which moves two miles away is completely lost to view. They never write, and there is no time and no money for visiting. Neighbours forget them. It was not mere personal liking which united them; it was a kind of mutual respect in the face of trouble. Even relatives cease to be actively interested in their fate. A fish-fryer lost his job in Lambeth owing to the business being sold and the new owner bringing in his own fryer. The man had been getting 26s. a week, and owed nothing. His wife's brothers and parents, who lived near by, combined to feed three of the four children; a certain amount of coal was sent in; the rent was allowed to stand over by a sympathetic landlady to whom the woman had been kind in her confinement; and at last, after nine weeks, the man got work at Finsbury Park at 24s. a week. Nearly £3 was owing in rent, but otherwise there was no debt. The family stayed on in the same rooms, paying 3s. a week extra as back rent, and the man walked daily from south of Kennington Park to Finsbury Park and back. He started at five in the morning, arrived at eight, and worked till noon, when he had four hours off and a meal. He was allowed to lie down and sleep till 4 p.m. Then he worked again till 10 p.m., afterwards walking home, arriving there at about one in the morning. A year of this life knocked him up, and he left his place at Finsbury Park to find one in a fish-shop in Westminster at a still slightly lower wage. The back rent is long ago paid off, and the family, now with five children, is still in the same rooms, though in reduced circumstances. When questioned as to why he had remained in Kennington instead of moving after his work, the man pointed out that the back rent would seem almost impossible to pay off at a distance. Then there was no one who knew them at Finsbury, where, should misfortune overtake them again, instead of being helped through a period of unemployment, they would have nothing before them but the 'house.'

It is obvious that, in London at any rate, the wretched housing, which is at the same time more than they can afford, has as bad an influence on the health of the poor as any other of their miserable conditions. If poverty did not mean wretched housing, it would be shorn of half its dangers. The London poor are driven to pay one-third of their income for dark, damp rooms which are too small and too few in houses which are ill-built and overcrowded. And above the overcrowding of the house and of the room comes the overcrowding of the bed—equally the result of poverty, and equally dangerous to health. Even if the food which can be provided out of 22s. a week, after 7s, or 8s. has been taken for rent, were of first-rate quality and sufficient in quantity, the night spent in such beds in such rooms in such houses would devitalise the children. It would take away their appetites, and render them more liable to any infection at home or at school. Taken in conjunction with the food they do get, it is no wonder that the health of London school-children exercises the mind of the medical officials of the London County Council.

MAUDE PEMBER REEVES, *Round about a Pound a Week*, 1913

AT THE ALBERT HALL

29 June 1914

Went with R——— to the Albert Hall to the *Empress of Ireland* Memorial Concert with massed bands. We heard the Symphonie Pathétique, Chopin's Funeral March, Trauermarsch from Götterdammerung, the Ride of the Valkyries and a solemn melody from Bach.

This afternoon I regard as a mountain peak in my existence. For two solid hours I sat like an Eagle on a rock gazing into infinity—a very fine sensation for a London Sparrow. . . .

I have an idea that if it were possible to assemble the sick and suffering day by day in the Albert Hall and keep the Orchestra going all the time, then the constant exposure of sick parts to such heavenly air vibrations would ultimately restore to them the lost rhythm of health. Surely, even a single exposure to—say Beethoven's Fifth Symphony—must result in some permanent reconstitution of ourselves body and soul. No one can be quite the same after a Beethoven Symphony has streamed thro' him. If one could *develop* a human soul like a negative the effect I should say could be seen. . . . I'll tell you what I wish they'd do— seriously: divide up the arena into a series of cubicles where, unobserved and in perfect privacy, a man could execute all the various movements of his body and limbs which the music prompts. It would be such a delicious self-indulgence and it's torture to be jammed into a seat where you can't even tap one foot or wave an arm.

The concert restored my moral health. I came away in love with people I was hating before and full of compassion for others I usually contemn. A feeling of immeasurable well being—a jolly bonhomie enveloped me like incandescent light. At the close when we stood up to sing the National Anthem we all felt a genuine spirit of camaraderie.

Just as when Kings die, we were silent musing upon the common fate, and when the time came to separate we were loath to go our several ways, for we were comrades who together had come thro' a great experience. For my part I wanted to shake hands all round—happy travellers, now alas! at the journey's end and never perhaps to meet again—never. . . .

R—— and I walked up thro' Kensington Gardens like two young Gods!

'I even like that bloody thing,' I said, pointing to the Albert Memorial.

We pointed out pretty girls to one another, watched the children play ring-a-ring-a-roses on the grass. We laughed exultingly at the thought of our dismal colleagues . . . tho' I said (as before!) I loved 'em all—God bless 'em—even old——. R—— said it was nothing short of insolence on their part to have neglected the opportunity of coming to the Concert.

Later on, an old gaffer up from the country stopped us to ask the way to Rotten Row—I overwhelmed him with directions and happy descriptive details. I felt like walking with him and showing him what a wonderful place the world is.

After separating from R—— very reluctantly—it was horrible to be left alone in such high spirits, walked up towards the Round Pond, and caught myself avoiding the shadows of the trees—so as to be every moment out in the blazing sun. I scoffed inwardly at the timorousness of pale, anæmic folk whom I passed hiding in the shadows of the elms.

At the Round Pond, came across a Bulldog who was biting out great chunks of water and in luxuriant wastefulness letting it drool out again from each corner of his mouth. I watched this old fellow greedily (it was very hot), as well pleased with him and his liquid 'chops' as with anything I saw, unless it were a girl and a man lying full length along the grass and kissing beneath a sunshade. I smiled; she saw me, and smiled, too, in return, and then fell to kissing again.

W. N. P. BARBELLION, *The Journal of a Disappointed Man*, 1919

GOBLINS IN THE QUEEN'S HALL

It will be generally admitted that Beethoven's Fifth Symphony is the most sublime noise that has ever penetrated into the ear of man. All sorts and conditions are satisfied by it. Whether you are like Mrs Munt, and tap surreptitiously when the tunes come—of course, not so as to disturb the others—or like Helen, who can see heroes and shipwrecks in the music's flood; or like Margaret, who can only see the music; or like Tibby, who is profoundly versed in counterpoint, and holds the full score open on his knee; or like their cousin, Fräulein Mosebach, who remembers all the time that Beethoven is 'echt Deutsch'; or like Fräulein Mosebach's young man, who can remember nothing but Fräulein Mosebach: in any case, the passion of your life becomes more vivid, and you are bound to admit that such a noise is cheap at two shillings. It is cheap, even if you hear it in the Queen's Hall, dreariest music-room in London, though not as dreary as the Free Trade Hall, Manchester; and even if you sit on the extreme left of that hall, so that the brass bumps at you before the rest of the orchestra arrives, it is still cheap.

'Who is Margaret talking to?' said Mrs Munt, at the conclusion of the first movement. She was again in London on a visit to Wickham Place.

Helen looked down the long line of their party, and said that she did not know.

'Would it be some young man or other whom she takes an interest in?'

'I expect so,' Helen replied. Music enwrapped her, and she could not enter into the distinction that divides young men whom one takes an interest in from young men whom one knows.

'You girls are so wonderful in always having—Oh dear! one mustn't talk.'

For the Andante had begun—very beautiful, but bearing a family likeness to all the other beautiful Andantes that Beethoven had written, and, to Helen's mind, rather disconnecting the heroes and shipwrecks of the first movement from the heroes and goblins of the third. She heard the tune through once, and then her attention wandered, and she gazed at the audience, or the organ, or the architecture. Much did she censure the attenuated Cupids who encircle the ceiling of the Queen's Hall, inclining each to each with vapid gesture, and clad in sallow pantaloons, on which the October sunlight struck. 'How awful to marry a man like those Cupids!' thought Helen. Here Beethoven started decorating his tune, so she heard him through once more, and then she smiled at her cousin Frieda. But Frieda, listening to Classical Music, could not respond. Herr Liesecke, too, looked as if wild horses could not make him inattentive; there were lines across his forehead, his lips were parted, his pince-nez at right angles to his nose, and he had laid a thick, white hand on either knee. And next to her was Aunt Juley, so British, and wanting to tap. How interesting that row of people was! What diverse influences had gone to the making! Here Beethoven, after humming and hawing with great sweetness, said 'Heigho,' and the Andante came to an end. Applause, and a round of 'wunderschöning' and 'prachtvolleying' from the German contingent. Margaret started talking to her new young man; Helen said to her aunt: 'Now comes the wonderful movement: first of all the goblins, and then a trio of elephants dancing'; and Tibby implored the company generally to look out for the transitional passage on the drum.

'On the what, dear?'

'On the *drum*, Aunt Juley.'

'No; look out for the part where you think you have done with the goblins and they come back,' breathed Helen, as the music started with a goblin walking quietly over the universe, from end to end. Others followed him. They were not aggressive creatures; it was that that made them so terrible to Helen. They merely observed in passing that there was no such thing as splendour or heroism in the world. After the interlude of elephants dancing, they returned and made the observation for the second time. Helen could not contradict them, for, once at all events, she had felt the same, and had seen the reliable walls of youth collapse. Panic and emptiness! Panic and emptiness! The goblins were right.

Her brother raised his finger: it was the transitional passage on the drum.

For, as if things were going too far, Beethoven took hold of the goblins and made them do what he wanted. He appeared in person. He gave them a little push, and they began to walk in major key instead of in a minor, and then—he blew with his mouth and they were scattered! Gusts of splendour, gods and demi-gods contending with vast swords, colour and fragrance broadcast on the field of battle, magnificent victory, magnificent death! Oh, it all burst before the girl, and she even stretched out her gloved hands as if it was tangible. Any fate was titanic; any contest desirable; conqueror and conquered would alike be applauded by the angels of the utmost stars.

And the goblins—they had not really been there at all? They were only the phantoms of cowardice and unbelief? One healthy human impulse would dispel them? Men like the Wilcoxes, or President Roosevelt, would say yes. Beethoven knew better. The goblins really had been there. They might return—and they did. It was as if the splendour of life might boil over and waste to steam and froth. In its dissolution one heard the terrible, ominous note, and a goblin, with increased malignity, walked quietly over the universe from end to end. Panic and emptiness! Panic and emptiness! Even the flaming ramparts of the world might fall.

Beethoven chose to make all right in the end. He built the ramparts up. He blew with his mouth for the second time, and again the goblins were scattered. He brought back the gusts of splendour, the heroism, the youth, the magnificence of life and of death, and, amid vast roarings of a superhuman joy, he led his Fifth Symphony to its conclusion. But the goblins were there. They could return. He had said so bravely, and that is why one can trust Beethoven when he says other things.

Helen pushed her way out during the applause. She desired to be alone. The music had summed up to her all that had happened or could happen in her career. She read it as a tangible statement, which could never be superseded. The notes meant this and that to her, and they could have no other meaning, and life could have no other meaning. She pushed right out of the building, and walked slowly down the outside staircase, breathing the autumnal air, and then she strolled home.

E. M. FORSTER, *Howards End*, 1910

TOO LATE

25 October 1914
Yesterday's ramble has left me very sore in spirit. London was spread out before me, a vast campagne. But I felt too physically tired to explore. I could just amble along—a spectator merely—and automatically register impressions. Think of the misery of that! I want to see the Docks and Dockland, to enter East End public-houses and opium-dens, to speak to Chinamen and Lascars: I want a first-rate, first-hand knowledge of London, of London men, London women. I was tingling with anticipation yesterday and then I grew tired and fretful and morose, crawled back like a weevil into my nut. By 6.30 I was in a Library reading the *Dublin Review!*

What a young fool I was to neglect those priceless opportunities of studying and tasting life and character in North ——, at Borough Council meetings, Boards of Guardians, and electioneering campaigns—not to mention inquests, police courts, and country fairs. Instead of appraising all these precious and genuine pieces of experience at their true value, my diary and my mind were occupied only with—Zoology, if you please. I ignored my exquisite chances, I ramped around, fuming and fretting, full of contempt for my circumscribed existence, and impatient as only a youth can be. What I shall never forgive myself is my present inability to recall that life, so that instead of being able now to push my chair back and entertain myself and others with descriptions of some of those antique and incredible happenings, my memory is rigid and formal: I remember only a few names and one or two isolated events. All that time is just as if it had never been. My recollections form only an indefinite smudge—odd Town Clerks, Town Criers (at least five of them in wonderful garb), policemen (I poached with one), ploughing match dinners (platters of roast beef and boiled potatoes and I, bespectacled student of Zoology, sitting uncomfortably among valiant trenchermen after their day's ploughing), election meetings in remote Exmoor villages (and those wonderful Inns where I had to spend the night!)—all are gone—too remote to bear recital—yet just sufficiently clear to harass the mind in my constant endeavours to raise them all again from the dead in my consciousness. I hate to think it is lost; that my youth is buried—a cemetery without even headstones. To an inquest on a drowned sailor—disclosing some thrilling story of the wild seas off the coast—with a pitiful myopia—I preferred Wiedersheim's *Comparative Anatomy of Vertebrates*. I used to carry Dr Smith Woodward's *Palæontology* with me to a Board of Guardians meeting, mingling *Pariasaurus* and Holoptychians with tenders for repairs and reports from the Master. Now I take Keats or Tchehov to the Museum!

London certainly lies before me. Certainly I am alive at last. Yet now my energy is gone. It is too late. I am ill and tired. It costs me infinite discomfort to write this entry, all the skin of my right hand is permanently 'pins and needles' and in the finger tips I have lost all sense of touch. The sight of my right eye is also very bad and sometimes I can scarcely read print with it, etc., etc. But why should I go on?

A trance-like condition supervenes in a semi-invalid forced to live in almost complete social isolation in a great whirling city like London. Days of routine follow each other as swiftly as the weaver's shuttle and numb the spirit and turn palpitating life into a silent picture show.

Everywhere always in the street people—millions of them—whom I do not know, moving swiftly along. I look and look and yawn and then one day as to-day I wake up and race about beside myself—a swollen bag ready to burst with hope, love, misery, joy, desperation.

W. N. P. BARBELLION, *The Journal of a Disappointed Man*, 1919

Yevgeny Zamyatin, whose futuristic novel We *inspired George Orwell to write* Nineteen Eighty-Four, *wrote two novellas about life in England. It should be clear from these excerpts that he does not work in the naturalistic vein.*

ON A SLEEPY ELEPHANT IN DELIRIOUS LONDON

The most wonderful thing in life is to be delirious and the most wonderful kind of delirium is being in love. In the morning mist, hazy and amorous, London was delirious. London squinted as it floated along, milky-pink, without caring where it was going.

Yesterday the slender columns of the druid temples had still been factory chimneys. The airy iron arches of the viaducts were now bridges from one mysterious island to another. The black cranes, like huge pre-historic swans, stretched out their necks, about to dive to the bottom for prey. Frightened, the brazen gold letters: 'Rolls-Royce Automobiles' flashed up at the sun and faded out. Once more forming a hushed, hazy circle: the lace of the sinking towers, the swaying web of cables, the slow dance of the slumbering tortoise-houses. And as the fixed axis of it all— the gigantic stone phallus of Nelson's column.

At the bottom of the milky-pink sea, Bailey the organist floated along the empty morning streets, without caring where he was going. He shuffled along the asphalt, getting his absurdly long feet entangled. He screwed up his eyes blissfully and, thrusting his hands into his pockets, he stopped in front of the shop windows.

Here were shoes. Brown leggings, enormous black wellingtons and tiny patent leather shoes for ladies.

'Great craftsman of shoes, divine poet of shoes . . .' Bailey the organist prayed before the shoemaker's window, 'Thank you for the tiny shoes . . . and for the chimneys and the bridges and Rolls-Royce and the mist and springtime. And if it's painful—for the pain too . . .'

On the back of a sleepy elephant—the first morning bus—Bailey the organist hurried home to Chiswick. The conductress, broad and motherly, like a bun (at home she had a heap of children), was keeping a benevolent eye on the passenger. Looks like he has been drinking, poor devil. There, his lips have fallen open.

The fat lips, which must have been as soft as a foal's, smiled blissfully. His head, with its comfortable ears, which stuck out and curled up at the edges, swayed slightly. Bailey the organist was floating.

'Hey, sir, isn't this your stop?'

The organist opened his eyes wide in surprise. What, already?

'Had a drop to drink have we, sir?'

The foal's lips opened. The organist shook his head and laughed happily. 'Drink? My dear lady, better than that!'

He started down the stairs of the bus. Below in the mist, the Craggs' window, washed for Sunday, squinted with embarrassment and shone with milky-pink lights. The sun was rising.

The organist turned to the conductress, silently pointed the windows out to her, and just as silently embraced and kissed her with his soft foal's lips. The conductress wiped her mouth with her sleeve, burst out laughing and rang the bell: what can you expect from someone like that?

The organist dived into an alleyway, quietly unlocked the back gate of his house and went into the yard. He stopped by the coal pile and looked up over the brick wall at the window of his neighbours, the Craggs. In the window a white curtain breathed evenly in the wind. His neighbours were still asleep.

Taking off his hat, he stood there until a faint shadow flitted across the curtain. It flitted across and a hand shone pink in the sun as it lifted the edge. Bailey the organist put on his hat and went into his house.

ZEPPELINS

Darkness. The door into the neighbouring room is not quite shut. A strip of light stretches through the crack in the door, across the ceiling. People are walking about by lamplight. Something has happened. The strip moves faster and faster and the dark walls move further and further apart, into infinity. This room is London and there are thousands of doors. The lamps dart about and the strips dart across the ceiling. And perhaps it is all delirium . . .

Something had happened. The black sky above London burst into fragments: white triangles, squares and lines—the silent geometric delirium of searchlights. The blinded elephant buses rushed somewhere headlong with their lights extinguished. The distinct patter along the asphalt of belated couples, like a feverish pulse, died away. Everywhere doors slammed and lights were put out. And the city lay deserted, hollow, geometric, swept clean by a sudden plague: silent domes, pyramids, circles, arches, towers, battlements.

The silence swelled out for a moment, stretching like a soap bubble and then burst. Far away bombs began to whine and stamp with iron feet. Growing taller and taller, reaching up to the sky, a delirious truncated creature—just legs and belly—stupidly and blindly stamped the bombs on to the ants and their square anthills below. Zeppelins . . .

The lifts did not have time to swallow them all. The ants poured down the emergency stairs. They clung on to the footboards and then with a roar sped along the tubes, without caring where they were going and got off without caring where they were. They crowded together in the delirious underground world with its concrete sky hanging over them, its confusion of caves, staircases, suns, kiosks, vending machines.

'Zeppelins over London! Extra! Extra!' The mechanical, clockwork boys scurried about.

THE FRENZIED CITY

The sun had driven London into a frenzy. London rushed onwards.

A torrent of top hats, of huge-brimmed white hats and impatiently open lips burst through the dam. The elephant buses sped along in a herd, in a fever from the spring. Lowering their heads, they sniffed each other like dogs. The street posters yelled out in raspberry, green and orange voices: 'Rolls-Royce', 'Waltz—the two of us', 'Automatic Sun'. And everywhere little boys in white collars ran quick as lightning between the flashing legs, letters and wheels with extra editions of the newspapers.

The top hats, the elephant buses, Rolls-Royce, Automatic Sun—all burst their banks and would of course have washed away the houses and the statues of policemen at the crossroads, if there had not been an outlet down into the Underground and the subterranean lines of the 'Tube'. The lifts swallowed one helping after another and lowered them into the sweltering belly. Here, the frenzied blood pulsated and sped more frantically along the resounding concrete tubes.

In a frenzy, London poured out wildly beyond the town into parks, on to the grass. People hurried, drove, walked and pushed newly-born infants in innumerable wicker prams.

> YEVGENY ZAMYATIN, *The Fisher of Men*, 1915, trans. Sophie Fuller and Julian Sacchi, 1984

Mrs Henedge, recently widowed by poor dear Leslie, *is holding a reception at her London house to celebrate the discovery, by Professor Inglepin, of a long-missing line by Sappho.*

A HOSTESS PREPARES

Mrs Henedge lived in a small house with killing stairs just off Chesham Place.

'If I were to die here,' she had often said, 'they would never be able to twist the coffin outside my door; they would have to cremate me in my room.' For such a cottage, the sitting-rooms, nevertheless, were astonishingly large. The drawing-room, for instance, was a complete surprise, in spite of its dimensions, being ocularly curtailed by a somewhat trying brocade of drooping lilac orchids on a yellow ground.

But to-day, to make as much space as possible to receive her guests, all the household heirlooms—a faded photograph of the Pope, a bust of *poor dear Leslie*, some most Oriental cushions, and a quantity of whimsies, had been carried away to the top of the house. Never before had she seen the room so bare, or so austere.

As her maid exclaimed: 'It was like a church.' If an entire Ode of Sappho's had been discovered instead of a single line she could have done no more.

In the centre of the room, a number of fragile gilt chairs had been waiting patiently all day to be placed, heedless, happily, of the lamentations of Thérèse, who, while rolling her eyes, kept exclaiming, 'Such wild herds of chairs; such herds of wild chairs!'

In her arrangements Mrs Henedge had disobeyed the Professor in everything.

Professor Inglepin had looked in during the week to ask that severity might be the key. 'No flowers,' he had begged, 'or, at most, placed beside the fragment (which I shall bring), a handful, perhaps, of——'

'Of course,' Mrs Henedge had replied, 'you can rely upon me.' And now the house was full of rambler roses and of blue sweet-peas.

A buffet, too, had arisen altar-like in her own particular sanctum, an apology to those whom she was unable to dine; nor, for toothsome curiosities, had she scoured a pagan cookery-book in vain. . . .

Glancing over the dinner list whilst she dressed, it seemed to her that the names of her guests, in neat rotation, resembled the cast of a play. 'A comedy, with possible dynamics!' she murmured as she went downstairs.

With a tiara well over her nose, and dressed in oyster satin and pearls, she wished that Sappho could have seen her then. . . .

RONALD FIRBANK, Vainglory, 1915

'UNREAL CITY'

Unreal City,
Under the brown fog of a winter dawn,
A crowd flowed over London Bridge, so many,
I had not thought death had undone so many.
Sighs, short and infrequent, were exhaled,
And each man fixed his eyes before his feet.
Flowed up the hill and down King William Street,
To where Saint Mary Woolnoth kept the hours
With a dead sound on the final stroke of nine.

T. S. ELIOT, from 'The Waste Land', 1922

PRITCHETT THE OFFICE BOY

We worked until seven in the evening. On Saturdays we left between two and four, this depending on the mail. In the evenings I went home from London Bridge Station. In *The Waste Land* T. S. Eliot wrote of the strange morning and evening sight of those thousands of men, all wearing bowlers and carrying umbrellas, crossing London Bridge in long, dull regiments and pouring into that ugly, but to me most affecting, railway station which for years I used. I was captivated by it as I suppose every office worker is by the station in the great city that rules his life. Penn Station in New York, St Lazare in Paris, Waterloo, Paddington and Liverpool Street, are printed on the pages of a lifetime's grind at the office desk. Each is a quotidian frontier, splitting a life, a temple of the inexorable. The distinction of London Bridge Station, on the Chatham side, is that it is not a terminus but a junction where lives begin to fade and then blossom again as they swap trains in the rush hours and make for all the regions of South London and the towns of Kent. The trains come in and go out over those miles of rolling brick arches that run across South London like a massive Roman wall. There were no indicators on the platforms in my day and the confusion had to be sorted out by stentorian porters who called out the long litanies of stations in a hoarse London bawl and with a style of their own. They stood on the crowded platform edge, detected the identifying lights on the incoming engine and then sang out. To myself, at that age, all places I did not know seemed romantic and the lists of names were, if not Miltonic, at any rate as evocative as those names with which the Georgian poets filled up their lines. I would stare admiringly, even enviously, at the porter who would have to chant the long line to Bexley Heath; or the man who, beginning with the blunt and challenging football names of Charlton and Woolwich would go on to comic Plumstead and then flow forward over his long list till his voice fell to the finality of Greenhythe, Northfleet and Gravesend; or the softer tones of St Johns, Lewisham, and Blackheath. And to stir us up were the powerful trains—travelling to distances that seemed as remote as Istanbul to me—expresses that went to Margate, Herne Bay, Rochester and Chatham. I saw nothing dingy in this. The pleasure of my life as an office boy lay in being one of the London crowd and I actually enjoyed standing in a compartment packed with fifteen people on my way to Bromley North. How pleasant it was, in the war years, to stop dead outside Tower Bridge and to see a maroon go off in an air-raid warning and, even better, for a sentimentalist, to be stuck in one of those curry powder fogs that came up from the river and squashed London flat in its windless marsh. One listened to the fog signals and saw the fires of the watchmen; there was a sinister quiet as the train stood outside the Surrey Docks. And when, very late, the train got to Bromley North and one groped one's way home, seeing the conductors with flares in their hands walking ahead of the buses, or cars lost and askew on the wrong side of the road, and heard footsteps but saw no person until he was upon you and asking where he was, one swanked to oneself that at last one had had a load of the traditional muck on one's chest.

The thing I liked best was being sent on errands in Bermondsey. They became explorations, and I made every excuse to lengthen them. I pushed down south to the Dun Cow in the Old Kent Road, eastward by side streets and alleyways to Tower Bridge. I had a special pleasure in the rank places like those tunnels and vaults under the railway: the smells above all made me feel importantly a part of this working London. Names like Wilde's Rents, Cherry Garden Street, Jamaica Road, Dockhead and Pickle Herring Street excited and my journeys were not simply street journeys to me: they were like crossing the desert, finding the source of the Niger. London was not a city; it was a foreign country as strange as India and even though I knew the Thames is a small river compared with the great ones of the world, I would patriotically make it wider and wider in my mind. I liked the Hide Market where groups of old women and children hung about the hide men who would occasionally flick off a bit of flesh from the hides: the children like little vultures snatched at these bits and put them in their mothers' bags. We thought the children were going to eat these scraps, but in fact it is more likely—money being urgent to all Londoners—they were going to sell them to the glue merchants. The glue trade haunted many busy Cockney minds. Owing to the loop of the river, Bermondsey has remained the most clannish and isolated part of London; people there were deeply native for generations. Their manner was unemotional but behind the dryness, there was the suggestion of the Cockney sob.

'What'll y'ave? Lovin' mem'ry or deepest sympathy?' the woman in the shop asked when I went to buy a mourning card for one of our office cleaners.

I would pass the Tanners Arms and wonder at the peculiar fact that the owner had a piece of tanned human skin 'jes like pigskin'. The evenings came on and a procession of women and children would be wheeling their mattresses up to the railway tunnels or the deep tube station to be safe from the occasional raids. I would see other office boys wearing their bowler hats as I wore mine: we were a self-important, cracked-voice little race, sheepish, yet cocky, regarding our firms with childish awe.

But my work was dull. The terrible thing was that it was simple and mechanical; far, far less difficult than work at school. This was a humiliation and, even now, the simplicity of most of the work in offices, factories and warehouses depresses me. It is also all trite child's play and repetition and the correcting of an infinitude of silly mistakes, compared with intellectual or professional labour. Most people seemed to me, then, and even now, chained to a dulling routine of systematized and tolerated carelessness and error. Whatever was going to happen to me, I knew I must escape from this easy, unthinking world and I understood my father's dogged efforts to be on his own, and his own master. In difficulty lay the only escape, from what for me seemed to be deterioration of faculty.

The dullness, the long hours, the bad food, the low pay, the paring away of pleasure to a few hours late on Saturday afternoon, the tedious Sundays brightened only by that brief hour at the Sunday School—all these soon stunned and stunted me in my real life however much they moved me to live in my imagination. I accepted, with the native London masochism, that these were hard times and that this was to be my life. London has always preferred experience to satisfaction. I saw myself a junior clerk turning into a senior clerk comfortable in my train, enjoying the characters of my fellow travellers, talking sententiously of the state of affairs in France, Hong Kong and Singapore and, with profound judiciousness, of the government. Over the years one would know these season ticket holders—perhaps not speaking to them—as well as the characters in a novel. Sometimes there was an oddity—the man who read Virgil as he travelled up and down. And there was always, for diversity, the girls who knitted for the soldiers and read novels. There was also the pride I felt in being enslaved in a city so world-famous, in being submerged in its brick, in being smoked and kippered by it. There was the curious satisfaction, in these months, of a settled fate and the feeling that here was good sense and, under the reserve, humour and decency.

V. S. PRITCHETT, A Cab at the Door, 1968

LONDON; THIS MOMENT OF JUNE

For having lived in Westminster—how many years now? over twenty,—one feels even in the midst of the traffic, or waking at night, Clarissa was positive, a particular hush, or solemnity; an indescribable pause; a suspense (but that might be her heart, affected, they said, by influenza) before Big Ben strikes. There! Out it boomed. First a warning, musical; then the hour, irrevocable. The leaden circles dissolved in the air. Such fools we are, she thought, crossing Victoria Street. For Heaven only knows why one loves it so, how one sees it so, making it up, building it round one, tumbling it, creating it every moment afresh; but the veriest frumps, the most dejected of miseries sitting on doorsteps (drink their downfall) do the same; can't be dealt with, she felt positive, by Acts of Parliament for that very reason: they love life. In people's eyes, in the swing, tramp, and trudge; in the bellow and the uproar; the carriages, motor cars, omnibuses, vans, sandwich men shuffling and swinging; brass bands; barrel organs; in the triumph and the jingle and the strange high singing of some aeroplane overhead was what she loved; life; London; this moment of June.

For it was the middle of June. The War was over, except for some one like Mrs Foxcroft at the Embassy last night eating her heart out because that nice boy was killed and now the old Manor House must go to a cousin; or Lady Bexborough who opened a bazaar, they said, with the telegram in her hand, John, her favourite, killed; but it was over; thank Heaven—over. It was June. The King and Queen were at the Palace. And everywhere, though it was still so early, there was a beating, a stirring of galloping ponies, tapping of cricket bats; Lords, Ascot, Ranelagh and all the rest of it; wrapped in the soft mesh of the grey-blue morning air, which, as the day wore on, would unwind them, and set down on their lawns and pitches the bouncing ponies, whose forefeet just struck the ground and up they sprung, the whirling young men, and laughing girls in their transparent muslins who, even now, after dancing all night, were taking their absurd woolly dogs for a run; and even now, at this hour, discreet old dowagers were shooting out in their motor cars on errands of mystery; and the shopkeepers were fidgeting in their windows with their paste and diamonds, their lovely old sea-green brooches in eighteenth-century settings to tempt Americans (but one must econom- ise, not buy things rashly for Elizabeth), and she, too, loving it as she did with an absurd and faithful passion, being part of it, since her people were courtiers once in the time of the Georges, she, too, was going that very night to kindle and illuminate; to give her party. But how strange, on entering the Park, the silence; the mist; the hum; the slow-swimming happy ducks; the pouched birds waddling; and who should be coming along with his back against the Government buildings, most appropriately,

carrying a despatch box stamped with the Royal Arms, who but Hugh
Whitbread; her old friend Hugh—the admirable Hugh!

'Good-morning to you, Clarissa!' said Hugh, rather extravagantly, for
they had known each other as children. 'Where are you off to?'

'I love walking in London,' said Mrs Dalloway. 'Really, it's better than
walking in the country.'

VIRGINIA WOOLF, *Mrs Dalloway*, 1925

'HURRY UP PLEASE ITS TIME'

When Lil's husband got demobbed, I said—
I didn't mince my words, I said to her myself,
HURRY UP PLEASE ITS TIME
Now Albert's coming back, make yourself a bit smart.
He'll want to know what you done with that money he gave you
To get yourself some teeth. He did, I was there.
You have them all out, Lil, and get a nice set,
He said, I swear, I can't bear to look at you.
And no more can't I, I said, and think of poor Albert,
He's been in the army four years, he wants a good time,
And if you don't give it him, there's others will, I said.
Oh is there, she said. Something o' that, I said.
Then I'll know who to thank, she said, and give me a straight look.
HURRY UP PLEASE ITS TIME
If you don't like it you can get on with it, I said.
Others can pick and choose if you can't.
But if Albert makes off, it won't be for lack of telling.
You ought to be ashamed, I said, to look so antique.
(And her only thirty-one.)
I can't help it, she said, pulling a long face,
It's them pills I took, to bring it off, she said.
(She's had five already, and nearly died of young George.)
The chemist said it would be all right, but I've never been the same,
You *are* a proper fool, I said.
Well, if Albert won't leave you alone, there it is, I said,
What you get married for if you don't want children?
HURRY UP PLEASE ITS TIME

Well, that Sunday Albert was home, they had a hot gammon,
And they asked me in to dinner, to get the beauty of it hot—
HURRY UP PLEASE ITS TIME
HURRY UP PLEASE ITS TIME
Goonight Bill. Goonight Lou. Goonight May. Goonight.
Ta ta. Goonight. Goonight.
Good night, ladies, good night, sweet ladies, good night, good night.

> T. S. ELIOT, from 'The Waste Land', 1922

MONET AND THE CHANGING THAMES

When I began, I was like everyone else, I thought two canvases were
enough, one for dull weather, one for sun. Then I painted some hayricks
which struck me and which made a splendid group, a little way from
here; one day I saw my light had changed and I asked my daughter-in-
law if she would mind going back to the house and bringing me another
canvas. She brought me one, but it wasn't long before the light had
changed again. Another canvas, and another! And I worked on each till
I had my effect—and that was that. Not very difficult to understand.

Where the process became really awful was on the Thames. Appearance changed all the time. At the Savoy Hotel or at St Thomas's Hospital, where I had my viewpoints, I kept almost a hundred canvases on
the go—for one subject. I would search feverishly through my sketches
till I found one not too different from what I could see. Then in spite
of everything I would change it entirely. When I finished work, I would
move the canvases and see that I had overlooked just the one which
would have served—there it was in my hand. That wasn't very bright!

> CLAUDE MONET, an interview, Feb. 1927, from *La Reine de l'art ancien
> et moderne*

'THROUGH THE EYES OF DEFOE'

Saturday, 12 April 1919
These ten minutes are stolen from *Moll Flanders*, which I failed to finish
yesterday in accordance with my time sheet, yielding to a desire to stop
reading and go up to London. But I saw London, in particular the view

of white city churches and palaces from Hungerford Bridge through the eyes of Defoe. I saw the old women selling matches through his eyes; and the draggled girl skirting round the pavement of St James's Square seemed to me out of *Roxana* or *Moll Flanders*. Yes, a great writer surely to be there imposing himself on me after 200 years. A great writer—and Forster has never read his books! I was beckoned by Forster from the Library as I approached. We shook hands very cordially; and yet I always feel him shrinking sensitively from me, as a woman, a clever woman, an up to date woman. Feeling this I commanded him to read Defoe, and left him, and went and got some more Defoe, having bought one volume at Bickers on the way.

VIRGINIA WOOLF, *A Writer's Diary*, ed. Leonard Woolf, 1953

THE OLD VIC IN THE 1920S AND 1930S

Nobody was ever allowed to forget the audience. A prime clue to the success of the Old Vic and the curious supremacy of Lilian Baylis lies in the character of the audience and Lilian's intimate understanding of it. This became manifest in the 1920s. To quote the *Daily Telegraph* in September 1921: 'To form part of an Old Vic audience is a real tonic. These people really love the theatre for itself: they love the plays, the acting, the players. They do not come to see, and be seen by, each other . . . It is really possible to tell, at the Old Vic, what the audience think of the play, and how deeply they understand it. And they *do* understand it.' This audience, said the same critic a month later, was 'not the least important factor' in the 'traditional' teamwork acting. By 1925 the *Sunday Times* was talking of it as 'members of a great family sharing a common inheritance'; *The Times*, in 1926, said that not only Shakespeare but 'his natural audience' was 'as much alive today as when he was writing'; in the same year the *Daily News* asked, rhetorically, 'Surely the greatest happiness that can come to a player must be to act before an audience at the Old Vic?'

What was so special about this audience? It came, said Margaret Webster, 'to enjoy itself and did so vociferously. It could criticize vocally too, and laugh with a mighty derision . . . The hard core . . . didn't read the critics and didn't care about an actor's previous successes. It still liked to make its own stars, and when it made them, they stayed made.'

Right through the 1920s there was 'a unique flavour of intimacy, loyalty, mutual friendship and proprietary pride'. It was not (as it once may have been) proletarian, but it was democratic. 'Nobody appeared in evening dress, and, as the difference in price between the stalls and gallery was very little, and the difference in comfort still less, the whole house seemed to acquire a unity of character that was to be observed in the Old Vic and nowhere else.' It was a *regular* audience, not one made up from the carriage trade and a floating population of tourists, on whom the London theatre now depends for survival. 'There will never be another audience quite like them,' said Joan Cross. 'They responded with understanding, devotion and loyalty. They partook, in the real sense of the word, and although not averse to offering criticism, they felt themselves part and parcel of the institution; it was *their* theatre as well as Miss Baylis's.' But it was Miss Baylis who created this audience, not only by 'constantly presenting them with excellent things' but 'by allowing her own personality to be felt all the time as something constant and human in a world of abstract values'. Some of these words were written after the 1920s were over, but they express the especial quality of the audience and of its manager; for Lilian managed not only the players and the singers, but the people before whom they performed. If, as John Gielgud said in later years, 'the spirit of the place seemed so much stronger than any of the separate personalities who served it', it was largely because of the custodian of the place, and the guardian of its spirit.

The audience changed as the years went by. In the 1930s it included—notably, in the gallery—a group of blimpish loyalists who, having discovered Shakespeare through the early Vic productions, found it hard to accept any subsequent interpretations of less roughness, less readiness and less patent 'sincerity'. This 'congregational element', as Harcourt Williams termed it, was both a tower of strength and a redoubt of resistance, and refused to welcome any newcomers until they had shown they were good enough for the Vic, to the satisfaction of the old guard. Their symbol was Miss Pilgrim, a tiny, shrill devotee who began going to opera in 1912, when she was fifty-four. She could not afford more than one visit to the gallery a week, at twopence, but she followed every season for twenty-five years. She became infected by a love of Shakespeare, and saved up so that she could go to the theatre *every* night, for opera and drama. She acquired so special a status that she never had to queue for a seat in the gallery: her accustomed place was always left for her. Every night, at the end of the performance, she sang 'God Save the King' in a cracked voice; and then she walked home to a tobacconist's shop in the Pentonville Road. That kind of devotion was part of the making of the Old Vic; and part, too, of the cross that directors and performers had to bear.

RICHARD FINDLATER, *Lilian Baylis: The Lady of the Old Vic*, 1975

SOME LONDON CHILDREN

There is one little picture which must be described, though the child and its mother were unknown. The visitor in Lambeth Walk met a thin, decent woman carrying a pot of mignonette. By her side, a boy about seven years old was hopping along with a crutch under one arm. His other arm encircled a pot in which was a lovely blooming fuchsia, whose flowers swung to his movements. The woman was looking straight ahead with grave, preoccupied eyes, not heeding the child. His whole expression was one of such glorified beatitude that the onlooker, arrested by it, could only feel a pang of sharpest envy. They went on their way with their flowers, and round the next corner the visitor had to struggle through a deeply interested crowd, who were watching a man being taken to prison.

Questions are often asked as to how these children amuse themselves. They are popularly supposed to spend their time at picture palaces. As far as close observation could discover, they seemed to spend their play-time—the boys shrilly shouting and running in the streets, and the girls minding the baby and looking on. They played a kind of hop-scotch marked out in chalk, which reminded the visitor of a game much beloved by her in extreme youth. Boys whose parents were able to afford the luxury seemed to spend hours on one roller skate, and seemed to do positive marvels when the nature of the roadway and the nature of the skate are considered. Girls sometimes pooled their babies and did a little skipping, shouting severe orders as they did so to the unhappy infants. One party of soldiers, whose uniform was a piece of white tape round the arm and a piece of stick held over the shoulder as a weapon, marched up and down a narrow street for hours on the first day of the August holidays, making such a noise of battle and sudden death that the long-suffering mothers inside the houses occasionally left their work to scream to them to be quiet. The pathways were full of hatless girls and babies, who looked on with interest and envy. Needless to state, no notice was taken of the mothers' remonstrance. The best game of all is an ambulance, but that needs properties, which take some finding. A box on wheels, primarily intended for a baby's perambulator, and with the baby inside, makes a wonderful sort of toboggan along the paved path. The boy sits on one corner and holds with both hands on to the edges, the baby occupies the centre, and off they go, propelled by vigorous kicks.

In holiday-time elder brothers or sisters sometimes organise a party to Kennington Park or one of the open spaces near by, and the grass becomes a shrieking mass of children, from twelve or thirteen years of age downwards. The weary mother gives them bread and margarine in a piece of newspaper, and there is always a fountain from which they can drink. When they come home in the evening, something more solid is added to their usual tea. On Bank Holiday these children are taken by their parents to the nearest park. The father strolls off, the mother and children sit on the grass. Nobody talks. There is scolding and crying and laughing and shouting, and there is dreary staring silence—never conversation.

Indoors there are no amusements. There are no books and no games, nor any place to play the games should they exist. Wet holidays mean quarrelling and mischief, and a distracted mother. Every woman sighs when holidays begin. Boys and girls who earn money probably spend some of it on picture palaces; but the dependent children of parents in steady work at a low wage are not able to visit these fascinating places— much as they would like to. Two instances of 'picktur show, 2d.' appeared in the budgets. One was that of a young, newly married couple. The visitor smilingly hoped that they had enjoyed themselves. ''E treated me,' said the young wife proudly. 'Then why does it come in your budget?' asked the visitor. The girl stared. 'Oh, I *paid*,' she explained; 'he let me take 'im.' The other case was that of two middle-aged people, of about thirty, where there were four children. A sister-in-law minded the children, they took the baby with them, and earnestly enjoyed the representation of a motor-car touring through the stars, and of the chase and capture of a murderer by a most intelligent boy, 'not bigger than Alfie.' Here again the wife paid.

The outstanding fact about the children was not their stupidity nor their lack of beauty—they were neither stupid nor ugly—it was their puny size and damaged health. On the whole, the health of those who lived upstairs was less bad than that of those who lived on the ground-floor, and decidedly less bad than that of those who lived in basements. Overcrowding in a first-floor room did not seem as deadly as overcrowding on the floor below. It is difficult to separate causes. Whether the superior health enjoyed by a first baby is due to more food, or to less overcrowding, or to less exposure to infection, is impossible to determine; perhaps it would be safe to say that it is due to all three, but whatever the exact causes are which produce in each case the sickly children so common in these households, the all-embracing one is poverty. The proportion of the infantile death-rate of Hampstead to that of Hoxton—something like 18 to 140—proves this to be a fact. The 42 families already investigated in this inquiry have had altogether 201 children, but 18 of these were either born dead or died within a few hours. Of the remaining 183 children of all ages, ranging from a week up to sixteen or seventeen years, 39 had died, or over one-fifth. Out of the 144 survivors 5 were actually deficient, while many were slow in intellect or unduly excitable. Those among them who were born during the investigation were, with one exception, normal, cosy, healthy babies, with good appetites, who slept and fed in the usual way. They did not, however, in spite of special efforts made on their behalf, fulfil their first promise. At one year of age their environment had put its mark upon them. Though superior to babies of their class, who had not had special nourishment and care, they were vastly inferior to children of a better class who, though no finer or healthier at birth, had enjoyed proper conditions, and could therefore develop on sound and hygienic lines.

MAUDE PEMBER REEVES, *Round about a Pound a Week*, 1913

IN PIMLICO

As I look back on the days of my youth, one of the things that most impresses me about them is the absence of meddling. Except for a nice old lady who said, 'My dear, I hope you won't sleep alone,' I don't recollect anyone showing concern over my future when I left home to set up in London. My father was recently dead, my mother was occupied in being a widow and removing to Devonshire where she would be able to grow gentians. The Carnegie United Kingdom Trust had enlarged its activities from distributing organs to benefiting music in wilder ways. Among these was a project of research into Tudor Church Music. An Editorial Committee had been formed with its headquarters in Westminster, and I from pure inconspicuous merit, or possibly through the unaccountable machinery of fate, had been adjuncted to it, with a salary of three pounds a week and travelling expenses: First Class.

So all that remained was to find myself somewhere to live in London. That was left to me.

Free to enjoy the calm unbridled licence which made everything so much easier in those unmeddlesome days, and with well-defined notions of what I wanted or imperatively did not want, I made expeditions to London, considering neighbourhoods, looking for notice-boards of *To Let* and visiting House Agents, who listened to my simple wants (quiet street, self-containment, enough room for a grand piano, low rental, no church within earshot—for if I was to concentrate on Tudor Church Music I did not want to be distracted by Anglican choir-practices), and gave me orders to view. Some of the places would have suited me admirably, if I had been rich enough to afford them. Others were above fried-fish-shops, dance-halls, or in Ealing. Others just smelled.

At an agents called with simplicity Smith, Smith & Smith, a clerk who seemed to be developing a fatherly feeling towards me, from seeing me so often perhaps, or perhaps from not wanting to see me ever again, suggested that I might be better suited in a hostel. I contained myself and said I thought not. My legs might feel discouraged but my principles were unshaken and life in a hostel was one of the things I imperatively did not want. Resounding with self-respect, I went to a firm called Lomax and Gladstone. Their earlier orders to view proved visionary, but had promise about them. This time I was asked if I would have any objections to Pimlico: there was a flat in Pimlico, just come in that morning, second-floor, self-contained, view of the river, really a unique opportunity, splendid fittings, marble bath, modern geyser . . . I should go at once, for it was bound to be snapped up. I went at once, smirking at this prompt accolade to my principles. Pimlico, too, when one had got to it, had the peculiar appeal of a locality which had begun life with grand ambitions and never achieved them—the sort of place where one would be irresistibly impelled to quotations from Baudelaire.

I was halfway up the stairs when I saw Robert coming down. 'Robert!'

'Sylvia! What on earth are you doing here?'

'I've come to look at a flat.'

'You can't possibly live here.'

'But I think Pimlico's charming.'

'I'm not talking about Pimlico. I'm talking about this house. You cannot possibly take a flat in this house.'

'It's got a marble bath.'

'Marble bath!'

'To lie in a marble bath listening to the tugs hooting on the river. What could be—'

'It *would* have a marble bath.'

'Do they all have marble baths? And how do you know? Robert! Have you just taken my flat? Is that why you were looking so pleased with yourself—and now so taken aback?'

For he had been looking uncommonly pleased with himself—as though he had just come away from a looking-glass. Robert could have hung with credit in any picture gallery: *Portrait of a Young Man, by Sir Joshua Reynolds*; a young man with that slight velvety embonpoint which Sir Joshua conveys so appreciatively; and in Robert's case Sir Joshua, positively licking his lips, had included the mole, black as the black eyes, on his left cheek.

A new light shone on the situation. I exonerated Robert from any designs on my flat. Unless the lady craved for intellectual conversation, she must have found him pleasurable.

Robert was a year younger than me. I felt a tutelary affection for him and hoped in time to make him rather less of an idiot.

'Taken aback? I should jolly well think I was taken aback. And when you talked about taking a flat here—'

'You'd find it embarrassing?'

He shot me a grateful glance. 'I don't see how I could go on coming here.'

I had been reading *The Republic* of Plato. It struck me that the Socratic method might forward my ambition of making Robert rather less of an idiot.

'Do I often embarass you?'

'Well, yes, from time to time. But I get over it.'

'But meeting me here would always embarrass you?'

'Well, what do you expect?'

'Would you be equally embarrassed if I made a point of always using the back stairs?'

'I don't know if there is a back stairs. Besides, there are landings.'

'True. So it is the bodily confrontation with me which you would be embarrassed by?'

'If you must put it that way.'

'If you met four editors of Tudor Church Music coming upstairs, would that be as bad?'

'But why should they come here?'

'To visit me—I shall be in my flat by then—to discuss conjectural readings and *musica ficta* in Taverner's *Salve Intemerata*.'

'That must be screaming fun.'

'What is your idea of fun, Robert?'

'Ordinary fun. Ordinary human fun, nothing clever about it.'

'But if you heard us discussing *musica ficta* in Taverner's *Salve Intemerata*, would you be embarrassed?'

'Yawn my head off, more likely.'

'But you would not be embarrassed?'

'I don't see why I should be.'

'Good. We seem to have got that much settled. And if you came in and found us eating—say—winkles—'

'Winkles? What on earth are you driving at?'

'You'll see.'

For some one inexperienced in the Socratic method, Robert was coming along pretty well. In a few minutes more I'd have brought him to admit that fornication and musicology could go on under the same roof and neither parties feel the worse for it. Socrates would have carried it further, but I thought I'd leave it at that.

'Do you like winkles?' I continued.

'Not particularly. Aren't they supposed to be good for the brain?'

'Then it would seem that there are two approaches to eating winkles: one, to improve the intellect, the other because you like the taste.'

'Might bring off both.'

'And that the approaches are different—you admit as much, for you say "both". Well, suppose you found me and the editors of Tudor Church Music in my flat eating winkles—'

'That's enough about your flat! I tell you, you can't possibly take a flat in this house. It's impossible, it's out of the question, it won't do. If you don't drop the idea—'

'Yes?'

'I'll tell your mother.'

As I looked at him the mole twitched. We broke into wild laughter, and laughed and laughed till an acrid voice from above said 'Hush!' and we stole away. A couple of days later I found a flat in Bayswater. It was draughty and incommodious, but had ample room for the grand piano.

SYLVIA TOWNSEND WARNER, *Scenes of Childhood and Other Stories*, 1981

WAUGH THE INVIGILATOR

7 March 1927

The school in Notting Hill is quite awful. All the masters drop their aitches and spit in the fire and scratch their genitals. The boys have close-cropped hair and steel-rimmed spectacles bound around with worsted. They pick their noses and scream at each other in a cockney accent. For the first three days I had nothing to do but 'invigilate' while one of the urchins did an exam . . . On Friday I went by appointment to the editor of the Daily Express. He will take me for three weeks' trial at the end of term at £4 a week . . . On Saturday there was a party at Oliver Messel's . . . Robert Byron made an ostentatious entry as Queen Victoria. The Earl of Rosse and I cut each other throughout the evening.

The Diaries of Evelyn Waugh, 1976

TUDOR ESTATES AND ODEONS

In our area of this scene of headlong change, there was a mixture of housing estates and light industry, with small factories built along the ten-mile stretch of the Kingston bypass, a road opened in 1927 and extended during the thirties out to Esher and Guildford, a highway that was recognised in the estate business as a magnet for the land speculators and builders of bijou properties.

Huge new estates were spreading fast across the rural acres, street after street of Tudor-type semi-detacheds with their brand-new railway stations, pubs and gleaming art-deco Odeons. My family's house was on one of these estates. It was a thriving, comfortably-off region of Britain. Thirty years earlier, the area around Raynes Park itself had been the centre of the greatest increase in population of all the London suburbs:

between the two census returns of 1901 and 1911 the populations of Merton and Morden had shot up by 156 per cent. In the thirties, another boom was happening: between 1931 and 1939 the population of the area rose by another 75 per cent, with more and faster trains and buses going into the centre of town from the new communities that were nevertheless within striking distance of the countryside and the sea.

It wasn't only the improved transport that made these new settlements so popular. The air was purer, too, with prevailing winds blowing from the open rural counties. Jobs were easier to find in the small factories on the edge of south-west London: it was one of the areas that had escaped the worst of the depression. Life was cleaner and more comfortable: electricity was on tap, whereas in the Victorian and Edwardian terraces of the inner city many households still relied on gas. There were new gadgets to keep the house clean and the family fed: electric cookers (their sales trebled between 1930 and 1935), electric kettles, electric fires and vacuum cleaners. And the customers for these commodities, as for the houses themselves, were the better-paid factory employees and white-collar workers in banks and offices and shops.

New communities, built mainly by private developers with no special concern for any principles of town planning, had settled into haphazard networks of new residential roads, generally handy for not much else than the local railway station. Shopping 'parades' had established themselves on some of the estates, with brief rows of 'nice' shops whose proprietors generally lived above in a flat, meeting some but not all the basic needs of the local households, usually at extra cost.

PAUL VAUGHAN, *Something in Linoleum*, 1994

THE THAMES FLOODS

10 *January 1928*

A gusty day, turning to rain, so in the afternoon, having tried on clothes I decided to go down to the river to look at the high tide. On Westminster Bridge there was a large crowd watching the water lapping against the lawn under Big Ben, and hawkers were selling Old Moore's Almanack, declaring that he had prophecied the flood. Very probably, as he is as inclusive as an all-in insurance policy. Thence I walked to view the damage in Grosvenor Road, very smelly and low-tide looking, and through the warren of streets behind the Tate, where there were quantities of broken basements. A large flock mattress, saturated with Thames, was lying flop on the pavement outside one house, a lugubrious object.

The Tate announced that the only picture likely to be badly damaged is Blake's Nelson. Now I suppose, having damaged it irreparably they will have it irreparably repaired.

SYLVIA TOWNSEND WARNER, Diaries, 1994

88 ACRE LANE

No 88 Acre Lane was a tall three-storied late Georgian house with a basement. When it was built, in the 1820s, the surroundings must have been very different. It had been part of a terrace which had been demolished, leaving only No 88 and its semi-detached neighbour, No 86. At the back, the house had a large window opening onto a curved balcony: a hundred years earlier, a person standing on it must have had a view of meadows sloping down to a valley where lay the village of Stockwell. In the distance, you would have seen the spires of the city churches and the great dome of St Paul's.

Now, in the 1920s, buildings came right up to the back of the house. There was no back garden, only a small concreted yard, without a plant in sight, not even a weed. No view, no vista, only a high brick wall, shutting off a view of the small terraced Edwardian houses that had swarmed up the sloping terrain between Acre Lane and the railway line, the former London, Chatham and Dover Railway running to Victoria.

To reach the front door of No 88, with its handsome fanlight, you ascended a wide flight of seven stone steps. In front of this was the garden, a generous space with a wide gravelled path set around a circular flower bed. A brick wall, about waist high but with a privet hedge, gave us some seclusion from the passers-by and the traffic going up and down to Lambeth Town Hall or westward to Clapham Common. Open-topped buses honked along the road, and a few cars, and trade vehicles delivering milk, bread, or coal.

Immediately next to a cobbled passage at the side of our house, the Acre Lane shops began, each with its characteristic smell. The first shop was an off licence: I recall its dank, beery odour and the clink of bottles. A Mrs Clay kept the premises, a small, cheery woman with pink cheeks and absurdly prominent front teeth. Her husband was seldom visible and was understood to suffer from some mysterious and possibly shameful ailment connected to his trade. Next to Clay's was the shop kept by Mr Godden the chemist, a courteous, white-haired, well-scrubbed man in gold-rimmed spectacles whose orderly displays of coloured liquids and long-forgotten household remedies (Zam-Buk, Zubes and Zoids) also had a unique smell—sharp, clinical, and good for you. A little way along was David Greig's the grocer's, where men in black serge coats with white sleeve protectors up to the elbow sold ham, Gorgonzola cheese, fresh coffee, and biscuits dispensed from square glass-fronted boxes ranged before the counter, and where the bacon slicer gave out a sinister hiss as it peeled off slice after slice of home-cured streaky. Further along still was the ironmonger's, smelling of tarred rope, paraffin and bundles of sticks for lighting the fire; then a baker, Bamford's, whose manageress was said to have been glimpsed doing bit parts in the films we saw at the Brixton Pavilion. 'Look,' my mother would excitedly exclaim, 'There's Mrs Bamford!' I cannot believe she wasn't making this up.

PAUL VAUGHAN, *Something in Linoleum*, 1994

'MIDNIGHT ORGIES AT NO. 10'

There were about a dozen people left at the party; that hard kernel of gaiety that never breaks. It was about three o'clock.

'Let's go to Lottie Crump's and have a drink,' said Adam.

So they all got into two taxicabs and drove across Berkeley Square to Dover Street. But at Shepheard's the night porter said that Mrs Crump had just gone to bed. He thought that Judge Skimp was still up with some friends; would they like to join them? They went up to Judge Skimp's suite, but there had been a disaster there with a chandelier that one of his young ladies had tried to swing on. They were bathing her forehead with champagne; two of them were asleep.

So Adam's party went out again, into the rain.

'Of course, there's always the Ritz,' said Archie. 'I believe the night porter can usually get one a drink.' But he said it in the sort of voice that made all the others say, no, the Ritz was too, too boring at that time of night.

They went to Agatha Runcible's house, which was quite near, but she found that she'd lost her latchkey, so that was no good. Soon some one would say those fatal words, 'Well, I think it's time for me to go to bed. Can I give any one a lift to Knightsbridge?' and the party would be over.

But instead a little breathless voice said, 'Why don't you come to *my* house?'

It was Miss Brown.

So they all got into taxicabs again and drove rather a long way to Miss Brown's house. She turned on the lights in a sombre dining-room and gave them glasses of whisky and soda. (She turned out to be rather a good hostess, though over-zealous.) Then Miles said he wanted something to eat, so they all went downstairs into a huge kitchen lined with every shape of pot and pan and found some eggs and some bacon and Miss Brown cooked them. Then they had some more whisky upstairs and Adam fell asleep again. Presently Vanburgh said, 'D'you mind if I use the telephone? I must just send the rest of my story to the paper.' Miss Brown took him to a study that looked almost like an office, and he dictated the rest of his column, and then he came back and had some more whisky.

It was a lovely evening for Miss Brown. Flushed with successful hospitality, she trotted from guest to guest, offering here a box of matches, there a cigar, there a fruit from the enormous gilt dishes on the sideboard. To think that all these brilliant people, whom she had heard so much about, with what envy, from Miss Mouse, should be here in papa's dining-room, calling her 'my dear' and 'darling'. And when at last they said they really had to go, Miss Runcible said, 'Well, *I* can't go, because I've lost my latchkey. D'you mind awfully if I sleep here?'

Miss Brown, her heart in her mouth, but in the most natural way possible, said, 'Of course not, Agatha darling, that would be divine.'

And then Miss Runcible said, 'How too divine of you, darling.'

Rapture!

At half-past nine the next morning the Brown family came down to breakfast in the dining-room.

There were four quiet girls (of whom the Miss Brown who had given the party was the youngest), their brother worked in a motor shop and had had to get off early. They were seated at the table when their mama came down.

'Now, children,' she said, 'do try to remember to talk to your father at breakfast. He was quite hurt yesterday. He feels out of things. It's so easy to bring him into the conversation if you take a little trouble, and he does so enjoy hearing about everything.'

'Yes, Mama,' they said. 'We do try, you know.'

'And what was the Bicesters' dance like, Jane?' she said, pouring out some coffee. 'Did you have a good time?'

'It was just too divine,' said the youngest Miss Brown.

'It was *what*, Jane?'

'I mean it was *lovely*, Mama.'

'So I should think. You girls are very lucky nowadays. There were not nearly so many dances when I was your age. Perhaps two a week in the season, you know, but *none* before Christmas ever.'

'Mama.'

'Yes, Jane.'

'Mama. I asked a girl to stay the night.'

'Yes, dear. When? We're rather full up, you know.'

'Last night, Mama.'

'What an extraordinary thing to do. Did she accept?'

'Yes, she's here now.'

'*Well*. . . . Ambrose, will you tell Mrs Sparrow to put on another egg?'

'I'm very sorry, my lady, Mrs Sparrow can't understand it, but there *are* no eggs this morning. She thinks there must have been burglars.'

'Nonsense, Ambrose, who ever heard of burglars coming into a house to steal eggs?'

'The shells were all over the floor, my lady.'

'I see. That's all, thank you, Ambrose. Well, Jane, has your guest eaten all our eggs too?'

'Well, I'm afraid she has . . . at least . . . I mean.'

At this moment Agatha Runcible came down to breakfast. She was not looking her best really in the morning light.

'Good morning, all,' she said in Cockney. 'I've found the right room at last. D'you know, I popped into a study or something. There was a sweet old boy sitting at a desk. He *did* look surprised to see me. Was it your papa?'

'This is Mama,' said Jane.

'How are you?' said Miss Runcible. 'I say, I think it's quite too sweet of you to let me come down to breakfast like this.' (It must be remembered that she was still in Hawaiian costume.) 'Are you sure you're not *furious* with me? All this is really much more embarrassing for *me*, isn't it, don't you think . . . or don't you?'

'Do you take tea or coffee?' at last Jane's mother managed to say. 'Jane, dear, give your friend some breakfast.' For in the course of a long public life she had formed the opinion that a judicious offer of food eased most social situations.

Then Jane's father came in.

'Martha, the most extraordinary thing! . . . I think I must be losing my reason. I was in my study just now going over that speech for this afternoon, when suddenly the door opened and in came a sort of dancing Hottentot woman half-naked. It just said, "Oh, how shy-making," and then disappeared, and . . . oh . . .' For he had suddenly caught sight of Miss Runcible '. . . oh . . . how do you do? . . . How . . .'

'I don't think you have met my husband before.'

'Only for a second,' said Miss Runcible.

'I hope you slept well,' said Jane's father desperately.

'Martha never told me we had a guest. Forgive me if I appeared inhospitable . . . I—er . . . Oh, why doesn't somebody else say something.'

Miss Runcible, too, was feeling the strain. She picked up the morning paper.

'Here's something terribly funny,' she said, by way of making conversation. 'Shall I read it to you?'

'"*Midnight Orgies at No.* 10." My dear, isn't that divine? Listen, "*What must be the most extraordinary party of the little season took place in the small hours of this morning at No.* 10, *Downing Street. At about* 4 *a.m. the policemen who are always posted outside the Prime Minister's residence were surprised to witness*"—Isn't this too amusing—"*the arrival of a fleet of taxis, from which emerged a gay throng in exotic fancy dress*"—How I should have loved to have seen it. Can't you imagine what they were like?—"*the hostess of what was described by one of the guests as the brightest party the Bright Young People have yet given, was no other than Miss Jane Brown, the youngest of the Prime Minister's four lovely daughters. The Honourable Agatha* . . ." Why, what an extraordinary thing . . . Oh, my God!'

Suddenly light came flooding in on Miss Runcible's mind as once when, in her débutante days, she had gone behind the scenes at a charity matinée, and returning had stepped through the wrong door and found herself in a blaze of flood-lights on the stage in the middle of the last act of *Othello*. 'Oh, my God!' she said, looking round the Brown breakfast table. 'Isn't that just too bad of Vanburgh. He's always doing that kind of thing. It really would serve him right if we complained and he lost his job, don't you think so, Sir James . . . or . . . don't you?

Miss Runcible paused and met the eyes of the Brown family once more.

'Oh, dear,' she said, 'this really is all too bogus.'

Then she turned round and, trailing garlands of equatorial flowers, fled out of the room and out of the house to the huge delight and profit of the crowd of reporters and Press photographers who were already massed round the historic front door.

EVELYN WAUGH, *Vile Bodies*, 1930

BALLS

The last big party of 1929 was held at the Kit-Kat in aid of charity. Ever since the war hospitals relying on voluntary contributions had been finding it extremely difficult to collect enough money to keep going. The new poor could not contribute, the new rich had not yet been educated up to their responsibilities, and the idea of social advancement through charitable generosity had not yet sounded the final and absolute knell not only to post-war society, but to an exclusiveness even in Royal circles. That was to come. At the moment hospitals organized balls with expensive tickets and a few added attractions such as tableaux of famous people impersonated by titled amateurs, hoop-la and fishing for drinks, flowers and cigarettes sold by well-known actresses.

Mayfair never seemed to tire of dressing up. Besides the Bright Young People, who were getting older and rather boring with their now laboriously thought-out stunts, there were many fancy dress parties. The Prince of Wales had appeared in two different comic costumes at one given by the Duchess of Sutherland, when Mr Churchill had been a magnificent Cardinal Wolsey and Lord Ednam a buxom nurse. The Duchess repeated her balls two or three years running and on other occasions Lord Berners (music lover and author) was a 'monkey-bride', Lord Blandford (later the Duke of Marlborough) a female Channel swimmer, and Prince George a chef.

I therefore suggested a small but distinctive pageant when Mary Pitcairn, an efficient, energetic, charity organizer, consulted me about a dinner-dance to be given for Queen Charlotte's Hospital. A pageant had certainly never taken place at a dinner-dance before, in fact the latter was in itself a new departure from a begging point of view. But the ball organizers had chosen the Kit-Kat and that was one of the few places in London where a pageant could be staged, if it were not too large.

Eventually we evolved the idea of 'Queen Charlotte's Birthday Dinner,' and I asked 'Peter' Baxendale, a talented little artist who had recently held an exhibition of portraits in my house and who was later to make a great success with her circus pictures, to design the costumes. We started with an 'Oyster' and ended with Queen Charlotte herself and her Ladies in Waiting. Lady Dunn was 'White Wine' and her small daughter, Patricia Douglas, a 'Mince-pie.' Viscountess Castlerosse, wife of the *Sunday Express's* most brilliant columnist, was the 'fish,' Viscountess Scarsdale the 'goose.' I was 'champagne' in a dress of gold tissue covered in cellophane, a new transparent product made from wood pulp which in a few years was to be used for wrapping practically everything from kippers to cigarettes. I originally asked Lady Curzon to be Queen Charlotte, but she refused saying she hardly thought it a compliment as Queen Charlotte was an extremely ugly woman.

BARBARA CARTLAND, *The Isthmus Years*, 1943

MEMORIALS

I have an early memory of Armistice Day in 1929 or 1930. My mother and I are shopping in Brixton. Outside Lambeth Town Hall, everything suddenly stops. The trams come to a halt where they are, in the middle of the road, so do cars and lorries and the odd horse and cart. It is as if a magic spell has been cast over London. Pedestrians stand still, with their hats off, their eyes downcast, and a clock strikes eleven. In the distance, there comes the rumble of artillery fire. Dogs bark. 'Did you hear the guns?' whispers my mother. 'The guns in Hyde Park.' The guns! You could almost believe yourself back in The War again. I stand holding my mother's hand, thrilled by the idea of two minutes' silence observed by everybody and all of them, together, thinking about the same thing—that huge, mysterious and frightening event that all grown-ups knew about.

There were other reminders when we travelled about the city: the Cenotaph in Whitehall, where my father, like all the other men in the bus, would doff his hat. (He did the same, standing to attention, if a funeral procession passed by.) There were certain statues: Jagger's Artillery Memorial near Hyde Park Gate, with a gunner standing in steel helmet and gas cape with his arms outstretched on the parapet behind him, gravely regarding the passers-by; or the Royal Fusiliers' Memorial in Holborn, on which a fusilier in what my father taught me to call Field Service Marching Order, with rifle at the trail, stood silhouetted against the city skyline, one hand held out behind him as though to steady himself, perhaps to call his comrades to join him—or caution them against doing so. On our bus journeys round London I hoped we might pass one of these dramatic memorials so that I could register once more the fortitude, endurance and reproach of those stern figures.

Nevertheless, my father's tales of Army life, experienced mostly after the fighting was over and the last shot had been fired, were of a cheerful, optimistic kind, in which he featured as a debonair young infantry subaltern being cheeky to the Colonel or Adjutant. To my slight disappointment, nobody was ever killed in his stories. The discomfort, the boredom of service life, not to mention the hardship and mortal danger, had been forgotten. The comradeship, the jokes and freedom from domestic care all took precedence, as they did in the memory of many ex-soldiers, especially if they had managed to avoid the Front Line.

PAUL VAUGHAN, *Something in Linoleum*, 1994

THE CAFÉ ROYAL

Until the late Thirties, until the early season of the war, we still had in London the brasserie of the Café Royal. By all accounts it wasn't the Café Royal that it had been in the era of Sickert and Orpen and George Moore and Wilson Steer and William Rothenstein. All the same, you could revolve the doors from Regent Street, cross the carpeted foyer, skip the grill room, still the haunt of elders with money, and settle down with only cash enough for coffee and a drink or two, in the large red brasserie, finding yourself in a very mixed population of the famous and the obscure. Round the walls, under the mirrors you could eat without the distaste that assailed your more delicate senses in the vulgarity of Lyons Corner House; or with more privacy you could eat upstairs on the surrounding balcony floor. Baedeker of the time or a few years earlier (18th revised edition, 1923) gave the Café Royal a star and called it 'an artistic and Bohemian rendezvous'—the only one of its kind in that grand capital city of the world, Baedeker might have added, if you were in the know.

Faithful to the end, painters, novelists, poets, journalists crowded the brasserie. Among them were ghost figures out of a Ninetyish past, such as Lord Alfred Douglas, Arthur Symons or Richard le Gallienne. Had I known what he looked like, I am pretty sure I could have identified in the brasserie that London Frenchman Valéry Larbaud—

> *Après avoir aimé des yeux dans Burlington Arcade,*
> *Je redescends Piccadilly à pied, doucement.*
> *O bouffées de printemps mêlées à des odeurs d'urine,*
> *Entre les grilles du Green Park et la station des cabs,*
> *Combien vous êtes émouvantes!*

—who wrote under a London pseudonym Barnabooth, compounded from Barnes where he lived and Boot's at the end of his road.

Nightly habitués, older and younger, in fashion and out of fashion, included Wadsworth, Bomberg, Matthew Smith, Paul Nash, Teddy Wolfe, Epstein and his womenfolk, and Nina Hamnett, and Constant Lambert the composer. Cyril Connolly might be there, eating upstairs (downstairs wasn't his line) with authors he was going to entice down to Chelsea so that they could sign their books for him.

One or two habitués inclined to be touchy or even dangerous. It didn't do (it was one of the waiters who warned me of this) to stare in surprise at a giant of a woman, the poet Anna Wickham, author, incongruously, of a favourite anthology poem about a very wee or meek husband

> *I am a quiet gentleman*
> *And I would sit and dream;*
> *But my wife is on the hillside,*
> *Wild as a hill-stream.*

Anna Wickham would notice the unbelieving stare, take offence, stride between rows and tables and smite the offender.

The brasserie too was a refuge for political Bohemians. At an adjoining table next to my wife and myself there sat one evening Kerensky, one time head of the Russian revolutionary government, whom the Bolsheviks threw out into Europe, and Madame Kerensky. They left after a while, and Mme Kerensky left with the new black gloves my wife had bought that day. Perhaps she had been short of money to buy herself a new pair.

One of my stranger encounters in the Café was with a grey middle-aged bent man, shabbily dressed, whom I recognized soon enough as Edgar Wallace, though he never identified himself. For me it was a kind of sociological encounter, and I spent much of that late evening discovering how such a writer behaved, and what the nature was of such a best-selling author, such a famous lowbrow or middlebrow, as I should have called him then. It sounds priggish, but it is true that I humoured him and that he didn't suspect the fact when he instructed me in one way and another about, for instance, wise and foolish behaviour in the wickedness of London's West End.

I took out my pocket book which was rather stuffed with notes because I was off to Paddington on the way to Cornwall by a train after midnight. I took out a note for my bill. 'You don't know who I am,' said Edgar Wallace. 'You should be more careful. Never flash your money like that.' And he added 'Now I am going to show you a thing or two.' Protectively and educationally he took me round some dens, I suppose I should call them, below pavement level in the alleys at the back of the Café Royal. He was good company, and kind company, and I liked him. 'Remember what I've told you,' he said, holding the taxi door open when I took off for Paddington.

Equally well in the Café Royal I might have encountered an unfrocked priest or a brothel-keeper who had taken a first in Greats.

When we had come out short of money and unable to afford the Café Royal, I and my friends used to eat at a counter in a hole in the wall at the Piccadilly Circus end of Shaftesbury Avenue, where they sold first-class cups of creamy coffee and sandwiches of peppery, pink Liptauer cheese to the whores, who were everywhere around Piccadilly Circus, everywhere on the Soho side then. If you walked down Glasshouse Street, which runs more or less east and west, on a sunny evening, there was a golden glow in every doorway which sheltered a head of hair blonde from the bottle. It was rather a beautiful sight. Then, too, for a cheap meal and some of the best cooked rice imaginable, we went down some stairs of frayed lino off Denman Street into a bare room presided over by a very fat slow-moving Greek named Stelio. Greek or Cypriot restaurants, believe it or not, were uncommon still in the Thirties. They ministered to Greeks from the City, who raised their eyebrows rather at one's intrusion, but slowly became friends. In Stelio's shabby *hellenikon hestiatorion* there was no ornament except a faded photograph of the Parthenon hanging askew on the wall. There was no notice on the street up above.

The Café Royal was the thing, all the same, and the end of its brasserie as an 'artistic and Bohemian rendezvous' left London centreless in a fashion, contributing more than you would think, and just at a wrong time, to something of a new provinciality, which offset a growing sophistication and consciousness, in the arts, I mean. The closure, when it came, made for a lack of confidence in our own cultural abilities and sufficiency, even if some of the damage was undone or the weakness strengthened by the arrival of so many artists from Germany under the Nazis. And then the war came, with a London scattering which made matters worse for a while.

As a people we were unkind or less kind than we should have been, for our own good, to the new cultural emigrés and immigrants. We were jealous and failed to keep any of the best and most creative of them, who would rather have stayed with us, on the European side of the Atlantic, had we given them the chance prestigiously and economically.

It was something to go to Herbert Read's studio in Hampstead and meet handsome tall and grave Walter Gropius, for instance, and hear him interrogating Eliot on Swift and the form and clear language of *Gulliver's Travels*, the first book he read in English during his own enforced travels; but how long was it before Gropius was lost to us and swallowed up by the more appreciative Americans?

Kokoschka stayed for a while and was fun. 'Your hair is the colour of ripe strawberries,' he said at a crowded party in Highgate, spotting a girl he did not know who had arrived late and whose hair wasn't at all the colour of ripe strawberries. 'I kiss your hand,' he continued when he reached her side, and he began with kissing her elbow and coming down her forearm kiss by kiss, until he did reach her hand. The English didn't care for Kokoschka's Viennese baroque in paint or in behaviour, and thought it an odd thing to do (as it was, from our point of view, our Hampstead leaning to Picasso and Braque) when he painted a panoramic landscape of Polperro employing all the tricks of his Viennese manner. We never felt at ease with him, and he never felt at home with us, I would say, though he became an English citizen. The stiffness of some of the Germans and other central Europeans never relaxed, and I recall formal half-frozen evenings, for instance with Moholy-Nagy and his wife in Golders Green where emigré guests, who had once had to do with the Bauhaus, sat in their black suits and drank and talked a little too solemnly.

Anyhow it wasn't long before Moholy had gone, and was being firmly established by dollars in his Institute of Design at Chicago.

Maybe that the Americans who were so ready to pay for them, needed the German art emigrés more than we did in those years, on our fringe of Europe. I believe one of the few distinguished scholars from Germany to whom—was it Oxford, was it Cambridge?—gave a post was a classicist.

One small item in this settlement, such as it was, afforded some pleasurable irony. I had as neighbour in Keats Grove towards the end of my time there the small sprightly emigré artist Fred Uhlmann, who illustrated a booklet I wrote about the Isles of Scilly, which were much visited by painters when Europe and its stimulus were denied them. Other painters to be encountered there, profiting by the marvellous light of the Islands, were, with Fred Uhlmann in their wake, John Craxton, and his friend Lucien Freud, and that elder and instructor who belonged to John Piper's generation and my own, Graham Sutherland.

Now that emigré artist had an English wife, and an English father-in-law; and that artist—think of it, an artist—was not merely an exile from Germany, he was a German-Jewish exile; and that German-Jewish or Jewish-German artist's wife's father and his father-in-law was not only a general and an MP, not only a Tory aristocrat with a castle, he was a minister of the crown about to become a peer, and one of the extreme right known to be or suspected of being not without sympathy for Nazis and Fascists: he was Sir Henry Page-Croft, of Croft Castle in the county of Herefordshire, Under-secretary of State for War. Ironic justice, surely.

GEOFFREY GRIGSON, *Recollections: Mainly of Writers and Artists*, 1984

A TICKET FOR THE READING ROOM

With a smile of secret triumph
    Seedy old untidy scholar,
Inkstains on his fingernails,
    Cobwebs on his Gladstone collar,

Down at heel and out at elbows
    Off he goes on gouty feet

(Where he goes his foxy smell goes),
  Off towards Great Russell Street.

Unaware of other people,
  Peace and war and politics,
Down the pavement see him totter
  Following his *idée fixe*.

Past the rowdy corner café
  Full of Cypriots and flies
Where the customers see daggers
  Looking from each other's eyes,

Past the sad but so-called Fun Fair
  Where a few immortal souls
Occupy their leisure hours
  Shooting little balls at holes,

Past the window full of booklets,
  Rubber goods and cures for piles,
Past the pub, the natty milk-bar
  Crowded with galactophiles,

Through the traffic, down the side-street
  Where an unfrocked parson thrives
('Palmist and Psychologist')
  Cutting short unwanted lives,

Through the shady residential
  Square in which a widow runs
A quiet gambling-hell, or 'bridge club',
  Fleecing other women's sons,

On he shuffles, quietly mumbling
  Figures, facts and formulae—
Bats are busy in the belfry,
  In the bonnet hums a bee.

At the Reading Room he settles
  Pince-nez on his bottle nose,
Reads and scribbles, reads and scribbles,
  Till the day draws to a close,

Then returns to oh, what squalor!
   Kippers, cake and dark brown tea,
Filthy sheets and filthier blankets,
   Sleep disturbed by mouse and flea.

What has the old man been doing?
   What's his game? Another book?
He is out to pour contempt on
   Esperanto, Vōlapük,

To fake a universal language
   Full of deft abbreviation
For the day when all mankind
   Join and form one happy nation.

In this the poor chap resembles
   Prosperous idealists
Who talk as if men reached for concord
   With their clenched or grasping fists.

WILLIAM PLOMER, *Collected Poems*, 1960

MR GOLSPIE LOOKS AT LONDON

Left to himself, with his cigars all safe, Mr Golspie ruminated for a
minute or two, then climbed to the upper deck, perhaps to decide what
it was that had been waiting so long.

He found himself staring at the immense panorama of the Pool. Dusk
was falling; the river rippled darkly; and the fleet of barges across the
way was almost shapeless. There was, however, enough daylight linger-
ing on the north bank, where the black piles and the white-washed wharf
edge above them still stood out sharply, to give shape and character to
the water front. Over on the right, the grey stones of the Tower were
faintly luminous, as if they had contrived to store away a little of their
centuries of sunlight. The white pillars of the Custom House were as
plain as peeled wands. Nearer still, two church spires thrust themselves
above the blur of stone and smoke and vague flickering lights: one was
as blanched and graceful as if it had been made of twisted paper, a salute
to Heaven from the City; the other was abrupt and dark, a despairing
appeal, the finger of a hand flung out to the sky. Mr Golspie, after a brief

glance, ignored the pair of them. They in their turn, however, were dominated by the severely rectangular building to the left, boldly fronting the river and looking over London Bridge with a hundred eyes, a grim Assyrian bulk of stone. It challenged Mr Golspie's memory, so that he regarded it intently. It was there when he was last in London, but was new then. Adelaide House, that was it. But he still continued to look at it, and with respect, for the challenge remained, though not to the memory. Both the blind eyes and the lighted eyes of its innumerable windows seemed to answer his stare and to tell him that he did not amount to very much, not here in London. Then his gaze swept over the bridge to what could be seen beyond. The Cold Storage place, and then, cavernous, immense, the great black arch of Cannon Street Station, and high above, far beyond, not in the city but in the sky and still softly shining in the darkening air, a ball and a cross. It was the very top of St Paul's, seen above the roof of Cannon Street Station. Mr Golspie recognised it with pleasure, and even half sung, half hummed, the line of a song that came back to him, something about 'St Paul's with its grand old Dome.' Good luck to St Paul's! It did not challenge him: it was simply there, keeping an eye on everything but interfering with nobody. And somehow this glimpse of St Paul's suddenly made him realise that this was the genuine old monster, London. He felt the whole mass of it, spouting and fuming and roaring away. He realised something else too, namely, the fact that he was still wearing his old brown slippers, the ones that Hortensia had given him. He had arrived, had crept right into the very heart of London, wearing his old brown slippers. He had slipped two hundred and fifty cigars past their noses and had not even changed into his shoes. James Golspie was surveying London in his slippers, and London was not knowing, not caring—just yet. These thoughts gave him enormous pleasure, bringing with them a fine feeling of cunning and strength: he could have shaken hands with himself; if there had been a mirror handy he would probably have exchanged a wink with his reflection.

He walked round the deck. Lights were flickering on along the wharf, immediately giving the unlit entrances a sombre air of mystery. A few men down there were heaving and shouting, but there was little to see. Mr Golspie continued his walk, then stopped to look across and over London Bridge at the near water front, the south bank. Such lighting as there was on this side was very gay. High up on the first building past the bridge, coloured lights revolved about an illuminated bottle, to the glory of Booth's Gin, and further along, a stabbing gleam of crimson finally spelt itself into Sandeman's Port. Mr Golspie regarded both these writings on the wall with admiration and sympathy. The sight of London Bridge itself too pleased him now, for all the buses had turned on their lights and were streaming across like a flood of molten gold. They brought another stream of pleasant images into Mr Golspie's mind, a bright if broken pageant of convivial London: double whiskies in crimson-shaded bars; smoking hot steaks and chops and a white cloth on a little corner table; the glitter and velvet of the music halls; knowing gossip, the fine reek of Havanas, round a club fender and fat leather chairs; pretty girls, a bit stiff perhaps (though not as stiff as they used to be) but very pretty and not so deep as the foreign ones, coming out of shops and offices, with evenings to spend and not much else: he saw it all and he liked the look of it. There was a size, a richness, about London. You could find anything or anybody you wanted in it, and you could also hide in it. He had been a fool to stay away so long. But, anyhow, here he was. He took a long and wide and exultant look at the place.

J. B. PRIESTLEY, *Angel Pavement*, 1930

Harry Daley was a policeman, stationed at Hammersmith, who was befriended by E. M. Forster and J. R. Ackerley. For some years he wrote a memoir, which was published after his death under the title This Small Cloud.

LONDON FASCISTS AT OLYMPIA

There now ran through our duties a pattern of hunger marches, demonstrations, political meetings and disorderly scenes outside Labour Exchanges. We marched so often with the unemployed that at last we identified ourselves with them, and trudged about wearily at the mercy of the organisers—men who seized on the situation to grind their own axes without really caring much about the hungry footsore unemployed—or the well-fed footsore coppers come to that.

After a long march round London and an interminable meeting in Hyde Park, hardly able to stand, we were often alleged to have declared unanimously our determination to march on to Wormwood Scrubs Prison to shout consoling slogans to some of Harry Pollitt's friends who were locked up inside—and off we would totter. One Sunday evening we were cheered by an incident almost too good to be true. Tens of thousands of people, with great trouble, were reduced to silence to allow Harry Pollitt to attempt contact with his friends in the cells. 'Can—you—hear—us—comrades?' 'Ye—ss—s—s—', came the faint reply. 'Have—you—a—message—for—us—comrades?' 'Ye—ss—s—s.' 'What—is—your—message—comrades?' Everyone held his breath and the reply floated into absolute silence—'Bol—lock—ss—s—s'.

Gangs of black-shirted louts now began to upset other people's meetings and their activities led up to the strangest of all our Olympia duties. In 1934, with Hitler flourishing in Germany and official England not seeming to mind very much, Oswald Mosley hired Olympia and *invited* thousands of his admirers to fill the hall, to roar their approval as he shouted insulting remarks about Jews and Negroes and other inoffensive people. Technically, in spite of its size, this was as much a private party as Mrs Jones' sing-song in her front room on the occasion of her daughter's wedding.

The party was staged in the Hitler manner, with a patriotic style of decoration on the platform, variations in lighting, dramatic entries, and scores of storm troopers in black shirts and jack-boots standing about as ushers. Unknown to us at first, many decent men had courageously gate-crashed the party and were scattered singly about the hall, from which, as trespassers, they could legally be ejected 'with no more force than necessary'.

We watched from a room with windows looking down on the hall, more or less imprisoned, having been forbidden to leave it under any circumstances. We had been paraded by our Chief Inspector, which was unusual, who told us that whatever we saw we were not to interfere. This warning was later twice repeated. Why were we there? Should we have been called into action had Mosley's limbs been endangered, or was some cowardly Home Office official insuring against future accusations in Parliament? A few years later, living in a Section House with some young Special Branch men, I was surprised at their enthusiastic zeal when enquiring into the activities of suspected Communists, whilst their attitude to the Fascists, whose gangs of louts were by then openly beating-up in the West End streets any Jew or Negro unfortunate enough to be caught on his own, ranged from indifference to approval. These young men were public school types and therefore not likely to think things out for themselves; there is no doubt they took their cue from much higher up.

From our room at Olympia we looked down at the preparations for Mosley's great entry. At last the lights were lowered, a spotlight shone on a doorway and through it came Mosley—I was going to say 'like Barbette', but unfortunately he was not in the least like that tolerant man—with a thug bodyguard, all giving the Fascist salute. They strode like ham actors to the platform by an unnecessarily long route, whilst the cheering audience, as befitted the sacred moment, rose as one man to their feet. We were unable to hear Mosley's words, but could see his exaggerated gestures. Now and again one of the decent intruders in the audience rose in his seat, apparently to question something Mosley had said. Each time ushers in force pounced on the offender and carried him from the hall. They passed through a passage under our room and, by crossing to the opposite windows, we could see what happened in the yard. We saw groups of black-shirts with their coshes violently beating the defenceless hecklers, who could do nothing but stand and cover their bowed heads with their arms and hands until they fell to the ground. Nobody, up to then, had ever seen anything like it. We were all shocked.

These brutal scenes had been organised by a prominent Englishman, and carried out in the most famous hall in the country under the noses of members of the Metropolitan Police, who three times had been ordered not to interfere under any circumstances. There is nothing more I can say about this shameful occurrence, because there is nothing more I know of it. Our consolation at the time was that there would be swift retribution. But no! There were proud boasts of our freedom of speech; things I had seen with my own eyes were denied officially in parliament; and Mosley was left free to organise his mischief-making rallies in the Jewish districts of the East End.

I was left to reflect that politics was a dirty business, and politicians, with their thick skins, their cowardice, broken promises and shiftiness, were not at all of the quality of my generous-minded costermonger and bricklayer friends in Hammersmith. Among the policemen witnessing these violent scenes were some of my critics, whom I confess were equally shocked by what they saw. I could not resist remarking that, as these thugs were obviously middle-class, no doubt I could associate with them without adverse comment.

> HARRY DALEY, *This Small Cloud: A Personal Memoir*, 1986; Harry Pollitt was head of the British Communist Party

The Danish architect and architectural historian Steen Eiler Rasmussen came to London in the 1930s and subsequently wrote London: The Unique City. *He gives many reasons for its uniqueness, but chief among them is the fact that London is a city of houses, however small, and not—like Paris, Rome, or his native Copenhagen—a city of apartments.*

'MY HOUSE IS MY CASTLE'

Just as we look to London as the originator of English ideals in the world, so is the manner in which people live, or try to live, in London the expression of the same world of thought . . . 'My house is my castle', the one-family house, open-air life and all that we others admire and are fain to imitate, is inseparable from the English mode of thought and life. One hardly knows whether to laugh or to cry on seeing a modernistic architecture, imported into London, which is far less suitable to the spirit of the age than the Georgian houses of about 1800. There is now a quantity of English books on the latest fashions in foreign architecture, but I have yet to find one English book dealing at length with the fine standardized type of Georgian town-house, the sight of which is one of the most remarkable experiences to the foreigner in London. Hardly anyone in London realizes that London is a first rate architectural city, and that Bedford Square is one of the finest squares in the world.

HAMPSTEAD HEATH: 1937

If you tell a Londoner what a fine park Hampstead Heath is he will look at you astonished and ask: 'Do you consider Hampstead Heath a park?' In fact he has never realized what Hampstead Heath is at all. To him it is a piece of uncultivated land which—for some unexplained reason —still lies there untouched in spite of the development of the town. He lives in the happy delusion, that it is a no-man's-land where every-body can do as he likes. And yet it is a public park with inspectors and gardeners, a place where trees and bushes are planted to emphasize the character of the place and to disguise the detrimental effect of new houses. In Hampstead Heath you will find beauty in all seasons. The undulating country is so full of variation that you find nearly all the artistic effects that European painters have depicted: in the damp atmosphere of the twilight the mirror of the Hampstead ponds behind the willows look just like a *Corot*, the flocks of sheep on the bare grass under solitary trees are *Millet*, and hills and bulky trees against a thundercloud are *Constable*. But those thousands who enjoy Hmpstead Heath do not look at it in this way. Their view has not been determined by art, they feel a much more primitive relation to Nature. They are not in an art gallery. They walk with delight in the high grass when they escape from the streets. They do not only see, they feel the forms of the land when they wearily plod up the hill. Here they are rewarded by the splendid view and in the ever-changing climate it is always of interest to try 'how far one can see to-day'. All the sports which are practised on Hampstead Heath may be looked upon as an attempt to perceive Nature in a more intensive way. Like Prospero in *The Tempest* the English want to know all the spirits of Nature, to understand them and to master them. On the top of Parliament Hill you see elderly gentlemen flying cleverly constructed kites. The taut string forms a sort of feeler hundreds of feet up in the air and makes space perceptible to him. From this hill the landscape slopes down on both sides into valleys at the bottom of which there is a series of ponds. On the flat plain towards the south, boys play football while others run up and down the hills kicking their balls about. In the cup-shaped valley towards Highgate there is a bandstand from which the hollow space can be filled with music and give an impression of the strange acoustics of Nature. In the lakes there is accommodation for swimming. Not, however, that the water is too tempting! And yet all the year round there are people who dive gracefully from the boards. The English love the raw sensation of the elements, to feel the wind and the moisture in their faces. That is why they swim in the lakes, dive down to muddy depths—becoming fishes in the coolness of the water.

The average visitor does not observe that there is a certain guiding principle in the apparently accidental planting of the park. He only knows how wonderful it is to saunter along the hedges of thorn, over the hills with the solitary oaks to the rounded tops of the heights and down through the grove of alders to the more cultivated Golders Hill Park passing all these characteristic types of planting, which in no place form an inarticulated mixture.

On Hampstead Heath the original nature is being ruined. The flora is simplified and vulgarized, the fauua is almost extinct. There are hills where the grass is worn off entirely, so that it most of all resembles a landscape with barren, sandy slopes. There is another place where a large and specially constructed ash area is laid out for the Bank Holiday booths and roundabouts. But even if original Nature has been spoiled in this way Hampstead Heath has yet to the advantage of great parts of London's population preserved its direct relation to her, not the rare and beautiful, but the primitive, to air and water, soil and plants. Everybody who walks here has some object or other, something to do, either kicking at a ball or diving into the lake or flying a kite and thereby keeps his own nature pure and unspoiled. He is not moved by second hand emotions, he does not love the place because it reminds him of something which he knows is considered refined and civilized. In Hampstead we have in the middle of the great city an instance of the right preservation of Nature—*the human nature*.

Steen Eiler Rasmussen, London: The Unique City, 1937

WHERE TO DINE: 1937

Every schoolboy of these precocious times knows how to pronounce the name of QUAGLINO'S, 16, Bury Street, off Jermyn Street. No more than eight years ago small, dapper Quaglino was head waiter at Sovrani's Restaurant. Now, with his brother, he has risen to the pinnacle of fame and success. He has constantly enlarged and extended his business, which has recently been formed into a Company. The decoration at Quaglino's is in the most colourful and exuberant modern style. There are painted mirrors and very pleasant lighting effects. The service is smooth and well organised.

As for food, everything is *à la carte*, and the prices are those of any restaurant de luxe. That is to say, that a good dinner for two may be had for about 25/-, exclusive of drinks. Here is a specimen dinner for the spring:

Caviar de Sterlet

Tortue Claire

Mousseline de Saumon aux Crevettes Roses
Suprême de Volaille sous Cloche Maison
Salade d'Asperges
Biscuit aux Avelines
Frivolités

Vodka should be drunk with the caviare. Château Margaux 1916 will fittingly accompany the salmon; Champagne, an Irroy 1923, may be served with the chicken; and an 1812 Napoleon Brandy will conclude a meal to satisfy even the most notorious of Charity hostesses.

Quaglino is to be congratulated on not troubling his guests overmuch with cabaret. There is but one turn, which comes on at midnight, and it lasts for only about twenty minutes. Dancing continues every night until 2.0 a.m., and the licence is extended until this hour on Wednesdays. On Sundays the entertainment is at 10.0 p.m.

In the kitchen M. Rossignol, perhaps the only bearded chef in London, presides over no less than twelve highly-qualified specialists in each branch of cooking. This great artist helped to build up the fame of Ciro's, and his skill has improved with the years.

For those not in evening dress there is a Grill Parisien next door in the basement. As in the Restaurant, dancing continues until 2.0 in the morning. The cabaret comes on shortly after midnight.

The SAN MARCO, Devonshire House, just opposite the Ritz, is the most amusingly decorated restaurant in Town. It has been designed by Oliver Messel as a sixteenth century Doge's palace. The colour scheme is in red, pale blue and pink; there is an illusion of the sun rising behind blinds; the Grand Canal is dramatically represented by means of light on an uneven surface, which creates the impression of running water; and there is a most intriguing little balcony with its table laid for a private supper which will never be eaten, as there is no visible means of approach. The lighting is particularly becoming for ladies.

Umberto, the charming *maître d'hôtel* from Ciro's at Monte Carlo and the Café de Paris, will guide your choice from an excellent cuisine. Specialities of the Restaurant are *Scampi Vénitiens*, which are Dublin prawns, *Volaille de Surrey Beauséjour*, or chicken done in casserole with rosemary, and *Crêpes Flambées Mandarinettes*. There is a minimum charge for supper of 12/6.

There is a single cabaret turn on all nights but Thursday, when there is an Amateur Hour, and the standard of entertainment is high. I hear, for instance, that the celebrated Dwight Fiske has been engaged for the Coronation.

The HUNGARIA, 14, Regent Street, really is Hungarian in atmosphere, music, food and wine. The walls are decorated with the crests of various Hungarian 'counties,' and there is that air of noisy revelry which one associates, rightly or wrongly, with the aforementioned country. There is a four-course lunch at 5/6 and a gigantic dinner at 12/6. Particularly to be recommended are the little snacks of caviare and what-not which are brought to you as you sip your Martini. Evening dress is essential and Tuesday is extension night.

The Grill downstairs is *à la carte*, and I am inclined to think that the food is slightly superior in this department. Perhaps that is only because you have the choice of such delightful dishes as Trout *à la Tatra*, Hungarian Turbot with onion and tomato and Paprika Chicken with the traditional pink sauce, instead of having French food chosen for you.

From 7.30 in the evening there are gipsy bands in both Restaurant and Grill, but dance bands come on at 9.30 p.m. In the Restaurant there is a cabaret at 10.45 p.m. and midnight, and in the Grill at 10.15 p.m. and 11.30 p.m. Kolopar, the xylophonist, is a great favourite of mine. He leers round the room in the friendliest possible manner while he is doing his turn. Incidentally, the Hungaria was several times visited by the Duke of Windsor as Prince of Wales and King, and many distinguished people are to be seen there.

The wine list deserves a word to itself, as it is sponsored by the Hungarian State as an advertising medium. Every kind of Hungarian wine is to be found on it, and many of them are excellent. There are all sorts of Tokays, ranging back to the year 1889, and there is an insidiously strong beverage called 'Bull's Blood.' Liqueurs and old brandies are a speciality.

'BON VIVEUR', *Where to Dine in London*, 1937

TRAMPS AND OTHERS

By dawn even the sexual sinners had gone to bed, the cleaners had refreshed the streets with their flooding fountains, and the beggars in their favourite nooks were left for a while to sleep in peace.

It was part of the Vine Street tradition not to badger the beggars; this originally may have been dictated by public opinion. When an old beggar-woman was arrested in Grafton Street outside the mansion of Mrs Willie James, one of the Great Hostesses, this dear lady was very upset and sent a stinker to the Commissioner of Police. 'I *like* to see her begging outside my house', she wrote. 'She is *not* to be arrested again.' This was the general attitude to our tramps and beggars. The rich saw them as poor humble creatures whose grovelling manners brought temporary feelings of graciousness and charity; the country visitors saw them as part of the scene they had come to stare at.

There were other reasons why they were not often arrested; they left the cells in such a lousy state that we hardly liked to invite a decent criminal in. A well known tramp, bearded and top-hatted, who pushed his possessions along in a pram, was lousy enough to have mice as well as the usual things. When he was arrested and brought to the station they ran from his pram like rats deserting a sinking ship. 'Don't ever dare to bring him here again', cried the station officer, and thus conferred on him the Freedom of the City.

The tramps, having gained public approval by public humility, did not feel it necessary to adopt this pose to policemen. They had their regular theatre doorways and other places to sleep in, and often called upon us to eject intruders. We usually left them alone, thankful to have them settled down, but in February it was the custom to speak to them before going off night duty. A frosty February often finished what a damp November had started, and a dead body in a theatre doorway took some explaining when the manager arrived at ten in the morning.

Before waking an old woman in the doorway of Daly's Theatre I reflected that she had slept here in the days of *The Waltz Dream*, *The Count of Luxembourg*, *The Dollar Princess* and *The Merry Widow*, through the long run of *The Maid of the Mountains* up to the over-patriotic *Young England*, which was now providing violent middle-class louts with a safe excuse to misbehave in public.

I woke her gently with a sort of apology. 'Oh, it's all right', she said. 'I wanted a policeman anyway—I want to report the loss of my furs.'

'Have you been to the police station? They may be there.'

'Don't talk so silly—how can I get to the station with my leg?'

She showed me her leg. It was frightful—quite raw and rotting from knee to ankle, with a dreadful smell. I begged to be allowed to take her to hospital, promising, dishonestly, that she would not be kept in.

'Never you mind about my leg', she said testily. 'You get off and look for my furs—that's what you're paid for.'

There was often trouble at the back of the Turkish Baths in Jermyn Street, where the hot steam floated up through the gratings and turned them into attractive beds. They were occupied by regulars and were so desirable that it was known who would succeed on the death of the holder. New homeless people sometimes found this haven by accident and once or twice I was called upon to give judgment. It was impossible. My sympathy was with the innocent newcomers, but I was obliged to murmur ambiguously something about first come first served and leave them to work it out for themselves. 'How can I get here earlier when I've got my dustbins to do?', cried one old man. Quite true. If one lives on the crumbs from the rich man's table, one must wait until the rich man finishes, and the best crumbs fall from the supper table.

All the hotel and restaurant dustbins were thoroughly sifted every night, not only for food but for other things that brought in a few coppers, several men being specialists. Some sought cigarette and cigar ends which fetched a few shillings for their nicotine content at Covent Garden next morning. To get the biggest haul, enough money to keep alive, it was necessary to wait until the restaurants were finally swept out. Police were aware of this and were not unsympathetic to the idea of reserved doorways and gratings.

The newcomers among the homeless, the unfortunate unemployed, got a raw deal all round. Not only were the best sleeping places occupied or booked, but being skilled workmen temporarily hungry and desperate, with no knowledge of the cringing art of begging, they got into trouble by openly asking for money when they saw it being wasted by revellers. Being by now merely shabby, still far from the picturesque filthy stage, they caused indignation and complaints, on the strength of which the snatchers were only too pleased to make arrests. They then became disillusioned and frightened and drifted out again to places like Hammersmith. The law authorised fingerprints of convicted beggers to be taken, and many honest men in Wales and the North, among those who survived the war, now back in their rightful place as heads of families, must have their convictions and fingerprints filed at Scotland Yard.

HARRY DALEY, *This Small Cloud: A Personal Memoir*, 1986

A BITTER PREDICTION

You English who come over to the Continent and see big residential quarters with miles and miles of tall houses in which the people live in dwellings piled one on top of the other, should try to realize that this unfortunate system is not the result of the need for good homes or the improvement of the conditions of traffic. The only reason for its existence is this: the landlord gets higher interest on his property. The thousands of human beings who live in dwellings so wretched that they are a danger to the community, are so doing in order to give the honest middle classes the opportunity of a good and safe investment.

You English should know that the Frenchman, Le Corbusier, is a modernist in his artistic form but a conservative in his planning of a city. When he plans to rebuild Paris with rows of sky-scrapers, he is merely keeping up the old tradition from the reigns of the Bourbons and the Bonapartes. To improve the health of Paris, the city has always been made more and more imposing and monumental, with less and less consideration for the manner in which a family can live under wholesome conditions. In England new slums largely develop in houses that have been given up by their middle-class owners. On the Continent we construct slums.

You English must also know that in all towns, in your own as well as others, there is a strong tendency to de-populate the most thickly populated areas. And this tendency is a right and wholesome one. But when replacing poor little houses by big blocks of flats, large sums are tied up in quarters which should normally de-populate, and wholesome evolution is thus hindered by the building of these large blocks. We on the Continent know something of this, for we have learnt it to our cost. To build flats in slums will not stem the current, London will continue to be a town of one-family houses, and it is tragic to see the enormous sums of money spent in this way and employed to a wrong purpose, for instead of planning the moving out of factories, business premises and private houses in connection with each other, living houses are being built with a quite un-English standard and according to types which are everywhere else recognized as inadequate.

The monumental city of antiquity, Peking, is ruined by the intrusion of houses of European types which destroy all the harmony of its plan. And now London, the capital of English civilization, has caught the

infection of Continental experiments which are at variance with the whole
character and tendency of the city! Thus the foolish mistakes of other
countries are imported everywhere, and at the end of a
few years all cities will be equally ugly and
equally devoid of individuality.
This is the bitter
END.

STEEN EILER RASMUSSEN, *London: The Unique City*, 1937

GRANADA, MITCHAM ROAD, TOOTING

Cecil Macey, 1938
The outside is any old cinema with a grandiose front and mean flanks.
The foyer is like a cross between Strawberry Hill and the Soane Museum;
for once the fantasy of films has been matched by fantasy in the cinema.
To argue that it is plaster deep is like arguing that *La Règle du Jeu* is just
a strip of celluloid. Ninety-nine cinemas may be a shoddy counterfeit and
so may ninety-nine films: but this is the hundredth. Gothic arches are all
around in the auditorium, dimly lit by reflections from the screen. When
the lights go up there is Aladdin's cave; and if you walk to the front for
a choc-ice or orange squash and turn round suddenly, the view may
literally make you gasp. Pinnacle after gilded pinnacle, to the back of the
gallery: one of the sights of London. Miss the Tower of London, if you
have to, but don't miss this.

IAN NAIRN, *Nairn's London*, 1966

LAVATORIES

It is worth adding that, as the months passed towards the outbreak of the
last war, the scribblings in London lavatories gradually became more
belligerous. This was most notable in the larger conveniences such as
those at Hyde Park Corner, and perhaps represent the folk mind letting
loose the dogs of war.

To return to Holborn. I made friends with the attendant [. . . ,] and
on my pointing out the resemblance of the water tanks to fish tanks, he
told me, to my delight, that a previous attendant had actually used them

for this purpose. It seemed to me that the fish must have been surprised to find their breathing space restricted and themselves coming down in the world each time the stalls were flushed, and what they made of the copper ball tap in their water I could not imagine. However, keeping fish in a lavatory tank is a delightfully rococo, or rather *fin de siècle*, idea, and might be copied with decorative results. There is also a certain logic about it which appeals to me, and it is wonderfully intriguing to imagine what the men using the place thought of the fish; more important, what the fish thought of the men. My attendant friend told me that there were very few old lavatories left in London (fewer still even today in the West End where the great landowners frowned on them). He called old conveniences 'Queen Victorias', a somewhat startling terminology. I was told that 'the lavatory in Charing Cross Road was the place to go if you want the writing on the wall . . . make your blood run cold, it would'. Charing Cross Road had been cleaned up before my tour of inspection, and so I found no writing on the wall. This lavatory, on an isolated site, is marked by one of the most splendid gas lamps in London, painted in black and gold and equalled only by the lamp at the back of St Clement Danes in the Strand and the pair in Trafalgar Square; the last, however, are now electrified. Holborn remains one of my favourites, for the gas jets are still intact over the water closets, and there are electric bulbs of Edwardian date which bend over like white tulips. The lavatory at the junction of Kings Cross Road and Pentonville Road was once, I believe, like the one in Rosebery Avenue, a privately owned affair—an odd way to make a living.

Yet another interesting lavatory is the one opposite the Brompton Oratory. From the isolation of the centre of the road, the ironwork makes a foreground to a view of the Italianate Oratory, dating from 1878. (Brompton Oratory is a sort of pastiche of Italian Baroque, built out of hard stone of an unsympathetic quality, but the front is interesting with its narthex and trumpeting angels. Seen in the fading light of a grey autumn evening with the lavatory rails in front, it creates a curious sensation, but under these conditions, the church is more attractive, a sort of Canaletto-like view strayed somehow into London.) The lavatory is reached by steep, narrow stairs, and the 'conveniences' inside are of boldly marked marble in brown and white. A tiled frieze of yellow-green acanthus runs above the white tile walls. These classical motifs have been made to suit some unusual purposes since they first saw the light of day, purposes that would have caused some consternation to the designers of the Periclean age. The Victorians were strong minded enough not to bother their heads over incongruous ornament, and made the Victorian lavatory, if not a thing of beauty, certainly a joy for ever. This Brompton one has a mosaic floor with a running leaf pattern in the border that gives one the feeling of behaving rather too freely in some corner of the Alhambra or in some delicately glimmering room in old Bagdad.

Other touches that give the place a comfortable period flavour are the cast iron plates fixed in the walls, with a hand pointing the way out. I like those pointing Victorian hands, often showing a nice bit of linen cuff, which showed (or shewed) so many ways to so many Victorians. They invariably occur in advertisements for patent medicines and cocoa, where the hand points to a warning against fraudulent imitations. The attendant's room has the windows covered with that transparent oiled paper in imitation of stained glass which was a characteristic invention of the Victorians who were addicted to semblances and simulations. Over the door is the final touch, a lace curtain—a badge, like the aspidistra, of conformity and utter respectability.

GEOFFREY S. FLETCHER, The London Nobody Knows, 1962

SUMMER, 1938

Regent's Park was
   Gay with ducks and deck-chairs,
Omens were absent,
   Cooks bought cloves and parsley;
O my love, to
   Stop one's ear to omens.

Pigeons courting, the cock
   Like an eighteenth-century marquis
Puffing his breast and dragging
   His fantail waltzwise;
O my love, the
   Southward trains are puffing.

Nursemaids gossiped,
   Sun was bright on pram-paint,
Gold in the breeze the arrow
   Swivelled on church-tops;

But Living drains the living
  Sieve we catch our gold in.

Toy sail skidding on Whitestone
  Pond at the peak of London,
Challenge of bells at morning,
  Crocus and almond;
O my love, my
  Thoughts avoid the challenge

But the rumbling summer rolls
  A register behind us—
March to April to May
  To denser summer—
And the road is dusty, the goal
  Unknown we march to.

Rampant on Europe headlines
  Herald beasts of fable;
Backward the eyes to ancient
  Codes—vellum and roseleaf;
From the moving train of time the
  Fields move backward.

And now the searchlights
  Play their firemen's hoses,
Evil their purport
  Though their practice lovely,
Defence and death being always
  Collateral, coæval.

And now the soldier
  Tightens belt and outlook,
Eyes on the target,
  Mind in the trigger-finger,
And a flight of lead connecting
  Self and horizon.

And now, and last, in London
  Poised on the edge of absence

I ask for a moment's mention
   Of days the days will cancel,
Though the long run may also
   Bring what we ask for.

LOUIS MACNEICE, from 'Trilogy for X', *Collected Poems 1925–1948*,
   1949

CHELSEA EMBANKMENT

Celia's course was clear: the water. The temptation to enter it was strong,
but she set it aside. There would be time for that. She walked to a point
about half-way between the Battersea and Albert Bridges and sat down
on a bench between a Chelsea pensioner and an Eldorado hokey-pokey
man, who had dismounted from his cruel machine and was enjoying a
short interlude in paradise. Artists of every kind, writers, underwriters,
devils, ghosts, columnists, musicians, lyricists, organists, painters and
decorators, sculptors and statuaries, critics and reviewers, major and minor,
drunk and sober, laughing and crying, in schools and singly, passed up
and down. A flotilla of barges, heaped high with waste paper of many
colours, riding at anchor or aground on the mud, waved to her from
across the water. A funnel vailed to Battersea Bridge. A tug and barge,
coupled abreast, foamed happily out of the Reach. The Eldorado man
slept in a heap, the Chelsea pensioner tore at his scarlet tunic, exclaiming: 'Hell roast this weather, I shill niver fergit it.' The clock of Chelsea
Old Church ground out grudgingly the hour of ten. Celia rose and
walked back the way she had come. But instead of keeping straight on
into Lot's Road, as she had hoped, she found herself dragged to the right
into Cremorne Road.

SAMUEL BECKETT, *Murphy*, 1938

AT THE KARACHI

The Karachi Hotel consists of two Kensington houses, of great height,
of a style at once portentous and brittle, knocked into one—or, rather,
not knocked, the structure might hardly stand it, but connected by
arches at key points. Of the two giant front doors under the portico, one

has been glazed and sealed up; the other up to midnight, yields to pressure on a round brass knob. The hotel's name, in tarnished gilt capitals, is wired out from the top of the portico. One former dining-room has been exposed to the hall and provides the hotel lounge; the other is still the dining-room, it is large enough. One of the first-floor drawing-rooms is a drawing-room still. The public rooms are lofty and large in a diluted way: inside them there is extensive vacuity, nothing so nobly positive as space. The fireplaces with their flights of brackets, the doors with their poor mouldings, the nude-looking windows exist in deserts of wall: after dark the high-up electric lights die high in the air above unsmiling armchairs. If these houses give little by becoming hotels, they lose little; even when they were homes, no intimate life can have flowered inside these walls or become endeared to them. They were the homes of a class doomed from the start, without natural privilege, without grace. Their builders must have built to enclose fog, which having seeped in never quite goes away. Dyspepsia, uneasy wishes, ostentation, and chilblains can, only, have governed the lives of families here.

In the Karachi Hotel, all upstairs rooms except the drawing-room, have been partitioned up to make two or three more: the place is a warren. The thinness of these bedroom partitions makes love or talk indiscreet. The floors creak, the beds creak; drawers only pull out of chests with violent convulsions; mirrors swing round and hit you one in the eye. Most privacy, though least air, is to be had in the attics, which were too small to be divided up.

ELIZABETH BOWEN, *The Death of the Heart*, 1938

REGENT'S PARK TERRACE

The noises round my house. On cobbles bounding
Victorian-fashioned drays laden with railway goods;
their hollow sound like stones in rolling barrels:
the stony hoofing of dray horses.

Further, the trains themselves; among them the violent,
screaming like frightened animals, clashing metal;
different the pompous, the heavy breathers, the aldermen,
or those again which speed with the declining

sadness of crying along the distant routes
knitting together weathers and dialects.

Between these noises the little teeth
of a London silence.

Finally the lions grumbling over the park,
angry in the night hours,
cavernous as though their throats were openings up from the earth:
hooves, luggage, engines, tumbrils, lions,
hollow noises, noises of travel, hourly these unpick
the bricks of a London terrace, make the ear
their road, and have their audience in whatever
hearing the heart or the deep of the belly owns.

BERNARD SPENCER, Collected Poems, 1965

SEPTEMBER 1940

A great provincial city like Sheffield could erect a dummy town in the neighbouring hills to attract and deceive the Luftwaffe, but the sprawling size of London made it impossible to disguise, and the U-shaped bend of the Thames round the Isle of Dogs, in the heart of Dockland, was unmistakable from the air.

Ten or a dozen miles from the centre of the capital, to north, south, west and east, lay the outer suburbs, from which office workers surged towards the centre in the morning, and to which they swarmed out again in the evenings. Harrow and Hornsey, Ealing and Richmond, Woodford, Wimbledon, Croydon and Bromley were the heartland of the English middle class, zones of tidy gardens, extensive green playing fields, quiet and propriety. Now tired commuters struggled home somehow on slow trains (when there were any) and went straight to their Andersons for the night, perhaps to read Trollope, whose pictures of the croquet lawns and country houses of the mid-Victorian age of equipoise were enjoying a marked but easily explained boom. Few footsteps, after darkness, echoed in the avenues. The warden's post was the liveliest social centre which the blacked-out, owner-occupied acres could afford. Within this outer ring of pebble dash, red brick and ornamental trees lay intermediate suburbs, shabbier genteel; then, to the north and west, older suburbs which gave flats and mansions to the well-to-do. Some, like Chelsea, were battered remorselessly. Others, like Hampstead, came off relatively lightly. Incendiaries would lodge in the rafters of mansions deserted by their owners, and burn them out. At the hub of the wheel lay the twin cities of London and Westminster. With Whitehall, Bloomsbury, Fleet Street, St Paul's, the Bank of England, the central area still concentrated within its few square miles Britain's cultural past, its commercial present and its legislative future. The raider could be sure that whatever he struck there was of objective or sentimental importance, and later this would become the most heavily blitzed area of all.

But on September 7th and the days which followed the bombs poured chiefly on Stepney, with its inimitable mixture of races, where nearly two hundred thousand people lived at an average of twelve per dwelling; on the tailors of Whitechapel; the factories, warehouses and gasworks of Poplar; the woodworking firms of Shoreditch; the docks of West Ham and Bermondsey. They poured on the sweated clothing trade, on the casual labour of the docks, on petty businesses Jewish and Gentile, on jerry-built Victorian slums, on marshy land which had made it hard to provide decent shelters. They poured on Cockneys who often knew little of the world beyond their immediate neighbourhood, who found their shops, their entertainments and their marriages near at home, who often spent their lives in the streets in which they had grown up, where two or three generations of the same family would commonly be found living in adjacent houses, where poverty and community flourished on the same stalk.

Here communism had found its best base in Britain outside a few mining districts. Here, in the mid-'thirties, Mosley had sought a foundation for his British Union of Fascists. The monotonous sequence of small bankruptcies in the tailoring and furnishing trades had given him his chance. Jews whose fathers had fled from the pogroms of eastern Europe had had their shop windows smashed and their lives threatened. When Mosley had limped through the narrow streets, thickets of arms had shot up on each side, though strong socialist feeling had thwarted the breakthrough he had needed.

'Everybody is worried about the feeling in the East End,' wrote Harold Nicolson in his diary on September 17th. '. . . There is much bitterness. It is said that even the King and Queen were booed the other day when they visited the destroyed areas.' Had the East End lost all heart, the chain reaction might have crippled London's morale. This nearly happened, but not quite, and after a few days the attack shifted noticeably westwards.

ANGUS CALDER, *The People's War*, 1969

LONDON'S NOSE

11 September 1940

A second raid on London almost as bad as the first. I have been wondering what is happening to St Paul's, and Gerald rang up with the same preoccupation. I suppose it is the Nose of London's familiar face (and everyone knows what noses stand for). It's disgusting to think of that familiar face being destroyed piecemeal.

FRANCES PARTRIDGE, *A Pacifist's War*, 1978

FIRE DUTY

Fire Duty was something that came round at regular intervals. It meant hanging about the building all night, fully dressed, prepared to go on the roof, if the Warning sounded, with the object of extinguishing incendiary bombs that might fall there. These were said to be easily dealt with by use of sand and an instrument like a garden hoe, both of which were provided as equipment. On previous occasions, up to now, no raid had occurred, the hours passing not too unpleasantly with a book. Feeling I needed a change from the seventeenth century and Proust, I had brought Saltykov-Schredin's *The Golovlyov Family* to read. A more trivial choice would have been humiliating, because Corporal Curtis turned out to be the accompanying NCO that night, and had *Adam Bede* under his arm. We made whatever mutual arrangements were required, then retired to our respective off-duty locations.

Towards midnight I was examining a collection of photographs taken on D-Day, which had not long before this replaced the two Isbister-like oil paintings. Why the pictures had been removed after being allowed to hang throughout the earlier years of the blitz was not apparent. Mime, now a captain, had just hurried past with his telegrams, when the Warning sounded. I found my way to the roof at the same moment as Corporal Curtis.

'I understand, sir, that we ascend into one of the cupolas as an action station.'

'We do.'

'I thought I had better await your arrival and instructions, sir.'

'Tell me the plot of *Adam Bede* as far as you've got. I've never read it.'

Like the muezzin going on duty, we climbed up a steep gangway of iron leading into one of the pepperpot domes constructed at each corner of the building. The particular dome allotted to us, the one nearest the river, was on the far side from that above our own room. The inside was on two floors, rather like an eccentric writer's den for undisturbed work. Curtis and I proceeded to the upper level. These Edwardian belvederes, elaborately pillared and corniced like Temples of Love in a rococo garden, were not in themselves of exceptional beauty, and, when first erected, must have seemed obscure in functional purpose. Now, however, the architect's design showed prophetic aptitude. The exigencies of war had transformed them into true gazebos, not, as it turned out, frequented to observe the 'pleasing prospects' with which such rotundas and follies were commonly associated, but at least to view their antithesis, 'horridly gothick' aspects of the heavens, lit up by fire and rent with thunder.

This extension of purpose was given effect a minute or two later. The moonlit night, now the melancholy strain of the sirens had died away, was surprisingly quiet. All Ack-Ack guns had been sent to the coast, for there was no point in shooting down V.1's over built-up areas. They would come down anyway. Around lay the darkened city, a few solid masses, like the Donners-Brebner Building, recognizable on the far side of the twisting strip of water. Then three rapidly moving lights appeared in the southern sky, two more or less side by side, the third following a short way behind, as if lacking acceleration or will power to keep up. They travelled with that curious shuddering jerky movement characteristic of such bodies, a style of locomotion that seemed to suggest the engine was not working properly, might break down at any moment, which indeed it would. This impression that something was badly wrong with the internal machinery was increased by a shower of sparks emitted from the tail. A more exciting possibility was that dragons were flying through the air in a fabulous tale, and climbing into the turret with Curtis had been done in a dream. The raucous buzz could now be plainly heard. In imagination one smelt brimstone.

'They appear to be heading a few degrees to our right, sir,' said Curtis.

The first two cut-out. It was almost simultaneous. The noisy ticking of the third continued briefly, then also stopped abruptly. This interval between cutting-out and exploding always seemed interminable. At last it came; again two almost at once, the third a few seconds later. All three swooped to the ground, their flaming tails pointing upwards, certainly dragons now, darting earthward to consume their prey of maidens chained to rocks.

'Southwark, do you think?'

'Lambeth, sir—having regard to the incurvations of the river.'

'Sweet Thames run softly . . .'

'I was thinking the same, sir.'

'I'm afraid they've caught it, whichever it was.'

'I'm afraid so, sir.'

The All Clear sounded. We climbed down the iron gangway.

'Do you think that will be all for tonight?'

'I hope so, sir. Just to carry the story on from where we were when we were interrupted: Hetty is then convicted of the murder of her child and transported.'

ANTHONY POWELL, The Military Philosophers, 1968

IN WESTMINSTER ABBEY

Let me take this other glove off
    As the *vox humana* swells,
And the beauteous fields of Eden
    Bask beneath the Abbey bells.
Here, where England's statesmen lie,
Listen to a lady's cry.

Gracious Lord, oh bomb the Germans.
    Spare their women for Thy Sake,
And if that is not too easy
    We will pardon Thy Mistake.
But, gracious Lord, whate'er shall be,
Don't let anyone bomb me.

Keep our Empire undismembered
    Guide our Forces by Thy Hand,

Gallant blacks from far Jamaica,
    Honduras and Togoland;
Protect them Lord in all their fights,
And, even more, protect the whites.

Think of what our Nation stands for,
    Books from Boots' and country lanes,
Free speech, free passes, class distinction,
    Democracy and proper drains.
Lord, put beneath Thy special care
One-eighty-nine Cadogan Square.

Although dear Lord I am a sinner,
    I have done no major crime;
Now I'll come to Evening Service
    Whensoever I have the time.
So, Lord, reserve for me a crown,
And do not let my shares go down.

I will labour for Thy Kingdom,
    Help our lads to win the war,
Send white feathers to the cowards
    Join the Women's Army Corps,
Then wash the Steps around Thy Throne
In the Eternal Safety Zone.

Now I feel a little better,
    What a treat to hear Thy Word,
Where the bones of leading statesmen,
    Have so often been interr'd.
And now, dear Lord, I cannot wait
Because I have a luncheon date.

JOHN BETJEMAN, Collected Poems, 1970

BROTHER FIRE

When our brother Fire was having his dog's day
Jumping the London streets with millions of tin cans
Clanking at his tail, we heard some shadow say

'Give the dog a bone'—and so we gave him ours;
Night after night we watched him slaver and crunch away
The beams of human life, the tops of topless towers.

Which gluttony of his for us was Lenten fare
Who mother-naked, suckled with sparks, were chill
Though cotted in a grill of sizzling air
Striped like a convict—black, yellow and red;
Thus were we weaned to knowledge of the Will
That wills the natural world but wills us dead.

O delicate walker, babbler, dialectician Fire,
O enemy and image of ourselves,
Did we not on those mornings after the All Clear,
When you were looting shops in elemental joy
And singing as you swarmed up city block and spire,
Echo your thought in ours? 'Destroy! Destroy!'

LOUIS MACNEICE, *Collected Poems 1925–1948*, 1949

'SNOW!'

When I first came to London, shortly after the end of the war, I found myself after a few days in a boarding-house, called a private hotel, in the Kensington High Street area. The boarding-house was owned by Mr Shylock. He didn't live there, but the attic was reserved for him; and Lieni, the Maltese housekeeper, told me he occasionally spent a night there with a young girl. 'These English girls!' Lieni said. She herself lived in the basement with her illegitimate child. An early postwar adventure. Between attic and basement, pleasure and its penalty, we boarders lived, narrowly.

I paid Mr Shylock three guineas a week for a tall, multi-mirrored, book-shaped room with a coffin-like wardrobe. And for Mr Shylock, the recipient each week of fifteen times three guineas, the possessor of a mistress and of suits made of cloth so fine I felt I could eat it, I had nothing but admiration. I was not used to the social modes of London or to the physiognomy and complexions of the North, and I thought Mr Shylock looked distinguished, like a lawyer or businessman or politician. He had the habit of stroking the lobe of his ear and inclining his head to listen.

I thought the gesture was attractive; I copied it. I knew of recent events in Europe; they tormented me; and although I was trying to live on seven pounds a week I offered Mr Shylock my fullest, silent compassion.

In the winter Mr Shylock died. I knew nothing until I heard of his cremation from Lieni, who was herself affronted, and a little fearful for the future, that she had not been told by Mrs Shylock of the event of the death. It was disquieting to me too, this secrecy and swiftness of a London death. And it also occurred to me that up to that time in London I had not been aware of death, had never seen those funeral processions which, rain or shine, had enlivened all our afternoons on the Caribbean island of Isabella. Mr Shylock was dead, then. But in spite of Lieni's fears the routine of his boarding-house did not change. Mrs Shylock didn't appear. Lieni continued to live in the basement. A fortnight later she invited me to the christening of her child.

We had to be at the church at three, and after lunch I went up to my narrow room to wait. It was very cold. It went dark in the room, and I noticed that the light outside was strange. It was dead, but seemed to have an inner lividness. Then it began to drizzle. An unusual drizzle: I could see individual drops, I could hear them strike the window.

Hectic feminine footsteps thumped up the stairs. My door was pushed open; and Lieni, half her face washed and white and bare, a bit of cosmetic-smeared cottonwool in her hand, said breathlessly, 'I thought you would like to know. It's snowing.'

Snow!

Screwing up her eyes, compressing her lips, she dabbed at her cheeks with the cottonwool—big hand, big fingers, small piece of cottonwool—and ran out again.

Snow. At last; my element. And these were flakes, the airiest crushed ice. More than crushed: shivered. But the greater enchantment was the light. I went out to the dark passage and stood before the window. Then I climbed up and up towards the skylight, stopping at each floor to look out at the street. The carpet stopped, the stairs ended in a narrow gallery. Above me was the skylight, below me the stair-well darkening as it deepened. The attic door was ajar. I went in, and found myself in an empty room harsh with a dead-fluorescent light that seemed artificial. The room felt cold, exposed and abandoned. The boards were bare and gritty. A mattress on dusty sheets of newspapers; a worn blue flannelette spread; a rickety writing-table. No more.

Standing before the window—crooked sashes, peeling paint-work: so fragile the structure up here which lower down appeared so solid—I felt the dead light on my face. The flakes didn't only float; they also spun. They touched the glass and turned to a film of melting ice. Below the livid grey sky roofs were white and shining black in patches. The bombsite was wholly white; every shrub, every discarded bottle, box and tin was defined. I had seen. Yet what was I to do with so complete a beauty? And looking out from that room to the thin lines of brown smoke rising from ugly chimneypots, the plastered wall of the house next to the bombsite tremendously braced and buttressed, looking out from that empty room with the mattress on the floor, I felt all the magic of the city go away and had an intimation of the forlornness of the city and of the people who lived in it.

V. S. NAIPAUL, *The Mimic Men*, 1967

BOMB DAMAGE

Crossing the road by the bombed-out public house on the corner and pondering the mystery which dominates vistas framed by a ruined door, I felt for some reason glad the place had not yet been rebuilt. A direct hit had excised even the ground floor, so that the basement was revealed as a sunken garden, or site of archæological excavation long abandoned, where great sprays of willow herb and ragwort flowered through cracked paving stones; only a few broken milk bottles and a laceless boot recalling contemporary life. In the midst of this sombre grotto five or six fractured steps had withstood the explosion and formed a projecting island of masonry on the summit of which rose the door. Walls on both sides were shrunk away, but along its lintel, in niggling copybook handwriting, could still be distinguished the word *Ladies*. Beyond, on the far side of the twin pillars and crossbar, nothing whatever remained of that promised retreat, the threshold falling steeply to an abyss of rubble; a triumphal arch erected laboriously by dwarfs, or the gateway to some unknown, forbidden domain, the lair of sorcerers.

Then, all at once, as if such luxurious fantasy were not already enough, there came from this unexplored country the song, strong and marvellously sweet, of the blonde woman on crutches, that itinerant prima donna of the highways whose voice I had not heard since the day, years

before, when Moreland and I had listened in Gerrard Street, the afternoon he had talked of getting married; when we had bought the bottle
labelled *Tawny Wine (port flavour)* which even Moreland had been later
unwilling to drink. Now once more above the rustle of traffic that same
note swelled on the grimy air, contriving a transformation scene to recast
those purlieus into the vision of an oriental dreamland, artificial, if you
like, but still quite alluring under the shifting clouds of a cheerless Soho
sky.

ANTHONY POWELL, *Casanova's Chinese Restaurant*, 1960

THE CALEDONIAN MARKET

A work-basket made of an old armadillo
   Lined with pink satin now rotten with age,
A novel entitled *The Ostracized Vicar*
   (A spider squashed flat on the title page),
A faded album of nineteen-oh-seven
   Snapshots (now like very weak tea)
Showing high-collared knuts and girls expectant   *dandies*
   In big muslin hats at Bexhill-on-Sea,
A gasolier made of hand-beaten copper
   In the once modern style known as *art nouveau*,
An assegai, and a china slipper,
   And *What a Young Scoutmaster Ought to Know* . . .

Who stood their umbrellas in elephants' feet?
   Who hung their hats on the horns of a moose?
Who crossed the ocean with amulets made
   To be hung round the neck of an ailing papoose?
Who paid her calls with a sandalwood card-case?
   From whose eighteen-inch waist hung that thin chatelaine?
Who smoked that meerschaum? Who won that medal?
   That extraordinary vase was evolved by what brain?
Who worked in wool the convolvulus bell-pull?
   Who smiled with those false teeth? Who wore that wig?
Who had that hair-tidy hung by her mirror?
   Whose was the scent-bottle shaped like a pig?

Where are the lads in their tight Norfolk jackets
   Who roistered in pubs that stayed open all day?
Where are the girls in their much tighter corsets
   And where are the figures they loved to display?
Where the old maids in their bric-à-brac settings
   With parlourmaids bringing them dinners and teas?
Where are their counterparts, idle old roués,
   Sodden old bachelors living at ease?
Where the big families, big with possessions,
   Their standards of living, their errors of taste?
Here are the soup-tureens—where is the ambience,
   Arrogance, confidence, hope without haste?

Laugh if you like at this monstrous detritus
   Of middle-class life in the liberal past,
The platypus stuffed, and the frightful epergne.
   You, who are now overtaxed and declassed,
Laugh while you can, for the time may come round
   When the rubbish *you* treasure will lie in this place—
Your wireless set (bust), your ridiculous hats,
   The photographs of your period face.
Your best-selling novels, your 'functional' chairs,
   Your primitive comforts and notions of style
Are just so much fodder for dealers in junk—
   Let us hope that they'll make your grandchildren smile.

            WILLIAM PLOMER, *Collected Poems*, 1960

A LONDON SURVIVOR: I

Christ Church, Commercial Street, Spitalfields

Nicholas Hawksmoor, 1723–9

Mighty; Hawksmoor's biggest and grandest church, all built up on the
scheme of the Venetian arch—three-part, with the centre higher than
the wings. But not 'composed'; transmuted somewhere right down in the
blood so that the whole building becomes a living idea (just as St Mary
Woolnoth is a living demonstration of cube inside cube: just as St Stephen
Walbrook, however brilliant, is a composition). Centre and wings in the

huge porch, in the relation of belfry to steeple; and, overwhelmingly, inside: aisles to central space, division of the chancel screen, divisions of the huge flat ceiling, the actual Venetian window at the east end: everything offered up: to God be the praise. Locked up whilst money is being collected for a restoration; if the Church lets it fall down it might as well present a banker's order for thirty pieces of silver. For here *is* the faith, manifest.

IAN NAIRN, *Nairn's London*, 1966

'SUNDAY DEATH'

Bernard looked down from the window of the flat on to Bloomsbury lying embalmed in its Sunday death. The rows of scarlet and lemon dahlias, the heliotrope carefully tended and the little green chairs carefully painted for Festival visitors decorated its stillness with a strange air of smartness—embalmed in best Sunday clothes, no doubt, to accord with the conventions of American visitors. From the ninth floor the sordid remnants of Saturday lost the squalor of greasy paper, refuse ends, dirt and spit which they showed to the pedestrian and merged into a general impression of dust and litter. The district was dead but recently, and these seemed the tag ends of life's encumbrance. But already the corpse was stirring into maggoty life—a paperman distributing the sheets that, crumpled and tired-looking, would add to the stuffy Sunday muddle of bed-sitting rooms and lounges; knots of earnest foreign tourists collected for an 'early start' on hotel steps; disconsolate provincial families already straggling and scratchy at the day before them; a respectable nineteenth-century couple, who Bernard hoped might be Irvingites bent on worship in Gordon Square.

ANGUS WILSON, *Hemlock and after*, 1952

LONDON'S SUPERIOR TRAFFIC SYSTEM

Dear Dale:

. . . I see in the current *New Yorker* that Sacheverell Sitwell, that visiting virtuoso of the quill pen, remarks that New York traffic is better managed than that in London, about as idiotic a remark as I have ever heard or read. New York traffic isn't managed at all. It is absolute chaos. London traffic, generally speaking and considering the fantastic pattern of the streets, is superbly managed. Of course the system wouldn't work in New York because it depends on a certain element of decency and obedience to the law. The only real fault I found with the London traffic system was their allowing left turns from places like Oxford Circus during rush hours. With which gripe I conclude.

Yours ever,

RAYMOND CHANDLER, letter to Dale Warren, 13 November 1952,
from *Selected Letters of Raymond Chandler*, ed. Frank MacShane, 1981

A LONDON SURVIVOR: 2

Apothecaries' Hall, Blackfriars Lane

Nowhere better to see one colour of London's spectrum. The outside is a heavy-lidded brick building overlooked by the new *Times* offices and nudged in front by the same viaduct which makes such a bewildering place out of Ludgate Circus. Under the entrance arch there is complete serenity, yellow stucco unrolling itself with all the time in the world around a courtyard. You could walk all day in New York and not find this kind of contrast, which is one of the ways that cities stay sane. You enjoy the calm after the hubbub; but you also enjoy the hubbub after the calm. Maybe New Towns should have oases of noise just as this is an oasis of quiet. The buildings are seventeenth-century underneath, and were given their present bland covering in 1786.

IAN NAIRN, *Nairn's London*, 1966

FROM THE ZOO TO THE ZOO

The final side-show, when one has done the superb museums and art galleries, the cathedrals and churches, the libraries and monuments, the Zoo, Hampstead Heath on Bank Holiday, the Cup Final, is the population of eccentrics. We, of course, hardly notice them and never have. Hazlitt said 180 years ago that you could dress up in fantastic clothes or behave in fantastic fashion in the street and not a soul would take any notice of you—on the general ground that it was your business and nobody else's. Our public eccentrics are not exhibitionists, they are not trying to draw a crowd—as has happened often in Paris. They are doing the very opposite: they are—and we understand this—withdrawn deeply into private life. The so-called King of Poland, who, a few years back, was often seen walking barefoot down the Strand in red velvet robes, golden hair down to his waist, and a royal wreath on his head, was never gaped at. A bus conductor might wink at another bus conductor or nod his head—but no more; and these acknowledgements expressed pleasure. On the Number 6 going down Edgware Road one sometimes met a merry baggage who carried a spare hat in a brown paper bag and changed it in the bus, singing out, as she did so:

> 'He called me his Popsy Woopsy
> But I don't care.'

And she got out at the Haymarket to dance a little on the pavement if she was in the mood. There is a native rattiness or dottiness among the pavement artists. David Burton—one of the most gifted: 'Gastric and duodenal Pains for 14 years' was the substance of his appeal—used to make war on a rival who had a gramophone and a dog to do his begging for him from the dog-lovers, cat-strokers, duck-feeders, horse-sugarers, bird-lovers of Hampstead and the Finchley Road and would scrawl in large chalk letters on the pavement, 'Worship God not Animals.' Burton had his religious side. He had a natural naïve gift. He turned out the Blessed Babe at Christmas and once said to me when I admired it: 'I done the lady all right but I couldn't get the kid.'

Burton was the son of a cab driver. His mother was dead. The father used to leave the house saying to the boy, 'Paint a lake.' The boy painted a circle and filled it in with blue. 'That int a lake,' said the father, giving him a clout, when he came back, and, getting a tin of salmon, he scissored out the fish on the label, gave it a lick, and slapped it on the drawing. 'That's a lake,' said Dad. Not a bad lesson, but Burton always claimed he had been punched and belted into the pavement-artist business against his will.

Burton's oddity was simply more productive than the elegance of the Hampstead tree-slasher, the Negro bird-warbler, the solitaries with imaginary military careers who reel off the record, click their heels, salute, and depart, or the clergyman who, exalted, marches down the street shouting 'It's all in the Book.' One has to distinguish between the mad and the people pursuing a stern individual cause: the elderly lady who arrives in white shorts on a racing bicycle at the British Museum every morning, winter and summer. She is a scholar. In another way so is that taxi driver who answers you in Latin, having, he says, picked it up taking bishops to and from the Athenaeum. Camden Town has its well-known misers. And any decent London club will produce for you among its members men of esoteric habit and information: Sinologists who have never crossed the Channel, old gentlemen who, by some freak, speak Lithuanian, and others who can be heard having scholarly quarrels, quoting chapter and verse, in a library where, when you nervously open the door, they are by themselves. And the fanatical eccentrics: the peer who always carried a couple of concealed bottles of beer to the Garden Party at Buckingham Palace and lowered them in one of the lakes on a piece of string, so that he could sneak off for a drink when the coast was clear. On—one reflects—what a coast! One has only to search for furnished rooms or to live in board residence to find oneself among peculiar rebels. They are really conformists, conforming steadfastly to something that exists only in their minds. There is the extraordinary host of old ladies with port-wine voices; there were those unshakeable Britannias who used to sit under the glass roof of the Langham Hotel during the Blitz doing the crossword puzzle; those landladies in something like Oriental dress who 'take a little something' in their tea, and have long sad love affairs with overfed dogs and hysterical canaries. London is a zoo.

V. S. PRITCHETT, *London Perceived*, 1962

A WEST INDIAN GIRL IN LONDON

One bright Sunday morning in July I have trouble with my Notting Hill landlord because he ask for a month's rent in advance. He tell me this after I live there since winter, settling up every week without fail. I have no job at the time, and if I give the money he want there's not much left. So I refuse. The man drunk already at that early hour, and he abuse me— all talk, he can't frighten me. But his wife is a bad one—now she walk in my room and say she must have cash. When I tell her no, she give my suitcase one kick and it burst open. My best dress fall out, then she laugh and give another kick. She say month in advance is usual, and if I can't pay find somewhere else.

Don't talk to me about London. Plenty people there have heart like stone. Any complaint—the answer is 'prove it'. But if nobody see and bear witness for me, how to prove anything? So I pack up and leave. I think better not have dealings with that woman. She too cunning, and Satan don't lie worse.

I walk about till a place nearby is open where I can have coffee and a sandwich. There I start talking to a man at my table. He talk to me already, I know him, but I don't know his name. After a while he ask, 'What's the matter? Anything wrong?' and when I tell him my trouble he say I can use an empty flat he own till I have time to look around.

This man is not at all like most English people. He see very quick, and he decide very quick. English people take long time to decide—you three-quarter dead before they make up their mind about you. Too besides, he speak very matter of fact, as if it's nothing. He speak as if he realize well what it is to live like I do—that's why I accept and go.

He tell me somebody occupy the flat till last week, so I find everything all right, and he tell me how to get there—three-quarters of an hour from Victoria Station, up a steep hill, turn left, and I can't mistake the house. He give me the keys and an envelope with a telephone number on the back. Underneath is written 'After 6 p.m. ask for Mr Sims'.

In the train that evening I think myself lucky, for to walk about London on a Sunday with nowhere to go—that take the heart out of you.

I find the place and the bedroom of the downstairs flat is nicely furnished—two looking glass, wardrobe, chest of drawers, sheets, everything. It smell of jasmine scent, but it smell strong of damp too.

I open the door opposite and there's a table, a couple chairs, a gas stove and a cupboard, but this room so big it look empty. When I pull the blind up I notice the paper peeling off and mushrooms growing on the walls—you never see such a thing.

The bathroom the same, all the taps rusty. I leave the two other rooms and make up the bed. Then I listen, but I can't hear one sound. Nobody come in, nobody go out of that house. I lie awake for a long time, then I decide not to stay and in the morning I start to get ready quickly before I change my mind. I want to wear my best dress, but it's a funny thing—when I take up that dress and remember how my landlady kick it I cry. I cry and I can't stop. When I stop I feel tired to my bones, tired like old woman. I don't want to move again—I have to force myself. But in the end I get out in the passage and there's a postcard for me. 'Stay as long as you like. I'll be seeing you soon—Friday probably. Not to worry.'

JEAN RHYS, 'Let Them Call It Jazz', from *Tigers Are Better Looking*, 1968

A LONDON SURVIVOR: 3

Bart's Hospital, West Smithfield

This is one of London's peculiar places whose character needs to be safeguarded as jealously as though it were the Temple or St James's Park. The hospital, in all its classical sobriety, with never a pointed arch all through the nineteenth-century additions, faces Smithfield Market's endearing fussy face. (The pubs around here, as at Covent Garden, open in the early morning.) The open space between hospital and market turns out to be a spiral ramp, which leads down to black tunnels calling themselves Smithfield Goods Station though they look much more likely to lead straight to the Old Bailey. On the east side is the entrance to St Bart's-the-Great. A sonata for oboe, tuba, cello, xylophone, and clavichord, and good stuff too.

Bart's itself has a grand entrance: a tough, compact building of 1702 by Wren's mason, Edward Strong Jun. This is Wren's Hampton Court style returned nearer to Holland and gaining from it, every swag and window-pediment making its point; above the arch, Henry VIII looks out with a splendid po-face.

Through the arch and on the left is another London surprise—St Bartholomew-the-Less, the hospital church. Above the door-knocker is a notice saying *Try this—it works*. It does, an object lesson to all the timid lockers-up of London's churches. The building was rebuilt by Dance in 1787 and again by Hardwick in 1823, a jolly Gothic octagon, one of the most cheerful buildings in London. The plan is still Dance's, with the octagon inscribed in a square and the gloomy corners given noble blind arches—an idea which Dance took further in his church at Micheldever near Winchester. It is easy to see how much his pupil Soane must have learnt from this gruff quixotic designer whose best buildings have all disappeared. Newgate Gaol, the best of all, was a few yards away on the site of the Old Bailey.

Through the next arch is the main quad of the Hospital. On the left through an open door is a brown-and-gold stairwell, designed by Gibbs and laughably painted by Hogarth, who was completely at odds with the generalized sentiments expected of him. Perhaps you shouldn't be here, but nobody seems to turn you out: a bit of the real London.

IAN NAIRN, *Nairn's London*, 1966

J. R. Ackerley was the at first reluctant owner of an Alsatian bitch called Queenie. She features in two of his books—in the novel We Think the World of You *and the memoir* My Dog Tulip. *He came to love her, bestowing on her literary immortality.*

A MAN AND HIS DOG AMONG THE DEAD

Whenever I take Tulip out, therefore, I always offer her opportunities to relieve herself in places relatively inoffensive to humanity before entering the busy streets of crowds and shops. To start with there is the Embankment, to which I have already referred. Although this is a carriageway, it is popularly used as a promenade by the people of Putney, who stroll up and down it by the river with their dogs, often on the street for the simple reason that its single footpath is discontinuous, interrupted for long stretches by boating ramps, and frequently submerged by the flooding tide. So little distinction, in fact, can be made between street and pavement that I consider none where Tulip is concerned. If she does not take immediate advantage of this, we dawdle on in the direction of Putney Bridge (we are generally making for a bus in the High Street) where another narrow ramp slants obliquely down into the mud of the foreshore. Here, amid the flotsam and jetsam of wood, cork, bottles, old tin cans, french letters, and the swollen bodies of drowned cats, dogs and birds left by the tide, she is often moved to open her bowels. If not, we pass on again (hurriedly now, for some fifty yards of pavement separate us from our next objective) to another species of refuse dump on the other side of the bridge, the ancient cemetery of Putney Church. The dead are less particular and more charitable than the living. It is a charming little cemetery; the few pretty nineteenth-century head-stones on the water side lean under acacia trees upon a grassy bank that slopes to a low river wall: swans float below. At the back of the church, where Hotpoint House now stands, lived 'that excellent woman, Mrs Catherine

Porten, the true mother of my mind as well as of my health', as her nephew, Gibbon, who passed much of his youth in her house, described her. Strangely peaceful and secluded, although it lies just below the busy bridge, this small churchyard draws others, besides Tulip and myself, for their private purposes: upon the flattened grass beneath the tombstones in summertime I occasionally find coins, which, unnoticed in the darkness, have slipped out of trouser pockets, and other indications that the poor fleeting living, who have nowhere of their own, have been there to make love among the dead. To what better use could such a place be put? And are not its ghosts gladdened that so beautiful a young creature as Tulip should come here for her needs, whatever they may be? Here, springing from their long-forgotten bones, rankly grow her medicinal grasses, the coarse quitch grass which she searches out to pluck and eat when she wishes to make herself sick, and that other sort of grass she uses to bind and cleanse her bowels; and here too, I hope—it is our last chance—she will unburden herself beside the mortal remains of Caroline, Dowager Countess of Kingston (d. 1823) or of Mr Stephen Robinson (d. 1827).

J. R. ACKERLEY, *My Dog Tulip*, 1965

A LONDON SURVIVOR: 4

Spitalfields

Doomed and grimly magnificent in its last tottering years, Spitalfields was an early-eighteenth-century New Town, just beyond the city. It went down as the East End grew up, and the big taciturn brick houses are now on their last legs: ironically it is the biggest area of its date left in London. Elder Street and Wilkes Street have hardly altered since 1750; unexpected treasure turns up, like the Great Synagogue in Fournier Street and the Georgian shopfront at 56 Artillery Lane—easily the best in London, with gusto as well as polish, now used as a storeroom. The whole area seems bound to go, not only because rehabilitation would be difficult, but quite simply because nobody loves it. Christ Church looms over the whole area, the meths drinkers lie around near by: charity is far enough away and compassion even farther. For tourists who visit the cheerful market at Petticoat Lane (Middlesex Street) on Sunday mornings, this sombre ghost is just beyond. It could even now be one of those living areas in the heart of cities over which so many pious words are spilt at conferences.

IAN NAIRN, *Nairn's London*, 1966

Barry Humphries, later to achieve international success as Dame Edna Everage, came to London from Australia in the 1960s. He secured a part in Lionel Bart's musical Oliver! *after many months of unemployment.*

MEETING THE KING OF RODONDA

Working in the West End at night and often during the day gave me an ideal opportunity to explore London. Now that I was earning money I could venture into secondhand bookshops, and sometimes, for very little, I could pick up a treasure like William Beckford's first book, *Extraordinary Painters*, written at the age of sixteen, and in orange wrappers a rare copy of *Zang Tuum Tuum*, Marinetti's Futurist Manifesto of 1913, belligerently inscribed by the author. Then there were the pubs. In Australia they were no more than licensed urinals, but in London they were often more comfortable and congenial than the basement flat in Notting Hill Gate. Right next to the theatre was the Salisbury, which had an Edwardian gin-palace glitter and a camp theatrical clientele, but I preferred the Lamb and Flag in Rose Court and I persuaded the more convivial members of the company to drink there between the matinée and evening performance on Wednesdays and Saturdays. The jovial publican began to greet me like a long-lost friend. On one occasion I found myself without enough money for an expensive round of drinks and he, at once, offered me something which to a dedicated drinker is more precious than love: namely, credit. I had only been in the West End for a few months, and I had a slate. At last I was beginning to feel like an adult human being.

Alan, our ballet-dancer boarder, sometimes drove us into the country-side in his small car, when it had not been borrowed by an opportunistic artist *manqué* from Sydney called Robert who had come to London in the hope of becoming a critic. Why were people from Sydney always so pushy? Probably the convict background, I reflected.

Around north Soho there were the beatnik pubs where my long hair was less noticeable in the throng of black-duffle-coated men and the barefoot hoydens with their lewd mascaraed glances. In a bar near the Portobello Road I met John Gawsworth, a sub-Drinkwater poet and self-styled King of Rodonda, a title he had inherited from M. P. Shiel, the 1890s writer of fantasy whose books I avidly collected. Shiel's ashes were in a biscuit tin on the mantelpiece in Gawsworth's old Westbourne Grove bed-sitting room. There he once made me, from cabbage leaves literally picked up off the vegetable end of Portobello Road and some cartilaginous scraps, a dubious stew, seasoned with a generous pinch of Shiel's incinerated residue. Gawsworth, charming and erudite in his rare moments of sobriety, was always on the cadge. Sliding deeper into alcoholism, he was rarely, as they say, 'in showroom condition'. But he had known so many of the authors I liked that we spent hours together in one pub or another talking about Havelock Ellis, Anna Wickham and Arthur Machen until he lapsed into total incoherence.

BARRY HUMPHRIES, *More Please: An Autobiography*, 1992

'FROZEN FACES'

Between Finchley Road and Wembley Park the train goes over a high viaduct system at Kilburn. Below, as far as you could see, lay cross-hatched streets of tall, run-down Victorian terraces. Half a dozen television aerials interwoven on every roof implied a honeycomb of plasterboard partitioning beneath. There were few cars in that sort of area at that time, and no visible greenery. A huge, regular, red-brick Victorian building stood in the middle: a monster school, infirmary, lunatic asylum— I never knew, nor wanted that sort of precision. The value of Kilburn depended on not knowing particularities, because it changed to the eye and the brain according to yourself, your mood and the day. On a late afternoon in winter, with the egg-white lamps faintly beginning to show, it was melancholy and frightening, the haunt of acid-bath murderers. On a clear, bright morning in summer, with almost no smog and lots of people visible, it was like a brave little slum in the Blitz: you half expected to see George VI poking around the few remaining bomb-sites with his umbrella. Kilburn could suggest to you the pullulating mass of the working class, who any moment might swarm like termites up the viaduct and take the pinstripes apart; equally, it could be a comforting proof that so many people could live together quietly at close quarters.

Toni and I got off at Wembley Park, changed platforms, and went back over the area. Then we did the same again.

'Christ, there're so many of them,' was Toni's eventual comment. Thousands of people down there, all within a few hundred yards of you; yet you'd never, in all probability, meet any of them.

'Well, it's an argument against God, isn't it?'

'Yeah. And for enlightened dictatorship.'

'And for art for art's sake.'

He was silent for a while, awed.

'Well, I take it back, I take it back.'

'Thought you might. There are others, but this is the best.' Toni silently got back on the next Baker Street train for his final run over the stretch.

From then on, I was not only interested in my journey, but proud of it. The termitary of Kilburn; the grimy, lost stations between Baker Street and Finchley Road; the steppe-like playing-fields at Northwick Park; the depot at Neasden, full of idle, aged rolling-stock; the frozen faces of passengers glimpsed in the windows of fast Marylebone trains. They were all, in some way, relevant, fulfilling, sensibility-sharpening. And what was life about if not that?

JULIAN BARNES, *Metroland*, 1981

'AN UNDERGROUNDER'

After leaving the office I would travel either to Sloane Square or to Liverpool Street to have a drink in the station buffet. In the whole extension of the Underground system those two stations are, as far as I've been able to discover, the only ones which have bars actually upon the platform. The concept of the tube station platform bar excited me. In fact the whole Underground region moved me, I felt as if it were in some sense my natural home. These two bars were not just a cosy after-the-office treat, they were the source of a dark excitement, places of profound communication with London, with the sources of life, with the caverns of resignation to grief and to mortality. Drinking there between six and seven in the shifting crowd of rush-hour travellers, one could feel on one's shoulders as a curiously soothing yoke the weariness of toiling London, that blank released tiredness after work which can somehow console even the bored, even the frenzied. The coming and departing rattle of the trains, the drifting movement of the travellers, their arrival, their waiting, their vanishing forever presented a mesmeric and indeed symbolic fresco: so many little moments of decision, so many little finalities, the constant wrenching of texture, the constant destruction of cells which shifts and ages the lives of men and of universes. The uncertainty of the order of the trains. The dangerousness of the platforms. (Trains as lethal weapons.) The resolution of a given moment (but which?) to lay down your glass and mount the next train. (But why? There will be another in two minutes.) *Ah qu'ils sont beaux les trains manqués!* as I especially had cause to know. Then once upon the train that sense of its thrusting life, its intent and purposive turning which conveys itself so subtly to the traveller's body, its leanings and veerings to points of irrevocable change and partings of the ways. The train of consciousness, the present moment, the little lighted tube moving in the long dark tunnel. The inevitability of it all and yet its endless variety: the awful daylight glimpses, the blessed plunges back into the dark; the stations, each unique, the sinister brightness of Charing Cross, the mysterious gloom of Regent's Park, the dereliction of Mornington Crescent, the futuristic melancholy of Moorgate, the monumental ironwork of Liverpool Street, the twining *art nouveau* of Gloucester Road, the Barbican sunk in a baroque hole, fit subject for Piranesi. And in summer, like an excursion into the country, the flowering banks of the Westbound District Line. I preferred the dark however. Emergence was like a worm pulled from its hole. I loved the Inner Circle best. Twenty-seven stations for fivepence. Indeed, for fivepence as many stations as you cared to achieve. Sometimes I rode the whole Circle (just under an hour) before deciding whether to have my evening drink at Liverpool Street or at Sloane Square. I was not the only Circle rider. There were others, especially in winter. Homeless people, lonely people, alcoholics, people on drugs, people in despair. We recognized each other. It was a fit place for me, I was indeed an Undergrounder.

IRIS MURDOCH, *A Word Child*, 1975

STEVIE SMITH AT THE PALACE

Tell me about your Queen's Gold Medal for Poetry?

It was last year. Of course I was very nervous. I thought 'I'm sure to be late, I'm always late.' So of course as a result I got there terribly early, when they were changing the guard. Crowds of people milling up against the rails, so I thought, 'Well, I've just got time to slip round to the gallery and get some picture postcards'. Which I did, and crammed my bag out with these picture postcards—a rather small bag. Then I went up to one of the police and he obviously didn't believe me, at least I thought he didn't. So I thought, 'I'd better go for another walk I suppose.' Then it came on to rain, and I suddenly got rather cross and thought, 'Well, I'm not going to walk round again.' So I just walked up, and said, 'Well, I'm supposed to be there, you know, an appointment with Her Majesty, to have this medal.' Then they did know about it, so I went in, and they were terribly nice. You go to the inner courtyard. I was met by rather a decorative young man in a naval uniform which was very nice, and he took me in, and then I sat in this outer room, whatever it's called, a huge room, alone with the lady-in-waiting who was a very agreeable gal and this young man, and we laughed and we had a very giggly time, because they'd obviously read it up a bit. They'd heard that I sang my poems as well, so they said could I sing one, so under my breath I hissed it at them. We had a very gay time. I adored that part of it. Well, then the one before me came out, a staggering-looking woman. Well, I thought, I'm not properly dressed for this. I looked at her. She was tremendously made-up. I thought, 'I don't think there was quite enough really. I think I ought to have something above the waist.' You curtsey when the door's flung open. The young man took me to the door, and far away—the room's as big as Trafalgar Square—standing against the mantelpiece was this charming figure—the Queen. You curtsey, and you make your way across the room. Then she comes forward and smiles—she's got a very gracious smile—and gives you the medal. And as she gave it to me she said, 'I don't know what you'll do with it,' and I looked at it and said, 'Well, I suppose I could have a hook put on it and wear it round my neck. It's very beautiful, isn't it?' 'Well,' she said, 'I don't know whether it's real', and I said, 'Beg your pardon'. 'Oh,' I said, 'I'm sure it is.' Then she motioned me—I think that's the expression—to sit down. There was a table between. They'd told me outside not to worry about when to come out because she'd ring a bell under the table. Well, the poor darling kept on asking me questions about poetry. I rather got the impression it wasn't her favourite subject. You feel you're with an enormously charming woman and a very professional Queen. I mean, the grip on things. She made me feel awfully like a schoolgirl again, being interviewed by a rather cordial headmistress, but knowing that headmistresses aren't always like that. Then we talked about poetry, and I got rather nervous and said, 'I don't know why, but I seem to have written rather a lot about murder lately', which was rather an unfortunate thing to say. I'd just written that very long one based on the moors murder case, so I started to tell her the story, and the smile got rather fixed. She is absolutely charming, a totally different sort of mind in the sense that it's not a poetical mind, but I mean on admin-istration and grasp of politics and economics and all that, she's fright-fully good, never a foot wrong. You can walk out backwards. When you get to the door you turn again and curtsey and come out, and then the young man and the girl get a taxi for you; and the taxi driver was very thrilled because he'd never been to the inner court before.

> KAY DICK, *Ivy and Stevie: Ivy Compton-Burnett and Stevie Smith, Conver-sations and Reflections*, 1971

THE SEAMEN'S CHURCH

Victor Harker walked beside the stagnant Thames. He had no fixed destination. He would follow his feet for a while.

They led him across Tower Bridge and into Rotherhithe, where he stopped to look at Tower Bridge Buildings. Those dozens of poky flats, built during Victoria's reign, were considered fit dwellings for the poor once. He heard a voice from that time, no one's in particular; a common voice, sharp as scissors, saying to a woman who might have been his grandmother: 'The height of luxury it is, Lil; you should see it. Like a bleeding palace it is after what me and Bert's been used to. You'll have to put on your finery when you pay us a visit.' ·

The poor occupied the Buildings still. They were out on the balconies enjoying the sun, reading the papers, drinking and lounging. A child waved to him. Embarrassed, feeling like a snooper, he moved on: he was an intruder now where once he would have been at home. In one dingy street after another he sensed that eyes were following him. Curtains twitched as he went by: behind them were Lils and Berts, Sids and Flos, and a Billy Harker or two perhaps.

He passed a housing estate, a modern counterpart to the Buildings— characterless concrete instead of oppressive brick—which some wit of a town planner had honoured with the name Charles Dickens. A grim joke, he thought, that the writer who had informed the English of the existence of Jo the crossing-sweeper should be celebrated in this way. He wondered how many of its residents, their heads stuck in tabloids this Sunday morning, had read those books that Stella and Victor Harker had loved so much.

He was thinking about retracing his steps when he saw a church. A few elderly worshippers were shaking hands with the clergyman in the portal. He would wait for everyone to leave before going in. He enjoyed churches when they were empty, and empty for him meant free from vicars and curates and wardens. He had never cared for men of the cloth—their breeziness gave him the shivers. He loathed their clockwork optimism. He hated that pitying look they assumed, that instant recognition of one's supposed fallen state. In his years of darkness he had needed the places they strutted in, not them.

Soon after entering St Mary's, Victor Harker fancied that he was in the presence of simple goodness. Wives had prayed here for the safe return of their sailor husbands, not heeding the carvings by Grinling Gibbons and the splendour of the organ. They were mere decorations: the progress of those ships across the Atlantic or the Pacific was what mattered. 'You *are* being fanciful,' he told himself, and yet he couldn't shake off the conviction that the atmosphere in this dockland church was suggestive of centuries of quiet, undemonstrative devotion. What grandeur St Mary's contained lay in its unoccupied pews, where ghosts now sang for him:

> O hear us when we cry to Thee
> For those in peril on the sea.

Hesitant voices were still singing faintly as he read the plaques on the walls. His notion seemed less fanciful with every dedication he looked at: a woman called Everilda Bracken had come from Sutton Coldfield to the shipbuilding village of Rotherhithe 'to relieve the sufferers from the cholera'; a certain Roger Tweedy, who died in 1655, decreed in his will that the sum of two shillings be distributed 'every Lords Day forever among twelve poor seamen or their widdows in bread', while other widows, of good character only, were remembered in the bequest of a Mr John Sprunt. He learned that Prince Lee Boo, the son of the ruler of the Pelau Islands, had died in Captain Wilson's house in Paradise Row in a smallpox epidemic. The captain had been shown great kindness by the prince's family when his ship, the *Antelope*, was wrecked on the shores of the Pelau in 1783 . . . Once again he saw hands clawing the air, and gold and brass wedding-rings glinting on the water.

'On Tuesday, yes.'

The face of the man he would never have granted an overdraft had suddenly appeared above the wreck of the *Antelope*, or was it the HMS *Captain*? It must have been the latter he was thinking of. Captain, Captain —he and that Standish individual had arranged to meet for dinner the day after tomorrow. Victor Harker would take his guest to a restaurant which the discerning few neglected to patronize.

Wandering back along the wharves, he tried to picture the prince, who had left somewhere like paradise only to die in a street on London's out-skirts that bore its name. Had he worn grass, or feathers, or both? Victor Harker thought of the captain's wife, who had not been widowed young, substituting sensible wool and cotton for the prince's showy clothing.

'He died of a fever, and no one could save him, and that was the end of poor Prince Lee Boo,' he sang under his breath.

PAUL BAILEY, *Old Soldiers*, 1980

ON THE UPPER DECK

His bus map told him that having taken the 127 to Gower Street he could change there to a 163 and, via Chelsea, Putney Bridge and Southfields, be transported to Colliers Wood. That was what he did. On this journey he had remembered to bring the *Times* crossword puzzle but the lurching and plunging of the vehicle at the various irregularities of the highway, together with the difficulty of the clues, led him to stop it soon. He was also distracted by the very loud unsteady wailing noise to be heard whenever the driver used his brakes. The view out of the win-dows south of the river, after the 163 had passed under a couple of dozen railway bridges in a mile or so, was definitely less attractive than what was to be seen from the 127. Here were derelict churches covered with grime, yards of hoardings with no posters on them, dining-rooms and small draper's shops such as he hadn't seen since the '30s, waste lots big enough to accommodate a shopping complex barely to be dreamed of and, beyond them, hulking greyish towers of offices or dwellings that loomed in the smoky distance. He supposed that people who lived here might well vote for or against somebody at an election, neither of which he had bothered to do since 1945 (Liberal). The ones he saw had an archaic look too, dumpy, dark-clothed, wearing hats: the infiltrators from Schleswig-Holstein had not reached here yet.

Sitting near the front of the bus on the upper deck he became aware by degrees that a sort of altercation was going on behind him, the sort, as it soon proved, in which only one voice was to be heard, a woman's, deep and powerful, projected with that pressure of the diaphragm used by actors.

'It isn't right, is it? I mean do you think it's right? After all these years and all I been through? I said I've had enough, I done everything you told me and I've had enough, I said, I told him straight. What's in it for me, I said, yeah, what's in it for me? I've had e-bloody-nough. Now that's my rights, isn't it? I reckon that's my rights, don't you? I said don't you?'

He looked over his shoulder to see what kind of unfortunate was having to put up with this, and found that nobody and everybody was, staring hard out of the window or at a newspaper or into space. The speaker wore a dark-brown coat flecked with green and a very pale lilac-coloured silk scarf round the neck. That neck looked too slender for the job of connecting the broad-shouldered trunk to the large round head. The woman's complexion was dull, her chin pointed, her nose thin, her hair straight and dry, standing out and up from her scalp. While she continued to talk she seemed never to look directly at anyone, always between people.

'I'm not going to stay there,' she repeated several times in the same tone as before, accusing rather than angry. 'I told him so. I said, I don't mind coming along, well I do, but I will. I don't mind coming along but I'm not going to stay. I've had enough of that. Where's it got me, that's what I'd like to know. It's not fair, it's taking advantage, that's what it is. He's got me where he wants me and there's nothing I can do about it. I been given a raw deal, haven't I, a raw bloody deal. Don't anybody think I've been given a raw deal?'

Jake had turned back to face his front after one good look. The sound-quality of the last couple of dozen words told him that the woman had got up and was moving towards the top of the stairs, presumably on the way to getting off the bus. On an impulse he didn't at once understand he shifted round in his seat and said, 'Yes, I do.'

Now she did look straight at someone and he saw with unusual clarity that everything about her face was wrong. The tip of her nose was a narrow white peak above a pair of ill-matched nostrils partly outlined in red; her eyes didn't so much protrude or glare as have no discernible sockets to lie in; her eyebrows were irregular streaks of bristle; her ears were set a little too far back on her skull; the borders of her lips were well marked at one corner and blurred at the other; the state of her skin showed him for the first time what it really meant to say that someone was pale and drawn. That's right, he thought to himself: they're not just mad inside their heads, they're mad to their fingertips, to the ends of their hair. And he had spoken to her to make her give him the straight look he had needed in order to see that in her.

What might have been the beginnings of a smile showed on the woman's face in the second before she stepped clumsily to one side and passed out of view down the stairs. Soon afterwards the bus stopped and from his position above the pavement he saw her walk away, swinging her arms a lot. Some distance ahead lay a small piece of park or public garden, a grassy triangle where, with a show of energy unexpected in these latitudes, a group of men in helmets and jerkins were attacking some trees. Products of their labours were strewn about them in the shape of much sound timber and vigorous foliage. The peevish wavering groan of their saws could be clearly heard through the noise of the traffic. At first idly, then with concern, Jake took in a rusty street-sign that said Trafalgar Place. Distracted by the incident of the madwoman, he was about to overshoot the stopping-point he had picked out on his de luxe A *to* Z. He toiled his way downstairs at his best speed but no kind of speed shown by him would have affected the progress of the bus, which finally dropped him a couple of hundred yards beyond the turning he wanted.

KINGSLEY AMIS, *Jake's Thing*, 1978

A LONDON SURVIVOR: 5

Spanish and Portuguese Synagogue, Bevis Marks

Mr Avis, 1700

A quiet courtyard behind the street (usually locked—go to the vestry in Heneage Lane) and, once inside, a great luminous room, compassionate light streaming in through big clear-glass windows on to a set of curly brass chandeliers from Amsterdam that are almost at eye level. Nothing has fretted or worried it for two hundred and fifty years, and the force of undisturbed goodness is as tangible as the marbling on the gallery pillars. The designer was a Quaker who gave his fee to the congregation, and this is exactly what the building conveys: that the real parts of all religions are identical.

IAN NAIRN, *Nairn's London*, 1966

The 'cottagers' in this poem are not the occupants of cottages, but frequenters of gentlemen's urinals.

WAILING IN WANDSWORTH

Lovers who would pet and fondle
All along the River Wandle,
Running down through Wandsworth Town
    Leafily, are gone.
Factory excreta tumble,
Gangs prowl, sniffing out a rumble,
    And the cops move on
Cottagers disposed to fumble
In their lowly dwelling, humble
    Public jakes or john.

Where the lovers used to ramble
Adult Aid chain owners amble,
Strolling down through Wandsworth Town,
    Counting up the cash.
By the bridge, his fourteenth tipple
Claims the drunk, who takes a triple
    Length-and-value slash,
And the alders wind would ripple,
Poplar, beech rain loved to stipple,
    Are not even ash.

> Still and all, I shouldn't grumble,
> I who sit alone and mumble,
> Writing down in Wandsworth Town
>   My troubled Double Dutch.
> I would never cause to stumble
> From its grave, but let it crumble,
>   Ancient pain, as such.
> By the waters of the Wandle
> Where the lovers used to fondle,
> Where I craft this rhubarb rondel,
>   Life is better: much.

KIT WRIGHT, Bump-Starting the Hearse, 1983

BEFORE THE MATCH, AND AFTER

At one time I really wanted to be the first Indian centre-forward to play for England and the school sent me for trials with Millwall and Crystal Palace. Spurs were our team, though, and as their ground was far away in North London, Ted and I didn't get to see them often. But when they were at home to Chelsea I persuaded Ted to take me. Mum tried to stop me going, convinced that the Shed boys would ensure me a sharpened penny in the skull. Not that I was too crazy about live matches. You stood there in the cold with icicles on your balls, and when someone was about to score the entire ground leapt in the air and all you could see were woolly hats.

The train took Ted and me and our sandwiches up through the suburbs and into London. This was the journey Dad made every day, bringing keema and roti and pea curry wrapped in greasy paper in his briefcase. Before crossing the river we passed over the slums of Herne Hill and Brixton, places so compelling and unlike anything I was used to seeing that I jumped up, jammed down the window and gazed out at the rows of disintegrating Victorian houses. The gardens were full of rusting junk and sodden overcoats; lines of washing criss-crossed over the debris. Ted explained to me, 'That's where the niggers live. Them blacks.'

On the way back from the match we were squashed into the corner of the carriage with dozens of other Spurs fans in black and white scarves.

I had a football rattle I'd made at school. Spurs had won. 'Tottenham, Tottenham!' we chanted.

The next time I looked at Ted he had a knife in his hand. He jumped on to his seat and smashed the lightbulbs in the carriage. Glass flew into my hair. We all watched as Ted carefully unscrewed the mirrors from the carriage partitions—as if he were removing a radiator—and lobbed them out of the train. As we moved around the carriage to make way for him—no one joined in—Ted stabbed the seats and tore the stuffing out of them. Finally he thrust an unbroken lightbulb at me and pointed at the open window.

'Go on, enjoy yerself, it's Saturday.'

I got up and flung the lightbulb as far as I could, not realizing we were drawing into Penge Station. The lightbulb smashed against a wall where an old Indian man was sitting. The man cried out, got up and hobbled away. The boys in the train jeered racist bad-mouth at him. When Ted brought me home Mum pointed at me and asked Ted if I'd behaved myself.

HANIF KUREISHI, *The Buddha of Suburbia*, 1990

NORWOOD NOW

Although the Case of the Norwood Builder was not one of Sherlock Holmes' more spectacular adventures, William liked to think that it conferred a certain sinister distinction on his part of London. Less leafy, more urban now than then, and than when Camille Pissarro painted Norwood, Dulwich and Crystal Palace, the suburb is still full of blossom in the spring. Buses lumber in heavy traffic up the hill where carriage lamps once glittered in black rain and snow blurred the pale green streetlamps. Pissarro's brother lived on the site of West Norwood Woolworths, on the opposite side of the road from the cemetery where the dead stare disconcertingly from coloured photographs or lie in the splendour of decay in great flaunting mausoleums which prove the mortality of marble and mortar and the supremacy of grass, briar and bush. Beyond Knight's Hill are secretive parks and half-hidden walks through what were once the gardens and woods of large houses; somewhere, lost, is Beulah Spa, a fashionable watering-place whose brilliance gushed briefly, and trickled away.

SHENA MACKAY, *Dunedin*, 1992

A SHORT TRIP ON THE TUBE

It should have been a simple enough journey. First of all I had to walk
to the tube station, which meant going through the park, across the
Albert Bridge, past the fortress-like homes of the super-rich on Cheyne
Walk, up Royal Hospital Road and into Sloane Square. I stopped only
once, to get myself some chocolate (a Marathon and a Twix, if memory
serves). It was another viciously hot morning, and there was no escaping
the palls of thick black smog which issued from the backsides of cars,
trucks, lorries and buses, hanging heavy in the air and all but forcing me
to hold my breath whenever I had to cross the road at a busy junction.
But then, when I arrived at the station and rode down on the escalator,
as soon as the platform came into view I could see that it was absolutely
packed. There was some fault with the service and there couldn't have
been a train for about fifteen minutes. Even though the line at Sloane
Square isn't deep, the steady downward motion of the escalator made me
feel like Orpheus descending to the underworld, confronted by this throng
of pale and sad-looking people, the sunlight which I'd just left behind
already a distant memory.

Four minutes later a District Line train arrived, every inch of every
carriage filled with sweating, hunched, compacted bodies. I didn't even
try to get on, but in the pandemonium of people fighting past each other
I managed to manœuvre my way to the front of the platform in readiness
for the next train. It came after a couple of minutes, a Circle Line train
this time, just as full as the last one. When the doors opened and a few
red-faced passengers had forced their way out through the waiting crowd,
I squeezed inside and took my first mouthful of the foul, stagnant air:
you could tell, just from that one taste, that it had already been in and
out of the lungs of every person in the carriage, a hundred times or more.
More people piled in behind me and I found myself squashed between
this young, gangly office worker—he had a single-breasted suit and a
pasty complexion—and the glass partition which separated us from the
seated passengers. Normally I would have preferred to stand with my
nose up against the partition, but when I tried it that way I found there
was a huge slimy patch, exactly at face-level, an accumulation of sweat
and grease off the back of the earlier passengers' heads where they had
been rubbing up against the glass, so I had no choice but to turn round
and stare eyeball-to-eyeball at this corporate lawyer or swaps dealer or

whatever he was. We were pushed up even closer after the doors closed, on the third or fourth attempt, because the people who had been standing half in and half out of the train now had to cram themselves inside with the rest of us, and from then on his pallid, pimply skin was almost touching mine, and we were breathing hot breath into each other's faces. The train shunted into motion and half the people who were standing lost their balance, including a builder's labourer who was pressed against my left shoulder and was wearing nothing on top except a pale blue vest. He apologized for nearly falling on top of me and then he reached up to hang on to one of the roof-straps, so I suddenly found that my nose was right inside his moist, gingery armpit. As unobtrusively as I could I put my fingers up to my nostrils and started breathing through my mouth. But I consoled myself, thinking, Never mind, I'm only going as far as Victoria, one stop, that's all it is, it'll be over in a couple of minutes.

But the train was already slowing down, and when it finally came to a standstill in the pitch dark of the tunnel I reckoned that it had only travelled three or four hundred yards. As soon as it stopped you could feel the atmosphere grow tense. We can't have been there for more than a minute, perhaps, or a minute and a half, but already it seemed like an eternity, and when the train started crawling forward there was visible relief on all our faces. But it turned out to be short-lived. After only a few seconds the brakes came on again, and this time, as the train shuddered to a decisive halt, it was with a terrible sense of finality. At once everything seemed very quiet, except for the hiss of a personal stereo further up the carriage, which grew louder as the passenger in question took her headphones off to listen for announcements. In no time at all the air had grown unbearably warm and clammy: I could feel the uneaten chocolate bars turning to liquid in my pocket. We looked around anxiously at each other—some passengers raising despairing eyebrows, others tutting or swearing under their breath—and anyone who was carrying a newspaper or a business document started using it as a fan.

I tried to look on the bright side. If I were to faint—which seemed entirely possible—then there was no chance of falling over and sustaining an injury, because there was nowhere to fall. Similarly, there was little danger of death by hypothermia. It was true that the charms of my neighbour's armpit might begin to pall after an hour or two: but then again perhaps, like a mature cheese, it would improve upon acquaintance. I looked around at the other passengers and wondered who would be the first to crack. There were several possible candidates: a rather frail and wizened old man who was clinging weakly to a pole; a slightly plump woman who for some reason was wearing a thick woollen jumper and had already gone purple in the face; and a tall, asthmatic guy with an earring and a Rolex who was taking regular gulps from his inhaler. I shifted my weight, closed my eyes and counted to one hundred very slowly. In the process, I noticed the level of noise in the carriage increasing perceptibly: people were beginning to talk to one another, and the woman in the woollen jumper had started moaning softly to herself, saying Oh God Oh God Oh God Oh God—when suddenly, the lights in the carriage went out, and we were thrown into total darkness. A few feet away from me a woman let out a little scream, and there was a fresh round of exclamations and complaints. It was a scary feeling, not only being immobilized but now completely unable to see, although at least I had the compensation that I was no longer required to stare at City Slicker's blackheads. But I could sense fear, now, fear all around me whereas before there had only been boredom and discomfort. There was desperation in the air, and before it proved contagious I decided to beat a retreat, as far as possible, into the privacy of my own mind. To start with, I tried telling myself that the situation could be worse: but there were surprisingly few scenarios which bore this out—a rat on the loose in the carriage, perhaps, or a busker spontaneously whipping out his guitar and treating us all to a few rousing choruses of 'Imagine'. No, I would have to try harder than that. Next I attempted to construct an erotic fantasy, based on the premise that the body I was pressed up against belonged not to some spotty stockbroker but to Kathleen Turner, wearing a thin, almost transparent silk blouse and an unbelievably short, unbelievably tight mini-skirt. I imagined the firm, ample contours of her chest and buttocks, the look of hooded, unwilling desire in her eyes, her pelvis beginning unconsciously to grind against mine—and all at once, to my horror, I was getting an erection, and my whole body went taut with panic as I tried to pull away from the businessman whose crotch was already in direct contact with mine. But it didn't work: in fact, unless I was very much mistaken, now *he* was getting an erection, which either meant that he was trying the same trick as me, or I was giving out the wrong signals and was about to find myself in very serious trouble.

Just at that moment, thank God, the lights flickered back on, and a muted cheer went up around the carriage. The speaker system also crackled into life, and we heard the laconic drawl of a London Underground guard who, without actually apologizing for the delay, explained that the train was experiencing 'operating difficulties' which would be rectified as soon as possible. It wasn't the most satisfying of explanations, but at least we no longer felt quite so irredeemably alone and abandoned, and now as long as nobody tried leading us into prayer or starting a singalong to keep our spirits up, I felt that I could cope with a few more minutes. The guy with the inhaler was looking worse and worse, though. I'm sorry, he said, as his breathing began to get faster and more frantic, I don't think I can last much more of this, and the man next to him started making reassuring noises but I could sense the silent resentment of the other passengers at the thought that they might soon have to deal with the problem of someone fainting or having a fit or something. At the same time I could also sense something else, something quite different: a strong, sickly, meaty sort of smell which was now beginning to establish itself above the competing bouquets of sweat and body odour. Its source quickly became apparent as the lanky businessman next to me squeezed open his briefcase and took out a paper bag with the logo of a well-known fast food chain on it. I watched him in amazement and thought, He isn't going to do this, he can't be going to do this, but yes, with the merest grunt of apology—'It'll go cold otherwise'—he opened his gaping jaws and crammed in a great big mouthful of this damp, lukewarm cheeseburger and started chomping on it greedily, every chew making a sound like wet fish being slapped together and a steady dribble of mayonnaise appearing at the corners of his mouth. There was no question of being able to look away or block my ears: I could see every shred of lettuce and knob of gristle being caught between his teeth, could hear whenever the gummy mixture of cheese and masticated bread got stuck to the roof of his mouth and had to be dislodged with a probing tongue. Then things started to go a bit hazy, the carriage was getting darker and the floor was giving way beneath my feet and I could hear someone say, Watch out, he's going!, and the last thing I can remember thinking was, Poor guy, it's no wonder, with asthma like that: and then nothing, no memory at all of what happened next, just blackness and emptiness for I don't know how long.

JONATHAN COE, *What a Carve Up!*, 1994

'THE CAPITAL OF ALL CAPITALS'

London is to us Continental people the successor of the self-governing townships of the Middle Ages—the Dutch civilian towns. London is the capital of all capitals which has resisted absolutism and maintained the rights of the citizens within the state. England's contribution to European civilization, as seen from the Continent, is a whole world of ideas that could only arise and flourish in a community which had resisted absolutism. London has played a considerable part in the evolution of it. It has never been of greater importance than now that these ideals should continue to exist, in one country at least, in Europe.

STEEN EILER RASMUSSEN, *London: The Unique City*, 1937

LOST ONES

South Bank: Sibelius 5's
incontrovertible end—
five exhalations, bray of expiry,
    absolute silence . . .

Under the Festival Hall is a foetid
    tenebrous concert
    strobed by blue ambulance light.
    PVC/newspapers/rags
insulate ranks of expendables, eyesores,
    winos, unworthies,
one of which (stiff in its cardboard Electrolux
    box stencilled **FRAGILE**,
    STOW THIS WAY UP, USE NO HOOKS)
officers lug to the tumbril,
    exhaling, like ostlers, its scents:

            squit,

            honk,

            piss,

            meths,

            distress.

PETER READING, *Perduta Gente*, 1989

THE VIEW FROM BRIXTON

You can see for miles, out of this window. You can see right across the river. There's Westminster Abbey, see? Flying the St George's cross, today. St Paul's, the single breast. Big Ben, winking its golden eye. Not much else familiar, these days. This is about the time that comes in every century when they reach out for all that they can grab of dear old London, and pull it down. Then they build it up again, like London Bridge in the nursery rhyme, goodbye, hello, but it's never the same. Even the railway stations, changed out of recognition, turned into souks. Waterloo. Victoria. Nowhere you can get a decent cup of tea, all they give you is Harvey Wallbangers, filthy cappuccino. I said to Nora: 'Remember *Brief Encounter*, how I cried buckets? Nowhere for them to meet on a station, nowadays, except in a bloody knicker shop. Their hands would have to shyly touch under cover of a pair of Union Jack boxer shorts.'

ANGELA CARTER, *Wise Children*, 1991

ACKNOWLEDGEMENTS

The editor and publisher gratefully acknowledge permission to include the following copyright material:

J. R. Ackerley, from *My Dog Tulip* (Bodley Head, 1965). Reprinted by permission of David Higham Associates.

Kingsley Amis, from *Jake's Thing*, copyright © 1978 by Kingsley Amis (Hutchinson, 1978). Reprinted by permission of Random House UK Ltd. and Viking Penguin, a division of Penguin Books USA, Inc.

Paul Bailey, from *Old Soldiers*, © Paul Bailey 1980 (Jonathan Cape, 1980) and from *Gabriel's Lament* © Paul Bailey 1986 (Jonathan Cape, 1986). Reprinted by permission of the author, Random House UK Ltd. and Rogers, Coleridge & White.

W. N. P. Barbellion, from *The Journal of a Disappointed Man* (Hogarth Press, 1984). Reprinted by permission of the Estate of the author.

Julian Barnes, from *Metroland* (Jonathan Cape 1980/Random House Inc.). Reprinted by permission of Random House UK Ltd. and the Peters Fraser & Dunlop Group Ltd.

Samuel Beckett, from *Murphy*, copyright © Samuel Beckett 1938, 1963, 1977 and © the Samuel Beckett Estate, 1993. Reprinted by permission of the Samuel Beckett Estate and the Calder Educational Trust, London. Also used by permission of Grove/Atlantic, Inc.

Max Beerbohm, from *The Letters of Max Beerbohm 1892–1956* ed. Rupert Hart-Davis (John Murray, 1988). Reprinted by permission of John Murray (Publishers) Ltd.

John Betjeman, 'In Westminster Abbey' from *Collected Poems* (John Murray, 1970). Reprinted by permission of John Murray (Publishers) Ltd.

James Boswell, in *Boswell's London Journal 1762–1863* ed. Frederick A. Pottle, copyright © 1950 by Yale University. Reprinted by permission of Yale University Press and Edinburgh University Press.

Elizabeth Bowen, from *The Death of the Heart*, copyright 1938 and renewed 1966 by Elizabeth D. C. Cameron (Jonathan Cape/Alfred Knopf, 1938). Reprinted by permission of Random House UK Ltd. and Alfred A. Knopf Inc.

Angus Calder, from *The People's War* (Jonathan Cape, 1969). Reprinted by permission of Random House UK Ltd. and the Peters Fraser & Dunlop Group.

Angela Carter, from *Wise Children*, © Angela Carter, 1991 (Chatto & Windus 1991/Farrar, Straus & Giroux). Reprinted by permission of Rogers, Coleridge & White Ltd.

Barbara Cartland, from *The Isthmus Years* (Hutchinson, 1943). Reprinted by permission of Rupert Crew Ltd.

Raymond Chandler, in *Selected Letters of Raymond Chandler* ed. Frank MacShane (Jonathan Cape, 1981). Reprinted by permission of Ed Victor Ltd.

Charles Chaplin, from *My Autobiography* (Bodley Head, 1964). Reprinted by permission of Random House UK Ltd.

Geoffrey Chaucer, from *The Canterbury Tales* trans. David Wright (Oxford University Press, 1985) copyright © David Wright 1985. Reproduced by permission of the Peters, Fraser & Dunlop Group Ltd.

Kellow Chesney, from *The Victorian Underworld*, copyright © Kellow Chesney 1970 (Penguin, 1991). Reproduced by permission of Curtis Brown Group Ltd., London.

Richard Church, from *Over the Bridge* (Heinemann, 1956) and *The Golden Sovereign* (Heinemann, 1957). Reprinted by permission of Laurence Pollinger Ltd. on behalf of the Estate of Richard Church.

Jonathan Coe, from *What a Carve Up!* (Viking, 1994), copyright © Jonathan Coe, 1994 published in the USA under the title *The Winshaw Legacy* (Alfred Knopf). Reproduced by permission of Penguin Books Ltd. and Alfred A. Knopf Inc.

Harry Daley, from *This Small Cloud* (Weidenfeld & Nicolson, 1986). Reprinted by permission of the Orion Publishing Group Ltd.

Elizabeth David, from *An Omelette and a Glass of Wine* (Robert Hale, 1984). Reprinted by permission of Jill Norman.

André Derain, reprinted from *Britain Observed* by Geoffrey Grigson, © 1975 Phaidon Press Ltd., in accordance with the information given on the imprint page of the book, by permission of Phaidon Press Ltd.

Fyodor Dostoyevsky, from *Winter Notes on Summer Impressions*, trans. K. FitzLyon (Quartet, 1985, first published by Calder Books 1955, as *Summer Impressions*), copyright © Kyril Fitzlyon 1955, 1985. Reprinted by permission of Kyril FitzLyon.

T. S. Eliot, from 'The Waste Land', in *Collected Poems 1909–1962* (Faber, 1963), copyright 1936 by Harcourt Brace & Company, copyright 1964, 1963 by T. S. Eliot. Reprinted by permission of Faber & Faber Ltd. and Harcourt Brace & Company.

Richard Findlater, from *Lilian Baylis: The Lady of the Old Vic* (Allen Lane, 1975). Reprinted by permission of A. P. Watt Ltd. on behalf of Angela Findlater.

E. M. Forster, from *Howards End* (Edward Arnold, 1910). Reprinted by permission of King's College, Cambridge, and The Society of Authors as the literary representatives of the E. M. Forster Estate, and of Alfred A. Knopf Inc.

M. Dorothy George, from *London Life in the Eighteenth Century*. Reprinted by permission of Routledge, Publishers.

Walter Greaves, reprinted from *Britain Observed* by Geoffrey Grigson, © 1975 Phaidon Press Ltd., in accordance with the information given on the imprint page of the book, by permission of Phaidon Press Ltd.

Geoffrey Grigson, from *Recollections: Mainly of Writers and Artists* (Chatto & Windus, 1984). Reprinted by permission of David Higham Associates.

Joseph Haydn, in *Collected Correspondence and London Notebooks of Joseph Haydn* by H. C. Robbins Landor (Barrie & Rockliff, 1959). Reprinted by permission of Random House UK Ltd.

Alethea Hayter, from *A Sultry Month: Scenes of London Literary Life in* 1846 (Robin Clark, 1992, first published by Faber & Faber, 1965). Reprinted by permission of the author and of Quartet Books Ltd.

Alexander Herzen, from *My Past Thoughts: The Memoirs of Alexander Herzen* (Vol. 3) trans. Constance Garnett, revised by Humphrey Higgins (Chatto & Windus, 1968). Reprinted by permission of Random House UK Ltd.

Gerard Manley Hopkins, from *The Journals and Papers of Gerard Manley Hopkins* edited by Humphry House and Graham Storey (OUP, 1959). Reprinted by permission of Oxford University Press.

M. V. Hughes, from *A London Child of the Seventies* (OUP, 1934) and *A London Girl of the Eighties* (OUP, 1978). Reprinted by permission of Oxford University Press.

Barry Humphries, from *More Please* (Viking, 1992), copyright © Barry Humphries, 1992. Reproduced by permission of Penguin Books Ltd. and Ed Victor Ltd.

Henry James, from *The Notebooks of Henry James*, ed. F. O. Matthiessen and Kenneth B. Murdock, copyright 1947 by Oxford University Press, Inc., renewed 1974 by Kenneth B. Murdock and Mrs Peters Putnam. Reprinted by permission of the publisher.

Hanif Kureishi, from *The Buddha of Suburbia* (Faber, 1990), copyright © 1990 by Hanif Kureishi. Reprinted by permission of Faber & Faber Ltd. and Viking Penguin, a division of Penguin Books USA, Inc.

Valery Larbaud, 'London' from *Les Poésies de A. O. Barnabooth*, © Editions Gallimard. Reprinted by permission of Editions Gallimard.

Richard Le Gallienne, 'A Ballad of London' from *R. L. Stevenson and Other Poems*. Reprinted by permission of The Society of Authors as the literary representative of the Estate of Richard Le Gallienne.

Norman Longmate, from *King Cholera* (Hamish Hamilton, 1966). Reprinted by permission of the author.

Colin MacInnes, from *Sweet Saturday Night* (MacGibbon & Kee, 1967), © Colin MacInnes Estate. Reprinted by permission of Reg Davis-Poynter.

Shena Mackay, from *Dunedin*, © Shena Mackay, 1992 (Wm. Heinemann Ltd., 1992). Reprinted by permission of Reed Consumer Books and Rogers, Coleridge & White Ltd.

Louis MacNeice, 'Brother Fire' and extract from 'Trilogy for X' from *The Collected Poems of Louis MacNeice* (Faber, 1966). Reprinted by permission of Faber & Faber Ltd.

Leopold Mozart, from *The Letters of Mozart & His Family* ed. E. Anderson (Macmillan, 1966). Reprinted by permission of Macmillan Press Ltd.

Iris Murdoch, from *A Word Child*, copyright © 1975 Iris Murdoch (Chatto & Windus, 1975). Reprinted by permission of Random House UK Ltd. and Viking Penguin, a division of Penguin Books USA, Inc.

V. S. Naipaul, from *The Mimic Men* (Penguin Books, 1969, first published by André Deutsch), copyright © V. S. Naipaul, 1967. Reproduced by permission of Penguin Books Ltd. and Penguin USA, Inc.

Ian Nairn, from *Nairn's London*, revised by Peter Gasson (Penguin Books 1966, revised edition 1988), copyright © Ian Nairn, 1966. Reproduced by permission of Penguin Books Ltd.

Samuel Pepys, from *Diaries* ed. Robert Latham and W. Matthews. Reprinted by permission of the Peters Fraser & Dunlop Group Ltd.

William Plomer, 'The Caledonian Market' and 'A Visit to the Reading Room' from *Collected Poems* (Jonathan Cape, 1960). Reprinted by permission of Random House UK Ltd.

Beatrix Potter, from *The Journal of Beatrix Potter* transcribed from her code writing by Leslie Linder, copyright © Frederick Warne & Co., 1966, 1989. Reproduced by permission of Frederick Warne & Co.

Anthony Powell, from *Casanova's Chinese Restaurant*, © Anthony Powell, 1960 (Wm. Heinemann Ltd., 1960) and *The Military Philosophers*, © Anthony Powell, 1968 (Wm. Heinemann Ltd., 1968). Reprinted by permission of Reed Consumer Books and David Higham Associates.

J. B. Priestley, from *Angel Pavement* (Wm. Heinemann, 1930). Reprinted by permission of Reed Consumer Books.

V. S. Pritchett, from *The Cab at the Door* (Chatto, 1968) and *London Perceived* (Chatto, 1962). Reprinted by permission of the Peters Fraser & Dunlop Group Ltd.

Peter Reading, poem from *Perduta Gente*, copyright © Peter Reading, 1989 (Secker & Warburg Poetry, 1989). Reprinted by permission of the author.

Maude Pember Reeves, from *Round About a Pound a Week* (Virago, 1979). Reprinted by permission of Virago Press Ltd.

Jean Rhys, from 'Let Them Call it Jazz' in *Tigers are Better Looking* (Penguin Books 1972, first published by.André Deutsch), copyright © Jean Rhys, 1962. Reproduced by permission of Penguin Books Ltd.

George Rudé, from *History of London: Hanoverian London 1714–1808*, © 1971 by George Rudé (Martin Secker & Warburg 1971). Reprinted by permission of Reed Consumer Books.

J. W. Sellar and R. J. Yeatman, from *1066 And All That* (Alan Sutton, 1993), originally published by Methuen Publishers, London, 1930. Reprinted by permission of Reed Consumer Books.

George Bernard Shaw, from *Pygmalion*. Reprinted by permission of The Society of Authors on behalf of the Bernard Shaw Estate.

Stevie Smith, in *Ivy and Stevie: Ivy Compton-Burnett and Stevie Smith: Conversations and Reflections* by Kay Dick (Duckworth, 1971). Reprinted by permission of Gerald Duckworth & Co. Ltd.

Bernard Spencer, 'Regent's Park Terrace', copyright © London Magazine Editions from *Collected Poems* (Alan Ross Ltd., 1965). Reprinted by permission of Alan Ross.

Italo Svevo, in *Italo Svevo: the Man and the Writer* by P. N. Furbank, © 1966 by P. N. Furbank (Martin Secker & Warburg, 1966). Reprinted by permission of Reed Consumer Books, and Curtis Brown, London on behalf of the copyright owner.

Vincent Van Gogh, from *The Complete Letters of Vincent Van Gogh* (Thames and Hudson, 1958). Reprinted by permission of Thames & Hudson Ltd.

Paul Vaughan, from *Something in Linoleum*, © 1994 by Paul Vaughan (Sinclair Stevenson, 1994). Reprinted by permission of Reed Consumer Books.

Sylvia Townsend Warner, from *Diaries of Sylvia Townsend Warner* (Chatto & Windus, 1994) and from 'In Pimlico', from *Scenes of Childhood and Other Stories* (Chatto & Windus, 1981). Reprinted by permission of Random House UK Ltd.

Evelyn Waugh, from *The Diaries of Evelyn Waugh* (Weidenfeld & Nicolson, 1976). Reprinted by permission of the Orion Publishing Group Ltd; from *Vile Bodies* (Chapman & Hall, 1930), reprinted by permission of the Peters Fraser & Dunlop Group Ltd.

H. G. Wells, from *Kipps: The Story of a Simple Soul*. Reprinted by permission of A. P. Watt Ltd. on behalf of the Literary Executor of the Estate of H. G. Wells.

Angus Wilson, from *Hemlock and After*, copyright © Angus Wilson, 1952 (Martin Secker and Warburg, 1952). Reprinted by permission of Reed Consumer Books and Curtis Brown Ltd., London on behalf of the Estate of Angus Wilson.

Virginia Woolf, from *A Writer's Diary: Being Extracts from the Diary of Virginia Woolf* (Hogarth Press, 1953). Reprinted by permission of Random House UK Ltd.

Dorothy Wordsworth, from 'The Grasmere Journals' in *The Journals of Dorothy Wordsworth* ed. Mary Moorman (OUP 1971). Reprinted by permission of Oxford University Press.

Kit Wright, 'Wailing in Wandsworth' from *Bump-Starting the Hearse* (Hutchinson, 1983). Reprinted by permission of Random House UK Ltd.

Yevgeny Zamyatin, from 'The Fisher of Men' in *Islanders and the Fisher of Men*, trans. Sophie Fuller and Julian Saachi (Salamander Press, 1984). Reprinted by permission of Sophie Fuller.

Index of Authors

General Index